# The Essential New Testament

Dennis Beatty

Copyright © 2004 by Dennis Beatty

*The Essential New Testament*
by Dennis Beatty

Printed in the United States of America

ISBN 1-594674-79-5

All rights reserved by the author. The contents and views expressed in this book are solely those of the author and are not necessarily those of Xulon Press, Inc. The author guarantees this book is original and does not infringe upon any laws or rights, and that this book is not libelous, plagiarized or in any other way illegal. If any portion of this book is fictitious, the author guarantees it does not represent any real event or person in a way that could be deemed libelous. No part of this book may be reproduced in any form without the permission of the author.

## TRANSLATORS

| BOOK | NAME | DEGREE | SCHOOL |
|---|---|---|---|
| MATTHEW | Rogers Chenault | B.D. | Southern Baptist Theological Seminary |
| MARK | William E. Paul | B.Th. M.S.L. | Midwestern School Evangelism |
| LUKE | Donald A. Nash | A.B. | Kentucky Christian College |
| | | B.Div. | Butler University School of Religion |
| | | D.Div. | Kentucky Christian College |
| JOHN | Gary Hoag | M.Div | Talbot School Theology, Biola University |
| ACTS | Donald A. Nash | A.B. | Kentucky Christian College |
| | | B.Div. | Butler University School of Theology |
| | | D.Div. | Kentucky Christian College |
| ROMANS | Robert Tucker | B.D. | Eastern Baptist Theological |
| 1 CORINTHIANS | Robert Tucker | B.D. | Eastern Baptist Theological |
| 2 CORINTHIANS | Robert Tucker | B.D. | Eastern Baptist Theological |
| GALATIANS | Dennis Beatty | M.Div. | Western Seminary |
| | | D.Min. | Fuller Seminary |
| EPHESIANS | Richard S. Beal | Ph.D. | University of California Berkeley |
| PHILIPPIANS | Craig Gustafson | M.Div. | Talbot School Theology, Biola University |
| COLOSSIANS | David Fabarez | M.Div. | Western Seminary |
| 1 THESSALONIANS | William R. Pawson | M.Div. | Southwestern Seminary |
| | | Th.M. | Austin Presbyterian Seminary |
| 2 THESSALONIANS | Rogers Chenault | B.D. | Southern Baptist Theological Seminary |

# TRANSLATORS (cont.)

| BOOK | NAME | DEGREE | SCHOOL |
|---|---|---|---|
| 1 TIMOTHY | William R. Pawson | M.Div. | Southwestern Seminary |
| | | Th.M. | Austin Presbyterian Seminary |
| 2 TIMOTHY | Kevin McGhee | M.Div. | Talbot School Theology, Biola University |
| TITUS | John Delhousaye | M.Div. | Phoenix Seminary |
| | | Th.M. | Fuller Seminary |
| PHILEMON | William R. Pawson | M.Div. | Southwestern Seminary |
| | | Th.M. | Austin Presbyterian Seminary |
| HEBREWS | Donald A. Nash | A.B. | Kentucky Christian College |
| | | B.Div. | Butler University School of Theology |
| | | D.Div. | Kentucky Christian College |
| JAMES | Jeff Johnson | M.Div. | Southwestern Seminary |
| 1 PETER | William Paul | B.Th. | Midwestern School of Evangelism |
| 2 PETER | Bryan Galloway | M.S.L. | Bethel Seminary |
| 1, 2, 3, JOHN | Dennis Beatty | M.Div. | Western Seminary |
| | | D. Min. | Fuller Seminary |
| JUDE | John Ploog | M.Div. | Western Seminary |
| | | D.Min. | Trinity Seminary |
| REVELATION | Chuck Saletri | M.Div. | Denver Seminary |
| | | D.Min. | Western Seminary |

# TABLE OF CONTENTS

| | |
|---|---|
| Translators | ii – iii |
| Table of Contents | iv |
| Introduction | 1 |
| MATTHEW | 2 |
| MARK | 38 |
| LUKE | 64 |
| JOHN | 102 |
| ACTS | 129 |
| ROMANS | 165 |
| 1 CORINTHIANS | 179 |
| 2 CORINTHIANS | 193 |
| GALATIANS | 202 |
| EPHESIANS | 207 |
| PHILIPPIANS | 212 |
| COLOSSIANS | 216 |
| 1 THESSALONIANS | 220 |
| 2 THESSALONIANS | 223 |
| 1 TIMOTHY | 225 |
| 2 TIMOTHY | 229 |
| TITUS | 232 |
| PHILEMON | 234 |
| HEBREWS | 235 |
| JAMES | 246 |
| 1 PETER | 250 |
| 2 PETER | 256 |
| 1 JOHN | 259 |
| 2 JOHN | 263 |
| 3 JOHN | 264 |
| JUDE | 265 |
| REVELATION | 267 |

It takes a lot of men with a lot of faithfulness to translate the New Testament. My thanks to each one of them for their hard work. They are listed on the previous two pages. A special thanks to Dianne Flood who did all the data entry as well as making positive suggestions about English grammar and syntax.

The translation is called "The Essential New Testament" in that it is essential for those teaching baptism by immersion. It may be used in the pulpit or in the classroom to facilitate the immersion viewpoint of baptism. In this translation every time the word "baptism" (or its various grammatical forms) are found, it is translated "immersion" (or its appropriate English equivalent).

                                      Serving Christ Together,
                                      Dennis Beatty,
                                      General Editor,
                                      *The Essential New Testament*

## *The Gospel According to*
# Matthew

1 The book of the genealogy of Jesus Christ, Son of David, Son of Abraham. [2]Abraham generated Isaac, and Isaac generated Jacob, and Jacob generated Judah and his brothers, [3]and Judah generated Pharez and Zarah of Tamar, and Pharez generated Hezron, and Hezron generated Aram, [4]and Aram generated Amminadab, and Amminadab generated Nahshon, and, Nahshon generated Salmon, [5]and Salmon generated Boaz of Rahab, and Boaz generated Obed of Ruth, and Obed generated Jesse, [6]and Jesse generated David the King.

And David the King generated Solomon out of the wife of Uriah, [7]and Solomon generated Rehoboam, and Rehoboam generated Abijah, and Abijah generated Asa, [8]and Asa generated Jehoshaphat, and Jehoshaphat generated Jehoram, and Jehoram generated Uzziah, [9]and Uzziah generated Jotham, and Jotham generated Ahaz, and Ahaz generated Hezekiah, [10]and Hezekiah generated Manasseh, and Manasseh generated Amon, and Amon generated Josiah, [11]and Josiah generated Johoiachin and his brothers at the removal to Babylon.

[12]And after the removal to Babylon, Jehoiachin generated Shealtiel, and Shealtiel generated Zerubbabel, [13]and Zerubbabel generated Abiud, and Abiud generated Eliakim, and Eliakim generated Eliud, 15and Eliud generated Eleazer, and Eleazer generated Matthan, and Matthan generated Jacob, [16]and Jacob generated Joseph the husband of Mary, of whom Jesus was born who is called Christ.

[17]Therefore all the generations from Abraham until David are fourteen generations, and from David until the removal to Babylon are fourteen generations, and from the removal to Babylon until The Christ are fourteen generations.

[18]Now the birth of Jesus Christ was in this manner: for His mother Mary, who was promised in marriage to Joseph, was found with child by The Holy Spirit, before they came together; [19]and Joseph her husband being righteous and not willing to make her a public disgrace planned to divorce her secretly; [20]but as he thought on these things, behold an angel of the Lord appeared to him in a dream, saying, "Joseph, son of David, do not be afraid to take Mary your wife; for that which is in her is begotten by The Holy Spirit; [21]and she shall bring forth a son and you shall call His name Jesus, for He shall save His people from their sins." [22]Now all this has come to pass in order that The Word by The Lord through the prophet may be fulfilled, saying, [23]"Behold! The Virgin shall be with child and shall bring forth a Son, and they shall call His name Immanuel, which is by interpretation, God with us. [24]And Joseph having been aroused from sleep, did as the angel of The Lord commanded him, and took his wife, [25]and did not know her until she brought forth her first born son; and she called His name Jesus.

2 Now Jesus having been born in Bethlehem of Judea in the days of Herod the King, behold wise men from the East came into Jerusalem saying, [2]"Where is He who was born King of the Jews? For we saw His star in the East, and we came to worship Him." [3]But Herod the King having heard this, was troubled and all Jerusalem with him. [4]And having gathered together all the chief priests and scribes of the people, he inquired of them where the Christ should be

born. ⁵And they said to him, "In Bethlehem of Judea, for thus it has been written by the prophet, ⁶'And you, Bethlehem, in the land of Judah are by no means the least among the rulers of Judah, for out of you shall come forth a ruler who shall shepherd My people Israel.'"

⁷Then Herod having secretly called the wise men and inquired of them the exact time of the appearing star. ⁸And having sent them to Bethlehem said, "Go and search accurately concerning the young child, and when you find Him, bring word to me so that having come I may also worship Him." ⁹And having heard the king, the departed. And behold! The star which they saw in the East went before them until it came and stood over where the young child was. ¹⁰And having seen the star, they rejoiced with exceeding great joy. ¹¹And having come into the house, they saw the young child with Mary His mother. And having fallen down they worshipped Him, and having opened their treasure chests, they offered gifts to Him, gold and frankincense and myrrh. ¹²And having been instructed by God in a dream not to return to Herod, they departed another way into their own country.

¹³Now they having departed, behold an angel of The Lord appears in a dream to Joseph, saying, "Arise, take the young child and His mother and flee into Egypt, and stay there until I speak to you; for Herod is about to seek the young child to destroy Him." ¹⁴and having arisen, he took the young child and His mother by night, and withdrew into Egypt. ¹⁵And he was there until the death of Herod, in order that it might be fulfilled which was spoken by The Lord through the prophet, saying, "Out of Egypt I called My Son." ¹⁶Then Herod, having seen that he was tricked by the wise men, was furious, and having sent forth he killed all the make infants in Bethlehem and in all of her borders, from two years old and under, according to the exact time which he inquired from the wise men. ¹⁷Then was fulfilled that which was spoken through Jeremiah the prophet saying, ¹⁸"A voice was heard in Ramah, wailing and weeping, and great mourning, Rachel weeping for her children, and she would not be comforted, because they are no more.

¹⁹But Herod having died, behold an angel of The Lord appears in a dream to Joseph in Egypt saying, ²⁰"Having risen, take the young child and His mother and go into the land of Israel, for they have died who were seeking the life of the young child." ²¹And arising, he took the young child and His mother, and came into the land of Israel. ²²But having heard that Arachelaus rules over Judea in place of his father Herod, he was afraid to go there. And having been instructed by God in a dream, he withdrew into the regions of Galilee. ²³And he came and dwelt in a city called Nazareth. Thus was fulfilled that which was spoken through the prophet: "He shall be called a Nazarene."

3 And in those days John the Immerser comes preaching in the Wilderness of Judea, saying, ²"You repent for the Kingdom of the Heavens is at hand. ³For this is He who was spoken of by Isaiah the prophet, saying, "A voice crying in the wilderness, you prepare the way of The Lord, you make straight His paths.'"

⁴Now John himself had clothes from the hair of a camel, and a belt of leather around his waist, and his food was locusts and wild honey.

⁵Then went out to him Jerusalem, and all Judea, and all the regions around the Jordan. ⁶And they were immersed in the Jordan by him, confessing their sins. ⁷And having seen many of the Pharisees and Sadducees coming to his immersion he said to them, "Offspring of vipers, who

warned you to flee from the coming wrath? ⁸Therefore you produce fruits worthy of repentance. ⁹And do not think to say among yourselves, we have Abraham as a father. For I say to you that God is able from these stones to raise up children to Abraham. ¹⁰And already the ax lies at the root of the trees; therefore every tree not producing good fruit is cut down and cast into the fire. ¹¹I indeed immerse you in water for repentance; but the One who comes after me is stronger than I, whose sandals I am not fit to carry. He shall immerse you in The Holy Spirit and fire, ¹²whose winnowing shovel is in His hand, and He shall thoroughly cleanse His threshing-floor and shall gather together His wheat into the barn with unquenchable fire."

¹³Then comes Jesus from Galilee to the Jordan to John to be immersed by him. ¹⁴But John was restraining Him saying, "I have need to be immersed by You, and You come to me?" ¹⁵And having answered, Jesus said to him, "You permit it now, for it is thus proper for us to fulfill all righteousness." Then he permitted Him. ¹⁶And having been immersed, Jesus immediately went up from the water, and behold the Heavens were opened to Him. And He saw the Spirit of God descending as a dove, and coming upon Him. ¹⁷And behold a voice out of the Heavens, saying, "This is My Beloved Son in whom I am well pleased."

4 Then Jesus was led up into the wilderness by the Spirit, to be tempted by the Devil. ²And, having fasted forty days and forty nights, afterwards He hungered. ³And having come to Him the tempter said, "If you are the Son of God, speak in order that these stones might become bread." ⁴But He having answered, said, "It has been written, 'A man shall not live by bed only, but by every word that proceeds from the mouth of God.'" ⁵Then the Devil takes Him into the holy city, and places Him upon the top of the temple, ⁶and says to Him, "If You are the Son of God, cast Yourself down: For it has been written, 'He shall command His angels concerning You, and they will lift You on their hands lest You strike your foot against a stone.'" ⁷Jesus said to him, "Again, it has been written; 'you shall not tempt the Lord your God'." ⁸Again the Devil takes Him into an exceeding high mountain, and shows to Him all the kingdoms of the world, and the glory of them. ⁹And he said to Him, "I will give to You all these things if You having fallen down worship me." ¹⁰Then Jesus said to him, "Begone Satan, for it has been written; you shall worship the Lord your God and Him only you shall serve.'"
¹¹Then the Devil leaves Him, and behold angels came and ministered to Him.

¹²But Jesus having heard that John was delivered up, He withdrew into Galilee. ¹³And having left Nazareth, He came and settled in Capernaum beside the sea in the regions of Zebulun and Naphtali; ¹⁴in order that it might be fulfilled which was spoken by Isaiah the prophet, saying, ¹⁵"Land of Zebulun and land of Naphtali, by way of the sea on the other side of the Jordan, Galilee of the nations; ¹⁶The people who are sitting in darkness have seen a Great Light; and to those sitting in the region and shadow of death, to them has the Light arisen."

¹⁷From that time Jesus began to preach and to say, "Repent, for the Kingdom of the Heavens is at hand."

¹⁸And Jesus walking by the Sea of Galilee saw two brothers, Simon called Peter and Andrew his brother, casting a casting-net into the sea, for they were fishermen. ¹⁹And He says to them, "Come after Me, and I will make you fishers of men." ²⁰And immediately leaving the

nets they followed Him. ²¹And having gone forward from there He saw two other brothers, James the son of Zebedee, and John his brother, in the boat with Zebedee, their father, mending their nets; and He called them. ²²And immediately leaving the boat and their father they followed Him.

²³And Jesus went about all Galilee, teaching in their synagogues and preaching the gospel of the Kingdom and healing every disease and every sickness among the people. ²⁴And His fame went out into all Syria. And they brought to Him all those having illness, suffering various diseases and torments, and demoniacs, and lunatics, and paralytics; and He healed them.

²⁵And many crowds followed with Him from Galilee, and Decapolis, and Jerusalem, and Judea, and on the other side of the Jordan.

5 And having seen the crowds, He went up into the mountain, and having sat down His disciples came to Him. ²And having opened His mouth He taught them saying,

³"Blessed are the poor in spirit because theirs is the Kingdom of the Heavens; ⁴Blessed are the mourners because they shall be comforted;

⁵"Blessed are the meek because they shall inherit the earth; ⁶Blessed are the ones hungering and thirsting for righteousness because they shall be satisfied;

⁷"Blessed are the merciful because they shall receive mercy; ⁸Blessed are the pure in heart because they shall see God; ⁹Blessed are the peacemakers because they shall be called sons of God; ¹⁰Blessed are those who have been persecuted for the sake of righteousness because theirs is the Kingdom of the Heavens; ¹¹Blessed are you when they shall reproach and shall persecute you, and say every evil word against you falsely for My sake; ¹²You rejoice and be exceedingly glad, because your reward in the Heavens is great, for they in the same way persecuted the prophets who were before you.

¹³"You are the salt of the earth, but if the salt has become tasteless, with what shall it be salted, for it no longer has any power except to be cast outside, and to be trodden underfoot by men.

¹⁴"You are the light of the world, a city sitting upon a mountain is not able to be hidden. ¹⁵And they do not light a lamp and place it under the corn-measure, but upon the lampstand, and it gives light to all those in the house. ¹⁶Let your light thus shine before men, so that they may see your good works and may glorify your Father who is in the Heavens.

¹⁷"Do not think that I came to destroy the law or the prophets; I did not come to destroy but to fulfill. ¹⁸For truly I say to you, until the heaven and the earth pass away, one jot or one tittle shall in no wise pass from the law until all come to pass.

¹⁹"Therefore, whoever may break one of these least commandments, and teaches men thus, he shall be called the least in the Kingdom of the Heavens; but whoever does and teaches them the same shall be called great in the Kingdom of the Heavens. ²⁰For I say to you that except your righteousness greatly exceeds that of the Scribes and Pharisees, you shall in no wise enter into the Kingdom of the Heavens.

²¹"You have heard that is was said to the ancients, 'Do not murder, and whoever should murder shall be liable to the Judgment'. ²²But I say to you that every one who is angry with his brother without cause, shall be liable to the Judgment. And whoever may say to his brother,

Raca, shall be liable to the Council. And whoever may say, Fool, shall be liable to hell of fire.
²³"Therefore if you bring your gift to the altar, and there remember that your brother has something against you, ²⁴leave there your gift before the altar, and go, first be reconciled to your brother, and then go offer your gift. ²⁵Be agreeable quickly with your adversary while you are with him in the way, lest the adversary deliver you to the Judge, and the Judge deliver you to the officer, and you be cast into prison. ²⁶Truly I say to you, you shall not go out from there until you have paid the last kodrantes.

²⁷"You have heard that it was said by the ancients, 'Do not commit adultery'. ²⁸But I say to you, that every one who looks at a woman to lust after her has already committed adultery with her in his heart. ²⁹And if your right eye causes you to sin, pluck it out and cast it from you. For it is profitable to you that one of your members should be destroyed, and not that your whole body be cast into hell. ³⁰And if your right hand causes you to sin, cut it off and cast it from you. For it is profitable to you that one of your members should be destroyed, and not that your whole body be cast into hell. ³¹And it was said, 'Whoever may put away his wife, let him give her a bill of divorce'. ³²But I say to you that whoever may put away his wife, except for the cause of fornication makes her to commit adultery, and whoever may marry a divorced woman, commits adultery.

³³"Again, you have heard that it was said to the ancients, 'Do not swear falsely, but you shall discharge to the Lord your oaths'. ³⁴But I say to you not to swear at all, neither by Heaven because it is the throne of God, ³⁵neither by earth because it is the footstool of His feet, nor by Jerusalem because it is the city of the great King, ³⁶nor by your head should you swear, because you are not able to make one hair white or black. ³⁷But let your word be yes, yes, no, no. And what is more than these is from evil.

³⁸"You heard that was said, 'An eye for an eye and a tooth for a tooth'. ³⁹But I say to you not to resist evil; but whoever strikes you on the right cheek, turn to him also the other. ⁴⁰And to the one who wishes to sue you, and to take your undergarment, give to him also the outergarment. ⁴¹And whoever shall compel you to go one mile, go with him two.

⁴²"Give to the one who asks you, and do not turn away the one who wishes to borrow from you.

⁴³"You heard that it was said, 'You shall love your neighbor and you shall hate your enemy'. ⁴⁴But I say to you, love your enemies, bless those who curse you, do good to those who hate you, and pray for those who insult you and persecute you, ⁴⁵so that you may be sons of your Father in the Heavens; because He causes His sun to rise on the evil and the good, and He sends rain on the just and unjust. ⁴⁶For if you love those who love you, what reward do you have? Do not also the tax collectors do the same? ⁴⁷And if you greet your brothers only what more do you do? Do not also the tax collectors do thus? ⁴⁸Therefore you shall be perfect just as your Father Who is in the Heavens in perfect.

6 "Take heed not to do your alms-giving before men, to be seen of them, or else you have no reward from your Father Who is in the Heavens. ²Therefore, when you do almsgiving, do not sound a trumpet before you, as the hypocrites do in the synagogues and in the streets, that they may be praised by men. Truly, I say to you, 'They have their reward'. ³But when you do

almsgiving, do not let your left hand know what your right hand is doing, ⁴so that your almsgiving may be in secret, and your Father who sees in secret shall Himself pay you back openly.

⁵"And when you pray, you shall not be as the hypocrites, because they love to pray standing in the synagogues and on the corners of the streets, so that they may be seen by men. Truly I say to you, that they have their reward. ⁶But you, when you pray, enter into your secret room, and having shut your door, pray to your Father who is in secret, and your Father who sees in secret shall pay you back openly. ⁷And when you pray, do not use vain repetitions as the nations do, for they think that they shall be heard in their much speaking. ⁸Therefore do not be like them, for your Father knows what you have need of before you ask Him.

⁹Therefore you pray like this, 'Our Father Who is in the Heavens, let Your Name be holy, ¹⁰let Your Kingdom come, let Your will be done also on the earth, as it is in Heaven, ¹¹give to us today our daily bread, ¹²and forgive us our debts as we also forgive those who are indebted to us, ¹³and do not bring us into temptation, but rescue us from evil, because Yours is the Kingdom and the power and the glory unto the ages, Amen.'

¹⁴"For if you forgive men their trespasses your Heavenly Father shall also forgive you; ¹⁵but if you do not forgive men their trespasses, neither shall your Father forgive your trespasses. ¹⁶And when you fast, do not be as the hypocrites with a sad countenance; for they disfigure their faces that they may be seen fasting by men. Truly I say to you, that they have their reward. ¹⁷But when fasting, anoint your head and wash your face, ¹⁸so that you may not be seen fasting to men, but by your Father who is in secret; and your Father who sees in secret shall pay you back openly.

¹⁹"Do not treasure up for yourselves treasures upon the earth, where moth and corrosion consumes, and where thieves dig through and steal. ²⁰But treasure up for yourselves treasures in Heaven, where neither moth nor corrosion consumes, and where thieves do not dig through nor steal. ²¹For where your treasure is, there your heart will be also. ²²The lamp of the body is the eye. If therefore your eye is sound, your whole body shall be enlightened. ²³But if your eye is evil, then your whole body shall be dark. Therefore if the light which is in you is darkness, how great the darkness.

²⁴"No one is able to serve two lords, for either he will hate the one and love the other, or he will cleave to one and despise the other. You are not able to serve God and riches. ²⁵Because of this I say to you, do not be anxious for your life, what you should eat and what you should drink, nor yet for your body, what you should put on. Is not the life more than food, and the body more than clothing? ²⁶You look at the birds of the heaven, that they do not sow, neither do they reap nor gather into storehouses, but your Heavenly Father feeds them. Are you not much better than they? ²⁷And which of you being anxious is able to add one span to his life? ²⁸And why are you anxious concerning clothing? Consider well the lilies of the field, how they grow. They do not work, neither do they make clothes; ²⁹but I say to you that Solomon in all his glory was not clothed as one of these.

³⁰"But if God so clothes the grass of the field, which is today and tomorrow is cast into the oven, shall He not much more clothe you? O you of little faith!

³¹"Therefore, do not be anxious, saying, what should we eat, or what should we drink, or, what are we to be clothed with? ³²For the nations diligently seek all these. For your Heavenly

Father knows that you have need of all these. ³³But seek first the Kingdom of God and His righteousness, and all these shall be added to you. ³⁴Therefore, do not be anxious for the morrow, for the morrow shall be anxious about the things of itself. Each day has enough evil of its own.

7 "Do not judge, in order that you may not be judged, ²for with what judgment you judge, you shall be judged; and with what measure you measure, it shall be measured back to you. ³And how do you see the twig in your brother's eye, but do not perceive a log in your eye? ⁴Or how will you say to your brother, 'permit me to cast out the twig from your eye,' and behold the log is in your eye. ⁵Hypocrite, cast out first the log from your eye, and then you shall see clearly to cast out the twig from your brother's eye. ⁶Do not give that which is holy to dogs, neither cast your pearls before swine, lest they may trample them under with their feet, and having turned they may tear you to pieces.

⁷"Keep asking and it shall be given to you; keep seeking and you shall find; keep knocking and it shall be opened to you. ⁸For everyone who keeps asking receives, and the one who keeps seeking finds, and to the one who keeps knocking it shall be opened. ⁹Or what man is there of you, who if his son would ask of him bread, will give to him a stone? ¹⁰And if he would ask a fish, will give to him a serpent? ¹¹Therefore, if you being evil, know to give good gifts to your children, how much more shall your Father Who is in the Heavens give good things to those who ask Him? ¹²Therefore, all things whatsoever you may wish that men should do to you, in like manner also you do to them; for this is the law and the prophets.

¹³"You enter through the narrow gate because the gate is wide and the way is broad which leads into utter destruction, and many are those entering through it; ¹⁴because the gate is narrow and the way is narrow which leads to life and they are few who are finding it.

¹⁵"And be on your guard against false prophets who come to you in sheep's clothing, but within they are ravening wolves. ¹⁶From their fruits you shall fully know them. Neither do they gather up grapes from thorn bushes, or figs from thistles. ¹⁷So every good tree produces good fruits, but the corrupt tree produces bad fruits. ¹⁸A good tree is not able to produce bad fruits, nor is a corrupt tree able to produce good fruits. ¹⁹Every tree not producing good fruit is cut down, and is cast into the fire. ²⁰Therefore, from their fruits you shall fully know them.

²¹"Not everyone who says to Me, Lord, Lord shall enter into the Kingdom of the Heavens, but the one who is doing the will of my Father who is in the Heavens. ²²Many shall say to Me in that day, 'Lord, Lord, have we not prophesied in Your name, and in Your name cast out demons, and in Your name we have done many powerful things?' ²³and then I will confess to them, 'I never knew you; depart from Me, those who are working lawlessness.'

²⁴"Therefore, everyone who hears these words of mine and does them, I will liken him to a wise man who built his house upon the rock. ²⁵And the rain came down, and the floods came, and the winds blew and beat against that house, and it did not fall for it had been founded upon the rock. ²⁶And everyone who hears these words, and does not do them, shall be likened to a foolish man who built his house upon the sand. ²⁷And the rain came down and the floods came, and the winds blew and beat against that house, and it fell, and great was the fall of it."

²⁸And it came to pass, when Jesus finished these words, the crowds were amazed at His teaching. ²⁹For He was teaching them as having authority and not as the scribes.

8 And He having come down from the mountain, many crowds followed Him. ²And behold a leper having come was doing Him homage, saying, "Lord, if You will, You are able to cleanse me." ³And having stretched forth His hand, Jesus touched him, saying, "I will, be cleansed." And immediately he was cleansed of the leprosy. ⁴And Jesus says to him, "See that you tell no one, but go show yourself to the priest, and offer the gift which Moses commanded for a witness to them."

⁵And Jesus having entered into Capernaum, a centurion came to Him begging Him, ⁶and saying, "Lord, my servant, a paralytic lies in the house being grievously tormented." ⁷And Jesus says to him, "I will come and heal him."

⁸But having answered, the centurion said, "Lord, I am not worthy that You should enter under my roof; but only speak the word and my servant shall be healed.

⁹For I am also a man under authority, having under myself soldiers, and I say to this one, 'Go', and he goes, and to another, 'Come', and he comes; and to my slave, 'Do this' and he does." ¹⁰And Jesus having heard, He marveled, and said to those following, "Truly I say to you, I have not found even in Israel such great faith. ¹¹And I say to you, that many shall come from East and West and shall recline with Abraham and Isaac and Jacob in the Kingdom of the Heavens. ¹²But the sons of the Kingdom shall be cast out into outer darkness; there shall be the weeping and the gnashing of teeth." ¹³And Jesus said to the centurion, "Go, and as you believed so let it be to you." And his servant was healed in that hour.

¹⁴And Jesus having come into the house of Peter, He saw his mother-in-law lying down and with a fever.

¹⁵And He touched her hand and the fever left her; and she arose and served them.

¹⁶And evening having come, they brought to Him many demoniacs; and He cast out the spirits with a word, and He healed all those who were sick, ¹⁷so that it might be fulfilled which was spoken by the prophet Isaiah, saying, "He took our sicknesses and He bore our diseases."

¹⁸Now Jesus having seen the great crowds around Him, gave orders to go to the other side.

¹⁹And having come near, a certain scribe said to Him, "Teacher, I will follow You wherever You may go." ²⁰And Jesus says to him, "The foxes have holes and the birds of heaven have nests, but the Son of Man does not have where He may lay the Head." ²¹And another of His disciples said to Him, "Permit me first to go and bury my father." ²²But Jesus said to him, "Follow me and leave the dead to bury their own dead."

²³And He having entered into the boat His disciples followed Him. ²⁴And behold a great tempest arose in the sea, so that the boat was being covered by the waves. But He was sleeping. ²⁵And His disciples, coming to Him aroused Him, saying, "Lord, save us, we are perishing." ²⁶And He says to them, "Why are you fearful? O you of little faith!" Then having arisen, He rebuked the wind and the sea, and there was a great calm. ²⁷And the men marveled, saying, "What manner of man is this, that even the winds and the sea obey Him?"

²⁸And He having come to the other side, into the country of the Gergesenes, two demoniacs met Him, coming out of the tombs, exceedingly fierce, so that no one was able to pass by that way. ²⁹And behold, they cried out saying. "What is it to us and to You, Jesus Son of God? Have You come before time to torment us?" ³⁰And at a great distance from them was a herd of many swine grazing. ³¹And the demons begged Him, saying, "If You cast us out, permit us to go away into the herd of swine." ³²And He said to them, "Go". And they came out and went

away into the herd of swine. And behold the whole herd rushed down the precipice into the sea and died in the waters. But those who were grazing them fled, and having gone forth into the city they proclaimed all things, and the things of the demoniacs. And behold all the city went out to meet with Jesus, and having seen Him, they begged that He might depart from their borders.

9 And having entered into the boat, He crossed over and came into His own city. [2]And behold, they brought to Him a paralytic, lying upon a bed. And Jesus having seen their faith, said to the paralytic, "Be of good cheer, son, your sins have been forgiven." [3]And behold, some of the scribes said within themselves, "This one blasphemes." [4]And Jesus having known their thoughts, said, "Why do you think evil in your hearts? [5]For which is easier to say, your sins have been forgiven, or to say, arise and walk? [6]But in order that you may know that the Son of Man has authority on earth to forgive sins;" then He says to the paralytic, "Having arisen, take up your bed and go to your house." [7]And having arisen he departed to his house. [8]But the crowds having seen it, they marveled and glorified God who gave such authority to men.

[9]And Jesus passing by from that place saw a man sitting at the tax office, called Matthew, and says to him, "Follow me," and having arisen he followed Him.

[10]And it came to pass as He was reclining in the house, and behold, also many tax collectors and sinners having come, were reclining with Jesus and His disciples. [11]And the Pharisees having seen it, said to His disciples, "Why does your teacher eat with tax collectors and sinners?" [12]But Jesus having heard, said to them, "Those who are healthy have no need of a doctor, but those who are sick. [13]But having gone, learn what this is, I desire mercy, and not sacrifice, for I came not to call the righteous but sinners to repentance."

[14]Then the disciples of John came to Him saying, "Why do we and the Pharisees fast much, and your disciples do not fast?" [15]And Jesus said to them, "Are sons of the bridechamber able to fast as long as the bridegroom is with them? But the days shall come when the bridegroom shall be taken from them, and then they shall fast. [16]And no one puts a piece of unfinished cloth on an old garment for the fullness of it takes away from the garment, and a tear becomes worse. [17]Neither do they put new wine into old wineskins, and if so, the wineskins are torn to pieces, and the wine is poured out, and the wineskins shall be destroyed. But they put new wine into new wineskins, are both are preserved."

[18]While He was speaking these things to them, behold, one came, a ruler, giving Him homage, saying, "My daughter has just died, but come, place Your hand upon her and she shall live." [19]And having arisen, Jesus and His disciples followed him. [20]And behold, a woman who had a hemorrhage for twelve years came near behind and touched the fringe of His garment. [21]For she was saying within herself, "If only I may touch His garment I shall be made whole." [22]And Jesus having turned and having seen her said, "Be of good cheer, daughter, for your faith has made you whole." And the woman was made whole from that hour.

[23]And Jesus having come into the house of the ruler, and having seen the flute-players and the crowd lamenting, [24]He says to them, "Withdraw, for the girl did not die, but is sleeping." And they were deriding Him. [25]But when the crowd was put out, He having entered took hold

of her hand and the girl was raised up.

$^{26}$And this report went out into all that land.

$^{27}$And Jesus passing on from there, two blind men followed Him, crying out and saying, "Have mercy on us, Son of David." $^{28}$And having come into the house, the blind men came to Him and Jesus said to them "Do you believe that I am able to do this?" They say to Him, "Yes, Lord." $^{29}$Then He touched their eyes saying, "Let it be to you according to your faith."

$^{30}$And their eyes were opened. And Jesus sternly charged them saying, "See that you let no one know." $^{31}$But going out they published Him abroad in all that land.

$^{32}$And as they were departing, behold they brought to Him a dumb man, a demoniac. $^{33}$And the demon having been cast out, the dumb man spoke. And the crowds marveled saying, "Never was anything seen like this in Israel." $^{34}$But the Pharisees were saying, "By the prince of the demons He casts out the demons."

$^{35}$And Jesus went about all the cities and the villages, teaching in their synagogues and preaching the gospel of the Kingdom, and He was healing every disease and every malady among the people. $^{36}$But having seen the crowds He was moved with compassion concerning them because they were exhausted and scattered as sheep having no shepherd. $^{37}$Then He says to His disciples, "The harvest truly is great, but the workers are few, $^{38}$pray therefore the Lord of the harvest that He may send workers into His harvest.

**10** And having called to Him His twelve disciples, He gave to them authority over unclean spirits, so as to cast them out, and to heal every disease and every malady. $^{2}$And the names of the twelve apostles are these: First, Simon who is called Peter, and Andrew his brother; James the son of Zebedee, and John his brother; $^{3}$Philip, and Bartholomew, Thomas and Matthew the tax collector; James, the son of Alpheus, and Lebbeus who was surnamed Thaddeus; $^{4}$Simon the Canaanite, and Judas Iscariot, who also betrayed Him.

$^{5}$These twelve Jesus sent out, having commanded them saying, "Do not enter into the way of the nations, and do not enter into a city of the Samaritans; $^{6}$But rather go to the lost sheep of the house of Israel. $^{7}$And as you go, preach, saying, the Kingdom of the Heavens has come near. $^{8}$Heal the sick, cleanse lepers, raise the dead, cast out demons. Freely you received, freely give. $^{9}$Do not get gold, nor silver, nor copper for your belts, $^{10}$nor a wallet for your journey, neither two tunics nor sandals, neither staff; for the worker is worthy of his food. $^{11}$And into whatever city or village you may enter, search out who in it is worthy. You remain there until you should depart. $^{12}$And when you come into the house, greet it. $^{13}$And if indeed the house is worthy, let your peace return to you. $^{14}$And whoever may not receive you nor hear your words, as you go out of that house or city, shake off the dust of your feet.

$^{15}$"Truly I say to you, it shall be easier for the land of Sodom and Gomorrah in the day of judgment than for that city.

$^{16}$"Behold I am sending you out as sheep in the midst of wolves. Therefore, be wise as serpents and as sincere as doves. $^{17}$But guard yourselves from men, for they shall deliver you up to sanhedrins, and they shall flog you in their synagogues. $^{18}$And you shall also be led before governors and kings for My sake, for a witness to them and to the nations. $^{19}$But when they deliver you up, do not be anxious how or what you may speak, for it shall be given to you in that hour what you may speak; $^{20}$For you are not those who speak, but the Spirit of your

Father which speaks in you. ²¹And brother shall deliver brother to death, and father, child, and children shall rise up against parents and put them to death. ²²And you shall be hated by all because of My name; but the one who endures to the end shall be saved. ²³But when they persecute you in this city, flee to another; for truly I say to you, you shall by no means finish going through the cities of Israel until the Son of Man has come. ²⁴A disciple is not above the teacher, nor a slave above his lord. ²⁵It is sufficient for the disciple that he be as his teacher, and the slave as his lord. If they call the master of the house Beelzebub, how much more the members of his household? ²⁶Therefore you should not fear them, for nothing is hid which shall not be revealed, and secret which shall not be known. ²⁷What I say to you in the dark, you speak in the light; and what you hear in the ear, proclaim upon the housetops. ²⁸And you should have no fear from those who kill the body, but are not able to kill the soul; but you should rather fear the One who is able also to destroy both soul and body in hell. ²⁹Are not two sparrows sold for an assarion? And one of them shall not fall upon the ground without your Father.

³⁰"But even the hairs of your head are all numbered. ³¹Therefore, you should not fear; you are more valuable than many sparrows. ³²Therefore, anyone whoever shall confess Me before men, I will also confess him before My Father Who is in the Heavens. ³³But whoever may deny Me before men, I will also deny him before My Father Who is in the Heavens. ³⁴Do not think that I came to bring peace upon the earth; I did not come to bring peace but a sword. ³⁵For I came to set at variance a man against his father, and a daughter against her mother, and a daughter-in-law against her mother-in-law, ³⁶and a man's enemies shall be those of his own household. ³⁷The one who loving father or mother more than Me is not worthy of Me, and the one loving son or daughter more than Me is not worthy of Me. ³⁸And whoever does not take up his cross and follow after Me is not worthy of Me.

³⁹"The one who finding his life shall lose it, and the one having lost his life for my sake shall find it.

⁴⁰"The one receiving you receives Me, and the one receiving Me receives the One Who sent Me.

⁴¹"The one receiving a prophet in the name of a prophet shall receive a prophet's reward; and the one receiving a righteous one in the name of a righteous one shall receive the reward of a righteous one. 42And whoever should give drink to one of these little ones, only a cup of cold water in the name of a disciple, truly, I say to you, he shall not at all lose his reward."

11 And it came to pass, when Jesus finished giving orders to His twelve disciples, He departed from there to teach and to preach in their cities.

²But John having heard in prison the works of Christ, and having sent two of his disciples, ³one said to Him, "Are you the coming One, or may we look for another?" ⁴And having answered Jesus said to them "Having gone, tell John what you hear and see.

⁵The blind are receiving sight, and the lame are walking, lepers are being cleansed, and the deaf are hearing, the dead are being raised, and the poor are receiving the good news. ⁶And blessed is anyone who shall not be offended in Me."

⁷And as these were departing, Jesus began to say to the crowds concerning John, "What did you go out into the wilderness to see? A reed being shaken by the wind? ⁸But what did you go

out to see? A man who was clothed in soft clothing? Behold, those who wear soft clothing are in the houses of kings, [9]but what did you go out to see? A prophet? Yes, I say to you, and more than a prophet. [10]For this is the one about whom it has been written, 'Behold I send My messengers before Your face, who shall prepare Your way before You.' [11]Truly I say to you, there has not arisen among those born of women a greater than John the Immerser. But the smallest in the Kingdom of the Heavens is greater than he. [12]And from the days of John the Immerser until now, the Kingdom of the Heavens is being taken violently, and the violent snatch it away. [13]For all the prophets and the law prophesied until John. [14]And if you are willing to receive it, he is Elijah who is about to come, [15]the one who has ears to hear, let him hear. [16]But to what shall I liken this generation? It is like children sitting in the market-places and calling to their companions, [17]and saying, 'We piped to you and you did not dance, we mourned to you and you did not lament.' [18]For John came neither eating nor drinking, and they say, 'He has a demon'. [19]The Son of Man came eating and drinking, and they say, 'Behold, a man, a glutton and a wine-bibber, a friend of tax collectors and of sinners.' And wisdom was justified of her children."

[20]Then He began to upbraid the cities in which most of His mighty deeds were done because they did not repent. [21]"Woe, to you, Chorazin, woe to you Bethsaida because if the mighty deeds which were done in you had been done in Tyre and Sidon, they would have repented long ago in sackcloth and ashes. [22]But I say to you, it shall be more bearable for Tyre and Sidon in the day of judgment than for you. [23]And you, Capernaum who has been exalted to Heaven shall be cast down to Hades; because if the mighty deeds which were done in you had been done in Sodom, it would have remained until this day. [24]But I say to you, it shall be more bearable for the land of Sodom in the day of judgment than for you.

[25]Having answered at that time, Jesus said, "I thank You, Father, Lord of Heaven and of earth, because You hid these things from the shrewd and intelligent and revealed them unto babes. [26]Yes, Father, because in this way it was pleasing before You. [27]All things were given over to Me by My Father, and no one knows the Son except the Father, neither does anyone know the Father except the Son, and to whomever the Son plans to reveal Him. [28]Come to Me all those who are toiling and are being burdened, and I will give you rest. [29]Take My yoke upon you and learn from Me because I am meek and lowly in heart; and you shall find rest to your soul, [30]for My yoke is easy and My burden is light."

**12** At that time Jesus went through the grain-fields on the Sabbaths; and His disciples were hungry and they began to pluck the ears of corn and to eat. [2]And the Pharisees who saw it said to Him, "Behold, your disciples are doing what is not lawful to do on a Sabbath." [3]But He said to them, "Have you not read what David did when he himself was hungry and those with him? [4]How he entered into the house of God and ate the shewbread, which was not lawful for him to eat, nor for those with him, except for the priests only? [5]Or, have you not read in the law, that the priests on the Sabbaths profane the Sabbath and are not guilty? [6]But I say to you, that a greater than the temple is here. [7]but if you knew what this is, 'I desire mercy and not sacrifice', you would not have condemned the guiltless. [8]For the Son of Man is also Lord of the Sabbath."

[9]And having departed from there, He came into their synagogue. [10]And behold, there was a

man having the hand withered. And they asked Him saying, "Is it lawful to heal on the Sabbath?" in order that they may accuse Him. ¹¹But He said to them, "What man will there be of you, who will have one sheep, and if this one falls into a ditch on the Sabbaths, will he not lay hold of it and lift it out? ¹²Therefore, how much more valuable a man than a sheep. Therefore, it is lawful to do good on the Sabbaths." ¹³Then He says to the man, "Stretch forth your hand," and he stretched it forth, and it was restored whole as the other.

¹⁴But the Pharisees having gone out took counsel against Him, how they might destroy Him. ¹⁵But Jesus having known this withdrew from there, and many crowds followed Him; and He healed them all, ¹⁶and charged them in order that they may not make Him known, ¹⁷so that it may be fulfilled which was spoken through Isaiah the prophet, saying, ¹⁸"Behold, My Child Whom I chose, My Beloved, in Whom My soul is well-pleased, I will put My Spirit upon Him, and He shall proclaim judgment to the nations. ¹⁹He shall not strive nor cry aloud, neither shall anyone hear His voice in the streets. ²⁰A broken reed shall He not break off, and a smoking flax He shall not quench, until He sends forth judgment unto victory. ²¹And in His name the nations shall hope."

²²Then a blind and dumb demoniac was brought to Him, and He healed him so that the blind and dumb both spoke and saw. ²³And all the crowds were amazed and said, "Is not this the Son of David?" ²⁴But the Pharisees having heard it said, "This one does not cast out the demons except by Beelzebub the prince of the demons." ²⁵But Jesus knowing their thoughts said to them, "Every kingdom divided against itself shall be made desolate, and every city or house divided against itself shall not stand. ²⁶And if Satan casts out Satan he is divided against himself; there, how then shall his kingdom stand? ²⁷And, if I by Beelzebub cast out demons, by whom do your sons cast them out? Because of this they shall be your judges. ²⁸But if by the Spirit of God I cast out the demons, then the Kingdom of God has come upon you. ²⁹Or, how is anyone able to enter into the house of the strong one and plunder his goods, unless he first binds the strong one, and he shall plunder his house? ³⁰The one who is not with Me is against Me, and the one who is not gathering with Me scatters abroad. ³¹Because of this I say to you, every sin and blasphemy shall be forgiven to men, but the blasphemy of the Spirit shall not be forgiven to men. ³²And whoever may speak a word against the Son of Man, it shall be forgiven him, neither in this age nor the coming age. ³³Either you make the tree good and its fruit good, or you make the tree corrupt and its fruit corrupt; for the tree is known by the fruit.

³⁴"Generation of vipers, how are you able to speak good things, being evil? For out of the abundance of the heart the mouth speaks. ³⁵The good man out of the good treasure of the heart brings forth the good, and evil man out of the evil treasure brings forth evil. ³⁶And I say to you, that every idle word which men shall speak, they shall give account of it in the day of judgment. ³⁷For by your words you shall be justified, and by your words you shall be condemned."

³⁸Then some of the scribes and Pharisees answered, saying, "Teacher, we wish to see a sign from you." ³⁹But having answered He said to them, "An evil and adulterous generation seeks a sign, and no sign shall be given to it except the sign of the prophet Jonah. ⁴⁰For as Jonah was in the belly of the sea-monster three days and three nights so shall the Son of Man be in the heart of the earth three days and three nights. ⁴¹The men of Nineveh shall rise up in the judgment with this generation and shall condemn it because they repented at the preaching of

Jonah, and behold, a greater than Jonah is here. ⁴²The queen of the South shall rise up in the judgment with this generation and condemn it because she came from the ends of the earth to hear the wisdom of Solomon, and behold, a greater than Solomon is here. ⁴³And when the unclean spirit goes out from a man, he goes through waterless places seeking rest, and he does not find it. ⁴⁴Then he says, 'I will return unto my house from where I came.' And having come he finds it unoccupied, swept and furnished. ⁴⁵Then he goes and takes with him seven other spirits more evil than himself, and having entered, he dwells there; and the last of that man becomes worse than the first. Thus it shall also be with this evil generation."

⁴⁶But while He was still speaking to the crowds, behold His mother and brothers stood outside seeking to speak to Him. ⁴⁷And someone said to Him, "Behold your mother and brothers stand outside seeking to speak to you." ⁴⁸And having answered, He said to the one who spoke to Him, "Who is my mother and who are my brothers?"

⁴⁹And stretching out His hand to His disciples, He said, "Behold, my mother and my brothers; ⁵⁰for whoever may do the will of My Father Who is in the Heavens, this one is my brother and sister and mother."

13 And in that day, Jesus having gone out of from the house was sitting by the sea. ²And many crowds were gathered together with Him, so that He having entered into the boat was sitting down, and all the crowd stood upon the shore. ³And He spoke many things to them in parables, saying, "Behold the sower went out to sow.

⁴"And in his sowing, some indeed fell by the roadside, and the birds came and ate them up. ⁵But other seed fell upon the stony places where it did not have much earth; and immediately it sprang up because it had no depths of earth. ⁶And the sun having risen, it was scorched, and because it had no root it was withered. ⁷But other seed fell among the thorns, and they came up and the thorns choked them. ⁸But other seed fell upon the good earth, and brought forth fruit, some indeed a hundredfold, and some sixty and some thirty. ⁹The one who has ears to hear let him hear."

¹⁰And having come, the disciples said to Him, "Why do you speak to them in parables?" ¹¹And having answered He said to them, "Because it is given to you to know the mysteries of the Kingdom of the Heavens, but to them it has not been given. ¹²For whoever has, it shall be given to him, and he shall have abundance, but whoever has not, even what he has shall be taken from him.

¹³"Because of this I speak to them in parables, because seeing they do not see, and hearing they do not hear nor understand. ¹⁴And the prophecy of Isaiah is fulfilled in them, which says, 'Hearing you shall hear and not at all understand, and seeing you shall see and not at all perceive. ¹⁵For the heart of this people has become fat, and they heard with heavy ears, and they have closed their eyes, lest they see with the eyes, and hear with the ears, and understand with the heart, and they should be converted, and I should heal them.' ¹⁶But blessed are your eyes because they see, and your ears because they hear. ¹⁷For truly I say to you that many prophets and righteous ones have desired to see what you see, and they did not see it, and to hear what you hear and did not hear it.

¹⁸"Hear therefore the parable of the sower.

¹⁹"Everyone who hears the Word of the Kingdom and does not understand, the evil one

comes and snatches away that which has been sown in his heart. This is the seed sown by the roadside. ²⁰And the seed sown on the stony places, this is the one who hears the Word and receives it immediately with joy; ²¹but he has no root in himself, but is for a while, but tribulation or persecution having come because of the Word, he is immediately offended. ²²But the seed sown among the thorns, this is the one who hears the Word, and the cares of this age and the deceitfulness of riches choke the Word, and it becomes unfruitful. ²³But the seed sown upon the good earth, this is the one who hears the Word and understands, who indeed yields fruit, and one truly brings forth a hundredfold, and the one sixty-fold, and the one thirty-fold."

²⁴He set another parable before them, saying, "The Kingdom of the Heavens is likened to a man sowing good seed in his field. ²⁵But when the men were sleeping his enemy came and sowed darnel in the midst of the wheat and departed. ²⁶But when the plant sprouted and produced fruit, then also the darnel appeared. ²⁷And the slaves of the master of the house having come said to him, 'Lord, did you not sow good seed in your field? From where then has it the darnel?' ²⁸And he said to them, 'An enemy man did this.' And the slaves said to him, 'Do you wish then that having gone out we may gather them?' ²⁹But he said, 'No, no, lest when gathering the darnel you might uproot the wheat with them. ³⁰Permit both to grow until the harvest; and in the time of the harvest I will say to the reapers, gather first the darnel, and bind them into bundles in order to burn them, but gather the wheat into my barn.'"

³¹Another parable He set before them, saying, "The Kingdom of the Heavens is like a grain of mustard seed, which a man having taken sowed in his field, ³²which seed is truly smaller than all the seeds, but when it has grown it is greater than the vegetables, and become a tree, so that the birds of the heaven come and roost in its branches."

³³He spoke another parable to them: "The Kingdom of the Heavens is like leaven, which a woman having taken hid in three measures of flour, until the whole was leavened."

³⁴Jesus spoke all these things to the crowds in parables, and without a parable He spoke not to them.

³⁵Thus was fulfilled which was spoken by the prophet, saying, "I will open my mouth in parables, I will utter things which have been hidden from the foundation of the world."

³⁶Then sending away the crowds, Jesus went into the house. And His disciples came to Him, saying, "Explain to us the parable of the darnel of the field." ³⁷And having answered He said to them, "The One who sows the good seed is the Son of Man; ³⁸and the field is the world; but the good seed, these are the sons of the Kingdom; and the darnel are the sons of the evil one; ³⁹and the enemy who sowed them is the Devil; and the harvest is the end of this age; and the reapers are angels. ⁴⁰Therefore, as the darnel is gathered and burned with fire, so shall it be at the end of the age. ⁴¹The Son of Man shall send His angels and they shall gather out of His Kingdom all the offences and those who do lawlessness, ⁴²and they shall cast them into the furnace of fire, and there shall be the weeping and the gnashing of teeth.

⁴³"Then the righteous shall shine as the sun in the Kingdom of their Father. The one who has ears to hear, let him hear.

⁴⁴"Again, the Kingdom of the Heavens is like a treasure hidden in a field, which a man finding, hid, and from the joy of it he goes and sells all whatever he has and buys that field.

⁴⁵"Again, the Kingdom of the Heavens is like a merchant man seeking fine pearls, ⁴⁶who

having found one very valuable pearl, went and sold all whatever he had and bought it. ⁴⁷"Again, the Kingdom of the Heavens is like a large net cast into the sea, gathering all kinds of fish, ⁴⁸which when it was filled and having it drawn to shore, and having sat down, they gathered the good into vessels, but the rotten they threw out. ⁴⁹"So shall it be at the end of the age. The angels shall go out and separate the evil from the midst of the righteous, ⁵⁰and shall cast them into the furnace of fire. There shall be the weeping and the gnashing of teeth."

⁵¹Jesus says to them, "Do you understand all these things?" They said to Him, "Yes." ⁵²And He said to them, "Because of this every scribe instructed into the Kingdom of the Heavens is like to a man, who is a householder who brings out of his treasure-box new and old."

⁵³And it came to pass when Jesus finished these parables, He departed from there. ⁵⁴And having come into His own country He taught them in their synagogue so that they were astonished and said, "From where is this wisdom and mighty works to this one? ⁵⁵Is this not the son of the carpenter? Is not his mother called Mary, and his brothers, James, Joseph, Simon and Judas? ⁵⁶And are not all his sisters with us? Therefore, from where then are all these things to this one?" ⁵⁷And they were offended in Him. But Jesus said to them, "A prophet is not without honor except in his own country and in his own house. ⁵⁸And He did not do there many mighty works because of their unbelief.

14 At that time Herod the Tetrarch heard the report concerning Jesus, ²and he said to his servants, "This is John the Immerser; he has risen from the dead, and because of this, mighty deeds are working in him." ³For Herod, having seized John, bound him and put him in prison because of Herodias the wife of his brother Philip. ⁴For John was saying to him, "It is not lawful for you to have her." ⁵And wishing to kill him, he was afraid of the crowd because they held him as a prophet. ⁶But Herodias' birthday being celebrated, the daughter of Herodias danced and pleased Herod; ⁷Whereupon, with an oath he promised to give her whatever she may ask. ⁸But she being urged on by her mother, says, "Give to me here upon a platter the head of John the Immerser." ⁹And the king was grieved; but because of the oaths and those reclining with him, he ordered it to be given. ¹⁰And, he sent and had John beheaded in the prison. ¹¹And his head was brought upon a platter, and was given to the girl, and she brought it to her mother. ¹²And going forth his disciples came and took the body and buried it, and having come told Jesus. ¹³And Jesus having heard, withdrew from there in a boat into a desert place to be alone. And the crowds having heard, they followed Him on foot from the cities. ¹⁴And, Jesus having gone out, saw a great crowd, and He was moved with compassion upon them, and He healed their sicknesses.

¹⁵But evening having come, His disciples came to Him saying, "The place is desert and the hour has already passed. Send the crowds away in order that having gone into the villages they may buy themselves food." ¹⁶But Jesus said to them, "They have no need to go away; you give to them to eat." ¹⁷But they say to Him, "We do not have here anything except five loaves and two fishes." ¹⁸And He said, "Bring them here to me." ¹⁹And He having commanded the crowds to recline upon the grass, and having taken the five loaves and the two fishes, having looked up to Heaven, He gave blessing, and having broken He gave the loaves to the disciples, and the disciples to the crowds. ²⁰And all ate and were filled. And they took up twelve baskets

full of the pieces left over. ²¹And there were about five thousand men who ate without women and children.
²²And immediately Jesus urged His disciples to enter into the boat and to go before Him to the other side until He should send the crowds away. ²³And having sent the crowds away, He went up into the mountain alone to pray. And evening having come He was there alone. ²⁴But already the boat was in the midst of the sea, being tossed by the waves, for the wind was contrary. ²⁵But in the fourth watch of the night Jesus went to them walking on the sea. ²⁶But His disciples having seen Him walking upon the sea were troubled, saying, "It is a ghost!". And they cried out from fear. ²⁷But immediately Jesus spoke to them saying, "Be of good cheer, I am I, do not be afraid."
²⁸And having answered Him, Peter said, "Lord, if it is You, command me to come to You upon the waters."
²⁹And He said, "Come." And having come down from the boat, Peter walked upon the waters to go to Jesus.
³⁰But seeing the strong wind he was afraid; and beginning to sink he cried out saying, "Lord, save me". ³¹And immediately Jesus having stretched out the hand took hold of him, and says to him, "O, you of little faith, why did you doubt?" ³²And having come into the boat the wind ceased. ³³And those in the boat came and worshipped Him, saying, "Truly You are the Son of God."
³⁴And having crossed over, they came to the land of Gennesaret. ³⁵And having known Him, the men of that place sent into all that surrounding country, and they brought to Him all that were sick. ³⁶And they begged Him that they might only touch the border of His garment. And as many as touched it were completely healed.

15 Then scribes and Pharisees from Jerusalem came to Jesus, saying, ²"Why do Your disciples transgress the tradition of the elders? For they do not wash their hands when they eat bread." ³But He having answered said to them, "And why do you transgress the commandment of God because of your tradition? ⁴For God commanded saying, 'Honor your father and mother, and the one who curses father or mother, let him die the death.' ⁵But you say, whoever says to father or mother, what you would have gained from me is given to God, ⁶and he in no wise honors his father or his mother. And you have made void the commandment of God because of your tradition. ⁷Hypocrites, well did Isaiah prophesy concerning you, saying, ⁸'This people draws near to Me with their mouth, and they honor Me with the lips, but their heart is far from Me, ⁹and they do worship Me in vain, teaching for doctrines the commandments of men.'"
¹⁰And having called the crowd to Him, He said to them, "You hear and understand; ¹¹not what goes into the mouth defiles the man, but what goes out of the mouth, this defiles the man."
¹²Then, His disciples having come said to Him, "Do you know that the Pharisees having heard Your word were offended?" ¹³But He having answered said, "Every plant which My Heavenly Father did not plant shall be rooted up. ¹⁴Leave them alone. They are blind guides of the blind; but if a blind one guides a blind one both shall fall into the ditch." ¹⁵But having answered Peter said to Him, "Explain this parable to us." And He said, ¹⁶"Are you also still

without understanding? ¹⁷Do you not yet understand that everything that goes into the mouth passes into the stomach and is cast out into the waste place?
¹⁸But the things which go out of the mouth come out of the heart, and these defile the man. ¹⁹For out of the heart comes forth evil thoughts, murders, adulteries, fornications, thefts, false witnesses, blasphemies, ²⁰These are the things which defile the man. But to eat with unwashed hands does not defile the man."
²¹And having gone out from there, Jesus withdrew into the regions of Tyre and Sidon. ²²And behold a Canaanite woman having come out of those regions cried out to Him, saying, "Have mercy on me, Lord, Son of David. My daughter is miserably demon-possessed."
²³And He did not answer her a word. And His disciples having come were asking Him, saying, "Send her away because she cries out after us." ²⁴But having answered, He said, "I was not sent except to the lost sheep of the house of Israel." ²⁵But having come, she worshipped Him saying, "Lord help me." ²⁶And having answered He said, "It is not good to take the bread of the children and to cast it to the dogs." ²⁷But she said, "Yes Lord, for even the dogs eat from the crumbs which fall from their master's table." ²⁸Then, Jesus having answered said to her, "O woman, your faith is great, let it be to you as you desire." And her daughter was healed from that hour.
²⁹And having departed from there, Jesus came to the Sea of Galilee; and having gone up into the mountain He was sitting there. ³⁰And many crowds came to Him having with them the lame, blind, dumb, crippled and many others, and they cast them down at the feet of Jesus, and He healed them; ³¹so that the crowds wondered seeing the dumb speaking, the crippled whole, the lame walking and the blind seeing. And they glorified the God of Israel. ³²And Jesus having called to His disciples said, "I have compassion on the crowd because already they continue with me three days, and they have not anything they may eat; and I do not wish to send them away without food, lest they faint in the way." ³³And His disciples say to Him, "Where in a desert shall be for us so many loaves so as to feed so great a crowd? ³⁴And Jesus said to them, "How many loaves do you have?" And they said, "Seven and a few small fish." ³⁵And He commanded the crowds to recline upon the ground. ³⁶And having taken the seven loaves and the fish, having given thanks He broke them and gave them to His disciples and the disciples to the crowd. ³⁷And all ate and were filled. And they took up what was left over of the pieces, seven baskets full. ³⁸And those who ate were four thousand men without women and children. ³⁹And having sent the crowds away, He went up into the boat and came into the regions of Magdala.

**16** And the Pharisees and Zadducees having come tempting Him asked Him to show them a sign out of Heaven. ²But having answered He said to them, "Evening having come you say 'fair weather', for the sky is red, ³and in the morning, 'today, stormy weather', for the sky is red and gloomy. Hypocrites, indeed you know how to judge the face of the heaven, but the signs of the times you are not able to judge. ⁴An evil and adulterous generation seeks a sign. And no sign shall be given it except the sign of Jonah the Prophet." And having left them He went His way.
⁵And His disciples having come to the other side forgot to take loaves. ⁶And Jesus said to them, "Beware and take heed of the leaven of the Pharisees and Sadducees." ⁷But they were

reasoning among themselves, saying, "It is because we did not take loaves." [8]And Jesus having known their thoughts said to them, "Why do you reason among yourselves, you of little faith, because you did not take loaves? [9]Do you not yet understand nor remember the five loaves of the five thousand, and how many baskets you took up?
[10]Nor the seven loaves of the four thousand and how many baskets you took up? [11]How do you not understand that I spoke not about loaves to you to take heed from the leaven of Pharisees and Sadducees?" [12]Then they understood that He did not say beware of the leaven of bread, but of the teaching of the Pharisees and Sadducees.
[13]Now Jesus having come into the regions of Caesarea Philippi, asked His disciples, saying, "Whom do men say, Me, the Son of Man to be?" [14]And they said, "Some say John the Immerser, but others Elijah, and others Jeremiah or one of the prophets."
[15]He says to them, "But whom do you say Me to be?"
[16]And Simon Peter having answered, said, "You are the Christ, the Son of the living God."
[17]And having answered Jesus said to him, "You are blessed, Simon, son of Jonah, because flesh and blood did not reveal it to you but My Father who is in the Heavens. [18]But I also say to you that you are Peter, and upon this rock I will build My church. And the gates of Hades shall not prevail against it. [19]And I will give to you the keys of the Kingdom of the Heavens; and whatever you may bind upon earth shall have been bound in the Heavens, and whatever you may loose upon the earth shall have been loosed in the Heavens. [20]Then He charged His disciples that they should tell no one that He is Jesus the Christ."
[21]From that time Jesus began to show His disciples that it was necessary for Him to go unto Jerusalem and suffer many things from the elders and the chief priests and scribes and to be killed and to be raised up on the third day. [22]And Peter, having taken Him aside began to rebuke Him, saying, "God be merciful to you Lord, this shall in no wise be to you." [23]But being turned, He said to Peter, "You go behind Me, Satan, you are an offence to Me because you do not consider the things of God, but the things of men."
[24]Then Jesus said to His disciples, "If anyone wishes to come after Me, let him deny himself, and let him take up his cross, and let him follow Me. [25]For whoever may wish to save his life shall lose it, and whoever may lose his life for My sake shall find it. [26]For what does a man profit if he should gain the whole world and forfeit his life? Or what shall a man give in exchange for his life? [27]For the Son of Man is about to come in the glory of His Father with His angels, and then He shall reward each according to His deeds. Truly I say to you, there are some of those standing here who shall in no wise taste of death until they see the Son of Man coming in His Kingdom."

17 And after six days Jesus takes Peter and James and John his brother, and leads them up into a high mountain alone. [2]And He was transformed before them and His face shone as the sun, and His garments were white as the light. [3]And behold Moses and Elijah appeared to them, speaking with Him. [4]And Peter having answered said to Jesus, "Lord, it is good for us to be here. If You will, let us make here three tents, one for You, and one for Moses and one for Elijah."
[5]While he was still speaking with Him, behold a bright cloud enveloped them, and behold a voice out of the cloud, saying "This is My Beloved Son in whom I delight; hear Him." [6]And

hearing this the disciples fell on their faces and were greatly frightened. ⁷And having drawn near, Jesus touched them and said, "Arise and do not be frightened." ⁸And when they lifted up their eyes they saw no one except Jesus only.

⁹And as they were coming down from the mountain, Jesus charged them, saying, "Tell no one the vision until the Son of Man is raised from the dead" ¹⁰And His disciples asked Him, saying, "Why therefore do the scribes say it is necessary that Elijah come first?" ¹¹And having answered Jesus said to them, "Elijah indeed comes first and he shall restore all things.

¹²But I say to you that Elijah has already come, and they did not know him, but they did to him whatever they wished. So also the Son of Man is about to suffer by them." ¹³Then the disciples understood that He spoke to them about John the Immerser.

¹⁴And they having come to the crowd, a man came to Him, falling on his knees before Him and saying,

¹⁵"Lord, have mercy on my son because he is a lunatic and suffers grievously; for often he falls into the fire and often into the water. ¹⁶And I brought him to your disciples, and they were not able to heal him." ¹⁷And having answered Jesus said, "O faithless and perverse generation! How long shall I endure you? Bring him here to Me," ¹⁸And Jesus rebuked him and the demon went out from him and the child was healed from that hour.

¹⁹Then the disciples having come to Jesus alone said, "Why were we not able to cast him out?" ²⁰And Jesus said to them "Because of your unbelief. For truly I say to you, if you have faith as a gain of mustard seed, you shall say to this mountain, move from this place to that place and it shall move, and nothing shall be impossible for you. ²¹But this kind does not go out except by prayer and fasting."

²²And while they abode in Galilee, Jesus said to them, "The Son of Man is about to be delivered into the hands of the men, ²³and they shall kill Him, and on the third day He shall be raised up." And they were exceedingly sorrowful.

²⁴And they having come to Capernaum, those receiving the double didrachmas came to Peter and said, "Does not your teacher pay the double didrachmas?"

²⁵He says, "Yes." And having come into the house Jesus anticipated him, saying, "What do you think, Simon? From whom do the kings of the earth receive toll or tax? From their sons or from foreigners?"

²⁶Peter said to Him, "From foreigners." And Jesus said to him, "So then, the sons are free. ²⁷But in order that we may not offend them, go to the sea and cast a hook, and the first fish that comes up you take, and having opened his mouth, you shall find a stater. Taking that, give it to them for you and Me."

18 In that hour the disciples came to Jesus, saying, "Who therefore is the greatest in the Kingdom of the Heavens? ²And Jesus having called a little child, set it in the midst of them, ³and said, "Truly I say to you, unless you turn and become as little children you shall in no wise enter into the Kingdom of the Heavens. ⁴Whoever therefore shall humble himself as this little child, this one is the greatest in the Kingdom of the Heavens. ⁵And whoever receives one little child like this in My name receives Me. ⁶But whoever causes one of these little ones who believe on Me to stumble, it is profitable for him that a great millstone should be hanged about his neck, and he be sunk in the depths of the sea. ⁷Woe to the world because of

occasions for stumbling; for it is necessary that occasions for stumbling come, nevertheless, woe to that man by whom occasions for stumbling come. [8]And if your hand or your foot causes you to stumble, cut them off and cast them from you. It is profitable for you to enter into life lame or crippled than having two hands or two feet to be cast into eternal fire. [9]And if your eye causes you to stumble, pluck it out and cast it from you. It is profitable for you to enter into life with one eye than having two eyes to be cast into the hell of fire. [10]See that you do not despise one of these little ones, for I say to you, that their angels in the Heavens always see the face of My Father Who is in the Heavens.

[11]"For the Son of Man came to save that which was lost. [12]What do you think? If any man has a hundred sheep, and one of them be led astray, does he not leave the ninety and nine upon the mountains, and having gone he seeks the one who is straying. [13]And if it should be that he finds it, truly I say to you, that he rejoices over it more than over the ninety and nine which had not gone astray. [14]So it is not the will before your Father who is in the Heavens, that one of these little ones should perish.

[15]"And if your brother sins against you, go and reprove him between you and him alone. If he hears you, you have gained your brother. [16]But if he does not hear, take with you yet one or two others, that at the mouth of two or three witness every word may be established. [17]But if he does not hear them, tell it to the church. And also if he does not hear the church, let him be to you as the Gentile or the tax collector. [18]Truly I say to you, whatever you may bind upon the earth shall have been bound in Heaven, and whatever you may loose upon the earth shall have been loosed in Heaven. [19]Again I say to you, that if two of you should agree on earth to anything, whatever they should ask, it shall be done for them by My Father in the Heavens. [20]For where two or three are gathered together in My Name, there I am in their midst."

[21]Then Peter having come to Him, said, "Lord, how often shall my brother sin against me and I forgive him? Until seven times?" [22]Jesus says to him, "I do not say to you, until seven times, but until seventy times seven. [23]Because of this the Kingdom of the Heavens has been likened to a man, a king who wished to settle accounts with his slaves. [24]But when he began to settle accounts one was brought to him owing ten thousand talents. [25]And when he had nothing to repay, his lord commanded him to be sold, even his wife and the children, and everything he had, and to make payment. [26]Then having fallen down, the slave gives him homage, saying, "Lord, have patience with me and I shall repay to you everything." [27]And having been moved with compassion, the lord of that slave released him and forgave him the debt. [28]But that slave having gone out, found one of his fellow-slaves who was owing him one hundred denarii; and having seized him, he choked him saying, "Repay me what you owe." [29]Then his fellow-slave having fallen down at his feet, begged him, saying, "Be patient with me and I shall repay you everything."

[30]"But he would not, but having gone forth, he cast him into prison until he should repay what he owed. [31]But when his fellow-slaves saw the things which took place, they were exceedingly sorrowful, and having gone, they declared to their lord all the things which happened. [32]Then, his lord having called him, says to him, "Evil slave, all that debt I forgave you when you begged me. [33]Must you not also have mercy on your fellow-slave, as I also had mercy on you." [34]And his lord being angry, delivered him to the tormentors until he should repay all that he owed to him. And in like manner My Heavenly Father shall do to you if you

do not from your hearts forgive each his brother their trespasses."

**19** And it came to pass, when Jesus finished these words, He departed from Galilee and came into the regions of Judea on the other side of the Jordan. ²And many crowds followed Him, and He healed them there.

³And the Pharisees came to Him testing Him, and saying to Him, "Is it lawful for a man to put away his wife for every cause?" ⁴And having answered He said to them, "Have you not read that He who made them from the beginning made them male and female?" ⁵And He said, "For this cause a man shall leave behind father and mother and shall be joined to his wife, and the two shall be one flesh; ⁶so that they are no more two but one flesh. Therefore, what God has joined together, let no man separate." ⁷They say to Him, "Why then did Moses command to give her a bill of divorce, and put her away?" ⁸He says to them, "Because Moses in regard to the hardness of your heart permitted you to put away your wives; but from the beginning it was not so.

⁹"And I say to you, that whoever puts away his wife except for fornication and should marry another commits adultery, and he who should marry her who has been put away commits adultery." ¹⁰His disciples say to Him, "If this is the case of man with his wife, it is not profitable to marry." ¹¹But He said to them, "All are not able to receive this saying, but those to whom it has been given. ¹²For there are eunuchs who were born thus from their mother's womb, and there are eunuchs who were made eunuchs by men, and there are eunuchs who made themselves eunuchs because of the Kingdom of the Heavens. He who is able to receive this saying let him receive it."

¹³Then were brought to Him little children, that He might lay His hands upon them and pray. But the disciples rebuked them. ¹⁴But Jesus said, "Permit the little children to come to Me, and do not hinder them, for of such is the Kingdom of the Heavens." ¹⁵And having laid hands on them, He departed from there.

¹⁶And, behold, one having come said to Him, "Good teacher, what good deed shall I do that I may have eternal life?" ¹⁷And He said to him, "Why do you call Me good? No one is good except One, God. But if you wish to enter into life, keep the commandments." ¹⁸He says to Him, "Which?"; And Jesus said, "You shall not murder, you shall not commit adultery, you shall not steal. You shall not bear false witness; ¹⁹honor your father and mother, and you shall love your neighbor as yourself." ²⁰The young man says to Him, "All these have I kept from my youth. What do I yet lack?" ²¹Jesus said unto him, "If you wish to be perfect, go, sell your possessions and give to the poor, and you shall have treasure in Heaven, and come follow Me."

²²But the young man hearing the word went away sorrowful. For he had many possessions.

²³And Jesus said to His disciples, "Truly I say to you, that with difficulty shall a man enter into the Kingdom of the Heavens. ²⁴And again I say to you, it is easier for a camel to go through the eye of a needle than for a rich man to enter into the Kingdom of God." ²⁵But His disciples having heard this were greatly amazed, saying, "Who then is able to be saved?" ²⁶And looking up, Jesus said to them, "With men this is impossible, but with God all things are possible."

²⁷Then, Peter having answered said to Him, "Behold we have left all and followed You.

What then shall be ours?" ²⁸And Jesus said to them, "Truly I say to you, that you who have followed Me, in the regeneration, when the Son of Man sits upon the throne of His glory, you also shall sit upon twelve thrones, judging the twelve tribes of Israel. ²⁹And everyone who has left houses, or brothers, or sisters, or father, or mother, or wife, or children, or lands for My Name's sake shall receive a hundredfold, and shall inherit eternal life. But many who are first shall be last, ³⁰and the last shall be first.

20 "For the Kingdom of the Heavens is like a man, master of a house, who went out early in the morning to hire workers for his vineyard. ²And having agreed with the workers for a denarius for the day he sent them into his vineyard. ³And having gone out about the third hour, he saw others standing in the market place idle; ⁴and he said to them, 'You go also into the vineyard, and whatever is just I will give to you'; and they went. ⁵Having gone out again about the sixth and ninth hour he did likewise. ⁶And about the eleventh hour, having gone out he found others standing, and says to them, 'Why do you stand here all the day idle?' ⁷They say to him,' Because no one has hired us.' He says to them, 'You go also into the vineyard, and whatever is just you shall receive.'

⁸"And evening having come, the lord of the vineyard says to his steward, 'Call the workers and pay them the wage, beginning from the last until the first.'

⁹"And those hired about the eleventh hour, having come, received each a denarius. ¹⁰And the first having come, supposed that they would receive more. And they also received each a denarius. ¹¹And having received it they were murmuring against the master of the house, ¹²saying, 'These last worked one hour, and you made them equal to us who bore the burden and the heat of the day.' ¹³But having answered he said to one of them, 'Comrade, I do you no injustice; did you not agree with me for a denarius? ¹⁴Take what is yours and go. But I wish to give to this last as also to you. ¹⁵Or, is it not lawful for me to do what I wish with what is mine? Or, is your eye evil because I am good?' ¹⁶So the last shall be first, and the first last; for many are called, but few chosen."

¹⁷And Jesus, going up to Jerusalem, took the twelve disciples alone in the road and said to them,

¹⁸"Behold we go up into Jerusalem, and the Son of Man shall be delivered to the chief priests and the scribes, ¹⁹and they shall condemn Him to death. And they shall deliver Him up to the nations to mock and to flog and to crucify. And the third day He shall rise up."

²⁰Then the mother of the sons of Zebedee came to Him with her sons, kneeling and asking something from Him. ²¹And He said to her, "What do you wish?" She says to Him, "Say that these my two sons may sit, one on Your right and one on Your left in Your Kingdom. ²²But having answered, Jesus said, "You do not know what you ask. Are you able to drink the cup which I am about to drink, and to be immersed with the immersion I am immersed with?" They say to Him, "We are able."

²³And He says to them, "You shall indeed drink My cup, and you shall be immersed with the immersion I am immersed with. But to sit on My right and on My left is not Mine to give, but for those for whom it has been prepared by My Father." ²⁴And the ten having heard it, were indignant about the two brothers. ²⁵And Jesus having called them to Him said, "You know that the rulers of the nations lord it over them, and ²⁶the great ones exercise authority

over them. But it shall not be like this among you; but whoever among you may wish to be great, let him be your servant, ²⁷and whoever among you may wish to be chief let him be your slave; ²⁸even as the Son of Man did not come to be ministered to, but to minister and to give his life a ransom for many."

²⁹And as they were going out from Jericho, a great crowd followed Him. ³⁰And behold, two blind men sitting by the road, having heard that Jesus was passing by, cried out saying, "Lord have mercy on us, Son of David." ³¹But the crowd rebuked them that they might be silent. But they were crying out more, saying. "Lord have mercy on us Son of David." ³²And having stopped, Jesus called them and said, "What do you wish I should do for you?" ³³They say to Him, "Lord, that our eyes may be opened." ³⁴And moved with compassion, Jesus touched their eyes, and immediately their eyes received sight, and they followed Him.

## 21

And when they drew near to Jerusalem, and came to Bethphage near to the Mount of Olives, then Jesus sent two disciples, ²saying to them, "Go into the village over against you, and immediately you will find an ass tied and a colt with her. Having loosed them you bring to Me. ³And if anyone says anything to you, you shall say that the Lord has need of them. And immediately he shall send them. ⁴Now all this was done that it might be fulfilled which was spoken by the prophet saying, ⁵"Speak to the daughter of Zion, behold your King comes to you meek and mounted upon an ass and a colt, the son of a beast of burden." ⁶And the disciples having gone and having done just as Jesus commanded them, ⁷brought the ass and the colt, and they put their garments upon them, and He sat upon them.

⁸And most of the crowd spread their garments in the way; and others were cutting branches from the trees and were spreading them in the way. ⁹And the crowds, those going in front, and those following cried out, saying, "Hosanna to the Son of David, blessed is the One who comes in the name of the Lord, Hosanna in the highest." ¹⁰And having entered into Jerusalem all the city was shaken, saying, who is this? ¹¹And the crowds said, "This is Jesus the prophet, the One from Nazareth of Galilee."

¹²And Jesus having entered into the temple of God, and cast out all those selling and buying in the temple; and He overthrew the table of the money changers and the seats of those selling the doves. ¹³And He says to them, "It has been written, 'My House shall be called a house of prayer,' but you have made it a cave of robbers." ¹⁴And the blind and lame came to Him in the temple, and He healed them. ¹⁵But the chief priests and the scribes seeing the wonders which He did, and the little children crying in the Temple, and saying, "Hosanna to the Son of David"; they were indignant, ¹⁶and said to Him, "Do you hear what these are saying?" And Jesus says to them, "Yes, did you never read, 'Out of the mouth of infants and nursing babes you have perfected praises?'" ¹⁷And having left them He went out of the city to Bethany and spent the night there.

¹⁸But in the morning while returning to the city He hungered. ¹⁹And having seen one fig tree by the road, He went up to it, and found nothing on it except leaves only. And He says to it, "May there never be fruit from you unto the age." And immediately the fig tree was withered. ²⁰And the disciples having seen it marveled, saying, "How was the fig tree withered immediately?" ²¹And having answered Jesus said to them, "Truly I say to you, if you have faith and do not doubt, not only shall you do the wonder of the fig tree, but even if you say to

this mountain, be taken up and be cast into the sea it shall be done. ²²And all whatever you may ask in prayer, believing you shall receive."

²³And He having come into the temple, the chief priests and the elders of the people came to Him while teaching, saying, "By what authority do you do these things? And who gave You this authority?" ²⁴And having answered Jesus said to them, "I will also ask you one word, which if you tell Me, I also will tell you by what authority I do these things. ²⁵From where was the immersion of John? From Heaven or from men?" But they reasoned among themselves, saying, "If we say from Heaven, He will say to us, why then did you not believe him? ²⁶But if we say, from men, we fear the crowd, for all hold John to be a prophet." ²⁷And giving answer to Jesus, they said, "We do not know." And He said to them, "Neither am I telling you by what authority I do these things. ²⁸And what do you think? A man had two sons. And going to the first, He said, 'Go today, work in my vineyard.' ²⁹And having answered he said, 'I will not.' But afterwards having repented, he went. ³⁰And having gone to the second he spoke likewise. And having answered he said, 'I go lord,' and he did not go. ³¹Which of the two did the will of the father?" They say to Him, "The first." Jesus says to them, "Truly I say to you, that tax collectors and harlots go before you into the Kingdom of God. ³²For John came to you in the way of righteousness, and you did not believe him; but the tax collectors and the harlots believed in him; but having seen Him you did not afterwards repent to believe in him.

³³"You hear another parable. A certain man was a aster of a house who planted a vineyard, and he placed a hedge around it, and he dug in it a winepress and built a tower, and he rented it out to farmers and went far away. ³⁴And when the time for the harvesting of the fruits came, he sent his slaves to the farmers to receive his fruits. ³⁵And having taken his slaves the farmers beat one, and killed one and stoned one.

³⁶"Again he sent other slaves, more than the first, and they did to them likewise. ³⁷But afterwards he sent his son to them, saying, they will reverence my son. ³⁸But the farmers having seen the son, said among themselves, 'This is the heir, come, let us kill him, and let us seize his inheritance,' ³⁹And having taken him they cast him out of the vineyard and killed him. ⁴⁰When therefore the lord of the vineyard comes, what will he do to those farmers?" ⁴¹They say to Him, "He shall miserably destroy those wicked men and he shall rent the vineyard out to other farmers who shall give to him the fruits in their season."

⁴²Jesus says to them, "Did you never read in the Scriptures, 'a stone which the builders rejected, this one has become the head of the corner, this was done by the Lord, and it is wonderful in our eyes?' ⁴³Because of this I say to you, that the Kingdom of God shall be taken from you and it shall be given to a nation producing the fruits of it, and ⁴⁴the one who falls upon this stone shall be broken to pieces; but upon whomever it may fall it shall grind him to powder."

⁴⁵And having heard His parables, the chief priests and the Pharisees knew that He was speaking concerning them. And seeking to seize Him they feared the crowds because they held Him to be a prophet.

22 And having answered, Jesus again spoke to them in parables, saying, ²"The Kingdom of the Heavens is likened to a man, a king who made a marriage feast for his son. ³And he sent forth his slaves to call those who had been invited to the marriage feast, and they

would not come. ⁴Again he sent forth other slaves, saying, 'Say to those who are invited, behold I have prepared my dinner, my oxen and fatlings are killed, and all things prepared. Come to the wedding feast' ⁵But not caring they departed, one to his own field, one to his trade, ⁶but the rest having seized his slaves insulted and killed them. ⁷And the king having heard was angry, and having sent his armies he destroyed those murderers and burned their city.

⁸"Then he says to his slaves, 'Indeed the wedding feast is prepared, but those who had been invited were not worthy. ⁹Therefore, go into the byways of the roads and as many as you may find invite to the marriage feast.' ¹⁰And those slaves having gone out into the roads gathered together as many as they found, both evil and good. And the wedding was filled with guests. ¹¹But the king having entered to see the guests saw there a man who was not clothed in a wedding garment; ¹²and he says to him, 'Friend, how did you enter here not having a wedding garment?' And he was speechless. ¹³Then the king said to his servants, 'having bound his feet and hands take him away and cast him out into outer darkness. There shall be the weeping the gnashing of teeth.' ¹⁴For many are called but few chosen."

¹⁵Then having gone, the Pharisees took counsel how they might ensnare Him in speech. ¹⁶And they sent forth to Him their disciples with the Herodians, saying, "Teacher, we know that you are true, and teach the way of God in truth, and you do not care about anyone, for you do not regard the position of men.

¹⁷"Tell us therefore what you think. Is it lawful to give tribute to Caesar to not?" ¹⁸But Jesus knowing their wickedness said, "Why do you put me on trial, hypocrites?; ¹⁹show me the tribute money." And they brought a denarius to Him. ²⁰And He says to them, "Whose figure and inscription is this?" ²¹They say to him, "Caesar's." Then He says to them, "Give then to Caesar the things of Caesar and to God the things of God." ²²And having heard this, they marveled; and having left Him they departed.

²³On that day Sadducees, who say there is no resurrection, came to Him and asked Him, ²⁴saying, "Teacher, Moses said, 'If any man should die not having children, his brother shall marry his wife and shall raise up seed to his brother.' ²⁵Now there were with us seven brothers. And the first one having married died, and having no seed he left his wife to his brother. ²⁶And likewise the second and the third until the seventh. ²⁷And last of all the wife also died. ²⁸Therefore in the resurrection of which of the seven shall she be wife? For they all had her." ²⁹But having answered Jesus said to them, "You are going astray, not knowing the Scriptures nor the power of God. ³⁰For in the resurrection they neither marry nor are given in marriage, but are as the angels of God in Heaven. ³¹But concerning the resurrection of the dead, did you not read what was spoken to you by God, saying, ³²'I am the God of Abraham, and the God of Isaac, and the God of Jacob.' God is not God of the dead but of the living." ³³And having heard this the crowds were astonished at His teaching.

³⁴But the Pharisees having heard that He silenced the Sadducees, were gathered together. ³⁵And one of them, a lawyer, questioned Him, putting Him on trial, and saying, ³⁶"Teacher, what is the great commandment in the Law?" ³⁷And Jesus said to him, "You shall love the Lord your God with all your heart, and with all your soul, and with all your mind. ³⁸This is the first and great commandment. ³⁹And the second is like it, you shall love your neighbor as yourself.

⁴⁰"On these two commandments hang all the Law and the Prophets."
⁴¹But the Pharisees having been gathered together Jesus asked them, ⁴²saying, "What do you think about the Christ? Whose Son is He?" They say to Him "The son of David." ⁴³He says to them, "How then does David in the Spirit call Him Lord, saying, ⁴⁴'The Lord said to my Lord sit on My right hand until I place Your enemies as a footstool of Your feet.' ⁴⁵If therefore David calls Him Lord, how is He His son?" ⁴⁶And no one was able to answer a word, neither did anyone from that day dare to question Him any more.

23 Then Jesus spoke to the crowds and to His disciples, ²saying, "The scribes and the Pharisees sat upon the seat of Moses. ³Therefore all things whatever they may tell you to keep, you keep and do. But do not do according to their words. For they speak and do not. ⁴For they bind heavy burdens and hard to bear, and put them upon men's shoulders; but they do not wish to move them with their little finger. ⁵And they do all their works to be seen by men. And they broaden their phylacteries, and make large the fringes of their garments; 6and they love the chief place at the suppers, and the first seats in the synagogues, ⁷and the salutations in the market places, and to be called by men, Rabbi, Rabbi. ⁸But you are not to be called Rabbi; for one is your Teacher, the Christ, and all of you are brothers. ⁹And do not call anyone of you on the earth father, for one is your Heavenly Father. ¹⁰Neither should you be called teachers; for one is your Teacher, the Christ. ¹¹For the greater of you shall be your servant. ¹²And whoever shall exalt himself shall be humbled; and whoever will humble himself shall be exalted."

¹³"Woe to you scribes and Pharisees, hypocrites, because you devour the houses of widows, and for a pretense you pray long. Because of this you shall receive the greater judgment. ¹⁴But woe to you, scribes and Pharisees, hypocrites, because you shut the Kingdom of the Heavens in the face of men. For you do not enter, nor do you permit these who are entering to enter. ¹⁵Woe to you, scribes and Pharisees, hypocrites because you encompass the sea and the dry land to make one proselyte, and when he has become one, you make him a twofold more son of hell than you. ¹⁶Woe to you blind guides who say, 'Whoever may swear by the Temple it is nothing; but whoever may swear by the gold of the Temple, he is obligated.'
¹⁷"Fools and blind, for which is greater the gold, or the Temple which sanctifies the gold? ¹⁸'And whoever may swear by the altar, it is nothing; but whoever may swear by the gift upon it, he is obligated.' ¹⁹Fools and blind, for which is greater the gift or the altar which sanctifies the gift? ²⁰Therefore, the one who having sworn by the altar swears by it and all the things upon it. ²¹And the one who having sworn by the Temple swears by it and by Him who inhabits it.
²²"And the One who having sworn by Heaven swears by the Throne of God and by the One sitting upon it.
²³"Woe to you, scribes and Pharisees, hypocrites, because you tithe mint and dill and cumin, and you have left off the weightier things of the law, judgment, and mercy, and faith; it is necessary to do these things, and not to leave off those things.
²⁴"Blind guides, who strain out the gnat, but swallow the camel.
²⁵"Woe to you, scribes and Pharisees, hypocrites, because you cleanse the outside of the

cup and platter, but inwardly they are full of extortion and intemperance. ²⁶Blind Pharisee, cleanse first the inside of the cup and the platter in order that the outside of them may also become clean. ²⁷Woe to you, scribes and Pharisees, hypocrites, because you resemble whitened tombs which outwardly indeed appear beautiful, but within they are full of the bones of dead men and of all uncleanness. ²⁸In like manner also outwardly you indeed appear righteous to men, but inwardly you are full of hypocrisy and lawlessness."

²⁹"Woe to you, scribes and Pharisees, hypocrites, because you build the tombs of the prophets, and you adorn the monuments of the righteous, ³⁰and you say, 'If we had been in the days of our fathers we would not have been sharers with them in the blood of the prophets.' ³¹So you are witnesses to yourselves that you are sons of those who murdered the prophets.

³²"And you made full the measure of your fathers.

³³"Serpents, generation of vipers, how shall you flee from the judgment of hell? ³⁴Because of this, behold I send to you prophets and wise men and scribes; and certain of them you shall kill and crucify, and certain of them you shall scourge in your synagogues, and shall persecute from city to city. ³⁵In this way may come upon you all the righteous blood which was shed upon the earth from the blood of the righteous Abel until the blood of Zachariah son of Barachiah whom you murdered between the temple and the altar.

³⁶"Truly I say to you, all these things shall come upon this generation. ³⁷Jerusalem, Jerusalem, who killed the prophets and stones those sent to her. How often I would have gathered together your children as a hen gathers together her brood under her wings. And you would not. ³⁸Behold your house is left to you desolate. ³⁹For I say to you, you shall not see me any more from now until you say, 'Blessed is the One coming in the name of the Lord.'"

24 And having gone forth, Jesus went away from the temple, and His disciples came to show to Him the buildings of the temple. ²And Jesus said to them, "Do you not see all these things? There shall in no way be left here a stone upon a stone which shall not be thrown down."

³And as He was sitting on the Mount of Olives, the disciples came to Him privately, saying, "Tell us when shall these things be and what is the sign of Your coming, and of the end of the age?" ⁴And Jesus having answered said to them, "Take heed lest anyone leads you astray. ⁵For many shall come in My name saying, 'I am the Christ' and many shall be led astray.

⁶"And you shall begin to hear of wars and rumors of wars. See that you be not troubled; for it is necessary for all these things to come to pass, but the end is not yet. ⁷For nation shall rise against nation, and kingdom against kingdom; and there shall be famines and pestilences and earthquakes in many places. ⁸But all these things are a beginning of travail. ⁹Then they shall deliver you to tribulation and shall kill you; and you shall be hated by all nations because of My name. ¹⁰And then many shall be led astray, and they shall betray one another, and they shall hate one another. ¹¹And many false prophets shall arise and shall lead many astray. ¹²And because lawlessness has been multiplied the love of many shall grow cold; ¹³but the one who endures to the end, he shall be saved. ¹⁴And this gospel of the Kingdom shall be proclaimed in all the world for a witness to all nations, and then shall the end come. ¹⁵Therefore, when you see the abomination of desolation which was spoken by Daniel the prophet, standing in the holy place, the one who reads let him understand,

¹⁶"then let those who are in Judea flee to the mountains; ¹⁷the one on the housetop, let him not come down to take anything out of his house; ¹⁸and the one in the field, let him not turn back to take his clothes.

¹⁹"But woe to those who are with child, and to those giving suck in those days. ²⁰And pray that your flight may not be in winter, nor on the sabbath.

²¹"For then there shall be great tribulation such as has not been from the beginning of the world until now, neither shall by no means be. ²²And unless those days were shortened not any flesh would be saved; but because of the elect, those days shall have been shortened. ²³Then if anyone should say to you, 'Look, here is the Christ,' or 'here' do not believe it. ²⁴for there shall arise false christs and false prophets, and shall give great signs and wonders so as to lead astray, if possible even the elect. ²⁵Behold I have told you beforehand. ²⁶If then they say to you, 'Behold He is in the desert,' do not go out there. 'Behold He is in the secret chambers,' do not believe it. ²⁷For as the lightning comes from the east and shines to the west, so shall also the coming of the Son of Man be. ²⁸For where the corpse may be, there the eagles shall be gathered together. ²⁹And immediately after the tribulation of those days, the sun shall be darkened, and the moon shall not give her light, and the stars shall fall from heaven, and the powers of the heavens shall be shaken. ³⁰and then shall appear in the heaven the sign of the Son of Man, and then all the tribes of the earth shall weep and they shall see the Son of Man coming upon the clouds of the heaven with power and great glory. ³¹And He shall send His angels with a great sound of a trumpet; and they shall gather together His elect from the four winds, from the heights of the heavens to the uttermost parts of them. ³²But learn from the parable of the fig tree: when her branch has already become tender, and she puts forth leaves, you know that summer is near. ³³So also when you see these things you know that it is near, at the doors. ³⁴Truly I say to you, this generation in no way passes away until all these things come to pass. ³⁵The heaven and the earth shall pass away, but My words shall in no wise pass away.

³⁶"But concerning that day and the hour, no one knows, neither the angels of the Heavens, except My Father only. ³⁷But as were the days of Noah, so shall also be the coming of the Son of Man. ³⁸For as they were in the days before the flood, eating and drinking, marrying and giving in marriage, until the day that Noah entered into the ark ³⁹and they did not know until the flood came and took them all away so shall also be the coming of the Son of Man. ⁴⁰Then shall two be in the field, the one is taken, and the one is left. ⁴¹Two are grinding at the mill, one is taken and one is left. ⁴²Watch therefore, because you do not know what hour your Lord is coming. ⁴³But now this, that if the master of the house had known in what watch the thief is coming, he would have watched, and would not have permitted his house to be broken into. ⁴⁴Because of this you be ready also, because in such an hour you think not, the Son of Man is coming. ⁴⁵Who then is a faithful and wise slave, which his lord has set over his household to give them food in season? ⁴⁶That slave is blessed who when his lord comes shall find him so doing. ⁴⁷Truly I say to you, that he shall set him over all his possessions. ⁴⁸But if that wicked slave says in his heart, 'My lord delays to come,' ⁴⁹and should begin to beat the fellow slaves, and to eat and to drink with those who are drunk, ⁵⁰the lord of that slave shall come on that day which he does not expect, and in an hour which he does not know, and he shall punish him severely, and shall appoint his part with the hypocrites; there shall be the weeping and

gnashing of teeth."

**25** "Then the Kingdom of the Heavens shall be likened to ten virgins, who took their lamps and went out to meet the bridegroom. ²But five of them were wise, and five foolish. ³Those who were foolish, having taken their lamps, did not take oil with themselves. ⁴But the wise took oil in their vessels with their lamps. ⁵But the bridegroom lingering, they all slumbered and slept.

⁶"But at midnight there was a cry, 'Behold the bridegroom comes, go out to meet him.' ⁷Then all those virgins were aroused and trimmed their lamps.

⁸"And the foolish said to the wise, 'Give us of your oil, for our lamps are going out.' ⁹But the wise answered, saying, 'No, there may not be enough for us and you, but rather go to those who sell and buy for yourselves.' ¹⁰But when they were going to buy oil the bridegroom came, and those ready entered with him into the marriage feast, and the door was shut. ¹¹And afterwards, the remaining virgins also came, saying, 'Lord, Lord, open to us.' ¹²But he having answered said, 'Truly I say to you, I do not know you. ¹³Watch therefore, because you do not know the day or the hour in which the Son of Man comes.'

¹⁴"For it is as a man going into a foreign country, who called his own slaves and delivered to them his possessions. And to one he gave five talents, ¹⁵and to another he gave two, and to another, one, to each according to his own ability. And immediately he went on his journey. ¹⁶And having gone, the one having received the five talents did business with them, and made five other talents.

¹⁷"Likewise also the one with the two also gained another two. ¹⁸But the one having received the one, having departed dug in the earth and hid the money of his lord. ¹⁹And after a long time, the lord of those slaves comes and settles accounts with them. ²⁰And having come near, the one having received the five talents brought another five talents, saying, 'Lord, you delivered to me five talents. Look, I have gained five other talents besides them.' ²¹And his lord said to him, 'Well done good and faithful servant, you were faithful over a little, I will set you over much. You enter into the joy of your lord.' ²²And also having come near, the one having received the two talents said, 'Lord, you delivered to me two talents, look, I have gained two other talents besides them.' ²³His lord said to him, 'Well done good and faithful servant, you were faithful over a little, I will set you over much. You enter into the joy of your lord.'

²⁴"And also having come near, the one who had received the one talent said. 'I knew you that you are a hard man, reaping where you did not sow, and gathering where you did not scatter abroad. ²⁵And having been afraid, having gone, I hid your talent in the earth, see, you have what is yours.' ²⁶But having answered, his lord said to him, 'Evil and lazy slave, you knew that I shall reap where I did not sow, and I gathered where I did not scatter abroad; ²⁷therefore it was necessary for you to put my money to the bankers, and having come I could have received what is mine with interest. ²⁸Therefore take the talent from him and give it to him who has the ten talents. ²⁹For to everyone who has it shall be given and he shall have abundance. But from the one who has not, even what he has shall be taken from him. ³⁰And cast out this useless slave into the outer darkness. There shall be the weeping and the gnashing of teeth.'

³¹"But when the Son of Man comes in His glory, and all the holy angels with Him, then He shall sit upon the throne of His glory. ³²And all the nations shall be gathered before Him, and He shall separate them from one another as the shepherd separates the sheep from the goats. ³³And He shall place the sheep on his right, but the goats on the left. ³⁴Then the King shall say to those on His right, 'Come, the blessed of My Father, inherit the Kingdom prepared for you from the foundation of the world. ³⁵For I hungered and you gave Me to eat, I thirsted and you gave Me drink, I was a stranger and you took Me in, ³⁶naked and you clothed Me, I was sick and you visited Me. I was in prison and you came to Me.' ³⁷Then the righteous shall answer Him, saying, 'Lord, when did we see You hungering, and fed You, or thirsting, and gave You drink? ³⁸And when did we see You a stranger and gathered You in, or naked and clothed You? ³⁹And when did we see You sick, or in prison, and came to You?' ⁴⁰And having answered, the King shall say to them, 'Truly I say to you, forasmuch as you did it to one of these least of My brothers you did it to Me.' ⁴¹Then He shall say also to those on the left, 'Depart from Me, the cursed into the eternal fire, having been prepared for the devil and his angels. ⁴²For I hungered and you gave Me nothing to eat, I thirsted and you gave Me nothing to drink. ⁴³I was a stranger and you did not gather Me in, naked and you did not clothe Me, sick and in prison and you did not visit Me.' ⁴⁴Then they shall also answer Him saying, 'Lord, when did we see You hungry or thirsty, or a stranger, or naked, or sick, or in prison, and did not minister to You?' Then He shall answer them, saying, 'Truly I say to you, forasmuch as you did it not to one of these least, you did it not to Me. And these shall go into eternal punishment, but the righteous into life eternal.'"

26 And it came to pass when Jesus finished all these saying, He said to His disciples, ²"You know that after two days the Passover is coming, and the Son of Man is being delivered up to be crucified." ³Then the chief priests and the scribes and the elders of the people were gathered together to the court of the high priest who was called Caiaphas; ⁴and they took counsel that they might seize Jesus by guile and kill Him.

⁵But they said, "Not during the feast, in order that there may not be a riot among the people."

⁶Now when Jesus was at Bethany in the house of Simon the leper, ⁷there came to Him a woman having an alabaster vase of very expensive ointment, and she poured it upon His head as He reclined. ⁸But His disciples having seen this were indignant, saying, "For what is this waste? ⁹For this ointment could be sold for a large sum and be given to the poor."

¹⁰But Jesus knowing their indignation said to them, "Why do you cause trouble for the woman? For she has done a good work for Me. ¹¹For you always have the poor with you, but you do not always have Me. ¹²For she having poured this ointment upon My body did it for My burial. ¹³Truly I say to you, wherever this gospel may be proclaimed in all the world, what this one did shall also be spoken for a memorial of her."

¹⁴Then one of the twelve, the one called Judas Iscariot, having gone to the chief priests, ¹⁵said, "What are you willing to give me, and I will deliver Him to you." And they paid to him thirty pieces of silver. ¹⁶And from then he sought opportunity in order that he might betray Him.

¹⁷Now on the first day of unleavened bread the disciples came to Jesus saying to Him,

"Where do you wish we may prepare for You to eat the Passover?" [18]And He said, "You go into the city to a certain one and say to him, 'The teacher says, my time is near, with you I am observing the Passover with My disciples.'" [19]And the disciples did as Jesus commanded them and prepared the Passover.

[20]And evening having come, He reclined with the twelve. [21]And as they were eating He said, "Truly I say to you, that one of you shall betray Me. [22]And being exceedingly sorrowful they began each of them to say to Him, "Lord, is it I myself?" [23]And having answered, He said, "The one dipping the hand in the dish with Me, he shall betray Me. [24]Truly the Son of Man goes as it has been written concerning Him, but woe to that man through whom the Son of Man is betrayed. It was good for him if that man were not born." [25]And having answered, Judas, the one betraying Him said, "Rabbi, is it I myself?" He says to him, "You said it."

[26]And while they ate, Jesus having taken the bread and blessing it, broke it and gave to the disciples and said, "Take, eat, this is My body." [27]And taking the cup, and giving thanks, He gave to them, saying, "You all drink of it, [28]for this is My blood of the new Covenant which is being shed concerning many for forgiveness of sins. [29]But, I say to you, that I shall in no wise drink from now of the fruit of the vine until that day when I drink it new with you in the Kingdom of My Father. [30]And having sung a hymn they went out to the Mount of Olives.

[31]Then Jesus says to them, "All of you shall be offended in Me during this night. For it has been written, 'I will smite the shepherd, and the sheep of the flock shall be scattered.' [32]But after I am raised up I will go before you into Galilee." [33]And having answered, Peter said to Him, "Even if all shall be offended in You, I will never be offended."

[34]Jesus said to him, "Truly I say to you, that during this night before the rooster crows, you shall deny Me three times." [35]Peter says to Him, "Even if it be necessary for me to die with you, I will in no wise deny You." Also all the disciples spoke likewise.

[36]Then Jesus comes with them into a place called Gethsemane, and says to the disciples, "You sit here until having gone over there, I may pray." [37]And having taken Peter and the two sons of Zebedee He began to be sorrowful and to be distressed. [38]Then He says to them, "My soul is exceedingly sorrowful, even to death, you remain here and watch with Me." [39]And having gone forward a little, He fell upon His face, praying and saying, "My Father if it is possible let this cup pass from Me, nevertheless not as I will but as You will." [40]And He comes to the disciples and finds them sleeping, and He says to Peter, "So, were you not able to watch with Me one hour? [41]Watch and pray that you may not enter into temptation. The spirit indeed is willing but the flesh is weak." [42]And again a second time, having gone, He prayed saying, "My Father, if this cup is not able to pass from Me except I drink it, let Your Will be done."

[43]And having come, He finds them sleeping again, for their eyes were heavy. [44]And leaving them, having gone, again He prayed a third time, saying the same words. [45]Then He comes to His disciples and says to them, "Sleep on now, and take your rest; behold the hour has drawn near, and the Son of Man is betrayed into the hands of sinners. [46]Arise, let us be going, behold the one betraying Me has drawn near."

[47]And while He was yet speaking, behold, Judas one of the twelve came, and a great crowd with him, with many swords and staves, from the chief priests and elders of the people. [48]And

the one betraying Him gave them a sign, saying, "Whomever I may kiss is He, you seize Him." ⁴⁹And having come immediately to Jesus he said, "Hail Rabbi," and he fervently kissed Him. ⁵⁰But Jesus said to him, "Friend, why are you here?" Then having come near they laid the hands upon Jesus and seized Him. ⁵¹And behold, one of those with Jesus, stretching forth the hand drew his sword, and striking the slave of the high priest he cut off his ear. ⁵²Then Jesus says to him, "Put your sword back into its place, For all those who take the sword shall perish by the sword. ⁵³Or do you think that I am not able now to call upon My Father and He shall place beside Me more than twelve legions of angels? ⁵⁴How then should the Scriptures be fulfilled that it must be thus?"

⁵⁵In that hour Jesus said to the crowds, "Have you come out as against a robber with swords and staves to seize Me? Day by day I was sitting with you in the temple teaching, and you did not seize Me. ⁵⁶But all this came to pass in order that the Scriptures of the prophets might be fulfilled." Then all the disciples leaving Him, fled.

⁵⁷And those who seized Jesus led Him away to Caiaphas, the high priest, where the scribes and elders were gathered together. ⁵⁸And Peter was following Him from a great distance upon the court of the high priest; and having entered inside he sat with the officers to see the end. ⁵⁹And the chief priests and the elders and the whole Sanhedrin sought a false witness against Jesus, so that they might put Him to death. ⁶⁰And they found none; even though many false witnesses having come forward found nothing. But afterwards two false witnesses having come near, ⁶¹said, "This one said, 'I am able to destroy the Temple of God and to build it in three days.'" ⁶²And having arisen the high priest said to Him. "Do You answer nothing? What do these witness against You?"

⁶³But Jesus was silent, and having answered, the high priest said to Him, "I put You under oath by the living God in order that You may tell us if You are the Christ, the Son of God." ⁶⁴Jesus says to him, "You said it, moreover I say to you, henceforth you shall see the Son of Man sitting on the right hand of power and coming upon the clouds of Heaven." ⁶⁵Then the high priest tore his garments, saying, "He blasphemed, why do we yet have need of witnesses? See, now you heard His blasphemy, ⁶⁶What do you think?" And they having answered said, "He is guilty of death," ⁶⁷Then they spat in His face, and they beat Him with the fists and they smacked Him, ⁶⁸saying, "Prophesy to us, Christ, who is it who struck You?"

⁶⁹And Peter sat outside in the court; and one servant-girl came to him, saying, "And you were with Jesus of Galilee." ⁷⁰But he denied before all, saying, "I do not know what you say." ⁷¹And having gone out into the porch, another saw him and says to those there, "And this one was with Jesus of Nazareth." ⁷²And again he denied with an oath, "I do not know the man." ⁷³But after a little, those standing by coming near said to Peter, "Truly also you are of them, for even your speech makes you manifest." ⁷⁴Then he began to curse and to swear, "I do not know the man." And immediately a rooster crowed. ⁷⁵And Peter remembered the word of Jesus which had been spoken to him, "Before a rooster crows you shall deny Me three times." And having gone outside, he wept bitterly.

**27** And morning having come, all the chief priests and the elders of the people took counsel together against Jesus, as it were, to put Him to death. ²And having bound Him, they led Him away and delivered Him to Pontius Pilate, the governor.

³Then Judas, the one having betrayed Him, having seen that he was condemned, having repented, returned the thirty pieces of silver to the chief priests and the elders ⁴saying, "I have sinned, having betrayed innocent blood." But they said, "What is that to us? You shall see to it." ⁵And throwing the pieces of silver into the temple, he departed; and having gone forth he hanged himself. ⁶And the chief priests taking the pieces of silver, said, "It is not lawful to put them into the treasury, since it is the price of blood." ⁷And taking counsel, they bought of them the field of the potter for burial for the strangers.

⁸Therefore that field was called the Field of Blood till this day. ⁹Then was fulfilled what was spoken by Jeremiah the prophet, saying, "And they took the thirty pieces of silver, the price of Him who was priced, whom they priced from the sons of Israel, ¹⁰and they gave them for a field of the potter as the Lord directed me."

¹¹And Jesus stood before the governor; and the governor asked Him saying, "Are You the King of the Jews?" And Jesus said to him, "You are saying it." ¹²And being accused by the chief priests and the elders, He answered nothing. ¹³Then Pilate says to Him, "Do you not hear how many things they are witnessing against You?" ¹⁴And He did not answer him, not even to one word, so that the governor greatly marveled. ¹⁵Now at a feast the governor usually released one prisoner to the crowd whom they wished. ¹⁶And they then had a notable prisoner called Barabbas.

¹⁷Therefore when they were gathered together, Pilate said to them, "Whom do you wish I should release to you, Barabbas or Jesus who is called Christ?" ¹⁸For he knew that they delivered Him up because of envy.

¹⁹And while he was sitting upon the throne his wife sent to him, saying, "There is nothing to you and to that Just Man, for today I suffered many things in a dream because of Him." ²⁰But the chief priests and the elders persuaded the crowds, in order that they might ask for Barabbas and might destroy Jesus. And having answered, ²¹the governor said to them, "Which of the two do you wish I may release to you?" And they said, "Barabbas." ²²Pilate says to them, "What then should I do with Jesus who is called Christ?"

²³They all said to him, "Let Him be crucified." But the governor said, "For what evil has He done?" But they cried out more saying, "Let Him be crucified."

²⁴And Pilate having seen that he gains nothing, but rather a tumult begins, having taken water he washed his hands before the crowd saying, "I am innocent of the blood of this Righteous man, you shall see."

²⁵And having answered, all the people said, "His blood be upon us and upon our children." ²⁶Then he released Barabbas to them, and having Jesus flogged, he delivered Him over in order that He might be crucified.

²⁷Then the soldiers of the governor, having taken Jesus into the Praetorium gathered together against Him all the band. ²⁸And having stripped Him, they placed around Him a scarlet cloak, ²⁹and having plaited a crown of thorns, they placed it upon His head, and a reed in His right hand; and kneeling before Him, they mocked Him, saying, "Hail, King of the Jews;" ³⁰and having spit on Him, they took the reed and smote Him on His head. ³¹And when they had mocked Him they stripped the cloak from Him and put on Him His clothes; and they led Him away to crucify Him.

³²And while going out they found a man, a Cyrenian named Simon. They compelled this

one in order that he might bear His cross. ³³And having come to a place called Golgotha, which is called 'a place of a skull,' ³⁴they gave Him vinegar mixed with gall to drink, and having tasted it He would not drink. ³⁵And having crucified Him, they divided His garments, casting a lot in order that it might be fulfilled which was spoken by the prophet, "They divided My clothes among themselves and for My garment they cast a lot." ³⁶And sitting they watched Him there. ³⁷And they placed over His head His accusation, which had been written, "THIS IS JESUS THE KING OF THE JEWS." ³⁸Then two robbers were crucified with Him, one on the right and one on the left.

³⁹And those passing by blasphemed Him, shaking their heads ⁴⁰and saying, "The one destroying the Temple and building it in three days, save Yourself. If you are the Son of God, come down from the cross." ⁴¹And likewise also the chief priests, mocking him with the scribes and elders said, ⁴²"He saved others; He is not able to save Himself. If He is the King of Israel let Him now come down from the cross and we will believe in Him. ⁴³He trusted on God, let Him rescue Him now if He wants Him. For He said, "I am the Son of God." ⁴⁴And also the robbers who were crucified with him reviled Him, saying the same.

⁴⁵Now from the sixth hour there was darkness over all the earth until the ninth hour. ⁴⁶And about the ninth hour, Jesus cried with a great voice saying, "Eli, Eli, lama, sabachthani?" this is My God, My God, why have You forsaken Me? ⁴⁷And some of those standing there hearing, said, "This one calls Elijah." ⁴⁸And immediately one of them having run and taking a sponge, and filling it with vinegar, and putting it on a reed, gave Him to drink. ⁴⁹But the rest said, "Let it be, let us see if Elijah is coming to save Him."

⁵⁰And again Jesus crying with a great voice dismissed His spirit. And behold, ⁵¹the veil of the Temple was rent in two from top to bottom. And the earth was shaken and the rocks were rent, ⁵²and the tombs were opened, and many bodies of the saints who had fallen asleep arose, ⁵³and having gone out of the tombs after His resurrection, they entered into the holy city and appeared to many.

⁵⁴But the centurion and those watching Jesus with him, having seen the earthquake and the things done, they feared exceedingly, saying, "Truly this One was the Son of God." ⁵⁵And there were many women watching from a distance, who followed Jesus from Galilee, ministering unto Him, ⁵⁶among whom was Mary Magdalene, and Mary the mother of James and Joses, and the mother of the sons of Zebedee.

⁵⁷And evening having come, there came a rich man from Arimathea, named Joseph, who was also himself discipled to Jesus. ⁵⁸This one having gone to Pilate, asked for the body of Jesus. Then Pilate commanded the body to be given. ⁵⁹And having taken the body, Joseph wrapped it in clean linen, ⁶⁰and placed it in his tomb which he had hewn in the rock, and having rolled a great stone to the door of the tomb, he departed. ⁶¹And there was Mary Magdalene and the other Mary sitting opposite the sepulcher.

⁶²Now on the next day, which is after the preparation, the chief priests and the Pharisees were gathered together with Pilate, ⁶³saying, "Sir, we remembered that that deceiver said while yet living, 'After three days I will rise up.' ⁶⁴Therefore command the sepulcher to be made secure until the third day, lest His disciples coming by night might steal Him, and might say to the people, 'He has raised from the dead, and the last error shall be worse than the first.'" ⁶⁵Pilate said to them, "You have a guard, go make it as secure as you can." ⁶⁶And they having

gone, made the sepulcher secure, sealing the stone, and with the guard.

28 Now late on the Sabbath, as it was dawning into the first day of the week, Mary Magdalene and the other Mary came to see the sepulcher. ²And behold, there was a great earthquake, for an angel of the Lord came down from Heaven, and having come, he rolled away the stone from the door, and was sitting upon it. ³And His appearance was as lightning and His clothing white as snow. ⁴And from the fear of him, those keeping watch were shaken and became as dead men. ⁵But having answered, the angel said to the women, "Fear you not, for I know that you seek Jesus Who was crucified. ⁶He is not here, for He was raised just at He said. Come, see the place where the Lord was lying. ⁷And having gone quickly, tell His disciples that He was risen from the dead; and behold He goes before you into Galilee; you shall see Him there. Behold I have told you."⁸And having departed quickly from the tomb with fear and great joy, they ran to tell His disciples. ⁹And as they were going to tell His disciples, behold also, Jesus met them saying, "Hail," and having come to Him they took hold of His feet and worshipped Him. ¹⁰Then Jesus says to them, "Do not fear, go tell My brothers in order that they may go into Galilee, and there they shall see Me."

¹¹And as they were going, behold, some of the guard having come into the city told the chief priests all the things that happened. ¹²And having been gathered together with the elders and having taken counsel, they gave much money to the soldiers, ¹³saying, "Say that His disciples having come by night stole Him while we were sleeping. ¹⁴And if this is heard by the Governor, we will persuade him, and we will make you free from anxiety." ¹⁵And having taken the money they did as they were taught. And this word was spread abroad by the Jews until this day.

¹⁶And the eleven disciples went into Galilee unto the mount where Jesus appointed for them. ¹⁷And having seen Him they worshipped Him, but they doubted. ¹⁸And having come near, Jesus spoke to them saying, "All authority in Heaven and upon earth was given to Me. ¹⁹Therefore having gone, you disciple all the nations, immersing them into the name of the Father, and of the Son, and of the Holy Spirit; ²⁰teaching them to observe all things whatever I commanded you. And, behold, I am with you all the days until the consummation of the age." Amen

*The Gospel According to*
# Mark

**1** ¹This is how the good news about Jesus Christ, the Son of God, began. ²It was even written in Isaiah, the prophet, "Look, I am sending my messenger on ahead of you. He will prepare the way for you. ³He will be the voice of a man shouting out in the desert, urging people to make the road for the Lord ready to travel on to make a straight pathway for Him." ⁴John the Immerser came immersing people in the desert and proclaiming that those immersed on the basis of their repentance would receive the forgiveness of sins from God. ⁵And people from throughout all the regions of Judea and all of Jerusalem went out to John in the desert. And he immersed them in the Jordan River as they confessed their sins. ⁶John wore clothing made of camel's hair and he had a leather belt around his waist. He ate grasshoppers and wild honey. ⁷In his preaching John said, "One who is more powerful than I am will follow my ministry. I am not even worthy to stoop down and loosen the straps of His sandals, to serve as His slave. ⁸I am immersing you in water, but He will immerse you in the Holy Spirit."

⁹And it happened at that time that Jesus went from Nazareth, in Galilee south of Judea, where He was immersed by John in the Jordan River. ¹⁰And immediately upon emerging from the water, He saw the sky split open and the Holy Spirit descending on Him as a dove. ¹¹And a voice called out from heaven, saying, "You are my dearly loved Son. I am very pleased with you."

¹²Then right after that the Holy Spirit drove Jesus out into the desert. ¹³He spent forty days in this desert where He was put to the test by Satan. He was with wild animals, and angels ministered to His needs while there.

¹⁴Now after John was turned over to the authorities and imprisoned Jesus went back to Galilee preaching the good news from God ¹⁵and saying, "The appointed time has arrived and the kingdom of God is near. So, you people should repent, change your hearts and lives and believe the good news about the kingdom."

⁶And while walking along the shore of Lake Galilee, Jesus saw Simon Peter, and his brother Andrew casting their net in the lake, for they were fishermen. ¹⁷And Jesus said to them, "Come follow me and I will make you fishermen for people." ¹⁸So, they left their nets immediately and became His followers. ¹⁹Then, as He walked on a little farther, He saw James, the son of Zebedee, and his brother John, who were in their boat repairing nets. ²⁰Immediately He called them to become His followers and they left their father, Zebedee, and went along with Him.

²¹So, they went to Capernaum and on the first Sabbath day Jesus entered the synagogue and taught people. ²²They were amazed at His teaching for He taught them as one who had real authority, and not as the experts in the Law of Moses. ²³And just then there appeared in the synagogue a man dominated by an evil spirit. He shouted out, ²⁴"What business do we have with You, Jesus from Nazareth? Have You come to destroy us? I know who You are, You are God's Holy One." ²⁵Jesus spoke sternly to him, saying, "Be quiet, and come out of him." ²⁶And the evil spirit caused the man to have a convulsion, then shouted

with a loud voice and came out of him. ²⁷And all the people in the synagogue were so amazed they began asking one another, "What is this, some new teaching? And it is spoken with such authority! He even orders evil spirits, and they obey Him." ²⁸And news about Him quickly spread everywhere, even into all of Galilee and the surrounding regions.

²⁹And as soon as they left the synagogue, they went into the house of Simon Peter, and Andrew, taking James and John with them. ³⁰New Simon's mother-in-law was sick in bed with a fever. Immediately, Jesus was told about her condition ³¹so He went to her, took her by the hand and raised her up from bed. The fever left her and she began serving them.

³²When evening came and the sun had set, they brought to Jesus all those who were sick and those dominated by evil spirits. ³³And people from all over the city of Capernaum gathered at the door of the house, ³⁴and He healed many of those who were sick with various diseases and drove out many evil spirits to tell people who He was, because they knew who He was, the Christ.

³⁵Very early in the morning, even before daylight, Jesus woke up, left Simon's house and went out to a deserted place where He prayed. ³⁶And Simon and those who were with him, probably Andrew, James and John, followed him. ³⁷When they found Him, they said to Him, "Everyone is looking for you." ³⁸He said to them, "Let us go on to the next towns so that I can preach there also, for this was why I came out, Jesus was sent by God to preach to other town as well as Capernaum." ³⁹So, Jesus went into the Jewish synagogues throughout all Galilee, preaching the good news about the coming kingdom, and driving out evil spirits.

⁴⁰Then a person with an infectious skin disease came to Jesus and, kneeling down before Him, begged Him, saying, "If you want, you can heal me." ⁴¹And being moved with deep pity, Jesus reached out His hand, touching him and said, "I do want to; be healed." ⁴²And immediately the infections skin disease left him and he was healed. ⁴³Jesus sternly warned him, sending him directly out, ⁴⁴and saying to him, "Make sure you do not say anything to anyone. But go and show yourself to the priest and make an offering for your healing with whatever Moses ordered as evidence to people that you were completely healed." ⁴⁵But instead the man went out telling everyone about the miracle of healing and spreading the story widely, so that Jesus was not able to enter a town publicly but had to remain outside in deserted places. So, people went to Him there from all over the region.

2 After Jesus returned to Capernaum several days later, it because known that He was back at home, possibly at the house of Peter and Andrew, where He was staying. ²And there were so many people gathered to listen to His message that there was no room for any more in the courtyard around the doorway. Then some people came, bringing a man afflicted with paralysis, who was being carried by four friends. ⁴And when they were unable to get near Jesus, because of the large crowd, they removed a section of the roof directly above Him. And when they had broken open a sizable hole, they lowered the cot on which the paralyzed man was lying. When Jesus saw the evidence of their faith, He said to the paralyzed man, "Son, your sins are forgiven."

⁶But certain experts in the Law of Moses, who were sitting there, began reasoning in their minds, ⁷"Why does this man talk this way? He is speaking against God. Who can forgive sins except one, that is, God?" ⁸And immediately Jesus perceived in His spirit what they were

reasoning in their minds and said to them, "Why are you reasoning like this in your minds? ⁹Which is easier, to say to the paralyzed man, 'your sins are forgiven' or to say 'get up, pick up your cot and walk'? ¹⁰But, so you will know that the Son of man has authority on earth to forgive sins." He then said to the paralyzed man, ¹¹"I say to you, get up, pick up your cot and go home." ¹²So, he got up and immediately picked up his cot and walked out in front of them all, so that everyone was amazed and gave honor to God, saying, "We have never seen anything like this before."

¹³Then Jesus went out again, walking along the shore of the lake, and when all the crowd came out to Him, He taught them. ¹⁴And as He walked along He saw Levi, the same person as Matthew, the son of Alphaeus, sitting at the toll booth collecting taxes. He said to him, "Become my follower." And he got up and followed Him.

¹⁵And it happened that Jesus was having a meal at Levi's house and many tax collectors and worldly people sat down with Him and His disciples, for many of these kinds of people became His followers. ¹⁶And when the experts in the Law of Moses, being Pharisees, a strict sect of the Jewish religion, saw that He was eating with tax collectors and worldly people, they said to His disciples, "Why does Jesus eat and drink with tax collectors and worldly people?" ¹⁷When Jesus heard about this, He said to them, "People who are healthy do not need a doctor, but only sick people do. I did not come to call those who do right, but sinners instead."

¹⁸Now John's disciples and the Pharisees were fasting, going without food and/or drink for religious reasons. Some people came and asked Jesus, "Why do John's disciples and the Pharisees' disciples fast, but your disciples do not?" ¹⁹Jesus answered them, "Can the companions of the groom fast while the groom is still with them? As long as they have the groom with them they cannot fast. ²⁰But the time will come when the groom will be taken away from them. Then they will fast at that time.

²¹"No one sows a patch of unshrunk cloth on an old garment, because what was supposed to cover the hole actually makes it larger. The new piece of cloth tears away from the old one and the hole is made worse. ²²And no one puts freshly squeezed grape juice into bottles made of previously used animal skins. If he does, the grape juice will cause cracks and burst the dried-out animal skins and the grape juice will all leak out and be wasted, and the animal skin bottles will become useless. But people put freshly squeezed grape juice into newly prepared animal skin bottles."

²³And it happened that Jesus was walking through the grain fields on the Sabbath day and His disciples began picking off heads of grain to eat as they traveled along. ²⁴And the Pharisees asked Him, "Look, why are they, Jesus' disciples, doing what is against the Law of Moses on the Sabbath day?" ²⁵And He replied to them, "Did you never read what King David did when he and his men were hungry and needed something to eat? ²⁶Or how he entered the house of God, the Temple, when Abiathar was head priest, and ate the 'Bread of Presence' which was not permissible, according to the Law of Moses, for anyone but priests? He even gave some of it to those who were with him." ²⁷And Jesus said to them, "The Sabbath day was made for man's benefit, and not man for the Sabbath day's benefit. ²⁸So, the Son of man is Lord, has authority, even over the Sabbath day."

3 And Jesus entered the synagogue again and there He met a man with a deformed hand. ²And the Pharisees were watching Him to see if He would heal the man on the

Sabbath day, so that they could find a reason to accuse Him. ³And He said to the man whose hand was deformed, "Step forward." ⁴Then He said to the Pharisees, "Is it permissible by the Law of Moses to do something good, or something harmful on the Sabbath day? To save a life or to kill it?" But they did not reply. ⁵And when He had looked around at them with righteous indignation, being grieved over their stubbornness, He said to the man, "Reach out your hand." And when he reached it out, his hand was restored to normal use. ⁶And the Pharisees immediately went out and conferred with the Herodians against Jesus, plotting how they could kill Him.

⁷Then Jesus withdrew from there with His disciples and went to the Lake of Galilee, being followed by a large crowd from Galilee. Also, a large crowd from Judea, ⁸Jerusalem, Idumaea, the east side of the Jordan River, and from around Tyre and Sidon, cities on the northwest coast of Palestine, came to Him, having heard about the great things, miracles, He had been performing. ⁹He told His disciples to have a small boat waiting for Him, from which He could address the people to prevent His being thronged by the large crowd. ¹⁰For He had healed so many people that large numbers of them who were plagued with serious illnesses were crowding around Him in hope of getting to touch Him.

¹¹And whenever they saw Him, people possessed by evil spirits fell to the ground in front of Him, shouting, "You are the Son of God." ¹²But He sternly ordered them not to reveal His identity.

¹³He then went up into the mountain and summoned those He wanted to come to Him and they came. ¹⁴He appointed twelve apostles to travel with Him, whom He could send out to preach ¹⁵and have authority to drive out evil spirits. ¹⁶These apostles were: Simon, to whom He gave the added name Peter, ¹⁷James and his brother John, the sons of Zebedee, to when He gave the added name Boanerges, which means "Sons of Thunder," ¹⁸Andrew, Philip, Bartholomew, the same as Nathaniel, Matthew, the same as Levi, Thomas, the same as Didymus, James, the son of Alphaeus, Thaddaeus, the same as Judas, the son on James, Simon the Canaanean, the same as the Zealot, ¹⁹and Judas Iscariot, who also betrayed Him.

Then Jesus went into a house. ²⁰Soon a crowd assembled again so that they could not even eat a meal without people crowding all around them. ²¹When His relatives or friends heard about this, all that He was doing, they went out to take custody of Him for safety reasons for people were saying, "He has lost His mind."

²²And the experts in the Law of Moses who had come down from Jerusalem were saying, "He has Beelzebub in Him" and "He is driving out evil spirits by the power of the chief of evil spirits." ²³And He called them to Him and began speaking to them in parables, brief stories to illustrate His teaching, saying, "How can Satan drive out Satan? ²⁴And if a kingdom is plagued by internal division, it will never survive. ²⁵And if a household is divided by strife within, that household will never last. ²⁶And if Satan has risen up against himself, and is divided in aim and purpose he cannot survive, and his end has come. ²⁷But no one can enter a strong man's house and steal his belongings unless he first ties up the strong man. Only then will he be able to steal from his house. ²⁸Truly I tell you, all of mankind's sins and the abusive language that they use in speaking against God and man can be forgiven. ²⁹But the person who speaks against the Holy Spirit can never be forgiven, for he is guilty of a never ending sin." ³⁰Jesus said all this because these experts in the Law of Moses had been saying, "He has an evil spirit in him."

³¹Then Jesus' mother and half-brothers came and stood outside of a large house. They sent a message to Him, asking Him to come out to them. ³²Someone in the large crowd that was sitting around Him said to Him, "Look, your mother and your brothers are outside looking for you." ³³He answered them "Who is my mother and who are my brothers?" ³⁴Then He looked out over those gathered around Him and said, "Look, here are my mother and my brothers! ³⁵For whoever will do what God wants, that person is my brother, and sister and mother."

4 Jesus again began teaching along the shore of the lake of Galilee. A huge crowd gathered around Him so that He had to sit in a boat out in the lake to speak to them, while all the crowd stood on the shore. ²He taught the people many things using parables to illustrate His lessons. In His teaching He said to them, ³"Listen carefully! A farmer went out to plant seed, ⁴and it happened, as he sowed scattering the seeds by hand, some of it fell by the side of the road and birds came and ate it. ⁵And some seed fell on rocky ground where there was not much soil, and immediately it sprouted up because the soil was so shallow. ⁶But when the sun came up the newly sprouted plants were scorched, and because they had no roots, soon withered away. ⁷And other seeds fell among thorns which grew up and choked them so that they yielded no crop. ⁸Then other seeds fell into fertile soil, and growing up to maturity, they yielded an ever-increasing crop. They produced thirty, sixty and even a hundred times as much as was planted." ⁹And Jesus said, "Whoever has ears to hear with ought to listen to this carefully."

¹⁰And when He was alone those people gathered around him, along with the twelve apostles, asked Him what the parables meant. ¹¹He said to them, "You disciples are being given an understanding of the secret of the kingdom of God, but to outsiders everything will be told in parables. ¹²This is so that even though they see, they will see and yet not perceive. And even though they hear, they will hear and yet not understand. For if they did, they would turn back to God again and receive forgiveness."

¹³And Jesus continued to speak to them, "Do you not know what this parable means? Then how can you understand any of the other parables? ¹⁴A farmer planted 'the word,' the message of God. ¹⁵Some of the seed that fell along the roadside represents where 'the word' was sown, preached. When these people have heard, immediately Satan comes and takes away 'the word' which had been sown in them. ¹⁶And in the same way, some of the seed that was sown on rocky soil represented those who heard 'the word' and immediately accepted it gladly, ¹⁷but since they had such shallow roots, they continued on for only a little while. Then, when trouble and persecution arose over obeying 'the word,' immediately they stumbled and fell away from God. ¹⁸And other seeds represent those who are sown among thorns. These are people who heard 'the word,' ¹⁹but worry over things of the world, and the deceitfulness of material wealth, and the evil desires for other things entered their hearts and choked the effectiveness of 'the word,' so that it did not yield a crop in their lives. ²⁰Then there were those who were sown on fertile soil. These represent people who heard 'the word,' accepted it and yielded a crop of thirty, sixty and even a hundred times as much as was planted."

²¹Then He said to them, "Is a lamp brought in to be put under a bushed-sized container, or under the bed, instead of on its stand? ²²For there is nothing that is hidden that should not be

exposed. Neither is anything covered up that should not be exposed. Neither is anything covered up that should not be revealed. $^{23}$If anyone has ears to hear with, he ought to listen to this carefully." $^{24}$And He said to them, "Pay attention to what you are hearing from Me. The standard you use in giving to others is the standard they will use on you, with even more added. $^{25}$For to the person who already has something, more will be given, and from the person who has almost nothing, even the little he has will be taken away from him."

$^{26}$And Jesus said, "The kingdom of God is like a farmer who scattered seed on the ground, $^{27}$then went to bed and got up the next day to find that the seed had sprouted and grown, yet he did not know how it happened. $^{28}$The soil yields its crop, first the green sprout, then the ears of grain, and then the kernels in the ears. $^{29}$But when the grain ripens the farmer wields his sickle because harvest time has come."

$^{30}$And He continued to speak, "What shall I compare the kingdom of God to? Or, what parable will best illustrate it? $^{31}$It is similar to a seed from the mustard tree which, when planted in the ground, $^{32}$even though it is the least significant of all seeds on earth, becomes larger than all other plants. It develops huge branches so that the birds of the sky can roost in their shade."

$^{33}$And He spoke 'the word' to the crowds with as many such parables as they were able to receive. $^{34}$And He did not speak to them concerning the kingdom without using a parable, but He explained everything to His own disciples privately.

$^{35}$When evening came that day He said to the disciples, "Let us go over to the other side, the east side, of Lake Galilee." $^{36}$And leaving the crowd, the disciples took Him in their boat just the way He was, this probably means without His making provision for the trip. They were accompanied by other boats also. $^{37}$Then a violent windstorm arose on the lake and huge waves began splashing into the boat until it began to fill with water. $^{38}$Jesus was sleeping on a pillow in the stern of the boat. They awakened Him, shouting, "Teacher, do you not care that we are sinking?" $^{39}$He immediately awoke and spoke sternly to the wind and called out to the water. "Be peaceful and still." Immediately the wind stopped blowing and a great calm came over the water. $^{40}$And He said to His disciples, "Why are you so afraid? Do you not still have any faith?" And they were extremely afraid, and said to one another, "Who can this man be that even the wind and water obey Him?"

5 Then Jesus and His disciples finally arrived on the other side of the lake, the east side, in the district of Geresa, $^{2}$When Jesus left the boat, immediately a man with an evil spirit came from the graveyard to meet Him. $^{3}$This man had been living in the graveyard and not one had been able to keep him tied up, not even with a chain. $^{4}$He had often been bound with ropes and chains but had broken the chains off and torn the ropes to pieces. And no one had enough strength to subdue him. $^{5}$And night and day, in the graveyard and in the mountains, he was always shouting out and cutting himself with sharp rocks. $^{6}$When he saw Jesus from far away he ran to Him and worshiped Him. $^{7}$And shouting with a loud voice, he said, "What do you want with me, Jesus, Son of the Most High God? I beg you, in God's name, do not torture me." $^{8}$For Jesus was saying to the evil spirit in him, "Come out of this man, you evil spirit." $^{9}$Then He asked the evil spirit, "What is your name?" And he answered Him, "My name is 'Legion,' for there are many of us, evil spirits." $^{10}$Then the spirits begged Jesus earnestly not to send them away out of the region.

[11]On the side of a nearby mountain, a large herd of wild hogs was grazing. [12]The evil spirits begged Him, saying, "Send us into those wild hogs, so we can enter their bodies." [13]And He gave them permission to do it. So, the evil spirits went out of the man's body and entered the bodies of the wild hogs. The herd then rushed down the cliff into the lake. There were about two thousand that drowned in the lake. [14]Those who had been feeding them ran and told what all occurred in the town and around the countryside and so people came to find out what had happened. [15]And when people came to Jesus, they saw the man who had been dominated by 5,000 to 6,000 evil spirits sitting down with his clothes on and perfectly sane, and they were afraid. [16]Those who saw this told the people what had happened to the man dominated by the evil spirits and about the wild hogs. [17]So, they began begging Jesus to leave that region.

[18]As He entered the boat the man who had been dominated by evil spirits begged for permission to be allowed to go with Him. [19]But Jesus would not allow him, saying to the man, "Go home to your friends and family and tell them about the great things the Lord has done for you and how He had pity on you." [20]But the man went away and began telling people throughout Decapolis about all of the great things Jesus had done for him.

[21]When Jesus had crossed over again in a boat to the other side, the northwest shore of the lake, probably in the vicinity of Capernaum, a large crowd gathered around Him along the shore of the lake. [22]About then a man named Jairus, one of the officials of the synagogue, came to Jesus and, upon seeing Him, fell to the ground at His feet. [23]He begged Him earnestly, saying, "My little daughter is about to die; please come and place your hands on her so she may be healed and live." [24]So, Jesus went along with the man, and was being thronged by a large crowd that followed Him.

[25]Then a woman, who had been bleeding for twelve years, came to Him. [26]She had suffered much at the hands of many doctors, through treatments and medication that only increased her discomfort and had spent all her money on medical bills and yet got worse instead of better. [27]She had heard what Jesus was doing so came from the crowd behind Jesus and touched His robe. [28]For she had told herself, "If only I can touch His clothing, I will be healed." [29]And immediately her flow of blood stopped and she felt healed in her body from the affliction. [30]Just then Jesus perceived in Himself that healing power had gone out from Him so turned to the crowd and asked, "Who touched my clothing?" [31]And His disciples said to Him, "You see the large crowd thronging you and yet you ask "Who touched me?" [32]Then He looked around to see who had done this, touched Him and received healing. [33]But the woman became afraid and trembled with fear, for she knew what had happened to her, the healing, so she came and fell down in front of Jesus and told Him the whole truth. [34]And He said to her, "Daughter, your faith has made you well. Go in peace and remain healed from your affliction."

[35]While Jesus was still speaking, someone came from the synagogue official's house and said to the official, "Your daughter is dead; why are you bothering the Teacher any more?" [36]But Jesus disregarded what the person said and told the official, "Do not be afraid; just believe in my power to restore your daughter." [37]He did not allow anyone to follow Him to the official's house except Peter, James and his brother John. [38]And when they arrived at the synagogue official's house He saw a commotion there, with many people crying and wailing

loudly. ³⁹And when He entered the house He said to them, "Why are you making such a commotion and crying? The child is not really dead, but only sleeping." ⁴⁰They laughed at Him scornfully. But after having all the people wait outside He took the child's father and mother, along with those who came with Him, Peter, James and John, and went in to where the dead child lay. ⁴¹And taking the child by the hand He said to here, "*Talitha cumi*," which means "Little girl, I tell you, get up." ⁴²And immediately the little girl arose and walked, for she was twelve years old. Upon seeing this the people were completely amazed. ⁴³But He strictly ordered them not to tell anyone about this; then He told them to give the girl something to eat.

6 Then Jesus went out from there and came to His home town, Nazareth, and His disciples went with Him. ²And when the Sabbath day came, He began teaching in the synagogue and many who heard Him was amazed, and asked such questions as, "Where did this man get these things, knowledge, miracles, etc.?" and "What kind of wisdom has been given to Him?" And "What do these supernatural powers He performs mean? ³Is not this the carpenter, the Son of Mary and brother of James, Joseph, Judas and Simon? And are not His sisters living here among us?" And they were led to doubt His true identity. ⁴Then Jesus said to them, "A prophet does not go without receiving honor, except in His own home town, and among His own relatives, and among His own family members." ⁵And He could not perform any supernatural deed there because of their lack of faith in Him except He placed hands on a few sick people accompanied by prayer and healed them. ⁶But He marveled at the people's lack of faith. So He traveled and taught throughout the surrounding villages.

⁷Then Jesus called to Him the twelve apostles and sent them out two by two. He gave them authority over evil spirits ⁸and ordered them not to take anything with them during their travels, except a walking stick. They were to take no food, no traveling bag for personal belongings, and no money in their money belts, ⁹but were to wear sandals and take only one coat. ¹⁰And He said to them, "Wherever you enter a house, stay there until you leave that place. ¹¹And the people from whatever place that does not welcome you or listen to you, when you leave there, shake the dust off from under your shoes as evidence against them." ¹²Then they went out and preached that people should repent, change their hearts and lives. ¹³And they drove out many evil spirits and applied olive oil to the heads of many sick people and healed them.

¹⁴Now King Herod heard about what Jesus was doing, because His name had become well known. He said, "John the Immerser has risen from the dead and it is his powers that are at work in Jesus." ¹⁵But others said, "He is the prophet Elijah." While others said, "He is a prophet like one of the prophets of old." ¹⁶But when King Herod heard about Jesus he said, "John whom I had decapitated, has risen." ¹⁷For it was Herod himself who had sent for John and had him arrested and chained up in prison. He did this to please Herodias, who had been his brother Philip's wife, but whom Herod had married. ¹⁸For John had said to Herod, "It is unlawful for you to marry your brother's wife." ¹⁹Now because of this Herodias had a grudge against John and wanted to kill him, but had not been able to. ²⁰It was because Herod was afraid of John, knowing he was a righteous and holy man, so he protected him. And Herod became very disturbed whenever he listened to John, yet he heard him gladly.

²¹Then an ideal opportunity arose for Herodias to do away with John when Herod gave a dinner on his birthday for his influential friends, military commanders and the prominent officials of Galilee. ²²And when Herodias' daughter came in and danced in front of them, sensually, she pleased Herod and his party guests so much that the king said to the young woman, "Ask me for whatever you want and I will give it to you." ²³And he vowed to her, "I will give you whatever you ask me for, up to one half the wealth of my kingdom." ²⁴So, she went out and said to her mother, "What shall I ask for?" And her mother said, "Ask for the head of John the Immerser." ²⁵At once she hurried in the king and said, "I would like you to give me the head of John the Immerser on a large platter right away." ²⁶And the king became very distressed over such a gruesome request, but because he had promised her with oaths, and to keep from looking bad in front of his party guests, he did not refuse her request. ²⁷And immediately the king sent a soldier who served as his guard and ordered him to bring John's head to him. So, he went and decapitated him in the prison, ²⁸and brought his head on a large platter and gave it to the young woman. She in turn gave it to her mother Herodias. ²⁹And when John's disciples heard what had happened they took his body and buried it in a grave.

³⁰Then the apostles got together with Jesus and told Him everything they had done and taught on their mission. ³¹He said to them, "You men, leave here and go to a deserted place and rest for awhile." For there were so many people coming and going to listen to preaching, receive healing, etc. that they had no opportunity even to eat. ³²So, Jesus and His apostles left by boat and went to a separate place where they could be alone. ³³But the people saw them going and, since many recognized them, these people ran on ahead of them from all the surrounding towns. ³⁴Then Jesus left His place of seclusion and, seeing the large crowd, He felt deep compassion for them because they were as disoriented as sheep without a shepherd, so He began teaching them.

³⁵And when the day was nearly over His disciples came to Him and said, "This place is deserted and the day is almost over; ³⁶send the crowd away so they can go into the surrounding countryside and towns to buy themselves something to eat." ³⁷But He answered them, "You men give them something to eat." And they replied, "Should we go and buy a supply of bread to give them to eat?" ³⁸And He said to them, "How many loaves of bread do you have? Go and see." And when had found out, they said, "Five barley loaves and two, fish." ³⁹And He ordered all of them to recline in groups on the green grass. ⁴⁰So, they reclined in groups of fifty and one hundred. ⁴¹Then He took the five loaves of bread and the two fish, and looking up to heaven, He asked God's blessing on them. Then He broke the loaves and gave them to His disciples to set in front of the people to eat. He divided the two fish among them also ⁴²and they all ate until they were full. ⁴³Then they gathered up twelve basketsful of broken pieces of bread and also some fish. ⁴⁴The number eating the loaves of bread was five thousand men.

⁴⁵And about then Jesus compelled His disciples to get into a boat and go on ahead of Him to the other side, the west side of the Lake Galilee, to Bathsaida while He Himself sent the crowd away. ⁴⁶And after He had left them He went into a mountain to pray.

⁴⁷When evening came the boat containing His disciples was in the middle of the lake while He remained alone on the shore. ⁴⁸When He saw how distressed His disciples were, rowing against an opposing wind, Jesus came to them between three and six o'clock in the

morning, walking on the water, and almost walked past them. ⁴⁹But when they saw Him walking on the water they thought it was a spirit, so shouted out, ⁵⁰becoming very frightened when they saw Him. But He immediately spoke to them and said, "Take courage, and do not be afraid, it is I." ⁵¹Then He got up into the boat with them and the wind immediately stopped. And His disciples were greatly amazed at this, ⁵²but they did not understand the miracle of the loaves because their minds were insensitive to the nature and power of Jesus.

53And when they had finally crossed over to the west side of Lake Galilee, they arrived in the district of Gennesaret and moored the boat on shore. 54As soon as they got out of the boat the people recognized Jesus 55As soon as they got out of the boat the people recognized Jesus 55and rushed around the whole direct to bring sick people on cots to where He was. 56And wherever He entered towns, cities or the countryside, they placed sick people at the open shopping markets and begged Him to allow them to touch even the edge of His robe. And all those who touched Him were made well.

7 The Pharisees and some experts in the Law of Moses, who had come from Jerusalem, gathered around Jesus. ²They had observed some of His disciples eating their food with contaminated, that is, ceremonially unwashed hands. ³For the Pharisees and all the Jews would not eat anything unless they first scrubbed their hands up to the wrists in accordance with the long-established tradition of the Jewish elders. ⁴And when they returned from the open shopping markets they refused to eat anything until they washed themselves or "it," that is, the food, thoroughly. There were also many other traditions which they strictly observed, like washing cups, pots and copper kettles thoroughly. ⁵The Pharisees and experts in the Law of Moses asked Jesus, "Why do your disciples not live according to the traditions of the Jewish elders, but instead eat their food with contaminated, ceremonially unwashed hands?" ⁶And He answered them, "Isaiah prophesied about you hypocrites very well when he wrote 'These people honor me with their lips by what they say, but their heart is far from honoring me. ⁷They are worshiping me for nothing because they are teaching principles which are merely the requirements of men.' ⁸You disregard the commandment of God and yet hang onto the traditions of men." ⁹And He said to them, "You are good at rejecting the commandment of God so you can keep your traditions. ¹⁰For Moses said, 'Give honor to your father and mother,' and 'Whoever says bad things about his father or mother should surely be put to death.' ¹¹but when you people say, 'If someone says to his father or mother, the money I could have helped with is *Corban*; in other words, it is given to God,' ¹²you are not allowing him to do anything for his father or mother anymore. ¹³You are making God's message useless by enforcing the tradition you have been following. And you do many things like that."

¹⁴Then He called the crowd to Him again and said to them, "Listen to me, all of you, and understand what I am saying. ¹⁵There is nothing that enters a person's body from the outside that can spiritually corrupt him, but it is what proceeds out of a person's life that spiritually corrupts him." ¹⁶[Verse 16 is absent from most ancient manuscripts.]

¹⁷And when He had gone into the house away from the crowd His disciples asked Him about this parable. ¹⁸He said to them, "Are you also as lacking in understanding as the others? Do you not understand that whatever enters a person's body from the outside cannot spiritually corrupt him? ¹⁹It is because it does not go into his heart, but into his stomach, and

eventually passes out into the toilet." By saying this He made all foods ceremonially acceptable. [20]And He said, "Whatever proceeds out of a man's life is what spiritually corrupts him. [21]For from within, out of people's hearts, proceed evil thoughts, sexual immorality, stealing, murder, extramarital affairs, [22]greedy desires, wickedness, deceit, unrestrained indecency, envy, slander, arrogance and foolishness. [23]All these evil things proceed from within man's heart and spiritually corrupt him."

[24]And from there Jesus got up and went away into the region of Tyre and Sidon. He entered a house but did not want anyone to know it. However, He could not keep it secret. [25]But just then a woman whose little daughter was dominated by an evil spirit heard about Jesus and came and fell down at His feet. [26]Now the woman was a Greek Gentile, a Syrophoenician by nationality. She begged Him to drive out the evil spirit from her daughter. [27]So, He said to her, "Children should be the first ones to eat until they are full, for it is not proper to take the children's food and throw it to the dogs." [28]But she answered Him, "Yes Lord, but even the dogs under the table eat the crumbs dropped by the children." [29]And He said to her, "Because you have said this, go on your way; the evil spirit has left your daughter." [30]And she went away to her house and found her child lying on her bed with the evil spirit gone from her.

[31]Again He left the region of Tyre and traveled north through Sidon, then back south to Lake Galilee, and through the middle of Decapolis. [32]And they brought to Him a deaf man who had a speech impediment and they begged Him to place His hand on him for healing. [33]So, Jesus took him away from the crowd by himself and put His fingers into the man's ears. Then He spit and touched the man's tongue with His saliva [34]and, looking up to heaven, He sighed and said, "*Ephphatha*," which means, "Be opened." [35]And immediately the man's hearing was restored, his speech impediment was removed and he began speaking clearly. [36]Then Jesus ordered the people who witnessed the miracle not to tell anyone about it, but the more He urged them not to, the more widely they publicized it. [37]And they were utterly amazed, saying, "He has done everything just right; He makes even the deaf to hear and the mute to speak."

**8** In those days, when a large crowd again assembled to listen to Jesus' teaching and did not have anything to eat, Jesus called His disciples and said to them, [2]"I feel deep pity for this crowd because they have continued listening to me for three days now and have nothing left to eat. [3]And if I send them home hungry they will become weak on the way, because some of them have come a long distance." [4]And His disciples replied to Him, "Where will a person get enough bread to feed these people in such a deserted place like this?" [5]And He asked them, "How many loaves of bread do you have?" And they answered, "We have seven loaves." [6]Then He ordered the crowd to sit down on the ground; He took the seven loaves, and after giving thanks to God for them, He divided the food and gave it to His disciples to set in front of them. They in turn set it in front of the crowd. [7]They also had a few small fish and after asking God's blessing on them, He ordered these also to be set in front of them. [8]And they all ate until they were full, then gathered up seven baskets of broken pieces which were left over. [9]The number who ate was about four thousand men besides women and children. Then Jesus sent them away. [10]Immediately He boarded a boat with His disciples and crossed to the west side of the lake to the region of Dalmanutha.

¹¹The Pharisees and Sudducees, these were strict sects of the Jewish religion, came out and began disputing with Jesus, asking for a supernatural sign from Him, in an attempt to test Him. ¹²Then He sighed deeply in His spirit and said, "Why does this generation of people look for a supernatural sign? Truly I tell you, there will not be any supernatural sign given to this generation." ¹³Then He left them and boarded a boat again and sailed to the other side, the east side of Lake Galilee.

¹⁴Now Jesus' disciples had forgotten to take any food with them, and had only one loaf of bread in the boat. ¹⁵Then Jesus ordered them, saying, "Pay attention and watch out for the leavening effect of the Pharisees and Herod." ¹⁶And they began reasoning with one another, saying, "Why be concerned about yeast since we do not have any bread?" ¹⁷Jesus, being aware of what they were thinking, said, "Why are you reasoning about not having any bread? Have you not yet perceived or understood? Have your hearts become insensitive? ¹⁸Even though you have eyes, do you not see? And even though you have ears, do you not hear? And do you not remember? ¹⁹When I divided the five loaves of bread among the five thousand persons, how many baskets full of broken pieces did you gather up?" They said to Him, "Twelve baskets full." ²⁰He again asked, "And when the seven loaves were divided among the four thousand persons, how many large basketfuls of broken pieces did you gather up?" And they said to Him, "Seven large basketfuls." ²¹Then He said to them, "Do you not understand yet?"

²²And when they came to Bethsaida some people brought a blind man to Jesus and begged Him to touch him for healing. ²³So, He took hold of the blind man by his hand and brought him out of the village. When Jesus spit and put His saliva on his eyes and placed His hands on him for healing. He asked him, "Can you see anything?" ²⁴The man looked up and said, "Yes, I see people, but they look like trees walking around." ²⁵Then Jesus again placed His hands on his eyes; the man stared intently, then his sight was completely restored and he was able to see everything clearly. ²⁶Then Jesus sent him home, saying, "Do not even go through the village on your way."

²⁷Now Jesus and His disciples went out to the villages in the vicinity of Caesarea Philippi. On their way, He asked His disciples, "Who are people saying that I am?" ²⁸And they answered Him, "Some say you are John the Immerser; others say the prophet Elijah, but others say you are one of the prophets." ²⁹Then He asked them, "But who do you say that I am?" Peter answered Him, "You are the Christ, God's specially chosen One." ³⁰Then He ordered them not to tell anyone about His identity.

³¹Jesus then began teaching them that the Son of man must suffer very much, be rejected by the Jewish elders, leading priests, and experts in the Law of Moses and be killed, but rise again from the dead after three days. ³²And He spoke about this freely. But Peter took Jesus aside and began rebuking Him for saying such things. ³³But He turned around, and looking at His disciples, He rebuked Peter, saying to him, "Get away from me, Satan; for you are not thinking about God's things but about men's."

³⁴And He called the crowd to Him, along with His disciples, and said to them, "If anyone wants to be my follower, he should deny himself of always having his own way and accept his cross, his responsibilities, with all their difficulties and then he can become my follower. ³⁵For whoever would try to save his life by neglecting spiritual things will lose it, miss out on the blessings of God. But whoever is willing to lose his life in commitment to God's service for

my sake and the work of the Gospel's sake, will save it, obtain both temporal and spiritual blessings. [36]For what would it benefit a person to gain the whole world of material things and give up his life of spiritual blessings? [37]Or what should a person give in exchange for his life? [38]For whoever will be ashamed of Me and of My words in this spiritually unfaithful and sinful generation, the Son of man will also be ashamed of him when He returns in the splendor of His Father, accompanied by the holy angels."

**9** And Jesus said to them, "Truly I tell you, there are some people standing here who will surely not experience death until they see that God's kingdom has come in a demonstration of power."
[2]And after six days had passed, Jesus took Peter, James and John aside alone and went up to a high mountain, probably Mt. Tabor, which was nearby. There His whole appearance was miraculously changed in front of them. [3]His clothing became dazzling and extremely white; whiter than anyone in the world could possibly launder them. [4]Then Elijah, along with Moses, appeared to them and they were talking with Jesus. [5]And Peter said to Jesus, "Rabbi, Teacher, it is good for us to be here. Let us build three small shelters, one for you, one for Moses and one for Elijah." [6]For he did not know what to day, because they all became very afraid. [7]Just then a cloud engulfed them and a voice spoke out of the cloud saying, "This is my dearly loved Son, listen to Him." [8]And suddenly they looked all around them, but the only one they saw with them was Jesus.
[9]And as they were coming down from the mountain Jesus ordered His disciples not to tell anyone what they had seen until after the Son of Man was raised again from the dead. [10]So, they kept what He told them to themselves, discussing only among themselves what "rising again from the dead" meant. [11]Then His disciples asked Him, "Why is it, since you are obviously the Messiah, that the experts in the Law of Moses say that Elijah must come first?" [12]Jesus answered them, "Elijah truly will come first and restore all things to their proper perspective concerning the Messiah. And it is also written in the Scriptures about the Son of Man, that He would suffer very much and be rejected. [13]But I tell you, Elijah has already come, and they did to him what they wanted to, just like it was written about him in the Scriptures."
[14]And when Peter, James and John returned to the rest of the disciples, they saw a large crowd gathered around them, and the experts in the Law of Moses disputing with them. [15]And immediately, upon seeing Jesus, the entire crowd ran to greet Him in great amazement, possibly over His sudden appearance. [16]And He asked the crowd, "What are you arguing about with my disciples?"
[17]And someone in the crowd answered Him, "Teacher, I brought to you my son, who is dominated by a spirit which causes him to be a mute. [18]Wherever it seizes him, it throws him down and he foams at the mouth, grinds his teeth and stiffens out. I spoke to your disciples, asking them to drive it out, but they were not able to." [19]Jesus said to them, "You generation of faithless people! How long must I be with you before you understand? How long do I have to be patient with you? Bring the sick boy to me." [20]Then some people from the crowd brought the sick boy to Jesus, and when the spirit saw Him, it immediately caused the boy to have convulsions and to fall on the ground and roll around, foaming at the mouth. [21]Jesus asked the

boy's father, "How long has this been happening to him?" And he answered, "Since he was a small child. $^{22}$And frequently the evil spirit has tried to kill him, throwing him into a fire or into the water. But if you can do anything for him, have pity on us and help us." $^{23}$And Jesus said to him, "If you can. Everything is possible to the person who believes it can happen." $^{24}$Immediately the father of the boy cried out, "I do believe; help me to have more faith." $^{25}$When Jesus saw a crowd running together toward Him, He spoke sternly to the evil spirit in the boy, saying to it, "You deaf-mute spirit, I order you to come out of this boy and to never return to him again." $^{26}$The spirit shrieked and caused violent convulsions in the boy, then came out of him. The boy appeared to be dead, so that most of the people were saying, "He is dead." $^{27}$But Jesus grasped his hand and lifted him up, and he arose fully healed.

$^{28}$And when Jesus had come into a house, His disciples asked Him privately, "Why could we not drive out the evil spirit from the boy?" $^{29}$He answered them, "This kind of spirit cannot be driven out except by praying."

$^{30}$So, they left there and traveled through Galilee, but Jesus did not want anyone to know about it. $^{31}$For He taught His disciples, saying to them, "The Son of Man will be handed over to evil men and they will kill Him, and three days after He dies He will rise up again." $^{32}$But His disciples did not understand what He meant and were afraid to ask Him.

$^{33}$Then Jesus and His disciples came to Capernaum. When He and His disciples entered a house He asked them, "What were you discussing on the way here?" $^{34}$But they kept quiet for they had been arguing with one another over which one of them was the greatest. $^{35}$So, He sat down and called the twelve apostles and said to them, "If anyone of you should try to be first in importance he will end up being last, and become the servant of all the others." $^{36}$And He took a little child and placed it in front of them, and lifting the child up into His arms, He said to them, $^{37}$"Whoever welcomes one such little child as this for My sake, welcomes Me; and whoever welcomes Me, does not welcome Me only, but also the One who sent Me."

$^{38}$Then John the apostle said to Him, "Teacher, we saw someone driving out evil spirits by using your name, so we told him to stop doing it, because he was not following You with us." $^{39}$But Jesus said, "Do not try to stop him, for there is not anyone who performs a supernatural deed using My name who will be able to quickly say something bad about Me.

$^{40}$"For the person who is not against us is for us. $^{41}$Truly I tell you, whoever will give you even a cup of water to drink because you belong to Christ will certainly not lose his temporal or eternal reward. $^{42}$And whoever causes one of these little ones, humble followers of the Lord, who believes in Me to be led astray from God, he would have been better off to have had a huge millstone tied around his neck and thrown into the ocean. $^{43}$And if your hand becomes the occasion for falling away from God, cut it off; it would be better for you to enter never ending life disabled, rather than keeping both hands and going to hell, into the fire that cannot be put out, all because it caused you to fall away from God. *[Verse 44 is absent from many manuscripts.]* $^{45}$And if your foot becomes the occasion for falling away from God, cut it off; it would be better for you to enter never ending life cripples, rather that keeping both feet and being thrown into hell. *[Verse 46 is absent from many manuscripts.]* $^{47}$And if your eye becomes the occasion for falling away from God gouge it out; it would be better for you to enter the kingdom of God with only one eye, rather that keeping both eyes and being thrown into hell, all because one of them caused you to fall away from God. $^{48}$For in hell the worm of those who are there will never die, their gnawing punishment will never cease and the fire there will never go out. ⁴⁹For everyone will be salted with fire.

⁵⁰"Salt is good, but if it loses its salty flavor, what will you use to restore it? It is difficult to restore the 'salt' of sacrificial commitment to God once it is lost. You should have salt in yourselves, develop the qualities of preserving, purifying, commitment to God and live peacefully with one another instead of in rivalry."

10 And Jesus left there and went to the region of Judea and east of the Jordan River. Again crowds gathered around Him and He continued teaching them, as was His custom.

²Some Pharisees, a strict sect of the Jewish religion, came to Him and attempted to test Him by asking, "Is it permissible by the Law of Moses for a man to divorce his wife?" ³And He answered them, "What did Moses command you to do?" ⁴They replied, "Moses allowed us to provide a legal divorce decree and then to divorce her." ⁵But Jesus said to them, "He wrote you this commandment only because of the rebellious spirit of you Jews. ⁶But from the beginning of creation God made mankind male and female. ⁷For this reason, since He made one woman for one man, a man will leave the home of his father and mother and will cling to his wife ⁸and the two of them will then become one flesh, united in such a close relationship as to constitute one body, so that upon becoming husband and wife they no longer function as two persons but as one body. ⁹Therefore, those whom God so joins together in the marriage bond, no person must ever separate."

¹⁰And when they were in the house, His disciples asked Him about this matter again. ¹¹And He said to them, "Whoever divorces his wife and marries another woman commits sexual unfaithfulness toward her. ¹²And if she herself divorces her husband and marries another man, she commits sexual unfaithfulness toward him."

¹³Then some parents were bringing their little children to Jesus so He could touch them, to bestow a blessing on them, but His disciples spoke harshly to these parents for doing this. ¹⁴But when Jesus saw it, He was moved with righteous indignation, and said to them, "Allow these little children to come to Me and stop trying to prevent them, for the kingdom of God belongs to such humble ones. ¹⁵Truly I tell you, whoever does not welcome the kingdom of God as a little child does, that person will by no means enter it." ¹⁶Then He lifted up the children into His arms, and placing His hands on them, He asked God's blessing on them.

¹⁷As Jesus was leaving to go on His way, a man ran to Him and kneeled down in front of Him and asked, "Good Teacher, what should I do in order to possess never ending life?" ¹⁸Jesus answered him, "Why are you calling Me good? Nobody is good except One, that is, God. ¹⁹You know the commandments: Do not murder. Do not be sexually unfaithful to your mate. Do not steal. Do not give false testimony. Do not cheat. Show honor to your father and mother." ²⁰And he replied, "Teacher, I have already been observing all these commandments since I was a young lad." ²¹And Jesus looked at Him, and filled with love, said to him, "There is one thing you still lack. Go and sell your possessions and give the money to poor people; become my follower, then you will have treasure in heaven." ²²But the man had a sad look on his face when he heard these words, and went away sorrowful, for he had many possessions.

²³Then Jesus looked around Him and said to His disciples, "How difficult it is for rich

people to enter the kingdom of God!" ²⁴And His disciples were amazed at what He said. But Jesus spoke to them again and said, "How difficult it is for anyone to enter the kingdom of God! ²⁵It is actually easier for a camel to pass through the eye of a needle than for a rich person to enter the kingdom of God." ²⁶And they were utterly amazed and said to Him, "Then who can possibly be saved?" ²⁷Jesus looked at them and said, "This would be impossible with men, but not with God, for everything is possible with God." ²⁸Peter began saying to Him, "Look, we have left everything, homes, jobs, family, to follow You." ²⁹Jesus said, "Truly I tell you, no one who has left his house, or brothers, or sisters, or mother, or father, or children or property for My sake and the Gospel's sake, to become a servant of the Lord, ³⁰but what he will receive back a hundred times as much now in this life – houses, and brothers, and sisters, and mothers, and children and property – yet with persecutions. And in the coming age he will receive never ending life. ³¹But many that appear to be first in importance and blessings will end up being last. And those appearing to be last will end up being first."

³²Now Jesus and His disciples were traveling along the road, going up to Jerusalem, with Jesus moving on ahead of the others. The disciples were amazed and they followed behind Him fearfully. He took the twelve apostles aside and began telling them about the things that were going to happen to Him. ³³He said, "Look, we are going up to Jerusalem and the Son of Man will be turned over to the leading priests and experts in the Law of Moses. They will condemn Him to death and turn Him over to the unconverted Gentiles. ³⁴They will mock Him, and spit on Him, and whip Him and finally kill Him, but after three days He will rise again from the dead."

³⁵Now James and John, the sons on Zebedee, came over to Jesus and said to Him, "We would like You to do for us whatever we ask You." ³⁶And He said to them, "What do you want Me to do for you?" ³⁷They answered Him, "Appoint one of us to sit at Your right side and the other at Your left side when You come in splendor." ³⁸But Jesus said to them, "You really do not know what you are asking for. Are you able to drink the cup of suffering that I will drink? Or are you able to be immersed with the immersion that I am to be immersed with, to be overwhelmed with agony?" ³⁹And they said to Him, "Yes, we are able to." And Jesus said to them, "The cup of suffering that I will drink, you also will drink. And the immersion with agony with which I am to be immersed, you also will be immersed. ⁴⁰But it is not My prerogative to appoint who sits at My right side and at My left, but those places are for people to whom it has been assigned by the Father." ⁴¹When the ten other apostles heard this, they became very upset with James and John. ⁴²Jesus called them, (probably all twelve apostles) to Him and said, "You are aware that those who are regarded as rulers among the unconverted Gentiles lord it over their own people, and their important men domineer over them as well. ⁴³But it is not to be this way among you, for whoever would like to become important among you will be your servant. ⁴⁴And whoever would like to be first in prominence among you, will be your slave. ⁴⁵For the Son of Man did not come to be served by others but to be the servant of others, and to sacrifice His life as a ransom price for many people, to purchase them back from Satan."

⁴⁶Then Jesus and the twelve apostles came to Jericho. As He left there with His disciples and a large crowd, they met a blind beggar named Bartimaeus, the son of Timaeus, sitting along side the road. ⁴⁷When he heard that it was Jesus from Nazareth passing by, he began

shouting, "Jesus, son of David, have pity on me." ⁴⁸Many people spoke harshly to the blind man, telling him to be quiet. But he shouted all the more loudly, "Son of David, have pity on me." ⁴⁹So, Jesus stopped and said, "Call that man to me." Then the crowd called the blind man, saying to him, "Cheer up, Jesus is calling you." ⁵⁰So, he threw off his robe, jumped up, and immediately went to Jesus. ⁵¹Jesus said to him, "What do you want me to do for you?" And the blind man answered, "*Rabboni*, Teacher, I want to have my sight restored." ⁵²And Jesus said to him, "Go on your way, your faith in Me has made you well." And immediately his sight was restored, and he began following Jesus along the road.

11 And when they all approached Jerusalem, and came close to Bethphage and Bethany, near the Mount of Olives, He sent two of His disciples on ahead, ²saying to them, "Go into the village just ahead of you and, upon entering it, you will find tied up there a colt that no one has ever ridden; untie it and bring it here. ³And if anyone says to you, 'Why are you doing this?' you should say, 'The Lord needs it,' and immediately he will send it back here." ⁴So, they went away and found a donkey's colt tied up at the gate, outside in the street, and untied it. ⁵Some bystanders said to them, "What are you doing, untying that colt?" ⁶But they answered him exactly what Jesus had told them to say, so the people let them go. ⁷Then they brought the colt to Jesus and spread their clothing on it and He mounted it. ⁸Many people spread their clothing on the roadway, while others spread leafy branches, which they had cut from the fields. ⁹And the people who walked ahead of Him and followed behind shouted, "*Hosanna*, may He who comes in the name by the authority of the Lord, be blessed. ¹⁰May the coming kingdom of our forefather David be blessed. *Hosanna* in the highest, may this blessing reach to the highest heaven."

¹¹Then Jesus entered the Temple in Jerusalem, and after looking around at everything there, He left for Bethany with the twelve apostles, since it was evening by then.

¹²On the next day, when they were going from Bethany to Jerusalem, Jesus became hungry. ¹³Upon seeing in the distance a leafy fig tree, He approached it in hope of finding something on it to eat. But when He got there He found nothing but leaves on it, for it was not the season for figs yet. ¹⁴Therefore, He said to the tree, "From now on no one will ever eat fruit from you." Now His disciples heard Him say this.

¹⁵Then they entered Jerusalem and Jesus went into the Temple and began to drive out those who bought and sold animals for sacrifice. He upset the table of the cashiers, those who exchanged foreign coins and the benches of those who sold pigeons for sacrifice. ¹⁶And He would not even allow anyone to carry a container of goods through the Temple area. ¹⁷Then He taught them, saying, "Is it not written, 'My house, the Temple, will be called a house of prayer for people of all nations'? But you have made it a hideout for thieves." ¹⁸The leading priests and experts in the Law of Moses heard this and began looking for some way to kill Jesus, because they were afraid of Him, since the whole crowd was amazed at His teaching.

¹⁹And each evening He left the city of Jerusalem, and went to Bethany for the night.

²⁰The next morning, as they returned to the city, they passed by the fig tree and saw that it had withered, clear down to its roots. ²¹Then Peter remembered what Jesus had done to the fig tree on a recent occasion, and said to Him, "Rabbi, Teacher, look, the fig tree you cursed the other day has withered up." ²²Jesus replied to him, "You should have faith in God. ²³Truly I

tell you, whoever will say to this mountain, 'Be lifted up and thrown into the ocean' and does not doubt in his heart, but believes that what he said will happen, he will have his request granted. $^{24}$Therefore I tell you, whatever things you ask for in prayer, believe that you have received them, and you will have every one of them. $^{25}$And whenever you stand praying, forgive whatever grievance you might have against anyone, so that your Father in heaven will also forgive you of your sins." *[Verse 26 is absent from many ancient manuscripts.]*

$^{27}$Jesus and His disciples again came to Jerusalem. As He was walking in the Temple area the leading priests, experts in the Law of Moses and Jewish elders came to Him $^{28}$and said, "By what authority are you doing these things, miracles and teaching? Or who gave You the authority to do these things?" $^{29}$Jesus answered them, "Let me ask you a question. And if you answer it, then I will tell you by what authority I am doing these things. $^{30}$Was the immersion of John authorized from heaven or from men? Give me an answer." $^{31}$So, they discussed this among themselves, saying, "If we say 'from heaven' He will say to us, 'Then why did you not believe his message?' $^{32}$But, should we say 'from men' instead?" Now they feared the people, for all of them considered John to be a true prophet. $^{33}$So, they answered Jesus and said, "We do not know where John got his authority to immerse." Jesus replied to them, "Then neither will I tell you by what authority I am doing these things, miracles and teaching."

12 Jesus began speaking to them, the leading priests and experts in the Law of Moses or, to the people, by using parables. He said, "A man planted a vineyard and built a fence around it. He dug a place for constructing a grape squeezing device, built a lookout tower near it, then leased it out to tenant farmers and went to another country. $^{2}$And when the grape harvest season came, the owner of the farm sent a slave to the tenant farmers asking them to deliver the grape crop to him. $^{3}$But they took the slave and beat him and sent him away empty-handed. $^{4}$Again the owner of the farm sent another slave, whom they wounded in the head and shamefully abused. $^{5}$He sent still another slave, whom they killed. He continued sending many more slaves; they beat some and killed others. $^{6}$The owner had one more person left to send, his dearly loved son. So he sent him to them last of all, reasoning to himself, 'Surely they will treat my son with respect.' $^{7}$But the tenant farmers said to one another, 'This is the heir to the vineyard. Come on, let us kill him and then the inheritance will be ours.' $^{8}$So they took him and killed him and threw his body out of the vineyard. $^{9}$What do you think the owner of the vineyard will do when he gets back?" Jesus asked. Then He continued, "He will come and kill those tenant farmers and give the vineyard to other people. $^{10}$Have you never read this Scripture, 'The building block rejected by the builders is the same one that was made the principal stone by which the entire building was aligned. $^{11}$This was planned by the Lord and is a marvelous thing to us'?"

$^{12}$And the leading priests and experts in the Law of Moses attempted to arrest Jesus, but hesitated because they feared what the crowd might do, for they understood that He was speaking the parable against them. So, they left Him and went away.

$^{13}$Then the Pharisees sent certain ones of their number along with the Herodians to attempt to trap Him by what He said. $^{14}$And when they arrived, they said to Him, "Teacher, we know that you are sincere, and that You do not fear or give in to anyone. For You do not allow the position of any person to influence You, but teach the truth about God's way. Is it lawful to pay taxes to Caesar, or not? ¹⁵Should we pay it, or should we not pay it?" But Jesus was aware of their hypocrisy and said to them, "Bring Me the coin so I can see it." ¹⁶So, they brought it to Him and He said to them, "Whose image and inscription are on this coin?" And they answered Him, "Caesar's." ¹⁷Then Jesus replied to them, "Pay to Caesar whatever belongs to Caesar and pay to God whatever belongs to God." And they greatly marveled at Him.

¹⁸Then some Sadducees, the ones who say there is no resurrection of the dead, came and asked Him, ¹⁹"Teacher, Moses wrote to us that if a man's brother dies, leaving his widow behind without having had any children, his brother should marry his widow and father children by her. These children would then be considered his dead brother's. ²⁰Now there were these seven brothers; the first one got married, but when he died he left no children behind. ²¹So, the second one married his widow, and at his death he too left no children behind. Then the third one did the same thing. ²²All seven left no children behind when they died. Finally, the woman also passed away. ²³Now whose wife will she be in the resurrected state, for all seven brothers were married to her?" ²⁴Jesus said to them, "Is not this the reason that you are so mistaken, that you do not know what the Scriptures teach or how much power God has? ²⁵For when people rise from the dead, men do not get married, and women are not given away in marriage, but all are like angels in heaven. ²⁶But concerning those who are raised from the dead, have you never read in the book of Moses, in the incident about the bush, how God spoke to him, saying 'I am Abraham's God, and Isaac's God, and Jacob's God?' ²⁷So, He is not God to those who are dead, but He is God to those who are alive. You are seriously mistaken."

²⁸Then one of the experts in the Law of Moses came and heard Jesus and the Sadducees discussing together the subject of the resurrection and knowing that Jesus had refuted the Sadducees successfully, asked Him, "Which commandment is foremost, above all the others?" ²⁹And Jesus answered, "The foremost one is this, 'Hear this, you Israelites, the Lord our God is the only Lord, ³⁰and you must love the Lord your God with all your heart, with all your soul, with all your mind and with all your strength.' ³¹The second one is this, 'You must love your neighbor the same way that you love yourself.' There is no other commandment greater than these, love for God and man." ³²The expert in the Law of Moses said to Jesus, "Truly, Teacher, You are right in saying that God is the only one and that there is no other God but Him. ³³And that to love Him with all one's heart, with all one's understanding, and with all one's strength, and to love one's neighbor the same way he loves himself, are far more important than all the burnt offerings and sacrifices in the world." ³⁴When Jesus saw that this man answered wisely, He said to him, "You are not very far from the kingdom of God." And after that, no one dared to ask Him any more questions.

³⁵As Jesus was teaching in the Temple, He responded to some Pharisees by asking, "How is it that the experts in the Law of Moses can say that the Christ is the son of David? ³⁶It was David himself who said by inspiration of the Holy Spirit, 'The Lord God said to my Lord Jesus, sit at My right side until I make Your enemies the footrest under Your feet.' ³⁷David himself called Him Lord, so how could He be his son?" And the large crowd listened to Him with pleasure.

³⁸In His teaching Jesus said, "Look out for the experts in the Law of Moses, who like to

walk around in long flowing robes and to receive special greetings at the open shopping markets [39]and to occupy the principal seats in the synagogues and the head places at dinner tables. [40]They consume widows' houses by foreclosing on them and then cover it up by offering lengthy prayers. These people will receive a more severe judgment."
[41]Then Jesus sat down over near the Temple treasury and watched how the crowd was throwing money into the treasury. Many rich people were throwing in lots of money. [42]A poor widow came and threw in two small copper coins. The total she gave was equivalent to a larger coin, worth twice as much. [43]Jesus called His disciples to Him and said to them, "Truly I tell you, this poor widow has thrown in more than all the rest who are throwing money into the treasury. [44]For all of them threw in from their abundance, but being very poor, she threw in everything she had, even all she had to live on."

13 As Jesus left the Temple, one of His disciples said to Him, "Teacher, look at the kind of stones these buildings are made of!" [2]And Jesus responded to him, "Do you see these huge buildings? There will not be one stone left on another here that will not be thrown down."
[3]As Jesus was sitting on the Mount of Olives, over near the Temple, Peter, James, John and Andrew asked Him privately, [4]"Tell us, when will these things you just spoke of happen? And what will be the sign that indicates when all these things are about to be fulfilled?"
[5]Then Jesus began saying to them, "Pay attention so that no one leads you astray from the truth. [6]For many false teachers will come, claiming to be Me, and saying, 'I am the Christ and they will lead many people astray. [7]And when you hear of wars going on and rumors of other wars pending, do not worry, for such things must necessarily happen. But the end has not yet come. [8]For nations will wage war against one another, and kingdoms will attack one another. And earthquakes will happen at various places in the world, and there will be famines. These things are only the beginning of terrible times.
[9]"But pay attention to yourselves, for people will turn you over to Jewish councils for judgment and you will be beaten in synagogues. You will stand trial before governors and kings for being loyal to me. This will afford you an opportunity for witnessing to them. [10]And the good news must first be preached to people of all nations. [11]And when they lead you into court, and hand you over to be judged, do not worry ahead of time about what you will say, but just say whatever you are told by God when the time comes. [12]And at that time a person will turn his brother over to be killed, and the father will do the same to his child. And children will rebel against their parents and will turn them over to be killed. [13]You will be hated by all people because you belong to Me, but the person who holds out, remains faithful to God until the end of this time of severe persecution, will be saved from destruction.
[14]"But when you see that disgusting thing that causes total destruction, the Roman army, standing where it ought not to be, surrounding the besieged city of Jerusalem, (let the reader understand what is meant by this) then those of you in Judea are to run away into the nearby mountains. [15]Also the person who is on a housetop should not go down into his house to take anything out when he flees. [16]The person who is in a field doing farm work should not return to his house to get his coat even. [17]It will be too bad for those who are pregnant and those who are nursing babies in those days. [18]And pray that your flight will not be in the winter. [19]There

will be great trouble during those days, such as has never been from the beginning of God's creation until the present, or even will be in the days to come. [20]And if the Lord had not kept those days as short as they were, no one would have been saved from the devastating destruction. But for the sake of the elect, God's people, whom He chose, He kept those days short. [21]And then if anyone says to you, 'Look, here is Christ,' or 'Look there He is,' do not believe him. [22]For false christs and false prophets will appear and they will perform miraculous signs and supernatural wonders in order to lead astray even the elect, if possible. [23]But pay attention, for I have told you all this ahead of time.

[24]"But after those days of terrible trouble, the next major event on God's calendar will be the sun will become dark, and therefore the moon will not be able to shed its reflected light, [25]and the stars will be falling from the sky and the forces of the heavens will be shaken. [26]And then they will see the Son of Man coming in the clouds with great power and splendor. [27]And He will send out His angels and gather His elect, God's people, from all directions, from the farthest part of the earth to the farthest part of the sky, from throughout the whole world.

[28]"Now learn this parable from the fig tree. When its tender sprouts appear and its leaves begin to develop, you know that summer is near. [29]In the same way also, when you see these things happening, you should know that He, Jesus, is as near as your front door. [30]Truly I tell you, the people of this generation will not all die off before all these things mentioned above happen. [31]Although the sky and the earth will pass away, My words will not pass away, they will certainly come true. [32]But no one knows when that day or that hour will come; not even the angels in heaven or the Son of God know, but only the Father does.

[33]"You should pay attention; be alert and pray, for you do not know when the time will come for the Lord to return. [34]It is like a man who left his house on a trip to another country. Before leaving he put his servants in charge of his affairs, giving each one a particular job to do, then he ordered the gatekeeper to stay alert while he was gone. [35]So, be alert, because you do not know when the owner of the house will return, whether some evening, at midnight, at dawn, or at mid-morning. [36]Be alert for he might come unexpectedly and find you asleep. [37]And what I am telling you, I am telling everyone. Be alert!"

**14** Now the Passover Festival and the Festival of Unleavened Bread were held two days later. And the leading priests and experts in the Law of Moses were looking for a way to take Jesus by trickery and kill Him. [2]But they reasoned, "We will not take Him during the Festival, because it might start a riot among the people."

[3]And while Jesus was in Bethany sitting at the dinner table in the house of Simon, the man with an infectious skin disease, a woman with an alabaster stone jar of very expensive perfume came to Him, broke the jar and poured the perfume on His head. [4]But some of the disciples were upset among themselves, saying, "What is the reason for wasting this perfume? [5]It might have been sold for a large sum of money and the money given to poor people." And they complained about her doing this. [6]But Jesus said, "Let her alone. Why are you bothering this woman? For she has done a kind deed to me. [7]You will always have poor people with you, and you can do something good for them whenever you want to, but you will not always have Me with you. [8]She has done what she could. She has applied this aromatic oil to My body in anticipation of My burial. [9]For truly I tell you, wherever the Gospel message will be preached

throughout the whole world, what this woman has done for Me will also be told about as a memorial of her kindness to Me."

¹⁰Now Judas Iscariot, who was one of the twelve apostles, left and went to the leading priests in order to make arrangements for turning Jesus over to them. ¹¹And when they, the leading priests, realized this, they were very pleased and promised to give him money. So, Judas began looking for a convenient way to turn Jesus over to these Jewish leaders.

¹²Now on the first day of the Festival of Unleavened Bread, the beginning of the Passover Festival week, when they sacrificed the Passover lamb, Jesus' disciples said to Him, "Where do you want us to go to make preparations for you to eat the Passover meal?" ¹³So, He sent two of His disciples, saying to them "Go into the city of Jerusalem and there a man carrying a pitcher of water will meet you; follow him. ¹⁴And wherever he enters a house follow him inside and say to the owner, "The Teacher says, where is My guest room where I can eat the Passover meal with My disciples?" ¹⁵And the owner himself will show you a large upstairs room all furnished and ready. Make preparations for us there to observe the Passover meal." ¹⁶So, the disciples left and entered the city of Jerusalem. They found everything just as Jesus told them it would be, and they made preparations for the Passover meal.

¹⁷When evening came, Jesus arrived at the upstairs room with the twelve apostles. ¹⁸As they reclined at the table to eat, Jesus said, "Truly I tell you, one of you will turn Me over to the Jewish leaders, it is the one who is eating with Me." ¹⁹And they all began to be grieved and said to Him, one by one, "Am I the one?" ²⁰And He answered them, "It is one of you twelve, the one who is dipping his bread with Me in the sauce bowl. ²¹For the Son of Man is going to die, but it is too bad for that person who will turn Me over to the Jewish leaders! It would be better for that man if he had not been born."

²²And as they were eating He took a small loaf of bread, and when He had asked God's blessing on it, He broke it an gave pieces to His disciples and said, "Take this, it represents my physical body." ²³Then He took a cup, probably wine made from fresh or possibly preserved grape juice, and when He had given thanks to God, He passed it to them and they all drank from it. ²⁴And He said to them, "This represents My blood of the Agreement between God and mankind which is to be poured out for many people. ²⁵Truly I tell you, I will not drink of this fruit of the vine any more until that day when I will drink it again figuratively in the kingdom of God."

²⁶And after they had sung a hymn, they went up to the Mount of Olives.

²⁷Then Jesus said to His disciples, "All of you will have doubts about Me, for it is written 'I will strike down the shepherd and the sheep will be scattered everywhere.' ²⁸However, after I am raised up, I will go on ahead of you to Galilee." ²⁹But Peter said to Him, "Although everyone else will have doubts about You, I never will." ³⁰And Jesus said to him, "Truly I tell you, today, in fact this very night, before the rooster crows twice, you will deny knowing Me three times." ³¹But Peter kept insisting emphatically, "Even if I have to die with You, still I will not deny knowing You." And all the rest of the disciples spoke the same way.

³²Jesus and His disciples came to a place called Gethsemane. He said to His disciples, "You sit here while I go away and pray." ³³And He took Peter, James and John with Him and began to be troubled and deeply distressed. ³⁴He said to them, "My soul is extremely grieved, even to the point where I could die. Stay here and be alert in prayer." 35And He went on

ahead a short distance and fell to the ground and prayed for that hour that time of terrible grief to pass away from Him, if it were at all possible. ³⁶So, He said, "*Abba*, Father, everything is possible with You. Take this cup of suffering away from Me; however, let it not be what I want but what You want for Me."

³⁷And when He came back and found His disciples sleeping He said to Peter, "Simon, are you sleeping? Could you not stay alert in prayer for one hour? ³⁸Be alert and pray, so that you do not give in to temptation. The spirit of a person is truly willing to do a certain thing but his physical nature is often too weak to carry it out."

³⁹And He went away again and prayed, saying the same words. ⁴⁰Then He came back again and found His disciples still asleep, because they had not been able to keep their eyes open at all. ⁴¹And He came back a third time and said to them. "Go ahead and sleep now and get your rest. That is enough; the time has come. See, the Son of Man is about to be turned over into the hands of sinners. ⁴²Get up, let us be going. Look the one who will turn me over to the Jewish leaders is nearby."

⁴³And immediately, as Jesus was still speaking, Judas, one of the twelve apostles, came with a crowd who were carrying swords and clubs. They had come from the leading priests, the experts in the Law of Moses and the Jewish elders. ⁴⁴Now the one who turned Him over to the Jewish leaders, Judas, had given them a signal, saying, "Whoever I give a kiss of greeting to, He is the one; arrest Him and lead Him away under guard." ⁴⁵And when Judas came, immediately he went to Jesus and said, "Rabbi," and then kissed Him enthusiastically. ⁴⁶Then the soldiers and officers arrested Him and began taking Him away. ⁴⁷But a certain disciple that was standing nearby, Peter, drew his sword and struck the head priest's servant, Malchus, shearing off his ear. ⁴⁸Then Jesus said to them, "Have you come out to arrest Me with swords and clubs like you would a thief? ⁴⁹I was with you everyday, teaching in the Temple, and you did not come to take Me. But this has happened so that the Scriptures would be fulfilled." ⁵⁰And all of His disciples left Him and ran away.

⁵¹And a certain young man who had a linen outer garment thrown over his scantily clad body, was following Jesus until the soldiers and officers took hold of Him. ⁵²Then he ran away in his underclothing, leaving his linen outer garment behind.

⁵³Then they led Jesus away to the head priest, and all the leading priests, Jewish elders and experts in the Law of Moses came together with Him. ⁵⁴But Peter had followed Him from a distance, right into the courtyard of the head priest. He was sitting there with the Jewish officers, warming himself by the light of the fire.

⁵⁵Now the leading priests and the entire Council, called the "Sanhedrin", were looking for false witnesses to testify against Jesus in order to put Him to death, but did not find any. ⁵⁶For many persons gave false testimony against Him, but their stories did not harmonize. ⁵⁷Then two people stood up and gave false testimony against Him, saying, ⁵⁸"We heard Him say, "I will destroy this Temple, which was constructed by hand, and in three days I will build another one, not made by hand." ⁵⁹And not even in this attempt did their testimony harmonize.

⁶⁰The head priest stood up in front of them and asked Jesus, "Do You not have anything to answer? What about this charge being made against You by these people?" ⁶¹But Jesus kept quiet and did not give them any answer.

Again the head priest asked Him, "Are you the Christ, God's specially chosen One?"

⁶²And Jesus answered, "Yes, I am, and you will see the Son of man sitting at the right side of Power, God, Himself, and coming on the clouds of the sky." ⁶³And the head priest tore at his clothing as an expression of frustration and said, "What additional need do we have for witnesses? ⁶⁴You yourselves have heard Him speaking against God. What do you people think about such statements?"

And they all condemned Him as deserving the death penalty. ⁶⁵And some of them began to spit on Him, then to cover His face with a blindfold and hit Him with their fists saying, "Prophesy, tell who hit You." And the officers in charge of Him also struck Him with their hands.

⁶⁶Now when Peter was in the courtyard downstairs from where the Sanhedrin was having its meeting one of the head priest's servant girls came in, ⁶⁷and seeing Peter warming himself by the fire, she looked at him and said, "You were with Jesus from Nazareth, too." ⁶⁸But he denied it, saying, "I do not know or understand what you are talking about." Then he went out onto the porch and the rooster crowed. ⁶⁹When the servant girl saw him there, she again began saying to those nearby, "This man is one of them, a disciple of Jesus." ⁷⁰But again he denied it.

Then after a little while those standing nearby said to Peter again, "We know for sure that you are one of them because you are from Galilee." ⁷¹Then Peter began to curse and swear, saying, "I do not know this man you are talking about." ⁷²Immediately the rooster crowed for the second time and Peter was reminded of the words of Jesus, Who had said to him, "You will deny knowing Me three times before the rooster crows twice." And as he thought about this, he cried.

## 15

As soon as it was morning the leading priests, along with the Jewish elders and experts in the Law of Moses and the entire Council, held a conference. Then they tied Jesus up, led Him away and turned Him over to Pilate, the Roman governor. ²Pilate asked Him, "Are you the King of the Jews?" Jesus answered him, "You have said so."

³Then the leading priests accused Him of many things. ⁴So, Pilate again asked Him, "Do you not have any answer? Look at how many charges they are bringing against you." ⁵But still Jesus gave no answer to anything, so that Pilate was amazed.

⁶Now at the Passover Festival Pilate customarily released whatever prisoner the people asked him to. ⁷One prisoner, named Barabbas, was kept chained up in prison along with men who had committed murder during a rebellion. ⁸The crowd then went to Pilate and asked him to do what he was accustomed to doing for them, release a prisoner of their choosing during the Passover Festival. ⁹Pilate answered them, "Do you want me to release to you the King of the Jews, Jesus?" ¹⁰For he perceived that the leading priests had turned Jesus over to him out of envy. ¹¹But the leading priests stirred up the crowd to insist that Pilate release Barabbas to them instead. ¹²So Pilate again asked them, "Then what shall I do to this one you call the King of the Jews?" ¹³And they shouted out again, "Crucify Him!" ¹⁴And Pilate said to them, "Why should we, what wrong has He done?" But they shouted out even louder, "Crucify Him." ¹⁵So Pilate, wanting to satisfy the crowd, released Barabbas to them, and after he had Jesus flogged, he turned Him over to be crucified.

¹⁶Then the soldiers led Jesus away to the courtyard of the governor's headquarters, where they assembled the entire battalion. ¹⁷They placed a purple robe on Him, and making a wreath

out of thorns, they placed it on His head. ¹⁸Then they began "greeting" Him with "Hey, King of the Jews!" ¹⁹They beat His head with a stick, spat on Him, knelt down before Him and mockingly worshiped Him. ²⁰And when they had mocked Him, they took the purple robe off of Him and put His own clothing back on Him. Then they led Him out to crucify Him.

²¹They forced a passerby, named Simon of Cyrene, the father of Alexander and Rufus, who was coming in from the countryside, to go with them so he could carry Jesus' cross (probably only the crossbeam portion).

²²Then they brought Jesus to the place called *Golgotha* which, being interpreted, means "the place of the skull". ²³They offered Him wine, mixed with aromatic spices, but He refused to accept it. ²⁴So, they crucified Him and divided His clothing by gambling for them to decide what each soldier would get.

²⁵It was nine o'clock in the morning and they crucified Him. ²⁶The inscription, stating the charge against Him, was attached above His head to the upright portion of the cross. It read, "The King of the Jews." ²⁷And they also crucified two thieves with Him, one at His right side and one at His left. [Later manuscripts add verse 28.] ²⁹And those who passed by the cross shouted abuse at Him and shoot their heads in derision saying, "Ha, You who said You would destroy the Temple and rebuild it in three days, ³⁰save Yourself from dying and come down from the cross."

³¹In the same way, the leading priests also mocked Him among themselves, along with the experts in the Law of Moses, saying, "He saved other people, now He cannot even save Himself. ³²This 'Christ, the King of Israel,' let Him now come down from the cross so we can see it and believe in Him." And the thieves who were being crucified with Him also spoke abusively to Him.

³³And when it became noon there was darkness over the entire land until three o'clock in the afternoon. ³⁴Then at three o'clock Jesus shouted in a loud voice, *"Eloi, Eloi, lama, sabachthani?"* which being interpreted, means "My God, my God, why have You forsaken Me?" ³⁵And when some of those standing there heard this, they said, "Look, He is calling for Elijah." ³⁶Then one of the soldiers ran and filled a sponge full of sour wine, put it on a stick and gave it to Him to drink, saying, "Let Him alone; let us see if Elijah comes to take Him down from the cross." ³⁷Then Jesus spoke in a loud voice and gave up His spirit to God.

³⁸Then the Temple curtain was torn in two from top to bottom. ³⁹And when the military officer in charge of one hundred men, who was standing in front of Jesus, saw Him die like that, he said, "Truly this man was the Son of God."

⁴⁰And there were also some women watching all this from a distance. Among them were Mary from Magdala; Mary the mother of the younger James and his brother Joseph, probably the wife of Clopas and Salome the mother of James and John and wife of Zebedee. ⁴¹These women had ministered to Jesus' needs when they followed Him from Galilee. Others watching were many women who had come up to Jerusalem with Him.

⁴²When evening had come, and since it was the day of Preparation for the Passover Festival, being the day before the special Sabbath Day, ⁴³Joseph, from Arimathea, a highly respected member of the Jewish Council, who was expecting the kingdom of God, went boldly to Pilate, the Roman appointed governor, and asked him for the body of Jesus. ⁴⁴Pilate was amazed that Jesus had already died, and calling the military officer to him, asked how long He

had been dead. ⁴⁵And when he found out from the military officer, he granted the body to Joseph. ⁴⁶Joseph then brought a linen cloth, and after taking Jesus down from the cross, wrapped the linen cloth around His body and placed it in a gravesite that had been cut out of a ledge of rock. Then he rolled a huge stone across the entrance to the cave. ⁴⁷Now Mary from Magdala and Mary the mother of Joseph saw where the body was laid.

16 Now when the Sabbath day was over, after sunset on Saturday evening, Mary from Magdala; Mary the mother of James; the "other Mary", who was probably Jesus' mother, and Salome, the mother of James and John and wife of Zebedee bought spices consisting of aloes and other aromatic perfumes in order to apply them to His body as a means of embalming. ²And very early on the first day of the week, after sunrise on Sunday morning, they went to the gravesite. ³They were questioning among themselves, "Who will roll away the stone from the entrance of the cave for us?" ⁴And when they looked up, they saw that the stone had already been rolled away, and it was very large. ⁵As they were entering the cave, they were amazed when they saw a young man, dressed in a white robe, sitting at the right side of the entrance. ⁶He said to them, "Do not be amazed. You are looking for Jesus from Nazareth, who was crucified, are you not? He has risen from the dead. He is not here. Look at the place where they laid Him. ⁷So, go and tell His disciples and Peter, 'He is going on ahead of you to Galilee. You will see Him there, just as He told you.'" ⁸So, they left, running out of the cave, and trembling with amazement. And they said nothing to anyone about this for they were afraid.

⁹Now when Jesus arose from the dead early on the first day of the week, Sunday morning, He appeared first to Mary from Magdala, from whom He had driven out seven evil spirits. ¹⁰Then she went and told those disciples who had been with Him what had happened. They were sorrowful and began to cry. ¹¹And when they heard that Jesus was alive and had been seen by Mary from Magdala, they refused to believe it.

¹²After these things happened, Jesus showed Himself in a different form to two disciples as they were walking out into the countryside to the village of Emmaus, about seven miles northwest of Jerusalem. ¹³And these two men went and told about their encounter with Jesus to the rest of the disciples, but they did not believe them either.

¹⁴Later on Jesus showed Himself to the eleven apostles as they sat reclined, eating a meal. He scolded them for their lack of faith and stubbornness because they refused to believe those who had seen Him alive after His resurrection. ¹⁵Then He said to them, "You men go into the entire world and preach the good news to every person. ¹⁶The person who believes the Gospel and is immersed will be saved from condemnation, but whoever does not believe it will be condemned. ¹⁷And these miraculous signs will attend the conversion of those who believe. In My name, by My authority, they will drive out evil spirits; they will speak in languages supernaturally, ¹⁸they will pick up snakes without being harmed and if they happen to drink anything poisonous, it will not harm them; they will place hands on sick people with prayer and they will be healed."

¹⁹So then, after the Lord Jesus had spoken to them He was taken up to heaven, where He sat down at the right side of God. ²⁰And the apostles went out and preached everywhere. The Lord worked with them and confirmed the message, verified that it was true, by means of the miraculous signs which accompanied their ministry. May it be so.

*The Gospel According to*
# Luke

**1** Whereas since many have taken in hand to set forth in order a detailed account concerning the actual events having been fully accomplished among us, ²even as the eyewitnesses and the ones becoming ministers of the Word from the beginning handed them down to us; ³it seemed good to me also having investigated everything accurately, to write to you an orderly account, most excellent Theophilus, ⁴in order that you might know fully the reliability of the words concerning which you have been instructed.

⁵There was in the days of Herod, king of Judea, a certain priest by name Zacharias, of the priestly division of Abijah, and his wife of the daughters of Aaron, and her name was Elizabeth. ⁶And they were both righteous before God, walking in all the commandments and regulations of the Lord, blameless. ⁷And they were without a child, because Elizabeth was barren, and both were well advanced in their days.

⁸And it happened that when he was performing his priestly duties in the order of his division before God, ⁹according to the custom of the priestly duties, he was selected by lot to enter into the sanctuary of the Lord to burn incense, ¹⁰and all the multitude of the people were waiting outside at the hour of the burning of incense; ¹¹but an angel of the Lord appeared to him standing on the right of the altar of incense. ¹²And Zacharias seeing was troubled, and fear fell on him. ¹³And the angel said to him, "Zacharias, stop being fearful because your petition has been heard favorably, and your wife Elizabeth will give birth to a son, and you will call his name John. ¹⁴And he shall be to you joy and gladness, and many shall rejoice at his birth; ¹⁵for he shall be great before the Lord, and he will absolutely not drink wine and strong drink, and he shall be filled with the Holy Spirit from his mother's womb. ¹⁶and he will return many of the sons of Israel back to the Lord their God. ¹⁷And he will go before Him in the spirit and power of Elijah to turn the hearts of fathers to children, and the disobedient to the understanding of the righteous, to make ready a people having been prepared for the Lord."

¹⁸And Zacharias said to the angel, "According to what evidence will I know this? For I am old and my wife is well advanced in her days." ¹⁹And the angel answering said to him, "I myself am Gabriel, the one standing in the presence of God, and sent to speak to you, and to proclaim to you these good tidings; ²⁰and behold, you shall be silent and not having power to speak until the day in which these events happen, since you did not believe my words, which shall be fulfilled in their appropriate time." ²¹And the people were waiting for Zacharias, and were marveling at the time he spent in the sanctuary. ²²Coming out, he was not able to speak to them, and they realized that he had seen a vision in the sanctuary; and he was making signs of them, and remained mute. ²³And it happened that when the days of his priestly ministry were fulfilled, he departed to him home.

²⁴And after these days Elizabeth his wife became pregnant, and she hid herself five months saying ²⁵that, "Thus the Lord has done for me in the days in which He looked upon me with favor to take away my reproach among men."

²⁶And in the sixth month the angel Gabriel was sent from God to a city of Galilee by name of Nazareth, ²⁷to a virgin having been engaged to marry a man by the name of Joseph of

the house of David, and the virgin's name was Mary. ²⁸And going in to her, he said to her, "Hail, one having been favored, the Lord is with you." ²⁹But she was very troubled by the word, and was considering what manner of greeting this might be. ³⁰And the angel said to her, "Stop fearing, Mary, for you have found grace from God; ³¹and behold you will conceive in your womb, and bear a Son, and you shall call His name Jesus. ³²This one shall be great, and He shall be called the Son of the Most High, and the Lord God shall give to Him the throne of His father, David, ³³and He shall reign over the house of Jacob forever, and of His kingdom there shall be no end."

³⁴And Mary said to the angel, "How shall this be since I do not know a man?"

³⁵And answering, the angel said to her, "The Holy Spirit shall come upon you, and the power of the Most High shall overshadow you; wherefore also the Holy One being born will be called the Son of God. ³⁶And behold, your relative also herself has conceived a son in her old age, and this one being called barren is in her sixth month; ³⁷because nothing, not any word is impossible with God." ³⁸And Mary said, "Behold the female slave of the Lord; let it be to me according to your word." And the angel departed from her.

³⁹And Mary arising in those days, went with haste to the hill country to a city of Judah, ⁴⁰and entered into the house of Zacharias and greeted Elizabeth. ⁴¹And it happened as Elizabeth heard the greeting of Mary, the baby leaped in her womb, and Elizabeth was filled with the Holy Spirit. ⁴²And she spoke up with a loud cry and said, "Blessed are you among women, and blessed the fruit of your womb. ⁴³And wherefore this to me that the mother of my Lord comes to me? ⁴⁴For behold as the sound of your greeting came to my ears, the baby leaped with gladness in my womb. ⁴⁵And blessed be she believing that there will be a fulfillment of the words having been spoken to her by the Lord."

⁴⁶And Mary said, "My soul magnifies the Lord, ⁴⁷And my spirit rejoiced in God my Savior, ⁴⁸Because He considered the humility of His female slave, for behold from now on all generations shall consider me blessed; ⁴⁹Because the powerful One did great things for me, and holy is His name. ⁵⁰And His mercy is for generations and generations to those fearing Him. ⁵¹He did mighty deeds with His arms. He scattered the proud in the thought of their hearts. ⁵²He brought down the powerful from their thrones and lifted up the humble. ⁵³He filled the hungry with good blessings, and the rich He sent away empty. ⁵⁴He helped His servant Israel,
when He remembered mercy. ⁵⁵Even as He spoke to our fathers, to Abraham and His seed forever." And Mary remained with her about six months, and then returned to her house.

⁵⁷And the time for Elizabeth to deliver was fulfilled, and she gave birth to a son. ⁵⁸And her neighbors and relatives heard that the Lord had magnified His mercy with her, and they rejoiced with her. ⁵⁹And it happened on the eighth day they came to circumcise the child, and they were going to call it by the name of his father Zacharias. ⁶⁰And his mother answering said, "Not so! But he shall be called John." ⁶¹And they said to her, "There is no one of your relatives called by this name." ⁶²But they made signs to his father as to what he would desire it to be called. ⁶³And asking for a tablet, he wrote saying, "His name is John." And all were marveling. ⁶⁴And his mouth was opened instantly, and his tongue was loosed, and he was speaking blessings to God. ⁶⁵And fear came upon all those dwelling around them, and in the whole hill country of Judea all these words were being discussed. ⁶⁶And all the ones hearing

kept this in their heart, saying, "What therefore will this child be? For certainly the hand of the Lord was with him."

⁶⁷And his father Zacharias was filled with the Holy Spirit and prophesied saying, ⁶⁸"Blessed be the Lord God of Israel, because He visited and made redemption for His people. ⁶⁹And raised a horn of salvation for us, in the house of His servant, David, ⁷⁰even as He spoke through the mouth of His Holy prophets from the ages; ⁷¹salvatio n from our enemies, and the hands of all the ones hating us; ⁷²"To manifest mercy with our fathers, and to remember His holy covenant, ⁷³The oath which He swore to Abraham our father, ⁷⁴To give us, having been delivered out of the hands of our enemies, to serve Him without fear. ⁷⁵In purity and righteousness before Him all our days. ⁷⁶And even you, child, shall be called a prophet of the Most High, for you will go before the Lord to prepare His ways. ⁷⁷To give knowledge of salvation to His people in the forgiveness of their sins, ⁷⁸Through the compassionate mercy of our God, in which the Sunrise from on high will visit us. ⁷⁹To shine upon those who sit in the darkness and shadow of death, To guide our feet in the way of peace." ⁸⁰And the child grew, and became strong in spirit, and was in the deserted places until the days of his showing forth to Israel.

2 And it happened in those days a decree went out from Caesar Augustus that all the world be registered in a census. ²This first registration came when Quirinius was governor of Syria. ³And all were going to be registered, each to his own city. ⁴And Joseph went up from Galilee out of the city of Nazareth to Judea to the city of David, which is called Bethlehem because he was of the house and family of David, ⁵to be registered with Mary, the one being engaged to him, being with child. ⁶And it happened when they were there the days were filled for her to give birth. ⁷And she gave birth to her first-born Son; and wrapped Him in cloths, and placed Him in a manger, because there was no place for them in the inn.

⁸And shepherds were in the same country, staying out in the fields, keeping watch over their flock by night. ⁹And an angel of the Lord stood over them, and the glory of the Lord shone around them, and they became afraid with great fear. ¹⁰And the angel said to them, "Stop being fearful, for behold I announce good news to you of great joy, which shall be to all people, ¹¹that this day in the city of David a Savior was born to you, Who is Christ the Lord. ¹²And this is a sign to you, you will find a baby having been wrapped in cloth, and lying in a manger." ¹³And suddenly there came with the angel a multitude of heavenly host praising God and saying, ¹⁴"Glory to God in the highest, And on earth, peace among men of good will."

¹⁵And it happened that as the angels went away from there into heaven, the shepherds were saying to one another "Let us go now to Bethlehem, and see this word which the Lord has made known to us." ¹⁶And hurrying they came and found both Mary and Joseph and the baby laying in the manger. ¹⁷And seeing they made known the word of the one having spoken to them concerning this Child. ¹⁸And all the ones hearing were marveling concerning what was told by the shepherds to them. ¹⁹And Mary kept secure all these words, pondering them in her heart. ²⁰And the shepherds returned, glorifying and praising God for all which they heard and saw even as it was told to them.

²¹And when eight days were filled to circumcise Him, His name was called Jesus which was given by the angel before He was conceived in the womb.

²²And when the days were fulfilled for their cleansing according to the Law of Moses, they brought Him up to Jerusalem to present Him to the Lord, ²³even as it has been written in the Law of the Lord that "every male opening a womb shall be called holy to the Lord," ²⁴and to offer a sacrifice according to that having been spoken in the Law of the Lord, "A pair of turtle doves or two young pigeons." ²⁵And behold a man was in Jerusalem whose name was Simeon, and this man was righteous and devout, waiting for the consolation of Israel, and the Holy Spirit was upon him. ²⁶And it had been revealed to him by the Holy Spirit that he would not see death before he would see the Christ of the Lord. ²⁷And he came in the Spirit into the temple; and when the parents brought in the child Jesus to do concerning Him according to the custom of the Law; ²⁸then he received Him in his arms and blessed God and said, ²⁹"Now, Sovereign Lord, let Your slave depart in peace, according to Your word; ³⁰Because my eyes have seen Your salvation, ³¹Wlhich You prepared before the face of all the people, ³²A light for revelation to the Gentiles, and a glory for Your people, Israel."

³³And His father and mother were marveling at what was being spoken concerning Him. ³⁴And Simeon blessed them, and said to Mary His mother, "Behold, this One is placed for the fall and rising up of many people in Israel, and for a sign that will be spoken against ³⁵"and a sword shall pierce even your own soul, that the reasoning of many hearts will be revealed."

³⁶And there was a prophetess, Anna, a daughter of Phanuel, of the tribe of Asher; she had advanced in many days, having lived with her husband seven years from her virginity, ³⁷and she was a widow until eighty four years, who did not depart from the temple serving in worship with fasting and petitions night and day. ³⁸And at that same hour coming upon them, she was giving acknowledgment to God, and speaking concerning Him to the ones waiting the redemption of Jerusalem.

³⁹And when they had completed everything according to the Law of the Lord, they returned to Galilee to their own city of Nazareth. ⁴⁰And the child grew, and became strong, being full of wisdom, and the grace of God was upon Him.

⁴¹And His parents were going yearly to Jerusalem for the feast of Passover.

⁴²And when He became twelve years of age, they were going up at the Feast according to their custom. ⁴³And the days having been completed, when they were returning, the child Jesus remained in Jerusalem, and His parents did not know it. ⁴⁴But supposing Him to be in the caravan, they went a day's journey, and were seeking Him among their relatives and acquaintances. ⁴⁵And not finding Him, they returned to Jerusalem seeking Him. ⁴⁶And it happened after three days, they found Him in the temple, sitting among the teachers both listening to them and answering them. ⁴⁷And all the ones hearing Him were astonished at His understanding, and His answers ⁴⁸And seeing Him, they were perplexed and His mother said to Him, "Child, why did You do thus to us? Behold Your father and I were seeking You anxiously." ⁴⁹And He said to them, "Why were you seeking me? Did you not know that I must be in the affairs of my Father?" ⁵⁰But they did not understand the word He spoke to them.

⁵¹And He went down with them, and came to Nazareth, and was subject to them. And His mother kept secure all the words in her heart.

⁵²And Jesus progressed in wisdom and stature and in favor with God and men.

3 And in the fifteenth year of the government of Tiberius Caesar, Pontius Pilate being governor of Judea, and Herod being tetrarch of Galilee, and Philip his brother tetrarch

of the country of Iturea and Trachonitis, and Lysanias the tetrarch of Albania, ²during the high priesthood of Annas and Caiaphas the word of God came to John the son of Zacharias in the wilderness ³and he came into all the surrounding country of the Jordan preaching an immersion of repentance for forgiveness of sins, ⁴as it had been written in the book of the words of Isaiah the prophet, "A voice of one crying in the wilderness, Prepare you the way of the Lord, make His paths straight, ⁵Every valley shall be filled up, and every mountain and hill shall be brought low, and the crooked road shall be made straight, and the rough roads smooth. ⁶And all flesh shall see the salvation of God."

⁷Therefore, he was saying to the crowds coming out to be immersed by him, "Progeny of vipers, who warned you to flee from the coming wrath? ⁸Produce therefore fruit worthy of repentance; and do not begin to say within yourselves, 'We have Abraham as our father,' for I say to you that God is able of these stones to raise up children of Abraham. ⁹But even already the axe is placed at the root of the trees, therefore every tree not producing good fruit is cut down, and is cast into the fire."

¹⁰But the crowds were asking him saying, "What therefore shall we do?" ¹¹And answering he was saying to them, "The one having two tunics, let him share with the one not having any, and the one having foods, let him do likewise." ¹²And also tax collectors came to be immersed, and said to him, "Teacher, what shall we do?" ¹³And he said to them, "Never be collecting more for you than you are instructed." ¹⁴And also those serving in the army were asking him, saying, "What shall we also do?" And he said to them, "Do not take money from anyone by force, neither by false accusations, and be content with your wages."

15But as the people were waiting with expectation, and reasoning in their hearts concerning John whether he himself might be the Christ, 16John gave answer to all, "I indeed immerse you in water; but One stronger than I comes, of Whom I am not worthy to unfasten the thongs of His sandals; He shall immerse in Holy Spirit and fire; Whose winnowing shovel is in His hand to thoroughly cleanse His threshing ground and to gather the wheat into His barn but the chaff He will burn up with unquenchable fire."

18Indeed, therefore, with many other exhortations He was proclaiming good news to them.19But Herod the tetrarch, being reproved by him concerning Herodias, his brother's wife, and concerning all the wicked acts which Herod did, 20he added to all them this also, he shut John up in prison.

21And it happened when all the people were being immersed, Jesus also was immersed, and was praying, and the heaven was opened, 22and the Holy Spirit came down in bodily form as a dove upon Him, and a voice came out of heaven, "You are My beloved Son in Whom I am well pleased."

²³And Jesus Himself was beginning His ministry at about thirty years of age, being the son, as was supposed of Joseph the son of Heli, ²⁴the son of Matthat, the son of Levi, the son of Melchi, the son of Jannai, the son of Joseph, ²⁵the son of Mattathias, the son of Amos, the son of Nahum, the son of Hesh, the son of Naggai, 26the son of Maath, the son of Mattathias, the son of Semein, the son of Joseph, the son of Joda, ²⁷the son of Johanan, the son of Resa, the son of Zerubabbel, the son of Shealtiel, the son of Neri, ²⁸the son of Melchi, the son of Addi, the son of Cosam, the son of Elmadam, the son of Er, ²⁹the son of Joshua, the son of Eliezer, the son of Jorim, the son of Matthat, the son of Levi, ³⁰the son of Simeon, the son of

Judah, the son of Josech, the son of Jonam, the son of Eliakim, ³¹the son of Melea, the son of Menna, the son of Mattatha, the son of Nathan, the son of David, ³²the son of Jesse, the son of Obed, the son of Boaz, the son of Salmon, the son of Nahshon, ³³the son of Amminadab, the son of Admin, the son of Ram, the son of Hezron, the son of Perez, the son of Judah, ³⁴the son of Jacob, the son of Isaac, the son of Abraham, the son of Terah, the son of Nahor, ³⁵the son of Serug, the son of Reu, the son of Peleg, the son of Heber, the son of Shelah, ³⁶the son of Cainan, the son of Arphaxad, the son of Shem, the son of Noah, the son of Lamech, ³⁷the son of Methuselah, the son of Enoch, the son of Jared, the son of Mahalaleel, the son of Cainan, ³⁸the son of Enosh, the son of Seth, the son of Adam, the son of God.

4 And Jesus being filled with the Holy Spirit returned from the Jordan, and was led by the Spirit in the wilderness, ²being tempted by the devil forty days, and He did not eat anything in those days, and when they were completed He hungered. ³But the devil said to Him, "If You are the Son of God, tell this stone that it become bread." ⁴And Jesus answered him, "It has been written that, 'Man shall not live by bread only.' ⁵And leading Him up, he showed Him all the kingdoms of the world in a moment of time. ⁶And the devil said to Him, "I will give you authority over all this and the glory of them because they have been delivered over to me, and to whomever I desire to give it. ⁷"If therefore you worship before me, all shall be yours."⁸But Jesus answering said to him, "It has been written, 'You shall worship the Lord your God, and Him only shall you serve.' ⁹And he led Him into Jerusalem, and stood Him upon the pinnacle of the temple, and said to Him, "If You are the Son of God, cast Yourself down from here; ¹⁰for it has been written, 'He will command His angels concerning You to guard You carefully,' ¹¹and that, 'in their hands they will bear You up, lest You strike Your foot against a stone.'" ¹²And Jesus answering said to him that, "It has been said, 'You shall not test the Lord your God.'" ¹³And the devil having finished every temptation, left Him for a time.

¹⁴And Jesus returned in the power of the Spirit to Galilee and the fame concerning Him went out throughout the whole surrounding country. ¹⁵And He was teaching in their synagogues, being glorified by all.

¹⁶And He went to Nazareth where He was brought up, and according to His custom went on the Sabbath day into the synagogue, and stood up to read. ¹⁷And the book of the prophet Isaiah was given to Him, and opening the book He found the place where it was written, ¹⁸"The Spirit of the Lord is upon Me, because He anointed Me to announce good news to the poor; He sent Me to proclaim release to the captive And recovery of sight to the blind; To release those being oppressed, ¹⁹to proclaim the favorable year of the Lord." ²⁰And closing the book, returning it to the attendant, He sat down, and the eyes of everyone in the synagogue were gazing intently on Him. ²¹And He began to say to them that, "Today this Scripture has been fulfilled in your ears." ²²And all were testifying about Him, and were marveling at the words of grace coming forth from His mouth, and were saying, "Is not this Joseph's son?" ²³And He said to them, "Probably you will tell me this proverb 'Physician, heal yourself; whatever we heard was being done in Capernaum, do also here in your own home town.'" ²⁴And He said, "Surely, I say to you that no prophet is accepted in his home town. ²⁵Upon a truth I say to you there were many widows in the days of Elijah in Israel, when the heaven was

shut up for three years and six months as a great famine came upon the land. ²⁶And Elijah was sent to none of them, except to Zarepath of Sidon to a widow woman. ²⁷And there were many lepers in Israel at the time of Elisha the prophet, and none of them was cleansed except Naaman the Syrian." ²⁸And all in the synagogue were filled with anger hearing these words. ²⁹And arising they cast Him out of the city, and they led Him to the edge of the mount upon which their city was built so that they could throw Him down the cliff. ³⁰But going through the midst of them, He departed.

³¹And He went down to Capernaum, a city of Galilee, and was teaching them on the Sabbath days. ³²And they were astonished at His teaching, because His word was with authority. ³³And there was in the synagogue a man having a spirit of an unclean demon, and he cried out with a loud voice, ³⁴"Ha! What is there between us and You, Jesus the Nazarene? Do You come to destroy us? I know who You are, the Holy One of God." ³⁵And Jesus rebuked him saying, "Be silent, and go out of him." And the demon throwing him down in their midst went out of him, not doing him any harm. ³⁶And amazement came upon all, and they were talking to one another, saying, "What is this word, that with authority and power He commands the unclean spirits, and they come out?" ³⁷And the rumor concerning Him was going out into every place of the surrounding country.

³⁸But arising, He went out from the synagogue into the home of Simon. The mother-in-law of Simon was suffering from great fever, and they requested Him concerning her. ³⁹And standing over her, He rebuked the fever, and it left her; and instantly arising, she was ministering to them.

⁴⁰And as the sun was setting, all whoever had those being sick from various diseases, were bringing them to Him; and laying His hands on each one of them, He was healing them. ⁴¹And also He was casting out demons from many, crying and saying that, "You are the Son of God." And rebuking them He would not allow them to speak because they knew He was the Christ.

⁴²And when day came, going out, He went into a wilderness place; and the crowds were seeking Him, and came to Him and were keeping Him from going from them. ⁴³But He said to them that, "I must also preach good news of the kingdom of God to other cities, because for this I was sent." ⁴⁴And He was preaching in the synagogues of Judea.

5 And it happened when the crowd was pressing around Him, listening to the word of God, and He was standing beside the lake Gennesaret, ²and He saw two boats standing beside the lake; but the fishermen having come down from them were cleaning their nets. ³And getting into one of the boats, which was Simon's, He asked him to go out a little from the land, and sitting down, He was teaching the crowds from the boat. ⁴And when He stopped speaking, He said to Simon, "Go out into the deep, and let down your nets for a catch." ⁵And Simon answering said, "Master, toiling through the whole night, we took nothing, but on Your word I will let down the nets. ⁶And having done this, they enclosed a large multitude of fish, and their nets were tearing. ⁷And they signaled their partner in the other boat to come and help them; and they filled both the boats so that they were about to sink. ⁸And Simon Peter beholding, fell on his knees before Jesus saying, "Depart from Me, because I am a sinful man, Lord." ⁹For amazement gripped him and all those with him upon

the catch of fish which they had taken, [10]and likewise also James and John, sons of Zebedee, who were companions to Simon. And Jesus said to Simon. "Fear not for from now on you will be catching men." [11]And bringing their boats upon the land, leaving all they followed Him.

[12]And it happened that when He was in one of the cities, behold there was a man full of leprosy; and beholding Jesus, falling on his face, he pleaded with Him saying, "Lord, if You will You are able to cleanse me." [13]And stretching forth His hand, He touched Him saying, "I will, be cleansed"; and immediately the leprosy left him. [14]And He commanded him to tell no one, "But departing, go show yourself to the priest and make an offering for your cleansing, even as Moses commanded for a testimony to them." [15]But the word concerning Him was spreading more, and many crowds were assembling to hear Him, and to be healed from their sicknesses. [16]But He himself was withdrawing to the wilderness places, and praying.

[17]And it happened on one of the days that He was teaching, and Pharisees and teachers of the law were sitting, who had come out from all the villages of Galilee, and from Judea and Jerusalem; and power was with the Lord for Him to heal. [18]And behold, men bearing on a stretcher a man who was paralyzed, and they were seeking to bring him in and set him before Him. [19]And not finding how to bring him in on account of the crowd, taking him up upon the housetop, they let him down through the tiles upon his stretcher into the midst, before Jesus. [20]And seeing their faith, He said to him, "Man, your sins have been forgiven you." [21]And the scribes and the Pharisees began to reason saying, "Who is this who speaks blasphemies? Who has power to forgive sins except God alone?" [22]But Jesus knowing their reasoning, answering said to them, "Why do you reason in your hearts? [23]Which is easier to say, 'Your sins be forgiven,' or to say, 'Rise and walk'? [24]But in order that you may know that the Son of Man has the authority on earth to forgive sins." He said to the paralytic, "I say to you, rise, take up your stretcher, and go to your home." [25]And instantly arising before them, taking up what he had been lying on, he departed to his house, glorifying God. [26]And all were taken with amazement, and were glorifying God, and they were filled with fear saying that, "We saw unique deeds today."

[27]And after these events He went out, and observed a tax collector by name Levi, sitting at the tax collector's booth, and He said to him, "Follow Me." [28]And leaving behind everything, arising, he followed Him.

[29]And Levi made a great festive meal for Him in his home, and there was a large crowd of tax collectors and others, who were reclining at the meal with them. [30]And the Pharisees and their scribes were grumbling to His disciples saying, "Why do You eat and drink with tax collectors and sinners?" [31]And Jesus answering said to them, "The healthy do not have need of a physician, but the ones having sickness. [32]I have not come to call the righteous, but the sinners to repentance."

[33]But they said to Him, "The disciples of John fast often and make petitions, likewise also the disciples of the Pharisees' but your disciples eat and drink." [34]And Jesus said to them, "You can not make the sons of the bridegroom to fast while the bridegroom is with them can you? [35]But the days shall come when the bridegroom will be taken from them, and then they shall fast in those days." [36]And He was telling also a parable to them that, "No one tears a patch from a new garment, and places it upon an old garment; if one does, the new one also tears, and the old does not match the patch from the new. [37]And no one puts new wine into old

wineskins, if one does the new wine bursts the wineskins, and the wine will be poured out, and the wineskins destroyed. [38]But new wine is put into new wineskins. [39]And no one drinking old wine desires new wine; for he says, 'The old is better.'"

[6]And it happened on a Sabbath that He was going through a grain field, and His disciples were plucking and eating the heads of grain, rubbing them in their hands. [2]But certain of the Pharisees said, "Why do you do that which is unlawful on the Sabbath?" [3]And answering Jesus said to them, "Have you not read this which David did when he hungered and those being with him? [4]He went into the house of God, taking the show bread ate it, and gave to those with him, which was unlawful to eat except only the priests." [5]And He was saying to them, "The Son of Man is Lord of the Sabbath."

[6]And it happened on another Sabbath, He went into the synagogue, and was teaching; and a man was there, and his right hand was withered. [7]And the scribes and Pharisees were watching Him carefully to see if He heals on the Sabbath in order that they may find a reason to denounce Him. [8]But He Himself knew their reasoning and said to the man having the withered hand, "Rise and stand in the midst." And arising, he stood. [9]And Jesus said to them, "I ask you, is it lawful to do good on the Sabbath or to do evil, to save a life or to destroy it?" [10]And looking around on all of them, He said to him, "Stretch forth your hand." And he did, and his hand was completely restored. [11]But they themselves were filled with vehemence, and were discussing with one another what they could do to Jesus. [12]And it happened in these days, He went off into the mountain to pray, and He continued through the night in prayer to God. [13]And when day came, He called His disciples to Him, and selected from them twelve, whom He named apostles: [14]Simon, whom He also named Peter, and Andrew his brother, and James and John, and Philip and Bartholomew, [15]and Matthew and Thomas, and James the son of Alphaeus, and Simon the one being called Zealot, [16]and Judas the son of James, and Judas Iscariot, who became a traitor.

[17]And coming down with them He stood on a level place, and there was a large crowd of His disciples, and a large group of people from all of Judea and Jerusalem, and the seacoast of Tyre and Sidon, [18]which came to hear Him, and to be cured from their diseases; and the ones being distressed from unclean spirits were being healed [19]And all the crowd was seeking to touch Him because power was going out from Him, and He was curing all.

[20]And turning His eyes upon His disciples, He was saying, "Blessed are the poor, because yours is the kingdom of God, [21]"Blessed are the ones hungering now, because you shall be satisfied. "Blessed are the ones weeping now, because you shall laugh.

[22]"Blessed are you when men will hate you, and when they repudiate you, and denounce you, and cast out your name as wicked, for the sake of the Son of Man. [23]Rejoice in that day and leap for joy, for behold, great is your reward in heaven; for according to the same way they did to their fathers, the prophets.

[24]"However, woe to you, the ones being well filled now, because you will hunger.

[25]"Woe to the ones laughing now, because you will mourn and weep.

[26]"Woe when all men speak well of you, for according to the same way their fathers did to the false prophets.

[27]"But I say to you who are hearing, love your enemies, do good to those hating you.

²⁸Bless the ones cursing you, pray concerning the ones despitefully treating you. ²⁹To the one striking you on the cheek, present him the other also, and the one taking from your cloak, do not forbid your tunic. ³⁰To everyone asking you, give; and from the one taking what is yours, do not demand it back. ³¹And even as you desire that men may do to you, you do to them likewise.

³²"And if you love the ones loving you, what thanks is there to you? For even the sinners love those who love them. ³³And if you do good to the ones doing good to you, what thanks is there to you? Even the sinners do the same. ³⁴And if you lend to those from whom you wish to receive, what thanks is there to you? Even sinners lend to sinners in order that they may receive back an equal amount. ³⁵However, love your enemies, and do good, and lend not expecting any return, and your reward shall be much, and you shall be sons of the Most High because He Himself is good to the ungrateful and wicked people. ³⁶You become merciful even as your Father is merciful.

³⁷"And do not judge and you absolutely will not be judged; do not condemn and you absolutely will not be condemned. Pardon and you will be pardoned. ³⁸You give and it shall be given to you, good measure, having been pressed down, having been shaken, running over they shall give into your lap; for with what measure you measure, it shall be measured again to you."

³⁹And He spoke a parable to them, "A blind man is not able to guide a blind man is he? Will not both fall into a pit? ⁴⁰A disciple is not above his teacher, but everyone having been fully trained shall be as his teacher. ⁴¹Why do you see the chip in the eye of your brother, and do not consider the beam in your own eye? ⁴²How are you able to say to your brother, 'Brother, let me take out the chip in your eye,' when you yourself do not see the beam in your eye? Hypocrite, take out first the beam in your eye, and then seeing clearly the chip in your brother's eye, you can take it out.

⁴³"For a good tree does not produce rotten fruit, again neither does a rotten tree produce good fruit. ⁴⁴For each tree is known by its own fruit; for people do not gather figs from thorn bushed, nor do they pick grapes from a bramble-bush. ⁴⁵The good man out of the good treasures of his heat brings forth good work; the wicked man out of his wicked heart brings forth wicked work; for out of the abundance of the heart the mouth speaks. ⁴⁶Why do you call Me, 'Lord, Lord,' and do not do what I say? ⁴⁷Everyone coming to Me, and hearing My words, and doing them, I will point out to you to whom he is like. ⁴⁸He is like a man building a home, who dug and went deep and laid a foundation upon rock; and a flood coming, the river struck against that home, and it was not strong enough to shake it, because he had built it well. ⁴⁹But the one hearing, and not doing is like a man who built his home upon the earth without foundation, which the river struck against, and immediately it collapsed, and the destruction of that home was great."

7 Now when He had finished all His words in the hearing of the people, He entered into Capernaum. ²And the slave of a certain centurion, who was honored by him, was about to die. ³But hearing about Jesus, he sent to Him elders of the Jews asking Him that coming He might bring his slave through safely. ⁴And they having reached Jesus, were pleading earnestly, saying that, "He is worthy for you to accomplish this; ⁵for he loves our

nation, and he himself built us our synagogue." ⁶And Jesus was going with them. But when He was already not far from the house, the centurion sent friends, saying to Him, "Lord, do not trouble Yourself, for I am not deserving that You come in under my roof. ⁷Wherefore, I did not even consider myself worthy to come to You; but You say the word, and my servant will be cured. ⁸"For I also am a man myself being placed under authority, having soldiers under myself, and I say to this one, 'Go,' and he goes, and to another 'Come,' and he comes, and to my slave, 'Do this,' and he does." ⁹And Jesus having heard these words, was marveling at him, and having turned to the crowd following Him He said, "I say to you, I have not even found such a faith as this in Israel." ¹⁰And the ones having been sent, returning into the house found the slave being healthy.

¹¹And it happened that soon afterward He went into a city being called Nain, and His disciples were going with Him, and a great crowd. ¹²And as they were drawing near to the gate of the city, behold a dead man was being carried out, the only son born to his mother, and she was a widow, and a sizeable crowd out of the city was with her. ¹³And the Lord seeing her was filled with compassion towards her, and said to her, "Stop weeping." ¹⁴And coming to them He touched the coffin, and those carrying it stood still, and He said, "Young man, I say to you, arise." ¹⁵And the corpse sat up and began to speak, and He gave him to his mother. ¹⁶And fear came upon all, and they were glorifying God saying that, "A great prophet has risen among us," and that, "God has visited His people." ¹⁷And this word about Him went out in all Judea, and in all the surrounding country.

¹⁸And His disciples reported to John concerning all these events. And John, calling to him a certain two of his disciples, ¹⁹sent them to the Lord saying, "Are you the One coming or should we expect another different one?" ²⁰And arriving to Him, the men said, "John the Immerser sent us to you saying, 'Are You the One coming or should we expect another different one?'" ²¹In that hour He healed many from diseases and scourges and evil spirits, and He granted many blind to see. ²²And answering He said to them "Going, you report to John what you saw and heard; blind are restored sight, lame walk, lepers are cleansed, and deaf hear, dead are raised up, the poor have good news proclaimed to them; ²³And blessed is he who is not offended in Me."

²⁴And after the messengers of John departed, He began to speak to the crowd concerning John, "What did you go into the wilderness to observe? A reed shaken by the wind? ²⁵But what did you go out to see? A man having been dressed in fine garments? Behold, the ones possessing expensive garments and luxury are in the kings' palaces. ²⁶But what did you go out to see? A prophet? Yes, I say to you, and more than a prophet. ²⁷This is the one about whom it has been written, 'Behold I send My messenger before your face, Who shall prepare your way before you.'

²⁸I say to you of those being born of women there is none greater than John; yet the least in the kingdom of God is greater than he." ²⁹And all the people hearing, and the tax collectors, were justifying God, having been immersed by the immersion of John. ³⁰But the Pharisees and the lawyers rejected the will of God for themselves, not having been immersed of him.

³¹"To what then shall I compare the men of this generation and to what are they like? ³²They are like children sitting in the market place, and calling to one another, who say, 'We played the flute for you, and you did not dance;   We sang a dirge, and you did not mourn.'

³³For John the Immerser came not eating bread nor drinking wine, and you say, 'He has a demon.' ³⁴The Son of Man came eating and drinking, and you say, 'Behold a man who is a glutton and drunkard, a friend of tax collectors and sinners.' ³⁵And wisdom is declared right by all its children."

³⁶And a certain Pharisee asked Him that He might eat with him; and going into the Pharisee's house He reclined at the meal table. ³⁷And behold a woman who was in the city, a sinner, and when she became aware that He was reclining at the meal in the home of the Pharisee she brought an alabaster flask of ointment. ³⁸And standing behind Him at His feet, weeping, she began to wet His feet with her tears, and was wiping them with the hairs of her head, and was continually kissing His feet, and was anointing them with the ointment. ³⁹But the Pharisee having invited Him, beholding this, said within himself, "If this one were a prophet, He would know what manner of woman this was who was touching Him, that she is a sinner." ⁴⁰And Jesus answering said to him, "Simon, I have somewhat to say to you." And he said, "Speak Teacher."

⁴¹"Two men were debtors to a certain money lender. One owed five hundred denarti, but the other fifty. ⁴²They not having money to repay, he granted pardon to both. Which therefore of them will love him the most?" ⁴³Simon answering said, "I suppose that the one to whom the most was pardoned." And He said to him. "You judged rightly." ⁴⁴And turning to the woman, He said to Simon, "Do you see this woman? I came into your home; you did not give Me water for My feet; but she wet My feet with her tears, and dried them with her hair. ⁴⁵You gave Me no kiss; but she from when I came in did not cease kissing My feet. ⁴⁶You did not anoint My head with oil; but she anointed My feet with ointment. ⁴⁷On account of which, I say to you, her sins which were many are forgiven, because she loved much, but the one to whom little is forgiven, loves little." ⁴⁸He said to her, "Your sins are forgiven." ⁴⁹And those reclining together began to say to themselves, "Who is this who even forgives sin?" ⁵⁰And He said to the woman, "Your faith has saved you. Go in peace."

**8** It happened afterwards that He was traveling about among cities and villages preaching and proclaiming good news of the kingdom of God, and the twelve were with Him, ²and certain women who had been healed from evil spirits and diseases: Mary, the one being called Magdalene, from whom seven demons had been cast out, ³and Johanna, wife of Chuza, Herod's overseer, and Susanna and many others who were ministering to them out of their possessions.

⁴And when a great crowd was coming together, and the ones coming to Him from various cities, He spoke by a parable, ⁵"A sower went out to sow his seed, and in the sowing one seed indeed fell beside the road, and was trampled down, and the birds of the heaven devoured it. ⁶And another fell on the rocky soil, and having grown it withered, because it did not have moisture. ⁷And another fell in the midst of thorns, and growing up together, the thorns choked it. ⁸And another fell on the good earth, and growing produced fruit a hundred times more." As He was speaking these words, He was saying, "The one having ears to hear, let him hear."

⁹But His disciples were questioning Him as to what this parable might be. ¹⁰And He said to them, "To you it is given to know the mysteries of the kingdom of God, but to the others in parables, in order that, seeing they may not see, and hearing they may not understand. ¹¹But

this is the parable, the seed is the word of God. ¹²The ones falling beside the road are those hearing, then the devil comes and takes the word from their hearts in order that they may not believe and be saved. ¹³And the ones on the rock are those when hearing, with joy they receive the word, and these do not have root; they believe for a time, but in the time of temptation, they fall away. ¹⁴And the one falling among the thorns, these are the ones having heard, and going along they are choked by the cares, and riches and pleasures of life, and do not come to maturity. ¹⁵And the one on the good earth, these are the ones who with a good and fair heart, having heard the word, hold firm, and bear fruit with steadfastness.

¹⁶"But no one having lit a lamp covers it with a container or places it under a bed, but he places it on a lampstand in order that the ones coming in may see the light. ¹⁷For nothing is hidden which shall not become manifest, neither concealed which shall not absolutely be known, and come to be manifest. ¹⁸Therefore, you see how you hear; for whoever has more shall be give to him, but whoever does not have, even what he seems to have shall be taken from him."

¹⁹And His mother and His brothers came to Him, and they were unable to reach Him on account of the crowd. ²⁰And it was reported to Him, "Your mother and your brothers have stood without desiring to see You." ²¹And answering He said to them "These are My mother and My brothers, the ones hearing and doing the word of God."

²²And it happened on one of the days that He and His disciples embarked in a boat, and He said to them, "Let us go to the other side of the lake." And they set sail. ²³And as they were sailing, He fell asleep. And a storm of wind came down on the lake, and they were being swamped, and were in danger. ²⁴And coming to Him, they aroused Him saying, "Master, Master, we are perishing." But having arisen He rebuked the wind and the waves of water, and they ceased, and it became calm. ²⁵And He said to them, "Where is your faith?" And being fearful, they marveled, saying to one another, "Who then is this that He even commands the wind and the waves, and they obey Him?"

²⁶And they sailed down to the country of the Gerasenes, which is opposite Galilee. ²⁷And coming out upon the land, a certain man of the city met Him, being demon possessed; and for considerable time he had not put on garments, and did not remain in a home but in the tombs. ²⁸And beholding Jesus, crying out, he fell before Him and with a loud voice said, "What have You to do with me, Jesus, Son of the Most High God. I beg You do not torture me." ²⁹For Jesus was commanding the unclean spirit to come out from the man. For it had seized him many times, and he was bound with chains and shackles, being guarded, and breaking his bonds, he was driven by the demon into the wilderness. ³⁰But Jesus asked him, "What is your name?" And he said, "Legion"; for many demons had entered into him. ³¹And they were pleading with Him that He would not command them to depart into the abyss. ³²And there was a considerable herd of hogs feeding on the mountain; and they pleaded with Him that He would permit them to enter into those hogs; and He permitted them. ³³And the demons going out from the man, entered into the hogs, and the herd rushed down the cliff into the lake and were drowned.

³⁴And those feeding the hogs, seeing what had happened, fled, and reported it in the city and countryside. ³⁵And the people went out to see what had happened, and came to Jesus, and found the man from whom the demon went out being clothed and sound-minded, sitting at the

feet of Jesus, and they were afraid. ³⁶And the ones having seen reported to them how the one being possessed of demons was saved. ³⁷And all the multitude of people around the country of the Gerasenes were asking Him to depart from them for they were being held with great fear; and embarking in the boat, He returned. ³⁸But the man from whom the demons went out was begging Him to be with Him. But He released him saying, ³⁹"Return to your house, and relate fully what God did for you." And he went away and proclaimed throughout the whole city what Jesus did for him.
⁴⁰And when Jesus returned the crowd welcomed Him, for all were waiting for Him. ⁴¹And behold a man by name Jairus came, and this one was a ruler of the synagogue, and falling at the feet of Jesus, he pleaded with Him to enter into his house, ⁴²because his only daughter, about twelve years old, was dying. But as He was going the crowd was shoving against Him. ⁴³And a woman having a flowing of blood for twelve years, of which she was not able from anyone to be healed, ⁴⁴going behind, she touched the fringe of His garment, and instantly the flowing of her blood stopped. ⁴⁵And Jesus said, "Who is the one having touched Me." As all were denying, Peter said, "Master, the crowds are thronging and pressing against You." ⁴⁶But Jesus said, "Someone touched Me, for I myself knew power had been going out from Me." ⁴⁷And the woman seeing that she was not undiscovered came trembling, and falling prostrate before Him, she declared before all the people the reason she touched Him, and how she was cured instantly. ⁴⁸And He said to her, "Daughter, your faith has saved you; go in peace." ⁴⁹While He was still speaking, a certain one comes from the house of the ruler of the synagogue saying, "Your daughter died, no longer trouble the Teacher." ⁵⁰But Jesus, having heard answered him, "Do not fear, only believe, and she shall be saved." ⁵¹And going into the home, He did not permit anyone to go in with Him except Peter and John and James and the father and the mother of the child. ⁵²And all were weeping and lamenting her. But He said, "Stop crying, for she is not dead but sleeps." ⁵³And they were laughing at Him, knowing that she died. ⁵⁴And grasping her hand, He spoke saying, "Child arise!" ⁵⁵And her spirit returned, and she arose instantly, and He instructed that she be given food to eat. ⁵⁶And her parents were ecstatic; but He told them to tell no one what had happened.

9 And calling together the twelve He gave to them power and authority over all the demons, and to heal diseases. ²And He sent them to preach the kingdom of God, and to cure sicknesses. ³And He said to them, "Do not take anything for the journey, neither a staff, nor a knapsack, nor bread, nor silver, nor have two tunics. ⁴"And into whatever home you enter, stay there, and go out from there. ⁵And whoever does not receive you, going out from that city, shake from your feet the dust as a witness against them." ⁶And going out, they were going throughout the villages preaching good news, and healing everywhere.
⁷And Herod the tetrarch heard all that was happening; and was perplexed because it was said by certain ones that John had risen from the dead; ⁸and by some others that Elijah had appeared, and others that one of the ancient prophets had arisen. ⁹But Herod said, "I myself beheaded John; but who is this concerning whom I hear such as this?" and he was seeking to see Him.
¹⁰And the apostles returning, related fully to Him whatever they had done. And taking them He departed in private to the city being called Bethsaida. ¹¹But the crowd knowing this

followed Him. And welcoming them, He was speaking to them concerning the kingdom of God, and curing the ones having need of healing. ¹²And the day began to decline; and the twelve coming to Him said to Him, "Send the crowd away, so that going into the surrounding villages and farms they may lodge, and find provisions because here we are in a wilderness place." ¹³But He said to them, "You yourselves give them to eat." But they said, "We do not have more than five loaves and two fish, unless going we buy food for all these people." ¹⁴For there were about five thousand men. But He said to His disciples, "Have them recline for eating in groups of fifty each." ¹⁵And they did thus, and all were reclining to eat. ¹⁶And taking the five loaves and two fishes, looking up to heaven, He blessed them, and broke and was giving them to His disciples to set before the crowd. ¹⁷And they ate, and all were satisfied, and they took up of leftovers of them twelve baskets of fragments.

¹⁸And it happened that when He was praying alone, His disciples came to Him, and He questioned them saying, "Who do the crowds say that I am?" ¹⁹And answering they said, "John the Immerser, but others Elijah, and others that some ancient prophet has arisen." ²⁰But He said to them, "But who do you say that I am?" And Peter answering said, "The Christ of God."

²¹And having warned them, He commanded them to tell this to no one, ²²saying that, "It is necessary for the Son of man to suffer much, and be rejected by the elders and chief priests and scribes, and be put to death, and be raised up on the third day."

²³And He was saying to them all, "If anyone desires to come after Me, let him deny himself and take up his cross day after day, and let him follow Me. ²⁴For whoever desires to save his life shall lose it; and whoever shall lose his life on account of Me shall save it. ²⁵For what does a man profit gaining the whole world but loses or forfeits himself? ²⁶For whoever shall be ashamed of Me and My words, the Son of Man shall be ashamed of this one whenever He comes in His glory, and the glory of the Father and the holy angels. ²⁷And I say to you truly, there are certain ones of those standing here who will absolutely not taste death until when they see the kingdom of God."

²⁸And it happened about eight days after these words, taking Peter and John and James, He went up into the mountain to pray. ²⁹And it happened as He was praying, the appearance of His face became different, and His garment gleaming white. ³⁰And behold two men were talking with Him, who were Moses and Elijah, ³¹who appearing in glory were speaking of His departure, which was about to be fulfilled in Jerusalem. ³²But Peter and the ones with him were burdened with sleep, but having been thoroughly awakened, saw His glory and the two men standing with Him. ³³And it happened that as they were departing Peter said to Jesus, "Master, it is good for us to be here, and let us make three tents, one for You and one for Moses and one for Elijah" – not knowing what he is saying. ³⁴But as he was saying these words, a cloud came and overshadowed them; and they were afraid when they came into the cloud. ³⁵And a voice came out of the cloud saying, "This is My Son, the Chosen One, you hear Him." ³⁶And after the voice came, Jesus was found alone. And they were silent, and told no one in those days what they had seen.

³⁷And it happened on the next day when they came down from the mountain, a great crowd met Him. ³⁸And behold, a man from the crowd called loudly saying, "Teacher, I beg of you to look at my son, because he is my only begotten son. ³⁹And behold a spirit takes hold of

him, and suddenly he cries out, and it throws him into convulsions with foam at his mouth, and it bruises him, seldom departing from him. [40]And I begged your disciples that they might cast it out, but they were not able." [41]And Jesus answering said, "O faithless and perverted generation, until when shall I be with you, and put up with you? Bring your son here." [42]And while he was still approaching, the demon threw him to the ground, and into convulsions; but Jesus rebuked the unclean spirit, and cured the child, and presented him to his father. [43]And all were astonished at the greatness of God.

And as all were marveling at all which He was doing, He said to His disciples, [44]"You place these words in your ears, for the Son of Man is about to be betrayed into the hands of men." [45]But they did not understand this remark, for it had been hidden from them so that they were not able to perceive it, and they were afraid to ask Him concerning this remark.

[46]And a discussion started among them as to who would be greatest of them. [47]But Jesus knowing of the reasoning of their hearts, taking a child He stood it among them, [48]and said to them, "Whoever receives this child in My name receives Me, and whoever receives Me receives the One having sent Me; for the one being least among all of you, this is the great one."

[49]But John answering said, "Master, we saw someone casting out demons in Your name, and we forbid him because he does not follow with us." [50]But Jesus said to him, "Do not forbid him, for who is not against you is for you."

[51]And it happened the days were being fulfilled for His ascension, and He resolutely set His face to go to Jerusalem. [52]And He sent messengers before His face, and going they went into a village of Samaria so as to prepare for Him. [53]But they did not receive Him, because He was journeying with His face set toward Jerusalem. [54]And His disciples seeing this, James and John said, "Lord, do you desire that we call down fire from heaven and destroy them?" [55]But turning He rebuked them. [56]And they went to another village.

[57]And as they were going in the way, someone said to Him, "I will follow You wherever You go." [58]And Jesus said to him, "Foxes have holes, and the birds of heaven nests, but the Son of man has nowhere to recline His head." [59]And He said to another, "Follow Me." But he said, "Lord, permit me first to go and bury my father." [60]But He said to him, "Leave the dead to bury the dead for themselves." [61]And another also said, "I will follow You, Lord; but first permit me to bid farewell to those in my house." [62]But Jesus said, "No one putting his hand upon the plow, and looking to the things behind, is fit for the kingdom of God."

10 And after these events, the Lord appointed seventy others, and sent them forth two by two before His face in every city and place to which He was about to go. [2]And He was saying to them, "The harvest is abundant, but the laborers are few; request therefore the Lord of the harvest so that He will send out workers into His harvest. [3]Depart! Behold I send you forth as lambs in the midst of wolves. [4]Do not carry a purse, nor a knapsack, nor shoes, and do not greet anyone on the way. [5]And into whatever home you enter first say, 'Peace to this house.' [6]And if a son of peace be there, your peace will rest on him, but if not it will return to you. [7]But remain in the same home, eating and drinking what they provide, for the laborer is worthy of his wage. Do not go about from home to home. [8]And into whatever city you go, and they receive you, eat what is set before you; [9]Heal those sick in it, and say to

them, 'The kingdom of God has drawn near you.' ¹⁰And into whatever city you go, and they do not receive you, going out into the streets of it, say, ¹¹'Even the dust of your city clinging to our feet we wipe off against you; however, know this that the kingdom of God has drawn near.' ¹²I say to you that it shall be more endurable for Sodom in that day than for that city.

¹³"Woe to you Chorasin; woe to you Bethsaida; because if the miracles being done in you had been done in Tyre and Sidon they would have repented, sitting in sackcloth and ashes long ago. ¹⁴However, it shall be more endurable for Tyre and Sidon than you in the judgment. ¹⁵And you, Capernaum, you will not be exalted to heaven, will you? You will be brought down to Hades.

¹⁶"The one listening to you, listens to Me, the one who rejects you, rejects Me; the one rejecting Me, rejects the One having sent me."

¹⁷The seventy returned with joy saying, "Lord, the demons are subject to us in Your name." ¹⁸And He said to them, "I was beholding Satan falling, as lightning out of heaven. ¹⁹Behold, I have given you the authority to tread upon serpents and scorpions and over all power of the enemy, and absolutely nothing shall harm you. ²⁰However, do not rejoice in this, that the spirits are subject to you, but rejoice that your names have been engraved in heaven."

²¹In this hour He rejoiced in the Holy Spirit, and said, "I honor You, Father, Lord of heaven and earth, that You have hidden these truths from the wise and intelligent and revealed them to babies; yes, Father, because thus it was well pleasing before You. ²²Everything has been delivered by the Father to Me, and no one knows who the Son is except the Father, and who the Father is except the Son, and to whomever the Son wills to reveal Him."

²³And turning to the disciples He said privately, "Blessed are the eyes seeing what you see. ²⁴For I say to you that many prophets and kings desired to see what you see, and did not see and hear what you hear and did not hear."

²⁵And behold a certain lawyer stood up testing Him saying, "Teacher, what shall I do to inherit eternal life?" ²⁶And He said to him, "In the Law what has been written? How do you read it? ²⁷And answering he said, "You shall love the Lord your God out of your whole heart, and with your whole soul, and with your whole strength, and with your whole mind, and your neighbor as yourself." ²⁸And He said, "You have answered rightly. This do and you shall live."

²⁹But desiring to justify himself, he said to Jesus, "And who is my neighbor?" ³⁰Replying Jesus said, "A certain man went down from Jerusalem to Jericho, and fell among robbers, who also stripping and beating him left, leaving him half dead. ³¹And by coincidence a certain priest came down that road, and seeing him went by on the other side. ³²And likewise also a Levite, having come by that place, and seeing him, went by on the other side. ³³But a certain Samaritan on a journey came upon him, and seeing him, had compassion. ³⁴And coming to him, bound up his wounds, and poured on them oil and wine, and placing him on his own beast, took him to an inn, and cared for him. ³⁵And on the morrow taking out two denarii, he gave to the innkeeper, and said, 'Take care of him and whatever you spend more I will repay you when I return.' ³⁶"Which of these three does it seem to you became a neighbor to the one falling into the robbers' hands?" ³⁷And he said, "The one practicing mercy toward him." And Jesus said to him, "Go and you do likewise."

³⁸And as they journeyed, He entered into a certain village where a certain woman by

name Martha welcomed Him. ³⁹And she had a sister being called Mary, who also was sitting at the feet of the Lord, listening to His Word. ⁴⁰But Martha was distracted about much service, and came to Him and said, "Lord, do You not care that my sister has left me alone to serve? Tell her therefore to take a part with me to help." ⁴¹But the Lord answering said to her, "Martha, Martha, you are worried and bothered about many tasks, ⁴²but only one is necessary; for Mary chose the good part which shall not be taken from her."

11 And it happened that He was in a certain place praying, when He finished, one of His disciples said to Him, "Lord, teach us to pray even as John was teaching his disciples." ²And He said to them, "When you pray, you say, Father, let Your name be sanctified. Let Your kingdom come, ³Give us daily our necessary bread, ⁴And forgive our sins, For we ourselves also forgive all indebted to us. And do not lead us into temptation."
⁵And He said to them, "Who of you will have a friend and will go to him at midnight, and say to him, 'Friend, lend me three loaves, ⁶since my friend has come on a journey to me, and I do not have anything to set before him'; ⁷and that one within answering may say, 'Do not cause me trouble; already the door has been shut, and my children are with me in bed; I am not able to rise up to give to you.' ⁸I say to you, even if he does not arise and give to him because he is his friend, yet because of his intense persistence he arises, and gives to him whatever he needs. ⁹And I say to you, ask and it shall be given to you, seek and you will find, knock and it will be opened to you. ¹⁰For everyone asking receives, and the one seeking finds, and to the one knocking it is opened. ¹¹And which of you as a father if your son asks for a fish, and instead will give to him a serpent? ¹²Or also he shall ask for an egg, will give to him a scorpion? ¹³If therefore you being evil, know to give good gifts to your children, how much rather the Father in heaven will give the Holy Spirit to those asking Him."
¹⁴And He was casting out a demon, and it was dumb, but when the demon came out, the dumb man began speaking, and the crowds marveled. ¹⁵But certain of them said, "He casts out the demons by Beelzebul the ruler of demons." ¹⁶And others, testing Him were seeking a signal out of heaven from Him. ¹⁷But He knowing their thoughts said to them, "Every kingdom being divided against itself is devastated, and a house against a house falls. ¹⁸And if also Satan was divided against himself, how will his kingdom stand? Since you say I cast out demons by Beelzebul. ¹⁹But if I cast out demons by Beelzebul, by whom do your sons cast them out? For this reason they shall be your judges. ²⁰But if by the finger of God I cast out the demons, then the kingdom of God has come upon you. ²¹Whenever the strong man being fully armed guards his own palace, his goods are at peace, safe. ²²But if one stronger than he comes, he conquers him; he takes away all his armor in which he trusted, and divides up his spoils. ²³The one not being with Me is against Me, and the one not gathering with Me scatters.
²⁴"When the unclean spirit goes out of the man, it goes through waterless places seeking rest, and not finding any, it says, 'I will return to my house from where I went out.' ²⁵Having come, it finds the house having been swept and having been put in order. ²⁶Then it goes and takes with it seven other spirits more wicked that himself, and going in dwells there, and the last condition of the man becomes worse than the first."
²⁷And it happened when He was saying these words some woman out of the crowd raising her voice said to Him, "Blessed be the womb bearing You, and the breasts which You

nursed." ²⁸But He said, "Indeed, rather, blessed are the ones who hear the Word of God and keeping it."

²⁹And as the crowds were pressing upon Him, He began to say, "This generation is a wicked generation; it seeks a signal and no sign shall be given to it except the sign of Jonah. ³⁰For even as Jonah became a sign to the Ninevites, thus also the Son of Man shall be to this generation. ³¹The queen of the South shall be raised up in the judgment with the men of this generation, and shall condemn them, because she came from the ends of the earth to hear the wisdom of Solomon, and behold a greater than Solomon is here. ³²The men of Nineveh shall stand up in the judgment with this generation and condemn it; because they repented toward the preaching of Jonah and behold a greater than Jonah is here. ³³No one having lit a lamp puts it in a hidden place nor under a bushel but upon a lampstand in order that the ones going in may see the light. ³⁴The lamp of the body is your eye. Whenever your eye is clear, also your whole body is enlightened; but whenever your eye is wicked your body is darkened. ³⁵Look carefully, therefore, that the light that is in you is not darkness. ³⁶If therefore your whole body is enlightened, you do not have any part darkness; it shall be fully enlightened as when the lamp lights you with its ray."

³⁷And after He had spoken, a Pharisee asks Him that He eat with him; and going in He was seated. ³⁸And the Pharisee beholding, marveled that He did not first wash ceremonially before the meal. ³⁹And the Lord said to him, "Now, you Pharisees clean the outside of the cup and the platter, but on the inside of you, you are full of robbery and wickedness. ⁴⁰Foolish one, did not the One making the outside make also the inside? ⁴¹However, you give that within the dish as charity, and behold everything is clean to you.

⁴²"But woe to you, the Pharisees, because you pay tithe of mint, and rue, and every herb but disregard justice and the love of God; these it is necessary to do and those others not to neglect. ⁴³Woe to you, the Pharisees, because you love the first seats in the synagogues and the salutations in the market places. ⁴⁴Woe to you because you are as the unseen tombs, and men walking over them do not know it."

⁴⁵And one of the lawyers answering says to Him, "Teacher, saying these words you also insult us." ⁴⁶But He said, "Woe to you lawyers also because you burden men with burdens difficult to bear, and you yourselves will not touch the burdens with one of your fingers. ⁴⁷Woe to you because you build the tombs of the prophets, but your fathers killed them. ⁴⁸Therefore you are witnesses and approve the deeds of your fathers for they on the one hand killed them and you on the other hand build their tombs. ⁴⁹And on account of this the wisdom of God said, 'I will send to them prophets and apostles, and they will kill some of them and persecute others,' ⁵⁰in order that the blood of all the prophets being shed from the foundation of the world, may be charged to this generation, ⁵¹from the blood of Abel until the blood of Zacharias, the one perishing between the altar and the sanctuary. Yes, I say to you such shall be charged against this generation. ⁵²Woe to you, the lawyers because you took away the key of knowledge; you yourselves did not enter, and the ones trying to enter, you hindered."

⁵³And as He was leaving there, the scribes and Pharisees began to oppose Him vehemently, and to interrogate Him firmly concerning many subjects, ⁵⁴watching closely to trap Him in something which He might say.

**12** At this time as thousands of the crowd were assembling so that they were tramping on one another, He began first to speak to His disciples, saying, "Guard yourselves from the leaven of the Pharisees which is hypocrisy. ²But there is nothing having been veiled which shall not be revealed, and hidden which shall not be made known. ³Accordingly, whatever you said in the dark shall be heard in the light, and what you spoke in your private rooms shall be proclaimed on the housetops.

⁴"And I say to you, my friends, do not fear those killing the body, and afterward do not have any more they can do. ⁵But I will point out whom you should fear; fear the one after he kills has authority to cast into hell, yes, I say to you, this one you should fear. ⁶Are not five sparrows sold for two assarions? And not one of them is forgotten before God. ⁷But even the hairs of your head are all numbered. Do not fear; you are more valuable that many sparrows.

⁸"I say to you, everyone who confesses Me before men, the Son of Man also will confess before the angels of God. ⁹But the one denying Me before men will be denied before the angels of God. ¹⁰And everyone who speaks a word against the Son of Man, it will be forgiven him; but the one blaspheming the Holy Spirit, it shall not be forgiven. ¹¹And whenever they bring you before the synagogues and the rulers and the authorities, do not be anxious how you will defend yourselves, or what you will say; ¹²for the Holy Spirit will teach you in that hour what it is necessary to say."

¹³And a certain one out of the crowd said to Him, "Teacher, tell my brother to divide with me the inheritance." ¹⁴And He said to him, "Man, who appointed Me a judge or arbiter for you?" ¹⁵And He said to them, "Watch and guard yourselves from all manifestations of greed, because one's life is not in the abundance of his possessions." ¹⁶And He spoke a parable to them, saying, "The ground of a certain rich man produced well. ¹⁷And he was reasoning within himself saying, 'What shall I do because I do not have anywhere to store my fruits.' ¹⁸"And he said, 'I will do this; I will tear down my barns and build greater ones, and I will store there all my grain and goods. ¹⁹And I will say to my soul, "Soul you have many goods being laid up for many years, be at rest, eat, drink, be merry."' ²⁰But God said to him, 'You fool, this night your soul will be required from you; then what you prepared, whose shall it be?' ²¹Thus is the one treasuring up for himself, and not riches for God."

²²And He said to the disciples, "On account of this I say to you, do not be anxious for your life, what you will eat, nor your body, what you will wear. ²³For life is more than food and the body than clothing. ²⁴Consider the ravens that they do not sow, nor reap, nor have storerooms or barns, and the Father feeds them, how much more valuable are you than the fowls. ²⁵And which of you by being anxious is able to add one cubit to his stature? ²⁶Therefore, if you are not able to do anything about this little matter, why are you anxious about other matters? ²⁷Consider the lilies, how they grow; they do not spin nor weave but I say to you, even Solomon in all his glory was not arrayed as one of these. ²⁸But if God thus attires the grass in the field being here today, and tomorrow being cast into an oven, how much more will He clothe you, you of little faith? ²⁹Do not you seek what you shall eat, and what you shall drink, and do not continually worry. ³⁰For the Gentiles of the world seek after all these things, but your Father knows that you need these. ³¹However, you seek His kingdom, and all these shall be added to you.

$^{32}$"Stop fearing, little flock, your Father was pleased to give to you the kingdom. $^{33}$Sell your possessions and give charity; make yourselves purses which do not become old, an unfailing treasure in heaven where a thief does not draw near nor a moth destroy. $^{34}$For where your treasure is, there will your heart be also.

$^{35}$"Let your bodies be clothed, and your lamps burning. $^{36}$And you be like men, waiting their own lord when he returns from the wedding festivities, in order that when he comes and knocks they may immediately open to him. $^{37}$Blessed are those slaves who, when the lord comes he finds watching; surely, I say to you, he will dress himself appropriately, and set them at the table, and proceed to serve them. $^{38}$And even if he comes in the second watch of night, or even the third, and he finds them thus, blessed are those. $^{39}$But know this that if the householder had known at what hour the thief comes, he would not have let his house be broken into. $^{40}$And you be prepared, because the Son of Man comes at an hour which you do not suppose that He will come."

$^{41}$But Peter said to Him, "Lord, are You telling to us this parable or to everyone?" $^{42}$And the Lord said, "Who, therefore, is the faithful and wise steward whom the lord appoints over his servants to give them sustenance at the proper time? $^{43}$Blessed is that slave whom when the lord comes he finds doing thus. $^{44}$Truly I say to you he will appoint him over all his possessions. $^{45}$But if that slave says in his heart, 'My lord is taking his time coming,' and will begin to beat both the men servants and women servants, and to both eat and drink and be drunken. $^{46}$The lord of that slave will come in a day which he does not suppose, and in an hour which he does not know, and will cut him to pieces, and place his part with the ones not believing. $^{47}$But that slave having known the will of his lord, and not preparing or doing his will, he will beat with many blows. $^{48}$But the one not knowing, and doing deeds worthy of a beating, will receive a few blows. But everyone to whom much was given, much shall be asked of him.

$^{49}$"I came to cast fire upon the earth, and what do I desire if already it be ignited. $^{50}$But I have immersion in which to be immersed, and how distressed I am until it be accomplished. $^{51}$Do you consider that I came to give peace to the earth? Not so, I say to you, but rather division. $^{52}$For from now on five in one house will be divided, three against two and two against three. $^{53}$They shall be divided, father against son, and son against father, mother against the daughter, and daughter against the mother, mother-in-law against her daughter-in-law, daughter-in-law against the mother-in-law."

$^{54}$And He was also saying to the crowds, "Whenever you see a cloud arising in the west, immediately you say that 'A shower is coming,' and thus it happens. $^{55}$And when the south wind blows, you say that, 'It will be hot,' and it happens. $^{56}$Hypocrites, you know how to discern the face of the earth and the heaven, but you do not know how to discern this present time.

$^{57}$"And why even for yourselves do you not judge what is right. $^{58}$For as you go with your adversary to the magistrate, while you are on the way, make an effort to be reconciled with him, lest he drag you off to the judge, and the judge delivers you over to the officer, and the officer casts you into prison. $^{59}$I say to you, you absolutely will not go out from there until you repay the last cent."

**13** And there were some present at the same time reporting to Him concerning the Galileans whose blood Pilate mingled with their sacrifices. ²And answering He said to them, "Do you suppose these Galileans were sinners worse than all Galileans because they suffered these trials? ³Not so, I tell you, but if you do not repent, you all shall likewise perish! ⁴Or those eighteen upon whom the tower in Siloam fell and killed them, do you suppose that they were debtors more than all the men dwelling in Jerusalem? ⁵Not so, I say to you, but if you do not repent, you all in like manner shall perish."

⁶And He was telling this parable; "A certain man had a fig tree having been planted in his vineyard, and he went seeking fruit on it and found none. ⁷And he said to the vineyard keeper, 'Behold three years upon which I come seeking fruit in this fig tree. Cut it down; why should it even use up the ground?' ⁸But answering he says to him, 'Lord, let it be even this year until when I dig around it and fertilize it. ⁹And if indeed it makes fruit in the future, and if not you will cut it down.'"

¹⁰And He was teaching in one synagogue on the Sabbath. ¹¹And behold a woman having a spirit causing infirmity for eighteen years, and she was bent over, and not able to straighten up perfectly. ¹²And Jesus beholding her, spoke to her, and said to her, "Woman, you are released from your infirmity." ¹³And He put His hands on her, and instantly she was made erect, and was glorifying God. ¹⁴But the ruler of the synagogue answered, being indignant that Jesus healed on the Sabbath, saying to the crowd that, "There are six days in which it is necessary to work; in these therefore come to be healed, and not on the Sabbath." ¹⁵But the Lord answered him and said, "Hypocrites, does not each of you on the Sabbath loose his ox or his donkey from the stall, and lead away for watering? ¹⁶But this one being a daughter of Abraham, whom Satan bound, behold even eighteen years, is it not necessary to loose from this bondage on the Sabbath?" ¹⁷And He saying these words, all His adversaries were being put to shame, and all the crowd were rejoicing at all the glorious deeds being done by Him.

¹⁸Therefore, He was saying, "What is the kingdom of God like, and to what shall I compare it? ¹⁹"It is like a grain of mustard, which a man taking casts into his own garden, and it grew, and became a tree, and the birds of heaven nest in its branches."

²⁰And again He said, "To what shall I compare the kingdom of God? ²¹It is like leaven, which a woman taking hid in three sata of meal, until the whole was leavened." ²²And He was going through cities and villages one by one, teaching, and making His journey toward Jerusalem. ²³And a certain one said to Him, "Lord, are just a few going to be saved?" And He said to them, ²⁴"Struggle to go in through the narrow door because many, I say to you will seek to enter in, and they shall not be able. ²⁵From whenever the householder arises and shuts the door, and you begin to stand outside and knock on the door saying, 'Lord, open to us'; and answering he says to you, 'I know not you, from where you are.' ²⁶Then you will begin to say, 'We ate and drank in Your presence, and You taught in our streets'; ²⁷and He will speak to you saying, 'I know not you from where you are; depart from Me all workers of iniquity.' ²⁸There shall be weeping and gnashing of teeth, whenever you shall see Abraham, Isaac and Jacob, and all the prophets in the kingdom of God, and you having been cast out. ²⁹And they will come from east and west and from north and south and recline at the feast table in the kingdom of God. ³⁰And behold they that are last shall be first, and they that are first shall be last."

³¹In the same hour certain Pharisees came to Him saying, "Go out and journey from here because Herod desires to kill you." ³²And He said to them, "Go, tell that fox, 'Behold I cast out demons and accomplish cures today and tomorrow, and on the third day I will finish.' ³³However, it is necessary that today and tomorrow and the following day I proceed for it is not acceptable for a prophet to perish outside of Jerusalem. ³⁴Jerusalem, Jerusalem, the one killing the prophets and stoning those having been sent to her, how often I wanted to gather together your children in like manner as a hen gathers her own brood under her wings, but you were not willing. ³⁵Behold your home is left to you desolate. And truly I say to you, you shall not at all see Me until it comes when you say, 'Blessed is the One coming in the name of the Lord!'"

14 And it happened that when He went into the house of a certain ruler of the Pharisees on a Sabbath to eat bread, they were watching Him carefully. ²And behold a certain man suffering from dropsy was before Him. ³And Jesus answering spoke to the lawyers and Pharisees saying, "It is lawful on the Sabbath to heal or not?" ⁴But they remained silent. And taking hold of him, He cured him, and sent him away. ⁵And He said to them, "Which of you having a donkey or an ox fall into a well, and will not immediately raise it up on a Sabbath day?" ⁶And they were not able to reply to this. ⁷And He was telling a parable of those being invited, noticing how they were choosing the chief places at the table, saying to them, ⁸"Whenever you are invited by someone to a wedding feast, do not take the chief place lest a more honorable person than you has been invited by him the host. ⁹And coming, the one having invited you and him, says to you, 'Give place to this one,' and then you begin with shame to take the last place. ¹⁰But whenever you are invited, going, appropriate the last place so that whenever the one having invited you comes, he will say to you, 'Friend, proceed up higher'; then you will have honor before all the ones reclining at the feast table with you. ¹¹Because everyone that exalts himself shall be humbled, and everyone humbling himself shall be exalted."

¹²And He was saying to the one having invited Him, "Whenever you give a luncheon or dinner, do not call your friends nor your brothers neither your relatives nor your rich neighbors, lest they also invite you in return, and you are repaid. ¹³But whenever you have a festive meal, call the poor, the crippled, the lame, the blind; ¹⁴and you shall be blessed, because they do not have the means to repay you, for you shall be repaid in the resurrection of the righteous."

¹⁵And a certain one reclining at the table with Him hearing these words, said to Him, "Blessed is whoever eats bread in the kingdom of God." ¹⁶But He said to him, "A certain man was giving a great dinner, and invited many, ¹⁷and he sent his slave at the dinner hour to tell those having been invited, 'Come, because it is now prepared.' ¹⁸And they all alike began to make excuses. The first said to him, 'I bought a field and I have need to go out to see it; I ask you to excuse me.' ¹⁹And another said, 'I bought five yoke of oxen and I go to examine them; I ask you to excuse me.' ²⁰And another said 'I married a wife and on account of this I am not able to come.' ²¹And the slave returning, announced to his lord these excuses. Then becoming angry, the householder said to his slave, 'Go out quickly into the streets and lanes of the city, and the poor and the crippled and the blind and the lame bring in here.' ²²And the slave said,

'Lord, what you commanded has been done, and there is still room.' ²³And the lord said to the slave, 'Go out into the roads and hedges, and constrain people to come, in order that my house may be filled. ²⁴For I tell you that none of those men having been invited shall taste of my dinner.'"

²⁵And great crowds were going with Him, and turning, He said to them, ²⁶"If anyone comes to Me, and does not hate his own father and mother and wife and children and his brothers and his sisters, and yet even his own life, he is not able to be My disciple ²⁷And whoever does not carry his own cross and come after Me, is not able to be My disciple. ²⁸For which one of you, desiring to build a tower, does not first, sitting down, calculate the expense, if he has sufficient for completion? ²⁹Lest having laid his foundation, and not being able to complete it, everyone viewing it begin to ridicule him, ³⁰saying that, 'This man began to build, and was not able to complete.' ³¹Or what king going out to encounter another king in war, does not first, sitting down, determine if he is able with ten thousand men to withstand the one coming against him with twenty thousand? ³²And if not, while he is still far away, sending an embassage, he ask for peace. ³³Thus, therefore, all of you who do not surrender all of your own possessions, is not able to be My disciple.

³⁴"Salt therefore is good; but if even the salt becomes tasteless, by what shall it become salted? ³⁵It is not useful for the ground or for the manure pile; they cast it out.

15 And all the tax collectors and sinners were coming near to hear Him. ²And both the Pharisees and the scribes were grumbling that, "This one receives sinners and eats with them."

³But He told them this parable, saying, ⁴"What man among you having a hundred sheep and losing one of them, does not leave the ninety-nine in the wilderness, and goes after the lost one until he finds it? ⁵And having found it, he places it upon his shoulders, rejoicing. ⁶And going into the house, calls together his friends and his neighbors, saying to them, 'Rejoice with me because I found my lost sheep.' ⁷I say to you thus there shall be joy in heaven over one sinner repenting more than upon ninety-nine righteous ones who have no need of repentance.

⁸"Or what woman having ten drachmas, if she loses one drachma, does not light a lamp and sweep the home and seeks carefully until when she finds it? ⁹And finding rejoices with her friends and neighbors saying, 'Rejoice with me because I found the drachma which I lost.' ¹⁰Thus, I say, there is rejoicing before the angels of God over one sinner repenting."

¹¹And He said, "A certain man had two sons. ¹²And the younger of them said to his father, 'Give to me the share of the estate falling to me.' And he divided his livelihood to them. ¹³And after not many days, the younger son gathered every possession together, and journeyed into a far country, and there squandered his substance in profligate living. ¹⁴And he having spent all, a severe famine came in that country, and he began to be in need. ¹⁵And going he was joined with a citizen of that country, and he sent him into the fields to feed hogs. ¹⁶And he was longing to fill his belly with the husks which the hogs were eating, and no one was giving to him.

¹⁷"And having come to himself, he said, 'How many hired servants of my father have more than sufficient bread, and I myself perish here with hunger! ¹⁸Arising, I will go to my

father and say to him, "Father, I have sinned against heaven and before you, [19]I am no longer worthy to be called your son; make me as one of your hired servants."' [20]And arising he went to his own father. But while he was yet coming afar off, his father saw him, and was filled with compassion, and running fell on his neck and kissed him again and again. [21]And the son said to him, 'Father, I have sinned against heaven and before you, I am no longer worthy to be called your son.' [22]But the father said to his servants, 'Quickly, bring out the best flowing robe and clothe him, and give a ring for his hand and sandals for his feet, [23]and bring the fatted calf, kill it and eating, let us celebrate [24]because this my son was dead and became alive, was lost and was found,' and they began to celebrate.

[25]"But his older son was in the field; and as he was coming near the home, he heard music and dancing. [26]And calling to one of the servants, he was inquiring what these activities might be. [27]And he said to him, 'Your brother has come and your father has killed the fatted calf because he has received him back safe and sound.' [28]And he became angry and would not enter. But his father going out, was pleading with him. [29]But answering he said to his father, 'Behold, for so many years I am serving you, and never yet transgressed your commandment, but you have never yet given me a kid in order that I might celebrate with my friends. [30]But when this son of yours who devoured your livelihood with harlots came, you killed the fatted calf.' [31]But he said to him, 'Child, you are always with me, and all that is mine is yours; [32]but it is necessary to celebrate and rejoice, because this brother of yours was dead and is alive, and having been lost, was found.'"

**16** And He was also saying to His disciples, "There was a certain rich man who had a steward, and this steward was reported to him as squandering his possessions. [2]And calling him, he said to him, 'What is this I hear concerning you? Present an account of your stewardship, for you are no longer able to be steward.' [3]But the steward said to himself, 'What shall I do since my lord is taking away my stewardship from me? I am not strong enough to dig. I am ashamed to beg. [4]I know what I will do, in order that whenever I am removed of my stewardship, they shall receive me into their own houses.' [5]And calling in each one of his lord's debtors, saying to the first one, 'How much do you owe my lord?' [6]And he said, 'A hundred measures of oil.' And he said, 'Take your bill and quickly write fifty.' [7]Afterward he said to another, 'And how much do you owe?' and he said, 'A hundred measures of wheat.' And he says to him, 'Take your bill and write eighty.' [8]And the lord commended the unrighteous steward because he acted wisely; because the sons of this age are more wise toward their own generation than the sons of light. [9]And I say to you, you make for yourselves friends out of the mammon of unrighteousness, in order that whenever it fails, they shall receive you in the eternal dwellings.

[10]The one faithful in the least is also faithful in much, and the one unrighteous in the least is unrighteous in much. [11]If therefore you have not been faithful in the use of unrighteous mammon, who will trust you with the true spiritual riches? [12]And if you have not been faithful in the riches of another, who will give your own to you? [13]No house servant is able to serve two lords, for either he will hate the one and love the other, or he will cling to the one and despise the other. You are not able to serve God and mammon."

[14]And the Pharisees, being lovers of money, were hearing all these words, and were

sneering at Him. ¹⁵And He said to them, "You are the ones making yourselves righteous before men, but God knows your hearts, because that exalted by men is detestable before God.

¹⁶"The Law and the prophets were until John, since then the kingdom of God is being proclaimed, and everyone is forcing a way into it. ¹⁷But it is easier for the heaven and the earth to pass away than one stroke of the Law to fall.

¹⁸"Everyone divorcing his wife and marrying another practices adultery, and the one marrying a woman who has been divorced from her husband practices adultery.

¹⁹"But there was a certain rich man, and he was dressed in purple and fine linen, living every day sumptuously in splendor. ²⁰And there was a certain poor man, named Lazarus, laid by his gate full of sores, ²¹and longing to be filled with the crumbs falling from the table of the rich man; but even the dogs coming were licking his sores. ²²And it happened the poor man died, and was carried by the angels into the bosom of Abraham; and the rich man also died and was buried. ²³And in Hades lifting up his eyes, being in torment, he saw Abraham from afar, and Lazarus in his bosom. ²⁴And calling he said, 'Father Abraham, have mercy on me, and send Lazarus in order that he may dip the tip of his finger in water and cool my tongue, because in this flame I am suffering agony.' ²⁵And Abraham said, 'Child, remember that you received good things in your life, and Lazarus likewise the evil; and now here he is comforted, and you suffering agony. ²⁶And in all these circumstances between us and you a great chasm has been established, so that those desiring to go through from here to you are not able, and neither may anyone come from there to us.' ²⁷And he said, 'I ask you therefore, father, that you send him to the house of my father, ²⁸for I have five brothers, that he may witness strongly to them that they may not come to this place of torment.' ²⁹But Abraham says, 'They have Moses and the prophets, let them listen to them.' ³⁰But he said, 'Not so, father Abraham, but if someone from the dead go to them, they will repent.' ³¹But he said to him, 'If they do not listen to Moses and the prophets, neither will they be persuaded if someone from the dead arises.'"

17 And He said to His disciples, "It is impossible that stumbling blocks will not come, however, woe to the one through whom they come. ²It would be better for him if a millstone be hung about his neck, and he be thrown into the sea than that he cause one of these little ones to stumble. ³Take heed to yourselves, if your brother sins, rebuke him, and if he repents, forgive him. ⁴And if he sins against you seven times a day and returns seven times to you, saying, 'I repent,' forgive him."

⁵And the apostles said to the Lord, "Increase our faith." ⁶And the Lord said, "If you have faith as a grain of mustard, you would say to this sycamine tree, 'You be uprooted and be planted in the sea' and it would obey you.

⁷"And which of you having a slave plowing or shepherding, who coming in from the field, says to him, 'Come, sit down to eat?' ⁸But will he not say to him, 'Prepare something for me to dine, and clothe yourself properly to serve me while I eat and drink, and after this you eat and drink?' ⁹He does not have thanks for the slave because he did what was commanded, does he? ¹⁰Thus also you, whenever you do all that was commanded to you; you say, 'We are undeserving slaves who did what we ought to have done.'"

¹¹And it happened while He was going toward Jerusalem that He was going along the

border of Samaria and Galilee. ¹²And as He was entering a certain village, ten leprous men met Him, who stood at a distance, ¹³and raised their voices saying, "Jesus, Master, have mercy on us." ¹⁴And beholding them, He said to them, "Going, present yourselves to the priests." And it happened that as they were going, they were cleansed. ¹⁵And one of them, seeing that he was cured, returned with a loud voice glorifying God. ¹⁶And he fell on his face at His feet thanking Him; and he was a Samaritan. ¹⁷And Jesus answering said, "Were there not ten cleansed? Where are the nine? ¹⁸Were none found returning to give glory to God except this foreigner?" ¹⁹And He said to him, "Arising, go, your faith has saved you."

²⁰And having been questioned by the Pharisees about when the kingdom of God comes, He answered them and said, "The kingdom of God does not come with observation, ²¹neither saying, 'Behold here' or 'There'; for behold the kingdom of God is within you."

²²And He said to the disciples, "Days shall come when you will long to see one of the days of the Son of Man and you will not see. ²³And they will say to you, 'Behold there.' Or 'Behold here.' Do not go neither pursue them. ²⁴For even as lightning flashing out from a part of the heaven lights up another part of heaven, thus shall be the Son of Man in His day. ²⁵But first it is necessary that He suffer much and be rejected by this generation. ²⁶And even as it happened in the days of Noah, thus it shall be also in the days of the Son of Man. ²⁷People were eating, drinking, marrying, giving in marriage until the day in which Noah went into the ark, and the flood came and destroyed everything. ²⁸Likewise even as it happened in the days of Lot; they were eating, drinking, buying, selling, planting, building. ²⁹And on the day Lot went out from Sodom, it rained fire and sulfur from heaven and destroyed everything. ³⁰It shall be according to the same circumstances the day in which the Son of Man is revealed. ³¹On that day let not the one who is on the housetop and his possessions in the home come down to take them; and who is in the field, likewise let him not return for the things left behind. ³²Remember Lot's wife. ³³Whoever seeks to secure his life shall lose it but whoever loses his life shall keep it alive. ³⁴I say to you, in this night there shall be two upon one bed, one shall be taken away and the other shall be left. ³⁵There shall be two grinding at the same place, one woman shall be taken away and the other shall be left. ³⁶Two men in the field, one shall be taken away and the other shall be left." ³⁷And answering they said to Him, "Where Lord?" And He said to them, "Where the body is, there also the vultures will be gathered together."

18 And He was telling a parable to them that it is necessary always to pray, and not to be discouraged, ²saying, "There was a certain judge in a certain city, not fearing God, and not respecting man. ³And there was in that city a widow, and she kept coming to him saying, 'Give me justice from my adversary.' ⁴And he would not for a time, but afterwards he said within himself, 'Even if I fear not God nor respect men, ⁵yet because this widow causes me trouble, I will give her justice in order that by her continual coming she does not wear me out.'" ⁶And the Lord said, "You heard what the unrighteous judge says; ⁷and shall not God deal justly with His elect, crying out to Him day and night, and be longsuffering toward them. ⁸I say to you that He will practice justice for them quickly. However, therefore when the Son of Man comes, will He find faith upon the earth?"

⁹And He also told this parable to certain of those who had confidence in themselves that

they were righteous, and treated others with contempt. ¹⁰"Two men went up into the temple to pray, one a Pharisee and the other a tax collector. ¹¹The Pharisee standing, was praying to himself this, 'O God, I thank You that I am not as other men: plunderers, unrighteous, adulterers, or even as this tax collector; ¹²I fast twice a week, I pay a tithe of all I acquire.' ¹³But the tax collector, standing at a distance would not even raise his eyes to heaven but was thumping his breast saying, 'O God, be merciful to me the sinner.' ¹⁴I say to you, this one went down to his house having been justified rather than the other, because everyone exalting himself shall be humbled, but the one humbling himself shall be exalted."

¹⁵And they were bringing to Him also infants in order that He might touch them; but the disciples seeing this were rebuking them. ¹⁶But Jesus was calling them to Him, saying, "Permit the little ones to come to Me, and do not forbid them, for of such as this is the kingdom of God. ¹⁷Surely I say to you, whoever does not receive the kingdom of God as a little child, shall absolutely not enter it."

¹⁸And a certain ruler questioned Him saying, "Good Teacher, what shall I do that I may inherit eternal life?" ¹⁹But Jesus said to Him, "Why do you call Me good? No one is good except God. ²⁰You know the commandments; Do not commit adultery, Do not murder, Do not steal, Do not bear false witness, Honor your father and mother." ²¹And he said, "All these I have kept from youth." ²²And Jesus hearing this said to him, "Yet one thing you lack; sell all whatever you have, and distribute to the poor, and you will have treasures in heaven, and come follow Me." ²³And hearing this, he became very sorrowful for he was very rich. ²⁴And Jesus beholding him, becoming very sorrowful, said, "How difficult for the ones having riches to enter into the kingdom of God. ²⁵For it is easier for a camel to go through the eye of a needle than for a rich man to enter the kingdom of God." ²⁶And those hearing said, "Then who is able to be saved?" ²⁷And He said, "That which is impossible with men, with God is possible." ²⁸And Peter said, "Behold we, leaving our own families and houses, have followed You." ²⁹And He said to them, "Surely, I say to you that there is no one who left home or wife or brothers or parents or children on account of the kingdom of God, ³⁰who shall absolutely not receive back many times as much at this time, and in the coming age eternal life."

³¹And taking aside the twelve, He said to them, "Behold we go up to Jerusalem, and all having been written about the Son of Man through the prophets shall be completed. ³²For He shall be delivered up to the Gentiles, and shall be mocked and mistreated and spit upon, ³³and having been scourged they shall put Him to death, and on the third day He shall rise up." ³⁴And they did not understand any of these words, and the remark had been hidden from them, and they did not know the meaning of what was being spoken.

³⁵And it happened as He was drawing near to Jericho, a certain blind man was sitting beside the road, begging. ³⁶And hearing the crowd going by, he inquired what this might be; ³⁷they told him that Jesus the Nazarene was passing by. ³⁸And he shouted out, saying, "Jesus, Son of David have mercy on me." ³⁹And those leading the way rebuked him that he be silent; but he cried out more loudly, "Son of David, have mercy on me." ⁴⁰And Jesus standing still commanded him to be brought to Him. And as he drew near, He asked him, ⁴¹"What do you desire that I do?" And he said, "Lord, that I receive sight." ⁴²And Jesus said to him, "Receive sight! Your faith has saved you." ⁴³And instantly he received sight, and was following Him, glorifying God. And all the people seeing this, gave praise to God.

**19** And entering, He was passing through Jericho. ²And behold there was a man by name being called Zaccheus, and he was a chief tax collector, and he was rich. ³And he was seeking to see who Jesus is, and he was not able, because of the crowd because he was small in stature. ⁴And running ahead, he went up in a sycamore tree so that he might see Him because He was about to come by that way. ⁵And as He came to the place, Jesus looking up said to him, "Zaccheus, come down in a hurry for today I must stay in your house." ⁶And he came down in a hurry, and received Him rejoicing. ⁷And all seeing this were grumbling, saying that, "He went in to be a guest of a sinful man." ⁸But Zaccheus standing up said to the Lord, "Behold the half of my possessions, Lord, I give to the poor, and if I have taken anything falsely from anyone, I will repay him fourfold." ⁹And Jesus said to him that, "Today salvation has come to this house because he also is a son of Abraham. ¹⁰For the Son of Man came to seek and to save the lost."

¹¹And they hearing these words, proceeding, He told a parable because He was near Jerusalem, and they supposed that the kingdom of God was about to appear instantly. ¹²He said therefore, "A certain noble born man went to a far country to receive for himself a kingdom and return. ¹³And having called ten of his own slaves, he gave them ten minas and said to them, 'Use this in a practical way until I come.' ¹⁴But his citizens hated him, and sent an embassage after him saying, 'We do not want this one to reign over us.' ¹⁵And it happened when he returned, having received his kingdom, that he said that these slaves to whom he had given the silver be called to him in order for him to know what was gained through their practical use of it. ¹⁶And the first came before him saying, 'Lord, your mina produced ten more.' ¹⁷And he said to him, 'Well done, good slave, because you have been faithful in the least, you be in authority over ten cities.' ¹⁸And the second came saying, 'Your mina, lord, made five minas.' ¹⁹And he said also to this one, 'And you be over five cities.' ²⁰And the other came saying, 'Lord, behold your mina which I had put away in a piece of cloth. ²¹For I feared you, that you are an austere man, you take up where you did not put down, and you reap where you did not sow.' ²²He says to him, 'Out of your mouth I will judge you, wicked slave. You knew that I am an austere man, taking up where I have not laid and reaping where I did not sow; ²³on account of this why did you not put my silver on the table of the money-changers? And I having come could have exacted interest.' ²⁴And he said to those standing by, 'Take from him the mina, and give to the one having ten minas.' ²⁵And they said, 'Lord, he has ten minas already.' ²⁶I say to you that to everyone having it shall be given, but from the one not having it also shall be taken away. ²⁷However my enemies, those not desiring me to reign over them, you bring here, and slay them before me."

²⁸And having said these words, He was proceeding, going up to Jerusalem. ²⁹And it happened as He drew near to Bethphage and Bethany toward the mount being called Olivet, He sent two of His disciples, ³⁰saying, "Go into the opposite village, in which having gone you will find a colt being tied on which no one of men has ever sat, and loosing you bring it. ³¹And if anyone asks you, 'Why are you loosing it?' You say thus that, 'The Lord has need of it.'" ³²And going, the ones having been sent found it even as He said to them. ³³As they were loosing the colt, the owners said to them, "Why are you loosing the colt?" ³⁴And they said that, "The Lord has need of it." ³⁵And they brought it to Jesus, and casting their garments upon the colt, they placed Jesus on it. ³⁶And as He was proceeding, they were spreading their

garments in the road. ³⁷And as He was drawing near to the descent of the Mount of Olives, all the multitude of the disciples began to praise God, rejoicing with a loud voice concerning all miracles which they had seen, ³⁸saying, "Blessed is the King coming in the name of the Lord, peace in heaven and glory in the highest." ³⁹And certain of the Pharisees from the crowd said to Him, "Teacher, rebuke your disciples." ⁴⁰And answering He said, "I say to you, even if these were silent, the stones will cry out."

⁴¹And as He drew near, beholding the city He wept over it, ⁴²saying that, "If you knew in this day, even you, the way to peace, but now it has been hidden from your eyes, ⁴³because the days shall come upon you, and your enemies shall raise up an embankment around you, and encompass you, and hem you in completely, ⁴⁴and they will dash you to the ground, and your children within you, and they will not leave a stone on a stone in you since you did not know the time of your visitation."

⁴⁵And going into the temple He began to cast out the money changers, ⁴⁶saying to them, "It has been written, 'And My house shall be a house of prayer,' but you have made it a den of robbers."

⁴⁷And He was teaching daily in the temple. But the chief priests and the scribes and the first men of the city were seeking to destroy Him. ⁴⁸And they were not finding what they might do, for all the people hearing Him were hanging on to Him.

**20** And it happened to one of the days that He was teaching the people in the temple and announcing good news, the chief priests and the scribes with the elders stood over Him, ²and spoke saying to Him, "Tell us by what authority you do these deeds, or who is the one giving this authority to you?" ³And answering He said to them, "I will ask you also a question, and you tell Me; ⁴the immersion of John, was it from heaven or from men?" ⁵And they reasoned among themselves saying that, "If we say, 'From heaven,' He will say, 'Why then did you not believe him?' ⁶But if we say, 'From men,' all the people will stone us for they are persuaded that John was a prophet." ⁷And they answered that they knew not where it was. ⁸And Jesus said to them, "Neither will I tell you by what authority I do these."

⁹And He began to tell the people this parable; "A certain man planted a vineyard and rented it out to farmers and went on a journey for a considerable time. ¹⁰And in time he sent to the farmers a slave that they might give him from the fruit of the vineyard, but the farmers, beating him, sent him away empty-handed. ¹¹And he proceeded to send another slave; and that one also beating and treating dishonorably, they sent away empty-handed. ¹²And he proceeded to send a third; and also this one, wounding, they cast out. ¹³And the lord of the vineyard said, 'What shall I do? I will send my beloved son, perhaps they will respect this one.' ¹⁴But the farmers seeing him reasoned to one another, saying, 'This is the heir, let us kill him in order that the inheritance may be ours.' ¹⁵And casting him out of the vineyard, they killed him. What then shall the lord do to them of the vineyard? ¹⁶He shall come and shall destroy those farmers, and shall give the vineyard to others." And having heard this they said, "May it not be." ¹⁷But looking upon them He said, "What therefore is this having been written, 'The stone which the builders rejected' this became the head of the corner? ¹⁸Everyone falling upon that stone will be broken in pieces, and on whomever it falls, it will crush him into dust."

¹⁹And the scribes and the chief priests were seeking to cast their hands upon Him in the

same hour, but they were afraid of the people; for they knew that He told this parable about them. [20]And keeping a close watch over Him, they sent spies pretending themselves to be righteous, in order that they might grasp hold of His word, so that they might deliver Him to the rule and the authority of the governor. [21]And they questioned Him, saying, "Teacher, we know that You speak and teach rightly, and do not take people at face value, but You teach the way of God with truth. [22]Is it lawful for us to give tax to Caesar or not?" [23]But He, perceiving their craftiness, said to them, [24]"Show Me a denarius; whose image and superscription does it have?" And they said, "Caesar's." [25]And He said to them, "Then give back to Caesar that which is Caesar's, and to God what is God's." [26]And they were not able to refute His word before the people, and marveling at His answer they were silent.

[27]And certain of the Sadducees, those saying there is no resurrection, coming to Him asked, [28]saying, "Teacher, Moses wrote to us, if any brother dies having a wife, and this one be childless that his brother take his wife, and raise up seed for his brother. [29]Therefore, there were seven brothers, and the first taking a wife died childless; [30]and the second; [31]and the third took her, and likewise also the seven, not leaving children, and they died. [32]Afterward the wife also died. [33]Therefore, in the resurrection to which of them would she be a wife? For the seven had her as a wife."

[34]And Jesus said to them, "The sons of this age marry and give in marriage, [35]but those being worthy to attain to that eternal age, and the resurrection of the dead neither marry nor give in marriage; [36]for neither are they able to die any more, for they are as angels, and are sons of God, being sons of the resurrection. [37]But that the dead are raised up even Moses indicated at the bramble-bush, as he says, 'the Lord God of Abraham and the God of Isaac and God of Jacob' [38]But God is not the God of the dead but living, for all live in Him." [39]And answering certain of the scribes said, "Teacher, you spoke well." [40]For they no longer were daring to ask Him anything.

[41]And He said to them, "How do they say the Christ to be the son of David? [42]For David says in the book of Psalms, 'The Lord said to my Lord, Sit on My right hand, [43]Until whenever I place Your enemies A footstool for Your feet.' [44]David therefore calls Him Lord, then how is He a son?"

[45]And while all the people were listening, He said to His disciples, [46]"Take heed of the scribes, the ones desiring to walk in flowing robes, and take pleasure in salutations in the market places, and first seats in the synagogues, and first places at dinners, [47]who devour the houses of widows, and for display offer long prayers; these shall receive greater condemnation."

21 And looking up He saw the rich casting their gifts into the treasury-box. [2]And He saw a certain very poor widow casting there two lepta, [3]and said, "Truly, I say to you that this poor widow cast in more than all; [4]for all these out of their abundance cast in their gifts, but she out of her poverty cast in all the livelihood which she has."

[5]And as certain ones were speaking about the temple that it had been adorned with goodly stones and dedicated gifts, He said, [6]"The days shall come in which these stones which you view, not one stone shall be left upon a stone which will not be torn down." [7]And they asked Him saying, "Teacher, when therefore shall these events be, and what the sign whenever

these shall happen?" ⁸And He said, "Watch that you are not deceived; for many shall come in My name, saying, 'I am He.' And 'The time has drawn near,' Do not go after them. ⁹But whenever you hear of wars and revolutions, do not be terrified; for it is necessary for these to come first, but not immediately before the end."

¹⁰Then He was saying to them, "Nation will rise up against nation and kingdom against kingdom. ¹¹There will be great earthquakes and from place to place there shall be famines and pestilences, and there will be terrors and great signs from heaven. ¹²But before all these they will lay their hands upon you and persecute you, delivering you up to synagogues and prisons, being brought before kings and governors for the sake of My name. ¹³It will present to you a witness opportunity. ¹⁴Therefore, put it in your hearts not to consider before time how to defend yourselves. ¹⁵For I myself will give a message and wisdom which all your antagonists will not be able to withstand or refute. ¹⁶But you will be betrayed even by parents and brothers and relatives and friends, and some of you will be put to death. ¹⁷And you shall be hated by all on account of My name. ¹⁸And absolutely not a hair on your head will perish. ¹⁹By your perseverance you will gain your souls.

²⁰"And whenever you see Jerusalem being surrounded by armies, then know that her desolation has drawn near. ²¹Then let the ones in Judea flee to the mountains, and the ones in the midst of her, let them depart, and the ones in the country, let them not enter into her, ²²because these are days of retribution that all that has been written might be fulfilled. ²³Woe to those being pregnant, and those nursing babies in those days; for there shall be great distress upon the land, and wrath upon this people. ²⁴And they shall fall by the edge of the sword and shall be led away captive into all nations, and Jerusalem shall be trampled underfoot by Gentiles, until the times of the Gentiles be fulfilled.

²⁵"And there shall be signs in the sun and moon and stars, and upon the earth anxiety of nations in perplexity at the roaring of the sea and the waves, ²⁶men fainting from fear, and of the expectation of what is coming on the inhabited world for the powers of heaven shall be shaken. ²⁷And then they shall see the Son of man coming in a cloud with power and much glory. ²⁸But when these events begin to happen, straighten up, and lift up your heads, because your redemption draws near."

²⁹And He told a parable to them, "Behold the fig and all the trees; ³⁰whenever they already shoot forth leaves, seeing for yourselves, you know that already summer is near. ³¹Thus also you, whenever you see these things happening, you know that the kingdom of God is near. ³²Surely, I say to you that this generation absolutely will not pass away until all these happen. ³³The heavens and the earth shall pass away; but My Word shall absolutely not pass away.

³⁴"But take heed to yourselves so that your hearts be not beaten down with debauchery and drunkenness and in worries of livelihood, and that day stand upon you suddenly, ³⁵as a trap, for it shall come upon all who dwell on the face of all the earth. ³⁶And you be alert at all time, praying in order that you may be able to escape all these events being about to happen, and to stand before the Son of Man."

³⁷And He was teaching during the days in the temple, and at night going out, He lodged on the mount being called Olivet. ³⁸And all the people arose in the morning to come to Him in the temple to hear Him.

**22** And the Feast of Unleavened Bread being called Passover was drawing near. ²And the chief priests and the scribes were seeking how they might destroy Him, for they were fearing the people.

³And Satan entered into Judas, the one being called Iscariot, being of the number of the twelve. ⁴And going out he discussed with the chief priest and officers how he might betray Him to them. ⁵And they rejoiced and agreed with him to give him silver. ⁶And he consented, and was seeking an opportune time to betray Him to them, apart from the crowd.

⁷And the day of the Unleavened Bread came in which it was necessary to kill the Passover lamb. ⁸And He sent Peter and John saying, "Going, prepare for us the Passover in order that we may eat it." ⁹And they said to Him, "Where do you desire us to prepare it?" ¹⁰And He said to them, "Behold, as you go into the city, a man will meet you carrying a jar of water; follow him into the home into which he enters. ¹¹And say to the householder of the home, 'The Teacher says to you, "Where is the guest room where I may eat the Passover with My disciples?"' ¹²And that one will show you a large upper room having been furnished; you prepare it there." ¹³And departing, they found it even as He had said to them, and they prepared the Passover.

¹⁴And when the hour came, He sat down and His disciples with Him. ¹⁵And He said to them, "With desire, I earnestly desired to eat this Passover with you before I suffer. ¹⁶For I say to you that I will absolutely not eat it again until it is fulfilled in the kingdom of God." ¹⁷And receiving a cup He gave thanks, saying, "Take this and distribute it among yourselves; ¹⁸for I say to you that I will absolutely not drink from the fruit of the vine from now until when the kingdom of God comes." ¹⁹And having taken the bread, giving thanks, He broke it and gave it to them saying, "This is My body given on behalf of you; this do for My memorial." ²⁰And in the same manner the cup after the supper, saying, "This is the cup of the new covenant in My blood, having been shed on behalf of you. ²¹However, behold, the hand of the one betraying Me is with Me on the table. ²²Because, indeed the Son of Man goes as it has been determined, however, woe to that man through whom He is betrayed." ²³And they began to question among themselves who then would be the one of them being about to do this.

24And a rivalry also took place among them as to which of them seems to be the greatest. 25But He said to them, "The kings of the Gentiles lord over them, and the ones having authority over them are called benefactors. 26But you are not thus, but the one being greatest among you, let him become as the youngest, and the leader as the one serving. 27For who is the greatest, the one reclining at meal or the one serving? Is it not the one reclining? But I am in the midst of you as the One serving.

²⁸"And you are the ones having remained with Me through My trials. ²⁹And I commit to you a kingdom, even as My Father did to Me, ³⁰in order that you may eat and drink at My table in My kingdom, and sit upon thrones judging the twelve tribes of Israel.

³¹"Simon, Simon, behold, Satan has begged earnestly for you to sift you like wheat; ³²but I prayed for you that your faith may not fail, and then turning back you strengthen your brothers." ³³And he said to Him, "Lord, with You I am prepared to go to prison and to death." ³⁴But He said, "I say to you, Peter, this day a cock will not crow until you have denied Me three times."

³⁵And He said to them, "When I sent you out without a purse or knapsack or sandals, you

did not lack anything did you?" And they said, "Nothing." ³⁶And He said to them, "but now let the one having a purse take it and also a knapsack, and the one not having a sword, let him sell his robe and buy one. ³⁷"For I say to you that this having been written must be fulfilled in Me, 'And He was counted with the lawless'; for also that written concerning Me has an end." ³⁸And they said, "Lord, behold here are two swords." And He said to them, "It is sufficient."

³⁹And having gone out, He went according to His custom to the Mount of Olives, and His disciples also followed Him. ⁴⁰And arriving at the place, He said to them, "You pray not to enter into temptation." ⁴¹And He withdrew from them about a stone's throw, and kneeling was praying, ⁴²saying, "Father, if You are willing, take this cup from Me; however, let not My will but Yours be done." ⁴³And an angel from heaven appeared to Him, strengthening Him. ⁴⁴And being in agony, He was praying more fervently; and His sweat became as blood falling down upon the ground. ⁴⁵And having arisen from prayer, coming to His disciples, He found them sleeping from sorrow. ⁴⁶And He said to them, "Why do you sleep? Arising, pray in order that you may not enter into temptation."

⁴⁷While He was still speaking, behold, a crowd came, and the one being called Judas, one of the twelve, was leading them, and he drew near to Jesus to kiss Him. ⁴⁸But Jesus said to him, "Judas, do you betray the Son of Man with a kiss?" ⁴⁹And those around Him seeing what was about to happen, said, "Lord, shall we strike with a sword?" ⁵⁰And a certain one of them struck the slave of the high priest, and cut off his right ear. ⁵¹But Jesus answering said, "This is enough"; and touching his ear healed him. ⁵²And Jesus said to those coming against Him the chief priests, the officers of the temple, and elders, "Why do you come with swords and clubs as upon a robber? ⁵³I was daily with you in the temple, and you did not lay hands on Me; but this is your hour, and you have the power of darkness."

⁵⁴And capturing Him, they led Him away, and brought Him into the home of the high priest; but Peter was following at a distance. ⁵⁵And after they kindled a fire in the middle of the courtyard, and sat down together, Peter sat with them. ⁵⁶And a certain young servant girl seeing him sitting in the light, and gazing intently on him said, "And this one was with Him." ⁵⁷But he answered saying, "I know Him not, woman." ⁵⁸And after a while another seeing him, said, "And you are one of them." But Peter said, "Man, I am not." ⁵⁹And after about a one hour interval another definitely asserted saying, "Of a truth this one was also with Him, for he also is a Galilean." ⁶⁰But Peter said, "Man, I know not of what you speak." And instantly, while he was still speaking, a cock crowed. ⁶¹And turning the Lord looked upon Peter, and Peter remembered the word of the Lord as He said to him that, "Before a cock crows this day you will deny Me thrice." ⁶²And he went out and wept bitterly.

⁶³And the men holding Jesus were mocking, and beating Him. ⁶⁴And blindfolding Him they were asking Him, saying, "You prophesy, who is the one having slapped You?" ⁶⁵And many other blasphemous words they were saying to Him.

⁶⁶And when it became day, the council of elders of the people, both chief priests and scribes, was gathered together and they brought Him into their Sanhedrin, ⁶⁷saying, "If you are the Christ, tell us." And He said to them, "If I told you, you would absolutely not believe. ⁶⁸If I ask you a question, you would absolutely not answer. ⁶⁹But from now on the Son of Man shall be sitting on the right hand of the power of God." ⁷⁰And they all said, "Are You the Son of God?" And He said to them, "You say that I am." ⁷¹And they said, "Why do we still have need

of witness? For we ourselves have heard from His mouth."

**23** And all the group of them arising, brought Him to Pilate. ²And they began to accuse Him saying, "We found this One subverting our nation, and forbidding to give taxes to Caesar, and saying He Himself is Christ, a King." ³And Pilate asked Him saying, "Are you the king of the Jews?" And answering He said, "You say so." ⁴But Pilate said to the chief priests and the group, "I do not find any fault in this man." ⁵But they persisted, saying that, "He excites the people, teaching throughout the whole of Judea, even beginning from Galilee to here."
⁶And Pilate hearing this asked if the man is a Galilean. ⁷And learning that He is of Herod's authority, he sent Him to Herod. ⁸And Herod seeing Jesus was very glad for he was desiring to see Him for a long time because he had heard about Him, and was hoping to see some miraculous sign being done by Him. ⁹And he asked Him with many words; but He answered him nothing. ¹⁰But the chief priests and the scribes stood there, and accused Him vehemently. ¹¹Herod with his soldiers despising Him, mocked and placed on Him a gorgeous robe, and sent Him back to Pilate. ¹²And Herod and Pilate became friends with one another on that day, for before they were enemies toward each other.
¹³And Pilate calling together the chief priests and the rulers of the people, ¹⁴said to them, "You brought this man to me as a perverter of the people, and behold, examining Him before you, I found no fault in this Man of which you accuse Him, ¹⁵but neither has Herod, for he sent Him back to us; and behold, nothing has been done by Him worthy of death. ¹⁶Therefore, punishing, I will release Him." [¹⁷*Omitted in older manuscripts*].
¹⁸And all the multitude cried out saying, "Take this one away, and release to us Barabbas"; ¹⁹who was the one having been cast in the prison because of a certain insurrection happening in the city and for murder. ²⁰But again Pilate spoke to them, desiring to release Jesus. ²¹But they were calling out saying, "Crucify, crucify Him." ²²But the third time he said to them, "Why? For what evil did this one do? I found not one cause of death in Him; therefore, punishing, I will release Him." ²³But they insisted with loud voices, asking Him to be crucified, and their voices were prevailing. ²⁴And Pilate made judgment that their request be done. ²⁵And he released the one for whom they asked, the one having been cast into prison for insurrection and murder, but he delivered over Jesus to their will.
²⁶And as they led Him away, laying hold of a certain Simon a Cyrenean, coming from the country, they placed on him the cross to bear behind Jesus. ²⁷And there was following Him a great multitude of the people, and of women who were mourning and lamenting Him. ²⁸But turning to them, Jesus said, "Daughters of Jerusalem stop weeping for Me; however, weep for yourselves and for your children, ²⁹because behold, days are coming in which they will say, 'Blessed are the barren, and the wombs which did not give birth, and breasts which did not nurse.' ³⁰Then they will begin to say to the mountains, 'Fall upon us,' and to the hills, 'Cover us.' ³¹Because if they do these in the green tree, what may happen in the dry?"
³²And also two others, criminals, they were bringing with Him to be killed. ³³And when they came to the place being called The Skull, there they crucified Him and the criminals, one on His right hand and the other on His left. ³⁴And Jesus was saying, "Father, forgive them, for they do not know what they are doing." And they cast lots for His garments. ³⁵And the people

stood by beholding. And also the rulers were sneering, saying, "He saved others, let Him save Himself, if this is the Christ of God, the Chosen One." [36]And the soldiers also were mocking Him, coming to Him, offering Him vinegar wine, [37]and saying, "If you are the king of the Jews, save Yourself." [38]And there was also a superscription over Him, "This is the King of the Jews."
[39]And one of the criminals having been hung there, was blaspheming Him, saying, "Are You not the Christ? Save Yourself and us." [40]But the other one answering, rebuking him said, "Do you not fear God, that you are under the same condemnation? [41]And we indeed justly, for we are receiving retribution worthy of what deeds we did; but this One did nothing out of place." [42]And he was saying, "Jesus, remember me when You come in Your kingdom." [43]And He said to him, "Surely, I say to you, this day you will be with Me in Paradise."
[44]And it was about the sixth hour: and darkness came on the whole land until the ninth hour, [45]the sun failing; and the veil of the temple was split in the middle. [46]And calling with a great voice, Jesus said, "Father into Your hands I commit My spirit." Having said this He expired. [47]And beholding what was happening the centurion was glorifying God, saying, "Certainly this was a righteous Man." [48]And all the crowd having gathered together for this spectacle, having viewed what had happened, thumping their breasts, were returning. [49]And all those knowing Him, and the women having followed Him together from Galilee, had stood at a distance to watch these events.
[50]And behold a man by name Joseph, being a counselor, a good and righteous man, [51]this one had not been consenting with their purpose and action from Arimathea, a city of Judea, who was awaiting the kingdom of God. [52]This one coming to Pilate requested the body of Jesus. [53]And taking it down, wrapped it in linen, and placed Him in a tomb hewn in rock where no one was ever laid. [54]And it was the Day of Preparation, and Sabbath was about to dawn. [55]And the women having followed Him together, who were the ones coming together out of Galilee, beheld the tomb and how His body was placed. [56]and returning prepared spices and myrrh.

And indeed they rested on the Sabbath according to the commandment.

**24** But on the first day of the week while still very early in the morning they came to the tomb bearing spices which they prepared. [2]And they found the stone having been rolled away from the tomb. [3]And going in, they found not the body of the Lord Jesus. [4]And it happened that when they were perplexed concerning this, that behold, two men stood before them in apparel shining as lightning. [5]And the women becoming terrified and bowing their faces to the ground, the men said to them, "Why do you seek the living among the dead? [6]He is not here but has risen. Remember what He spoke to you being still in Galilee, [7]saying that it is necessary for the Son of Man to be delivered up into the hands of sinful men, and to be crucified, and on the third day to arise." [8]And they remembered His words. [9]And returning from the tomb, they announced all these things to the twelve and to all the rest. [10]And there were Mary Magdalene and Johanna and Mary the mother of James; also the other women with them were telling these things to the apostles. [11]And these words appeared before them as foolishness, and they did not believe them. [12]But Peter arising, ran to the tomb, and bending over he sees the linen wrappings only; and went away, marveling to himself at that having happened.

¹³And behold, two of them on the same day were going to a village by name Emmaus, being about sixty stadia from Jerusalem, ¹⁴and they were conversing with one another concerning all these events having taken place. ¹⁵And it happened as they were talking and discussing that Jesus Himself drawing near, began walking with them. ¹⁶But their eyes were being prevented from recognizing Him. ¹⁷And He said to them, "What are these words which you were exchanging with one another as you are walking?" And the stood still looking dreary. ¹⁸And one by name Cleopas, answering said to Him, "Are you alone visiting Jerusalem and knowing that having happened in it in these days?" ¹⁹And He said to them, "What things?" And they said to Him, "The things concerning Jesus of Nazareth, Who was a man, a prophet, mighty in deed and word before God and all the people, ²⁰so that both the chief priests and our rulers delivered Him over to the judgment of death, and crucified Him. ²¹But we were hoping that He is the One about to redeem Israel: but indeed also with all this, this is the third day since these things happened. ²²But also certain women among us excited us going early to the tomb. ²³and not finding His body, they came saying also they had seen a vision of angels, who said He is alive. ²⁴And certain of those with us went to the tomb and found it thus even as also the women said, but they did not see Him." ²⁵And He said to them, "O ignorant and slow of heart men to believe all which the prophets spoke. ²⁶Was it not necessary for the Christ to suffer these things, and to enter into His glory?" ²⁷And beginning from Moses and from all the prophets, He explained to them to all the Scriptures the things concerning Himself.

²⁸And they drew near to the village where they were going and He pretended to go farther. ²⁹And they persuaded Him, saying, "Remain with us, because it is near evening, and the day already has declined." ³⁰And it happened that as He reclined at the table with them, having taken the bread, He blessed it, and having broken it, was giving it to them. ³¹And their eyes were opened, and they recognized Him, and He became invisible to them. ³²And they said to one another, "Were not our hearts burning within us as He was speaking to us on the way, as He was opening the Scriptures to us?" ³³And arising at the same hour they returned to Jerusalem, and found collected together the eleven and those with them, ³⁴saying that the Lord was really risen, and was seen by Simon. ³⁵And they themselves were relating the events on the road, and how He was made known to them in the breaking of the bread.

³⁶And as they were relating these, He Himself stood in their midst, and says to them, "Peace to you." ³⁷And having been startled, and becoming frightened, they supposed they were seeing a spirit. ³⁸And He said to them, "Why have you been troubled and why does uncertainty arise in your heart? ³⁹Behold My hands and My feet that it is I Myself; touch Me and behold that spirit does not have flesh and bones, even as you see Me having." ⁴⁰And saying this, He showed them His hands and feet. ⁴¹And when they were still unbelieving from joy, and were marveling, He said to them, "Have you any food here?"⁴²And they handed to Him a piece of broiled fish. ⁴³And having taken, He ate before them.

⁴⁴And He said to them, "These are my words which I spoke to you still being with you, that it is necessary for all to be fulfilled having been written concerning Me in the Law of Moses and the Prophets and Psalms." ⁴⁵Then He opened their mind to understand the Scriptures. ⁴⁶And He said to them that, "Thus it has been written that the Christ should suffer and rise from the dead on the third day, ⁴⁷and that repentance and forgiveness of sins be

preached in His name to all nations, beginning from Jerusalem; ⁴⁸and you are witnesses of these things. ⁴⁹And behold I Myself send the promise of the Father upon you; but you remain in the city until when you are clothed with power from on high."

⁵⁰And He led them out until near Bethany, and raising His hands He blessed them. ⁵¹And it happened that as He was blessing them, He parted from them, and was taken up into heaven. ⁵²And they, worshipping Him, returned into Jerusalem with great joy, ⁵³And they were continually in the temple praising God.

## *The Gospel According to*
# John

1 In the beginning was the Word; the Word was with God, and the Word was God. ²He was with God in the beginning. ³Through Him all things were made; not one thing in all creation was made without Him. ⁴In Him was life, and this life was the light of mankind. ⁵The light shines in the darkness, and the darkness has not overcome it.

⁶There came a man sent from God; his name was John. ⁷His task was to tell people about the light, so that all would hear the message and believe. ⁸John was not the light; but he came in order to tell people about the light.

⁹The true light that gives light to every man was coming into the world. ¹⁰The Word was in the world and though the world was made through Him, the world did not recognize Him. ¹¹He came to His own people, and His own people did not receive Him. ¹²Some, however, did receive Him and believe in His name; to them He gave the right to become children of God— ¹³Children born not by natural means or related by human decision, but born of God.

¹⁴The Word became flesh and lived among us, and we have seen His glory – the glory of the one and only Son who came from the Father – full of grace and truth. ¹⁵John spoke about the Word. He cried out, saying, "This is the One I was talking about when I said, 'He who comes after is greater than I am, because He existed before I was born.'" ¹⁶Out of the fullness of His grace we have all received one blessing after another. ¹⁷The Law was given through Moses; grace and truth came through Jesus Christ. ¹⁸No one has ever seen God; the one and only Son; who is the same as God and is at the Father's side, has made Him known.

¹⁹This is the testimony of John: when the Jewish authorities of Jerusalem sent priests and Levites to ask him who he was, ²⁰John did not refuse to answer them, but shared openly, "I am not the Christ." ²¹"Who are you then? Are you Elijah?" They asked. "I am not." John answered. "Are you the Prophet?" They asked. "No." He replied. ²²Then they said to him, "Tell us who you are so that we can give an answer to those who sent us. What do you say about yourself?" ²³John answered them by quoting the prophet Isaiah: "I am the voice of one shouting in the wilderness, 'Prepare the way for the Lord!'" ²⁴The priests and Levites, who had been sent from the Pharisees, ²⁵then asked John, "Why then are you immersing, if you are not the Christ, nor Elijah, nor the Prophet?" ²⁶John replied, "I immerse people in water, but among you stands the one you do not recognize. ²⁷He is coming after me, and I am not worthy even to untie His sandals." ²⁸All this happened at Bethany, on the east side of the Jordan River, where John was immersing.

²⁹The next day John saw Jesus coming toward him and said, "Look, here is the Lamb of God, who takes away the sin of the world! ³⁰He is the One I was talking about when I said, 'After me, a Man is coming who is greater than I am, because He existed before I was born.' ³¹I personally did not know who He would be, but I came immersing people in water so that He might be revealed to the people of Israel." ³²John continued, saying, "I saw the Spirit come down from heaven and remain on Jesus. ³³I would not have recognized Him, but God, who sent me to immerse people in water, told me, 'He on whom you see the Spirit descend and

remain is He who will immerse you in the Holy Spirit.' ³⁴I have seen and testify that He is the Son of God."

³⁵The next day John was there again with two of his disciples. ³⁶When he saw Jesus walking along, he said, "Look, the Lamb of God!" ³⁷When the two disciples heard him say this, they followed Jesus. ³⁸Jesus turned around, saw that they were following Him, and asked, "What do you want?" They replied, "Rabbi" which translated means Teacher "Where are You staying?" ³⁹"Come and see." He said. They went and saw where He was staying; and they stayed with Him that day, for it was about the tenth hour. ⁴⁰Andrew, Simon Peter's brother, was one of the two who had heard what John had said and had followed Jesus. ⁴¹The first thing Andrew did was find his brother Simon and tell him, "We have found the Messiah" (which translated means Christ). ⁴²He brought him to Jesus. Jesus looked at him and said, "You are Simon, the son of John. You will be called Cephas" which is translated Peter.

⁴³The next day Jesus decided to go to Galilee. He found Philip and said to him, "Follow Me." ⁴⁴Philip, like Peter and Andrew, was from the town of Bethsaida. ⁴⁵Philip found Nathanael and said to him, "We have found the One whom Moses wrote about in the Law and about whom the Prophets also wrote – Jesus of Nazareth, the son of Joseph." ⁴⁶"Nazareth! Can anything good come from there?" Nathanael asked. "Come and see," said Philip. ⁴⁷When Jesus saw Nathanael coming to Him, He said about him, "Here is a true Israelite, in whom there is nothing false." ⁴⁸"How do you know me?" Nathanael asked. Jesus answered, "I saw you when you were under the fig tree before Philip called you." ⁴⁹Then Nathanael exclaimed, "Rabbi, You are the Son of God! You are the King of Israel!" ⁵⁰Jesus asked, "Do you believe because I said I saw you when you were under the fig tree? You will see greater things than this." ⁵¹Jesus then said, "I am telling you the truth: you will see heaven open and the angels of God ascending and descending on the Son of Man."

2 On the third day there was a wedding in the town of Cana in Galilee. Jesus' mother was there ²and Jesus and His disciples had also been invited to the festivities. ³When the wine was gone, Jesus' mother said to Him, "They have no wine left." ⁴Jesus said to her, "Woman, why do you want Me to get involved? My hour has not yet come." ⁵His mother said to the servants, "Do whatever He tells you." ⁶Now there were six stone water pots set there for the Jewish custom of purification which held 20 or 30 gallons each. ⁷Jesus said to the servants, "Fill the pots with water." And they filled them to the brim. ⁸Then He said to the servants, "Now draw some out and take it to the wedding coordinator." And so they did. ⁹The wedding coordinator tasted the water that had been turned into wine. Now he did not know where it had come from, though the servants who had drawn the water knew, so he called the groom aside, ¹⁰And said to him, "Everyone else serves the choice wine first and then the cheaper wine after the guests have had plenty to drink; but you have saved the best until now." ¹¹Jesus performed this, the first of His miraculous signs, in the town of Cana in Galilee. He revealed His glory and His disciples believed in Him.

¹²After this, Jesus went down to Capernaum with His mother and brothers, and His disciples. They stayed there a few days. ¹³It was almost time for the Passover Feast, so Jesus went up to Jerusalem. ¹⁴In the temple He found men selling cattle, sheep and doves, and also moneychangers sitting at their tables. ¹⁵He made a whip out of cords and drove them out of the

temple with the sheep and the cattle; He overturned the tables of the moneychangers and scattered their coins; [16]And to those who sold doves He said, "Get them out of here! Stop making My Father's house like a marketplace!" [17]His disciples remembered that it was written in the Scripture, "Zeal for your house, O God will consume Me." [18]Then the Jewish authorities demanded of Him, "What miraculous sign can You show us to prove Your authority to do all this?" [19]Jesus answered them, "Destroy this temple, and in three days I will raise it up." [20]"It took 46 years to build this temple." They replied. "And You are going to raise it up in three days?" [21]But the temple Jesus was talking about was His body. [22]After Jesus was raised from the dead, His disciples remembered what He had said. Then they believed the Scripture and what Jesus had said.
[23]Whle Jesus was in Jerusalem at the Passover Feast, many believed in His name as they saw the miraculous signs He performed. [24]But Jesus did not entrust Himself to them, for He knew all men. [25]He did not need anyone to tell Him what man was like, for He Himself knew what was in man.

3 Now there was a man named Nicodemus, who was a Pharisee and a ruler of the Jews. [2]One night Nicodemus came to Jesus and said to Him, "Rabbi, we know that You are a teacher who has come from God, for no one could perform the miraculous signs You are doing unless God was with Him." [3]Jesus answered and said to him, "I am telling you the truth: no one can see the Kingdom of God unless he is born again." [4]Nicodemus said to Him, "How can a grown man be born again? He cannot enter a second time into his mother's womb and be born, can he?" [5]Jesus replied, "I am telling you the truth: no one can enter the Kingdom of God unless he is born of water and the Spirit. [6]Flesh gives birth to flesh, and the Spirit gives birth to spirit. [7]So do not be surprised when I say, 'You must be born again.' [8]The wind blows where it pleases. You hear the sound of it, but do not know where it comes from or where it is going. So it is with everyone who is born of the Spirit." [9]"How can this be?" Nicodemus asked. [10]Jesus answered and said to him, "You are Israel's teacher, and you do not understand this? [11]I am telling you the truth: we are talking about what we know and we are sharing about what we have seen, and yet none of you is willing to accept our testimony. [12]If I told you earthly things and you do not believe; how then will you believe if I tell you heavenly things? [13]No one has ever gone up to heaven except the Son of Man, who came down from heaven. [14]Just as Moses lifted up the snake in the wilderness, so also must the Son of Man he lifted up, [15]that everyone who believes in Him may have eternal life.
[16]"For God loved the world so much that He gave His one and only Son, that whoever believes in Him should not die but have eternal life. [17]God did not send His Son into the world to condemn the world, but so that the world should be saved through Him. [18]Whoever believes in the Son is not condemned; whoever does not believe has already been condemned, because he has not believed in the name of God's one and only Son. [19]The basis of the judgment is this: the light has come into the world, but people loved darkness rather than the light because their deeds were evil. [20]Everyone who does evil hates the light and will not come to the light, because he does not want his evil deeds to be exposed. [21]But he who practices the truth will come to the light so that it may be clearly evident his works have been done through God."
[22]After this, Jesus and His disciples went out into the Judean countryside where He spent

some time with them and immersed. ²³Now John was also immersing in Aenon, near Salim, because there was plenty of water there and people were coming to be immersed. ²⁴John had not yet been thrown into prison. ²⁵An argument started between some of John's disciples and a Jew over the matter of ceremonial washing. ²⁶So they went to John and said, "Teacher, the One who was with you on the other side of the Jordan – the One you spoke about – well, He is immersing now, and everyone is going to Him." ²⁷John answered and said, "A man can receive only what is given to him from heaven. ²⁸You yourselves are my witnesses this I said, 'I am not the Christ, but I have been sent before Him.' ²⁹The bride belongs to the groom. The best man, who stands by and listens, rejoices greatly when he hears the groom's voice. This joy is mine, and now it is complete. ³⁰He must increase, but I must decrease.

³¹"He who comes from above is greater than all. He who is from the earth belongs to the earth and speaks about earthly matters. He who comes from heaven is above all. ³²He testifies to what He has seen and heard, but no one accepts His testimony. ³³He who receives His message confirms by this that God is true. ³⁴For He whom God has sent speaks God's words; because God gives Him the Spirit without measure. ³⁵The Father loves the Son, and has put everything in His control. ³⁶Whoever believes in the Son has eternal life; whoever disobeys the Son will not have life, but will remain under God's wrath."

4 Now when Jesus knew that the Pharisees had heard that He was making and immersing more disciples than John, ²although Jesus Himself was not immersing but His disciples were, ³He left Judea and went back to Galilee, ⁴and He had to go through Samaria. ⁵In Samaria, He came to a town called Sychar, which was near the field that Jacob gave to his son Joseph. ⁶Jacob's well was there, and Jesus, weary from His journey, sat down by the well. It was about the sixth hour.⁷When a Samaritan woman came to draw water, Jesus said to her, "Give me a drink." ⁸For His disciples had gone into town to buy food. ⁹The Samaritan woman said to Him, "You are a Jew and I am a Samaritan woman. How can You ask me for a drink?" For Jews did not associate with Samaritans. ¹⁰Jesus answered, "If you knew the gift of God and who it is that is saying to you, 'Give me a drink,' then you would have asked Him and He would have given you living water." ¹¹"Sir," the woman said to Him, "You have no bucket and the well is deep. Where can you get this living water? ¹²Are You greater than our father Jacob who gave us this well and drank from it himself, as did his sons and his cattle?" ¹³Jesus answered and said to her, "Everyone who drinks this water will be thirsty again, ¹⁴but whoever drinks the water I give him will never be thirsty again. For the water I give him will become in him a well of water springing up to eternal life." ¹⁵The woman said to Him, "Sir, give me this water, so I will not be thirsty and have to keep coming here to draw water." ¹⁶"Go, call your husband and come back," He said. ¹⁷The woman answered and said, "I don't have a husband." Jesus replied, "You are correct when you say that you don't have a husband. ¹⁸You have had five husbands, and the man you are with now is not your husband. You are telling Me the truth." ¹⁹"Sir," the woman said to Him, "I think You are a prophet. ²⁰Our Samaritan ancestors worshipped on this mountain, but you Jews say that Jerusalem is the place where we must worship." ²¹"Woman, believe me," Jesus replied, "the hour will come when you will worship the Father neither on this mountain nor in Jerusalem. ²²You Samaritans worship what you do not know; we worship what we do know,

for salvation is from the Jews. ²³But the hour is coming and has now come, when the true worshippers will worship the Father in spirit and truth; for they are the kind of worshippers the Father seeks. ²⁴God is spirit and those who worship Him must worship in spirit and truth." ²⁵The woman said to Him, "I know that Messiah is coming, He who is called Christ. When He comes, He will explain everything to us." ²⁶Jesus said to her. "I who speak to you am He."

²⁷At that moment Jesus' disciples returned and were surprised to find Him talking with a woman; yet no one asked, "What do You want?" or "Why are You talking with her?" ²⁸Then the woman left her water pot and went back into town and said to the people, ²⁹"Come and see the Man who told me everything I have ever done. Could He be the Messiah?" ³⁰They came out of the town and made their way toward Him. ³¹Meanwhile His disciples were urging Him, saying, "Rabbi, eat something." ³²But He said to them, "I have food to eat that you know nothing about." ³³Then His disciples said to one another, "No one brought Him food to eat, did he?" ³⁴Jesus said to them, "My food is to do the will of Him who sent Me and to accomplish His work. ³⁵Don't you have a saying, 'Four months more and then comes the harvest'? I am saying, Open your eyes and look at the fields! They are ripe for harvest. ³⁶He who reaps gets paid and gathers fruit for eternal life, so that the reaper and sower may be glad together. ³⁷Thus the saying holds true. 'One sows and another reaps.' ³⁸I sent you to reap in a field where you did not work; others worked there, and you have reaped the benefits of their labor."

³⁹Many of the Samaritans from that town believed in Him because of the woman's testimony: "He told me everything I ever did." ⁴⁰So when the Samaritans came to Him, they begged Him to stay with them, and He stayed two days. ⁴¹And many more believed in Him because of what He Himself said to them. ⁴²They said to the woman, "We no longer believe just because of what you said, now we have heard for ourselves, and we know that this One indeed is the Savior of the world."

⁴³After spending two days there, Jesus left town and went to Galilee. ⁴⁴For Jesus Himself had pointed out that a prophet is not respected in his own country. ⁴⁵So when He arrived in Galilee, the Galileans welcomed Him having seen all that He had done in Jerusalem at the Passover Feast, for they also had been there.

⁴⁶Once again He visited Cana in Galilee, where He had turned the water into wine. And there was a certain royal official, whose son was sick at Capernaum. ⁴⁷When this man heard that Jesus had come to Galilee from Judea, he went to Him and begged Him to come and heal his son, who was about to die. ⁴⁸Jesus said to him, "Unless you people see miraculous signs and wonders, you will not believe." ⁴⁹"Sir." The royal official said, "come down before my child dies." ⁵⁰Jesus replied, "Go, your son lives." The man took Jesus at His word and went. ⁵¹On his way home, his servants met him with the news that his son was living. ⁵²When he asked them what time it was that his son got better, they said to him, "Yesterday at the seventh hour the fever left him." ⁵³Then the father realized that this was the exact time at which Jesus said to him, "Your son lives." So he and all his household believed. ⁵⁴This was the second miraculous sign that Jesus performed having come from Judea to Galilee.

5 After these things there was a Jewish feast and Jesus went up to Jerusalem. ²Now there is a pool with five patios in Jerusalem by the Sheep Gate. In Hebrew it is called Bethesda. ³In the patios many people who were sick, blind, disabled and paralyzed would lay

waiting for the stirring of the water. ⁴For an angel of the Lord would come down at certain times and stir up the water. The first person in the pool after the water was stirred was healed of whatever disease he had. ⁵A man was there who had been sick for 38 years. ⁶Jesus saw him lying there and knew that He had been in that condition a long time, so He said to him, "Do you want to get well?" ⁷The sick man answered Him, "Sir, I have no one to put me in the pool when the water is stirred up. While I am trying to get in, somebody else gets there first." ⁸Jesus said to him, "Rise, pick up your mat and walk." ⁹Immediately the man was healed; he picked up his mat and walked. Now this happened on the Sabbath. ¹⁰So the Jewish authorities said to the man who had been healed, "It is the Sabbath, and you are not permitted to carry your mat." ¹¹But he replied, "The man who healed me said to me, 'Pick up your mat and walk.'" ¹²They asked him, "Who is the man who told you to pick up your mat and walk." ¹³The man who had been healed did no know who it was, for Jesus had slipped away into the crowd that was there. ¹⁴Later Jesus found him in the Temple and said to him, "Look, you are healed; stop sinning so that nothing worse will happen to you." ¹⁵The man left and told the Jewish authorities that it was Jesus who had healed him. ¹⁶For this reason the Jewish authorities persecuted Jesus, because He was doing these things on the Sabbath. ¹⁷Jesus said to them, "My Father is still at work, and I too must work." ¹⁸This remark made the Jewish authorities all the more determined to kill Him; not only was He breaking the Sabbath, but He was also calling God His own Father thus equating Himself with God.

¹⁹Therefore Jesus said to them, "I am telling you the truth: the Son can do nothing on His own; He does only what He sees His Father doing. What the Father does, the Son also does. ²⁰For the Father loves the Son and shows Him all that He Himself is doing. The Father will show the Son even greater things to do, and you will all be surprised. ²¹For just as the Father raises the dead and gives them life, in the same way the Son gives life to those He wants. ²²For the Father does not judge anyone, but He has entrusted all judgment to the Son, ²³So that all will honor the Son in that same way that they honor the Father. Whoever does not honor the Son does not honor the Father who sent Him. ²⁴I am telling you the truth: whoever hears My words and believes Him who sent Me has eternal life. He will not be condemned, but has already passed from death to life. ²⁵I am telling you the truth: the hour is coming and has now come when the dead will hear the voice of the Son of God, and those who hear it will come to life. ²⁶For just as the Father has life in Himself, in the same way, He has given to the Son also to have life in Himself. ²⁷And He has given the Son the authority to judge, because He is the Son of Man. ²⁸Do not be surprised at this. The hour is coming when all who are in their graves will hear His voice, ²⁹And will come out. Those who have done good will rise to live, and those who have done evil will rise and to be condemned.

³⁰"I can do nothing on My own initiative. I judge only as I hear, and My judgment is just, because I seek not My own will but the will of Him who sent Me. ³¹If I alone testify about Myself, My testimony is not valid. ³²There is another who testifies on My behalf, and I know that what he says about Me is true. ³³You have sent to John and he has testified to the truth. ³⁴Not hat I accept a man's testimony; but I say this that you may be saved. ³⁵John was the lamp, that was burning and shining, and you were willing for a while to enjoy his light. ³⁶But I have a testimony that is greater than John's: the works which the Father has given Me to accomplish – the very works that I do – testify that the Father has sent Me. ³⁷And the Father

who sent Me has Himself testified about Me. You have never heard His voice nor seen His form. ³⁸And you do not have His word abiding in you, for you do not believe Him whom He sent. ³⁹You study the Scriptures because you think that in them you will find eternal life, and the Scriptures testify about Me, ⁴⁰yet you are not willing to come to Me to have life. ⁴¹I do not receive glory from men. ⁴²But I know you, and I know that you do not have the love of God in you. ⁴³I have come in My Father's name and you do not receive Me; but if someone else comes in his own name, you will receive him. ⁴⁴How can you believe when you are looking for glory from one another and not the glory that comes only from God? ⁴⁵Don't think that I will accuse you before the Father; the one who accuses you is Moses, in whom you have put your hope. ⁴⁶If you believed Moses, you would believe Me; for he wrote about Me. ⁴⁷But since you do not believe what he wrote, how are you going to believe what I say?"

6 After these things, Jesus crossed to the other side of the Sea of Galilee also known as the Sea of Tiberias. ²A large crowd followed Him because they had seen the miraculous signs that He was performing on those who were sick. ³Jesus went up on the mountainside and sat down with His disciples. ⁴Now the Passover, the feast of the Jews, was near. ⁵When Jesus looked up and saw that a large crowd was coming to Him, He asked Philip, "How are we going to buy bread so that all these people may eat?" ⁶Jesus said this only to test him, for He Himself knew what He was going to do. ⁷Philip answered Him, "Two hundred denarii would not buy enough bread for each person to get a little." ⁸Another of Jesus' disciples, Andrew, Simon Peter's brother, said to Him, ⁹"There is a boy here who has five barley loaves and two fish, but how far will they go among so many?" ¹⁰Jesus said, "Have the people sit down." Now there was a lot of grass there. So the men, about 5,000 of them, sat down. ¹¹At this point, Jesus took the loaves, gave thanks to God, and distributed bread to all who were seated. He did the same with the fish. Everyone got as much as they wanted. ¹²When they were all full, Jesus said to His disciples, "Gather the pieces that are left over so that nothing goes to waste." ¹³So the disciples gathered them up and filled twelve baskets with the pieces of the five barley loaves that were left over after everyone had eaten. ¹⁴After the people saw the miraculous sign that Jesus performed, they said, "Surely this is the Prophet who is to come into the world!" ¹⁵Now Jesus, knowing that they intended to come and take Him by force to make Him king, went off again to a mountain by Himself.

¹⁶When evening came, Jesus' disciples went down to the sea, ¹⁷got into a boat and set off across the sea for Capernaum. By this time it was dark outside and Jesus had not yet come to them. ¹⁸Because a strong wind was blowing, the sea began to get rough. ¹⁹When they had rowed about three or four miles, they saw Jesus walking on the water coming toward the boat; and they were frightened. ²⁰Jesus said to them, "It is I; don't be afraid." ²¹Therefore they were willing to take Him in the boat, and immediately the boat reached the shore where they were going.

²²The next day the crowd that had stayed on the other side of the sea realized that there had been only one boat there. They knew that Jesus had not gone in the boat with His disciples, but that they had left without Him. ²³Then some boats from Tiberias came to the place where the people had eaten the bread after the Lord had given thanks. ²⁴Once the crowd realized that neither Jesus nor His disciples were there, they themselves got into the boats and

went to Capernaum in search of Jesus. ²⁵When the people found Jesus on the other side of the sea, they said to Him, "Rabbi, when did You get here?" ²⁶Jesus answered, "I am telling you the truth; you are looking for Me, not because you saw miraculous signs, but because you ate the bread and were filled. ²⁷Don't work for food that spoils; instead work for food that lasts for eternal life. This is the food the Son of Man will give you, for He is the One who bears the stamp of God the Father." ²⁸Therefore, they said to Him, "What must we do in order to do the works of God?" ²⁹Jesus answered, "This is the work of God; that you believe in the One whom He sent." ³⁰So they asked Him, "What miraculous sign then will You perform that we may see it and believe You? What will You do? ³¹Our ancestors ate manna in the wilderness, as it is written: 'He gave them bread from heaven to eat.'" ³²Jesus then said to them, "I am telling you the truth: it was not Moses who gave you bread from heaven; but it is My Father who gives you the true bread from heaven. ³³For the bread of God is He who comes down from heaven and gives life to the world." ³⁴Therefore they said to Him, "Sir, from now on give us this bread." ³⁵Jesus said to them, "I am the bread of life. He who comes to Me will never go hungry, and he who believes in Me will never be thirsty. ³⁶But as I told you, you have seen Me and still you do not believe. ³⁷All that the Father gives Me will come to Me, and whoever comes to Me, I will never turn away. ³⁸For I have come down from heaven not to do My will but to do the will of Him who sent Me. ³⁹And this is the will of Him who sent Me, that I should not lose any of all that He has given Me, but that I should raise them up at the last day. ⁴⁰For this is the will of My Father, that everyone who sees the Son and believes in Him will have eternal life; and I Myself will raise him up on the last day."

⁴¹At this point the Jews began to grumble about Him because He said, "I am the bread that came down from heaven." ⁴²They said, "Isn't this Jesus, the son of Joseph, whose father and mother we know? How can He now say, 'I came down from heaven'?" ⁴³"Stop grumbling among yourselves," Jesus answered. ⁴⁴"No one can come to Me unless the Father who sent Me draws him; and I will raise him up on the last day. ⁴⁵It is written in the Prophets: 'They will all be taught by God.' Everyone who has heard and learned from the Father comes to Me. ⁴⁶No one has seen the Father except the One who is from God; only He has seen the Father. ⁴⁷I am telling you the truth; he who believes has eternal life. ⁴⁸I am the bread of life. ⁴⁹Your ancestors ate the manna in the wilderness, and they died. ⁵⁰This is the bread that comes down from heaven, which a man may eat and not die. ⁵¹I am the living bread that came down from heaven. If anyone eats of this bread, he will live forever. This bread is My flesh, which I will give for the life of the world."

⁵²Then the Jews began to argue with one another, saying, "How can this man give us His flesh to eat?" ⁵³Jesus said to them, "I am telling you the truth: unless you eat the flesh of the Son of Man and drink His blood, you have no life in you. ⁵⁴Whoever eats My flesh and drinks My blood has eternal life, and I will raise him up on the last day. ⁵⁵For My flesh is true food, and My blood is true drink. ⁵⁶Whoever eats My flesh and drinks My blood abides in Me, and I in him. ⁵⁷Just as the living Father sent Me and I live because of the Father, in the same way, whoever feeds on Me will live because of Me. ⁵⁸This is the bread that came down from heaven. Your ancestors ate manna and died, but he who eats this bread will live forever." ⁵⁹These things he said as he taught in the synagogue in Capernaum.

⁶⁰After hearing this, many of His disciples said, "This teaching is hard to accept. Who

can?" ⁶¹But Jesus, aware that His disciples were having a tough time with this, said to them, "Does this cause you to stumble? ⁶²What if you were to see the Son of Man ascend to where He was before? ⁶³The Spirit gives life; the flesh counts for nothing. The words I have spoken to you are spirit and they are life. ⁶⁴Still there are some of you who do not believe." For Jesus knew from the start who would not believe and who would betray Him. ⁶⁵He went on to say, "This is why I told you that no one can come to Me, unless the Father has drawn him."

⁶⁶As a result of this many disciples turned away and no longer followed Him. ⁶⁷To the twelve, Jesus said, "You do not want to leave too, do you?" ⁶⁸Simon Peter answered Him, "Lord, to whom would we go? You have the words of eternal life, ⁶⁹And we believe and know that You are the Holy One of God." ⁷⁰Then Jesus replied, "I chose the twelve of you, didn't I? Yet one of you is a devil!" ⁷¹He was referring to Judas, the son of Simon Iscariot, for he, though one of the twelve, was going to betray Him.

7 After these things Jesus remained in Galilee; He would not go into Judea because the Jews were seeking to Kill Him. ²Now the Jewish Feast of Tabernacles was near, ³so Jesus' brothers said to Him, "Leave here and go to Judea, so that Your disciples may see the miracles You are performing. ⁴No one who wants publicity does anything in secret. Since You are doing these things, show Yourself to the world." ⁵For not even His brothers believed in Him. ⁶Therefore Jesus said to them, "My time has not yet come; but your time is always right. ⁷The world cannot hate you, but it hates Me, because I testify that what it does is evil. ⁸Go up to the feast yourselves. I'm not going up to the feast yet, because My time has not yet fully come." ⁹Having said these things to them, Jesus stayed in Galilee.

¹⁰After His brother's had gone up to the feast, then He Himself also went up – not publicly, but in secret. ¹¹Now at the feast, the Jews were looking for Him and asking, "Where is He?" ¹²Among the crowds there was mixed feelings about Jesus; some were saying, "He is a good man." Others said, "No, He is deceiving people." ¹³Yet no one would say anything publicly about Him for fear of the Jews.

¹⁴About halfway through the feast, Jesus went up into the temple and began to teach. ¹⁵The Jews were amazed and asked, "How does this man know so much when He has never been educated?" ¹⁶Therefore Jesus replied, "My teaching is not My own, but it comes from God, who sent Me. ¹⁷Whoever is willing to do God's will, he will know whether My teaching comes from God or whether I speak on My own authority. ¹⁸He who speaks on his own authority is trying to gain glory for himself, but He who wants glory for the one who sent Him is honest, and there is nothing false in Him. ¹⁹Moses gave you the Law, didn't he? Yet not one of you obeys the Law. Why are you seeking to kill Me?" ²⁰"You have a demon in you!" The crowd answered. "Who is seeking to kill You?" ²¹Jesus said to them, "I perform one miracle and you are all astonished. ²²Moses gave you circumcision though actually it did not come from Moses but from the patriarchs and so you circumcise a child on the Sabbath. ²³Now if a child can be circumcised on the Sabbath so that the Law of Moses may not be broken, why are you angry with Me for healing a man on the Sabbath? ²⁴Stop judging by external standards, and start judging by true standards."

²⁵At this point, some of the people in Jerusalem were saying, "Isn't this the man they are seeking to kill? ²⁶And here He is, speaking publicly, and they are not saying anything to Him.

Have the rulers really concluded that He is the Christ? ²⁷But we know where this man is from; when the Christ comes, no one will know where He is from." ²⁸Then Jesus, still teaching in the temple courts, cried out, saying, "Yes, you know Me and you know where I am from. I am not here on My own, but He who sent Me is true. You do not know Him, ²⁹But I know Him because I am from Him and He sent Me." ³⁰So they sought to seize Him, but no one laid a hand on Him, because His hour had not yet come. ³¹But many in the crowd put their faith in Him, saying, "When the Christ comes, He will not perform more miraculous signs than those which this man has, will He?"

³²The Pharisees heard the crowd muttering these things about Him. Then the chief priests and Pharisees sent temple guards to arrest Him. ³³Therefore Jesus said, "I will be with you for a little while longer, then I will go away to Him who sent Me. ³⁴You will look for Me, but you will not find Me, because where I am, you cannot come." ³⁵The Jews said to one another, "Where does this man intend to go that we cannot find Him? Will He go where our people live scattered among the Greeks, and teach the Greeks? ³⁶What did He mean when He said, 'You will look for Me, but you will not find Me, because where I am, you cannot come'?"

³⁷On the last and greatest day of the feast, Jesus stood and cried out, saying, "If anyone is thirsty, let him come to Me and drink. ³⁸Whoever believes in Me, as the Scripture has said, 'From within him will flow streams of living water.'" ³⁹By this He meant the Spirit, whom those who believed in Him were to receive. For the Spirit had not yet been given, since Jesus had not yet been glorified. ⁴⁰When they heard these words, some of the people were saying, "This must be the Prophet!" ⁴¹Others said, "This is the Christ!" But some asked, "The Christ isn't supposed to come from Galilee, is He? ⁴²Doesn't the Scripture say that the Christ will be a descendant of David and will come from Bethlehem, the town where David lived?" ⁴³So there was division in the crowd because of Jesus. ⁴⁴And some of them wanted to arrest Him, but no one laid a hand on Him.

⁴⁵Then the officers returned to the chief priests and Pharisees, who said to them, "Why didn't you bring Him?" ⁴⁶The officers answered, "No one has ever spoken like this man." ⁴⁷"Have you been led astray, too?" The Pharisees asked pointedly. ⁴⁸"No one of the rulers or Pharisees has chosen to believe in Him, has he? ⁴⁹No! As for this crowd that does not know the Law – there is a curse on them." ⁵⁰Nicodemus the man who came to Jesus earlier, who was one of them said to them, ⁵¹"Does our Law condemn anyone without first hearing from him to find out what he is doing?" ⁵²"Are you from Galilee, too?" They replied. "Search the Scriptures and you will see that no prophet comes from Galilee." ⁵³Then everyone went home.

8 But Jesus went to the Mount of Olives. ²Early the next morning Jesus returned to the temple. The people gathered around Him, and He sat down and began to teach them. ³The scribes and the Pharisees brought a woman who had been caught committing adultery and made her stand in front of everyone. ⁴They said to Him, "Teacher, this woman was caught in the act of adultery. ⁵In the Law, Moses commanded that such a woman must be stoned to death. So what do You say?" ⁶They said this to test Him in order that they might have grounds to bring a charge against Him. But Jesus bent down and wrote on the ground with His finger. ⁷When they kept on questioning Him, He straightened up and said to them, "If any one of you is without sin, let him be the first to throw a stone at her." ⁸Then again, He bent down and

wrote on the ground. ⁹At this point, those who heard it began to leave one by one, the older ones first, until only Jesus was left with the woman still standing there. ¹⁰Jesus straightened up and asked her, "Woman, where are they? Has no one condemned you?" ¹¹"No one, sir." She replied. Then Jesus said, "Neither do I condemn you. Go now and do not sin again."

¹²Again Jesus spoke to the Pharisees, saying, "I am the light of the world. Whoever follows Me will not walk in darkness, but will have the light of life." ¹³The Pharisees therefore said to Him, "Now You are testifying about Yourself. Your witness is not valid." ¹⁴Jesus answered and said to them, "Even if I testify on My own behalf, My witness is true, because I know where I came from and where I am going. But you have no idea where I came from or where I am going. ¹⁵You judge according to the flesh; I am not judging anyone. ¹⁶But even if I do judge, My judgment is true, for I am not alone, the Father who sent Me is with Me. ¹⁷It is written in your Law that the testimony of two men is true. ¹⁸I testify on My own behalf and My other witness is the Father, who sent Me." ¹⁹"Where is Your Father?" They asked Him. "You do not know Me or My Father." Jesus replied. "If you knew Me, you would know My Father also." ²⁰He spoke these words while teaching in the temple area near the place where the offerings were put. Yet no one seized Him because His hour had not yet come. ²¹Again Jesus said to them, "I am not going away, and you will look for Me, and die in your sin. Where I am going, you cannot come." ²²Then the Jews said, "He says that we cannot go where He is going. Does this mean that He will kill Himself?" ²³And Jesus said to them, "You are from below; I am from above. You are of this world; I am not of this world. ²⁴Now I told you that you would die in your sins, because unless you believe that I am, you will die in your sins." ²⁵They asked Him. "Who are You, anyway?" Jesus replied to them, "Who have I claimed to be from the beginning? ²⁶I have many things to say in judgment of you. But He who sent Me is true, and what I have heard from Him, I tell the world." ²⁷They did not realize that He was talking to them about the Father. ²⁸So Jesus said, "When you lift up the Son of Man, then you will know that I am and that I do nothing on My own, but speak these things as the Father taught Me. ²⁹And He who sent Me in with Me; He has not left Me alone, for I always do what is pleasing to Him." ³⁰As He shared these things, many came to believe in Him.

³¹To the Jews who had chosen to believe in Him, Jesus then said, "If you abide in My word, you are truly My disciples; ³²And you will know the truth, and the truth will set you free." ³³They answered Him, "We are Abraham's descendants, and have never been slaves to anyone. So, how can you say that we will be set free?" ³⁴Jesus replied, "I am telling you the truth; everyone who sins is a slave to sin. ³⁵Now a slave has no permanent place in a family, but a son belongs to it forever. ³⁶Even so, if the Son sets you free, you will be free indeed. ³⁷I know that you are Abraham's descendants; yet you are ready to kill Me, because My word has no place in you. ³⁸I speak about what I have seen with My Father, and you do what you have heard from your father." ³⁹They answered and said to Him, "Abraham is your father." Jesus replied. "If you were Abraham's children, you would do what Abraham did. ⁴⁰But as it is, you are determined to kill Me, a man who has told you the truth, which I heard from God. This is not what Abraham did! ⁴¹You are doing the things your father did." Then they protested. "We are not illegitimate children; we have one Father, God Himself." ⁴²Jesus responded, "If God were your Father, you would love Me, because I came from God. I have not come on My own

initiative, but He sent Me. ⁴³Why don't you understand what I am saying? It is because you cannot hear My message. ⁴⁴You are of your father the devil and you want to do your father's desires. He was a murderer from the beginning, and does not stand for truth, because there is no truth in him. When he lies, he is just doing what comes natural to him, for he is a liar and the father of lies. ⁴⁵Yet because I am telling the truth, you do not believe Me. ⁴⁶Can any of you prove that I am guilty of sin? If I am telling the truth, why don't you believe Me? ⁴⁷He who is of God hears the words of God. The reason you do not hear is because you are not of God."
⁴⁸The Jews retorted, "Aren't we right in saying that You are a Samaritan and have a demon?" ⁴⁹"I do not have a demon," Jesus answered, "but I honor My Father and you dishonor Me. ⁵⁰I am not trying to gain glory for Myself; but there is One who seeks it an He will be the judge. ⁵¹I am telling you the truth; if anyone obeys My teaching, he will never see death."
⁵²With this, the Jews exclaimed, "Now we know that You have a demon! Abraham died and so did the Prophets, yet You say that if anyone obeys Your teaching, he will never taste death. ⁵³Are You greater than our father Abraham? He died, and so did the Prophets. Who do You claim to be?" ⁵⁴Jesus answered, "If I glorify Myself, My glory is nothing. My Father, whom you claim as your God, glorifies Me. ⁵⁵Though you have not come to know Him, I know Him. If I said I did not know Him, I would b a liar like you; but I do know Him, and obey His teaching. ⁵⁶Your father Abraham rejoiced to see My day; he saw it and was glad." ⁵⁷The Jews therefore said to Him, "You are not yet fifty years old, and have You seen Abraham?" ⁵⁸Jesus replied, "I am telling you the truth; before Abraham was born, I am." ⁵⁹At this point, they picked up stones to stone Him; but Jesus hid Himself and slipped away from the temple.

9 As He walked by, Jesus saw a man blind from birth. ²And His disciples asked Him, "Rabbi, who sinned, this man or his parents that he was born blind?" ³Jesus answered, "Neither this man nor his parents sinned, but he is blind in order that the works of God might be displayed in him. ⁴As long as it is day, we must do the words of Him who sent Me. Night is coming, when no one can work. ⁵While I am in the world, I am the light of the world." ⁶After Jesus said this, He spat on the ground, made some mud with the spittle, and put it on the man's eyes, ⁷and said to him, "Go, wash in the pool of Siloam" which is translated Sent. So he went away and washed and came back seeing. ⁸Then his neighbors and those who had seen him before as a beggar, asked, "Isn't this the man who used to sit and beg?" ⁹Some said, "Yes." Others said, "No, but he looks like him." He kept saying, "I am the man." ¹⁰So they asked him, "How then were your eyes opened?" ¹¹He answered, "The man who is called Jesus made some mud, and put it on my eyes, and said to me, 'Go to Siloam, and wash'. So I went away and washed, and then I could see. ¹²"Where is He?" they asked. "I do not know." he replied.
¹³Then the man who had been blind was brought before the Pharisees. ¹⁴Now the day that Jesus made the mud and opened his eyes was a Sabbath. ¹⁵The Pharisees then asked him again how he had received his sight. And he said to them, "He put mud on my eyes, I washed, and now I can see." ¹⁶Therefore, some of the Pharisees were saying, "This man is not from God, because He does not observe the Sabbath law." But others were saying, "How can a man who is a sinner perform such miraculous signs?" And there was a division among them. ¹⁷So they turned to the blind man once more and asked, "What do you say about Him, since He opened your eyes?" The man replied, "He is a prophet." ¹⁸The Jews still did not believe that he had

been blind and had received his sight, until they called his parents, ¹⁹And questioned them, saying, "Is this your son, who you say was born blind? How is it that he now can see?" ²⁰"We know this is our son and that he was born blind," the parents answered. ²¹"But how he now can see, or who opened his eyes, we do not know. Ask him; he is old enough and can speak for himself. ²²His parents said this for fear of the Jews; because the Jews had already agreed that anyone who confessed that Jesus was the Christ would be thrown out of the synagogue. ²³This is the reason his parents said, "He is old enough; ask him."

²⁴So a second time they summoned the man who had been blind, and said to him, "Give glory to God. We know that this man is a sinner." ²⁵"Whether He is a sinner or not, I do not know." The man replied. "One thing I do know: I was blind, but now I see!" ²⁶Then they asked him, "What did He do to you? How did He open your eyes?" ²⁷He answered them, "I told you already, and you did not listen; why do you want to hear it again? Do you want to become His disciples, too?" ²⁸Then they hurled insults at him and said, "You are His disciple, but we are disciples of Moses! ²⁹We know that God spoke to Moses; but as for this Man, we don't even know where He is from." ³⁰The man answered, "Now this is amazing: you do not know where He is from, and yet He opened my eyes. ³¹We know that God does not hear sinners; but if anyone is God-fearing and does His will, He hears him. ³²Never, since the beginning of time, has it been heard that anyone opened the eyes of a man born blind. ³³If this Man were not from God, He could do nothing." ³⁴To this they replied, "You were born entirely in sins, and you are trying to teach us?" And they threw him out of the synagogue.

³⁵Jesus heard that they had thrown him out; and when He found him, He said, "Do you believe in the Son of Man?" ³⁶The man answered and said, "And who is He, Lord, that I may believe in Him?" ³⁷Jesus said to him, "You have seen Him, and He is the One who is speaking with you." ³⁸Then the man said, "Lord, I believe." And he worshipped Him. ³⁹And Jesus said, "For judgment I came into this world, so that the blind may see and those who see may become blind." ⁴⁰Some Pharisees who were with Him, heard these things, and said to Him, "We are not blind too, are we?" ⁴¹Jesus said to them, "If you were blind you would have no sin; but since you say that you can see, your sin remains."

10 Jesus said, "I am telling you the truth: the man who does not enter the sheep pen by the gate, but climbs in some other way, is a thief and a robber. ²The man who enters by the gate is the shepherd of the sheep. ³The watchman opens the gate for him, and the sheep hear his voice. He calls his own sheep by name and leads them out. ⁴When he has brought them out, he goes ahead of them, and they follow him because they know his voice. ⁵They will not follow a stranger; instead, they will run away from him, because they do not recognize his voice." ⁶Jesus told them this parable, but they did not understand what He was saying to them.

⁷So Jesus again said to them, "I am telling you the truth: I am the gate for the sheep. ⁸All who came before Me are thieves and robbers, but the sheep did not listen to them. ⁹I am the gate. Whoever enters through Me will be saved; he will come in and go out and find pasture. ¹⁰The thief comes only to steal, kill, and destroy; I have come that they might have life, and have it abundantly! ¹¹I am the Good Shepherd; the Good Shepherd lays down His life for the sheep. ¹²The hired hand is not the shepherd who owns the sheep. When he sees the wolf

coming, he abandons the sheep and runs away, and the wolf snatches and scatters them. ¹³Because he is a hired hand, he is not concerned about the sheep. ¹⁴I am the good shepherd; I know My sheep and My sheep know Me – ¹⁵Just as the Father knows Me and I know the Father – and I lay down My life for My sheep. ¹⁶And I have other sheep that are not of this fold. I must bring them also, and they too will hear My voice. There will be one flock and one Shepherd. ¹⁷For this reason the Father loves Me, because I lay down My life only to take it up again. ¹⁸No one takes it from Me, but I lay it down on My own initiative. I have authority to lay it down, and I have authority to take it up again. This commandment I received from My Father."

¹⁹Again, there was division among the Jews, because of these statements. ²⁰And many of them said, "He has a demon and is insane! Why listen to Him?" ²¹Others said, "These are not the sayings of a man possessed by a demon. Can a demon open the eyes of the blind?"

²²At that time the Feast of the Dedication took place in Jerusalem. ²³It was winter, and Jesus was walking in Solomon's Patio in the Temple, ²⁴When the people gathered around Him, saying, "How long will You keep us in suspense? If You are the Christ, tell us plainly." ²⁵Jesus answered them, "I have already told you and you do not believe. The works that I do in My Father's name speak for Me. ²⁶But you do not believe, because you are not My sheep. ²⁷My sheep hear My voice. I know them, and they follow Me, ²⁸and I give eternal life to them, and they will never die. No one can snatch them out of My hand. ²⁹My Father, who has given them to Me, is greater than all; no one can snatch them out of the Father's hand. ³⁰I and the Father are one."

31Again the Jews picked up stones to stone Him. 32Jesus answered them, "I have shown you many good works from the Father. For which of these do you want to stone Me?" ³³"We do not want to stone You for a good work," the Jews replied, "but for blasphemy, because You, a mere man, claim to be God." ³⁴Jesus answered them, "Isn't it written in your Law, 'I said, you are gods'? ³⁵If He called them gods, to whom the Word of God came – and the Scriptures cannot be broken – ³⁶do you say of Him whom the Father set apart as His very own and sent into the world, 'You are blaspheming,' because I said, 'I am the Son of God'? ³⁷If I do not do the works of My Father, do not believe Me; ³⁸but if I do them, though you do not believe Me, believe the works, that you may know and understand that the Father is in Me and I in the Father." ³⁹Again they tried to seize Him, and He eluded their grasp.

⁴⁰Then Jesus went back across the Jordan to the place where John was first immersing and He stayed there, ⁴¹And many people came to Him. They said, "Though John performed no miraculous signs, everything John said about this man was true." ⁴²And many believed in Jesus there.

11 Now a certain man named Lazarus was sick. He was from Bethany, the village of Mary and her sister Martha. ²This was the Mary who anointed the Lord with perfume and wiped His feet with her hair. It was her brother Lazarus who was sick. ³So the sisters sent word to Jesus, saying, "Lord, he whom You love is sick" ⁴But when Jesus heard it, He said, "This sickness is not unto death, but for the glory of God, that the Son of God may be glorified by it." ⁵Now Jesus loved Martha, and her sister, and Lazarus. ⁶Yet when He heard that Lazarus was sick, He stayed in the place where he was for two more days. ⁷The He said to

His disciples, "Let us go back to Judea." [8]"But Rabbi," they said, "the Jews just tried to stone you, and You want to go back there again?" [9]Jesus answered, "Are there not twelve hours of daylight? If anyone walks in the day, he does not stumble, because he sees the light of this world. [10]But if anyone walks in the night, he stumbles, because the light is not in him." [11]After He had said this, He went on to tell them, "Our friend Lazarus has fallen asleep; but I am going there to wake him up." [12]His disciples replied, "Lord, if he is just sleeping, he will get better." [13]Now Jesus had been speaking of His death, but His disciples thought He meant literal sleep. [14]So then He told them plainly, "Lazarus is dead, [15]and for your sakes I am glad I was not there, so that you may believe; but let us go to him." [16]Then Thomas, who is called the Twin, said to his fellow disciples, "Let us also go that we may die with Him." [17]Upon His arrival, Jesus found that Lazarus had already been in the tomb for four days. [18]Now Bethany was near Jerusalem, less than two miles away, [19]and many Jews had come to Mary and Martha to comfort them in the loss of their brother. [20]When Martha heard that Jesus was coming, she went out to meet Him, but Mary stayed at home. [21]"Lord," Martha said to Jesus, "If You would have been here, my brother would not have died. [22]But I know that even now God will give You whatever you ask." [23]Jesus said to her, "Your brother will rise again." [24]Martha answered, "I know he will rise again in the resurrection on the last day." [25]Jesus said to her, "I am the resurrection and the life. He who believes in Me will live, even though he dies; [26]and whoever lives and believes in Me will never die. Do you believe this?" [27]"Yes, Lord." She said to Him, "I believe that You are the Christ, the Son of God, who comes into the world." [28]After Martha said this, she pulled Mary her sister aside, and said, "The Teacher is here and He is calling for you." [29]When Mary heard this, she got up quickly and went to Him.

[30]Now Jesus had not yet entered the village, but was still at the place where Martha had met Him. [31]When the Jews who had been in the house with Mary, comforting her, noticed how quickly she got up and went out, they followed her, supposing that she was going to the tomb to mourn there. [32]So when Mary came to the place where Jesus was and saw Him, she fell at His feet, saying to Him, "Lord, if You had been here, my brother would not have died."
[33]When Jesus saw her weeping, and the Jews who had come along with her weeping too, He was deeply moved in spirit, and He Himself was troubled. [34]"Where have you laid him?" Jesus asked. "Come and see, Lord." They replied. [35]Jesus wept. [36]And so the Jews were saying, "See how much He loved him." [37]But some of them said, "Could not He who opened the eyes of the blind man have kept this man from dying?" [38]Jesus therefore again being deeply moved within, came to the tomb. It was a cave and stone was covering the entrance. 39"Remove the stone." Jesus said. "But Lord," said Martha, the sister of the deceased, "by this time he will smell for he has been there four days." [40]Jesus said to her, "Did I not say to you, if you believe, you will see the glory of God?" [41]So they removed the stone, and Jesus looked up and said, "Father, I thank You that You have heard Me, [42]and I know that You always hear Me. I said this for the benefit of the people standing here – that they may believe that You sent Me. [43]Therefore many of the Jews who had come to Mary and seen what Jesus had done, believed in Him. [44]The dead man came forth, bound hand and foot with wrappings, and a cloth was around his face. Jesus said to them, "Unbind him, and let him go."

[45]Therefore many of the Jews who had come to Mary and seen what Jesus had done, believed in Him. [46]But some of them went to the Pharisees and told them what Jesus had done.

⁴⁷So the chief priests and the Pharisees convened the Council and said, "What should we do? This man is performing many miraculous signs. ⁴⁸If we let Him go on like this, everyone will believe in Him, and then the Romans will come and take away both our place and our nation." ⁴⁹Then one of them, named Caiaphas, who was high priest that year, spoke up, "You know nothing at all! ⁵⁰Don't you realize that it is better for you that one man die for the people than that the whole nation die." ⁵¹And did not say this on his own initiative; but as high priest that year, He prophesied that Jesus was going to die for the nation, ⁵²And not only for that nation, but also for the children of God that are scattered abroad – to gather them together as one. ⁵³So from that day on, they plotted together to kill Him.

⁵⁴Therefore, Jesus no longer moved about publicly among the Jews. Instead, He withdrew to a region near the wilderness, to a village called Ephraim; and He stayed there with the disciples. ⁵⁵Now the Passover of the Jews was near, so many went up from the country to Jerusalem before the Passover, to purify themselves. ⁵⁶Therefore, they were looking for Jesus and saying to one another, as they stood in the temple, "What do you think? Will He not come to the feast at all?" ⁵⁷Now the chief priests and the Pharisees had given orders that if anyone found out where Jesus was, he should report it so that they might arrest Him.

12 Six days before the Passover, Jesus came to Bethany where Lazarus was, whom He had raised from the dead. ²There they made supper for Him. Martha was serving, and Lazarus was among those sitting with Him. ³Then Mary took a pound of pure nard, an expensive perfume, and anointed the feet of Jesus and wiped His feet with her hair. And the house was filled with the fragrance of the perfume. ⁴But one of His disciples, Judas Iscariot, who was going to betray Him, said, ⁵"Why wasn't this perfume sold for 300 denarii and the money given to the poor?" ⁶Now he said this not because he cared about the poor, but because he was a thief. As keeper of the moneybox, he used to take from what was put into it. ⁷Jesus therefore said, "Leave her alone! Let her keep what she has for the day of My burial. ⁸For you will always have the poor among you, but you will not always have Me."
⁹Meanwhile, a large crowd of Jews discovered that He was there; and they came, not for Jesus' sake only, but also to see Lazarus, whom He had raised from the dead. ¹⁰But the chief priests conspired to kill Lazarus as well, ¹¹because on account of him, many of the Jews were going away and believing in Jesus.

¹²On the next day, when the large crowd that had come to the feast heard that Jesus was on His way to Jerusalem, ¹³They took palm branches and went out to meet Him, shouting, "Hosanna, blessed is He who comes in the name of the Lord! He is the King of Israel!" ¹⁴Then Jesus, finding a young donkey, sat on it; as it is written, ¹⁵"Don't be afraid, O daughter of Zion! Look here, your King is coming, seated on a donkey's colt." ¹⁶At first His disciples did not understand all this. Only after Jesus was glorified did they realize that these things had been written about Him and that they had done these things to Him. ¹⁷And so the crowd that was with Jesus, when He called Lazarus out of the tomb and raised him from the dead, continued to tell others about Him. ¹⁸For this reason the crowd went to meet Him, because they heard that He had performed this miraculous sign. ¹⁹The Pharisees, at this point, said to one another, "You see, we are not succeeding at all. Look the world is following Jesus."

²⁰Now there were certain Greeks among those who went up to worship at the feast.

[21]They came to Philip, who was from Bethsaida in Galilee, and asked him, saying, "Sir, we wish to see Jesus." [22]Philip went and told Andrew. Andrew and Philip went and told Jesus. [23]Jesus answered them, saying, "The hour has come for the Son of Man to be glorified. [24]I am telling you the truth: unless a grain of wheat goes into the ground and dies, it remains only a single seed; but if it dies, it bears much fruit. [25]He who loves his life will lose it, and he who hates his life in this world will keep it for eternal life. [26]If anyone serves Me, let him follow Me; and where I am, My servant also will be. If anyone serves Me, the Father will honor him.

[27]"Now My soul is troubled, and what will I say, 'Father, save Me from this hour'? No, it was for this purpose I came to this hour. [28]Father, glorify Thy name." Then a voice came from heaven, "I have glorified it, and will glorify it again." [29]The crowd that was there and heard it, said that it had thundered. Others said, "An angel has spoken to Him." [30]Jesus answered and said, "This voice has not come for My sake, but for yours. [31]Now judgment is upon this world; now the ruler of this world will be cast out. [32]And when I am lifted up from the earth, I will draw all men to Myself." [33]He was saying this to indicate the kind of death by which He was going to die. [34]The crowd therefore answered Him, "We have heard from the Law that the Christ is to remain forever, so how can you say, 'The Son of Man must be lifted up'? Who is the Son of Man?" [35]Then Jesus told them, "For a little while longer the light is among you. Walk while you have the light, that darkness may not overtake you; he who walks in the darkness does not know where he is going. [36]While you have the light, believe in the light, in order that you may become sons of the light." When he had finished speaking, Jesus left and hid Himself from them. [37]Even though He had performed many miraculous signs before them, they were not believing in Him. [38]This was to fulfill the Word of Isaiah the prophet: "Lord, who has believed our message? And to whom has the Lord revealed His power?" [39]For this reason they could not believe, because Isaiah said again, [40]"God has blinded their eyes and hardened their hearts; lest they see with their eyes, and understand with their hearts, and turn to me to heal them." [41]Isaiah said these things because he saw Jesus' glory and spoke about Him. [42]Nevertheless many of the rulers even believed in Him, but because of the Pharisees they were not confessing their faith for fear they would be thrown out of the synagogue. [43]They loved the approval of men rather than the approval of God.

[44]Then Jesus cried out, "He who believes in Me, believes not in Me, but in Him who sent Me. [45]And he who sees Me, sees Him who sent Me. [46]I have come into the world as a light, so that everyone who believes in Me will not remain in darkness. [47]And if anyone hears My message and does not obey it, I do not judge him; for I did not come to condemn the world, but to save the world. [48]He who rejects Me, and does not accept My message, has one who will judge him; the Word I have spoken is what will condemn him on the last day. [49]For I did not speak on My own initiative, but the Father Himself who sent Me commanded Me what to say and how to say it. [50]And I know that His commandment is eternal life; therefore, whatever I say is just what the Father has told Me to say."

13 It was just before the Passover Feast. Jesus knew that the hour had come for Him to leave this world and go to the Father. Having loved His own who were in the world, He now showed them His love to the fullest extent. [2]By the time they were having supper, the devil had already put it into the heart of Judas Iscariot, son of Simon, to betray

Jesus. ³Knowing that the Father had put all things under His power, and that He had come from God and was returning to God, ⁴Jesus got up from the table, took off His garments, and wrapped a towel around His waist. ⁵Then He poured water into a basin and began to wash His disciples' feet, drying them with the towel that was wrapped around Him. ⁶He came to Simon Peter, who said to Him, "Lord, you're going to wash my feet?" ⁷Jesus answered and said to him, "You don't realize what I am doing now, but you will understand later." ⁸Peter exclaimed, "You will never wash my feet!" Jesus replied, "If I don't wash you, you have no part with Me." ⁹Simon Peter said to Him, "Lord, do not wash only me feet, then! Wash my hands and head, too!" ¹⁰Jesus said to him, "He who has had a bath is completely clean and needs only to wash his feet; and you are clean, though not all of you." ¹¹For He knew the one who was going to betray Him, and that is why He said, "Not all of you are clean."

¹²When Jesus had finished washing their feet, He put on His garments, and sat back down. He asked them, "Do you understand what I have done for you? ¹³You call Me 'Teacher' and 'Lord,' and you are right, for so I am. ¹⁴If I, your Lord and Teacher, have washed your feet, you also ought to wash one another's feet. ¹⁵I have set an example for you, so that you will do just what I have done for you. ¹⁶I am telling you the truth: a servant is not greater than his master; neither is one who is sent greater than the one who sent him. ¹⁷Now that you know these things, you will be blessed if you do them. ¹⁸I am not referring to all of you. I know the ones I have chosen, but this is to fulfill the Scripture: 'He who eats My bread has lifted up his heel against Me.' ¹⁹I am telling you this now, before it happens, so that when it does happen you will believe that I am. ²⁰I am telling you the truth: whoever receives anyone I send receives Me; and he who receives Me receives Him who sent Me."

²¹After Jesus had said this, He was troubled in spirit and testified, saying, "I am telling you the truth: one of you is going to betray Me." ²²The disciples looked at one another, at a loss to know of whom He spoke. ²³One of them, the disciple whom Jesus loved, was sitting close to Him. ²⁴So Simon Peter motioned to him, and said to him, "Ask Him who it is." ²⁵Leaning back against Jesus he asked, "Lord who is it?" ²⁶Jesus answered, "It is the one to whom I give this piece of bread after I have dipped it." So when He had dipped the bread, He gave it to Judas, son of Simon Iscariot. ²⁷As soon as Judas took the bread, Satan entered into him. Jesus therefore said to him, "What you are going to do, do quickly." ²⁸But none of the disciples sitting there understood why He had said this to him. ²⁹Because Judas kept the moneybox, some thought that Jesus was telling him to buy what was needed for the feast, or that he should give something to the poor. ³⁰As soon as Judas had taken the bread, he left immediately; and it was night.

³¹After Judas had left, Jesus said, "Now is the Son of Man glorified, and God is glorified in Him; ³²If God is glorified in Him, God will also glorify the Son in Himself, and will glorify Him immediately. ³³My children, I am with you a little while longer. You will look for Me; and just as I told the Jews, so I tell you now: where I am going, you cannot come. ³⁴A new commandment I give you: love one another. As I have loved you, so you must love one another. ³⁵By this all men will know that you are My disciples, if you love one another."

³⁶Simon Peter asked Him, "Lord, where are You going?" Jesus answered, "Where I am going, you cannot follow Me now, but you will follow Me later." ³⁷Peter said to Him, "Lord, why can't I follow You right now? I will lay down my life for You!" ³⁸Jesus replied, "Will

you lay down your life for Me? I am telling you the truth: before the cock crows, you will deny Me three times."

**14** "Don't let your hearts be troubled. Trust in God, trust also in Me. ²There are many rooms in My Father's house, and I am going to prepare a place for you. I would not tell you this, if it were not so. ³After I go and prepare a place for you, I will come again and take you to be with Me that you also may be where I am. ⁴And you know the way to where I am going."

⁵Thomas said to Him, "Lord, we don't know where You are going, so how can we know the way?" ⁶Jesus said to him, "I am the way, and the truth, and the life; no one comes to the Father except through Me." ⁷If you have come to know Me, you have come to know My Father also; from now on, you know Him and have seen Him."

⁸Philip said, "Lord, show us the Father and that will be enough for us." ⁹Jesus answered, "I have been with you a long time, and yet you have not come to know Me, Philip? He who has seen Me has seen the Father. So how can you say, 'Show us the Father'? ¹⁰Don't you believe that I am in the Father, and that the Father is in Me? The words that I say to you, I do not speak on My own initiative, but the Father, who is abiding in Me, is doing His work. ¹¹Believe Me when I say that I am in the Father, and the Father is in Me; otherwise, believe on account of the works themselves. ¹²I am telling you the truth: he who believes in Me will also do the works that I do. He will do even greater things than these, because I am going to the Father. ¹³And I will do whatever you ask in My name, so that the Son may bring glory to the Father. ¹⁴If you ask Me for anything in My name, I will do it. ¹⁵If you love Me, you will obey My commandments. ¹⁶And I will ask the Father, and He will give you another Counselor, that He may be with you forever – ¹⁷The Spirit of Truth, whom the world cannot receive, because it neither sees Him nor knows Him. But you know Him, because He abides with you and will be in you. ¹⁸I will not leave you as orphans: I will come to you. ¹⁹In a little while, the world will not see Me anymore, but you will see Me. Because I live, you also will live. ²⁰On that day you will realize that I am in My Father, and you are in Me, and I am in you. ²¹He who has My commandments and obeys them; he is the one who loves Me. He who loves Me will be loved by My Father, and I will love him and make Myself known to Him."

²²Then Judas not Judas Iscariot said, "Lord, how is it that you will make Yourself known to us, and not to the world?" ²³Jesus answered and said to him, "If anyone loves Me, he will obey My word. My Father will love him, and We will come to him and make Our home with him. ²⁴He who does not love Me does not obey My teaching. The word which you hear is not Mine but the Father's who sent Me.

²⁵I have shared these things with you while abiding with you. ²⁶But the Counselor, the Holy Spirit, whom the Father will send in My name, He will teach you all things, and remind you of all that I said to you. ²⁷Peace I leave with you; My peace I give to you; not as the world gives, do I give to you. Don't let your hearts be troubled, and don't be afraid. ²⁸You heard Me say to you, 'I am going away, and I will come back to you.' If you loved Me, you would be glad that I am going to the Father, for He is greater than I. ²⁹I have told you this now, before it happens, so that when it does happen you will believe. ³⁰I will not speak with you much longer, for the ruler of this world is coming. He has no power over Me, ³¹but that the world

may know that I love the Father and I do as the Father has commanded Me. Rise, let us go from here."

**15** "I am the true vine, and My Father is the gardener. ²Every branch in Me that does not bear fruit, He cuts off; and every branch that bears fruit, He prunes, so that it may bear even more fruit. ³You are already pruned because of the Word I have spoken to you. ⁴Abide in Me, and I will abide in you. As the branch cannot bear fruit by itself, unless it abides in the vine, so also you cannot bear fruit unless you abide in Me. ⁵I am the vine; you are the branches. He who abides in Me, and I in him, will bear much fruit; for apart from Me you can do nothing. ⁶If anyone does not abide in Me, He is like the branch that is thrown away and withers; such branches are picked up, thrown into the fire and burned. ⁷If you abide in Me and My words abide in you, ask whatever you wish, and it will be done for you. ⁸By this My Father is glorified, that you bear much fruit, showing yourselves to be My disciples. ⁹Just as the Father has loved Me, so have I loved you. Now abide in My love. ¹⁰If you obey My commandments, you will abide in My love; just as I have obeyed My Father's commandments, and abide in His love. ¹¹I have shared these things with you so that My joy may be in you and your joy may be complete.

¹²"This is My commandment; love one another, as I have loved you. ¹³Greater love has no one than this, that one lay down his life for his friends. ¹⁴You are My friends, if you do what I command. ¹⁵I no longer call you servants, because a servant does not know what his master is doing. Instead, I have called you friends, for everything that I have heard from My Father, I have made known to you. ¹⁶You did not choose Me, but I chose you and appointed you, that you should go and bear fruit – fruit that will endure. Then whatever you ask of the Father in My name, He will give it to you. ¹⁷This I command you: love one another.

¹⁸"If the world hates you, know that it hated Me before you. ¹⁹If you belonged to the world, it would love you as its own. But I chose you out of the world, and you do not belong to it; that is why the world hates you. ²⁰Remember what I told you: 'A servant is not greater than his master.' If they persecuted Me, they will persecute you also. If they obeyed My Word, they will obey yours also. ²¹They will do all these things to you because of Me, for they do not know the One who sent Me. ²²If I had not come and spoken to them, they would not have guilt. Now, however, they have no excuse for their sin. ²³He who hates Me hates My Father also. ²⁴If I had not performed miraculous signs among them, they would not have guilt. But now they have both seen the works and hated Me and My Father. ²⁵In order to fulfill what is written in their Law, 'They hated Me for no reason.'

²⁶"When the Counselor comes, whom I will send to you from the Father, the Spirit of Truth who comes from the Father, He will testify about Me. ²⁷And you will too, because you have been with Me from the beginning.

**16** "I have shared these things with you, so that you will not stumble. ²They will throw you out of the synagogue; in fact, an hour is coming when anyone who kills you will think he is offering service to God. ³They will do these things, because they have not know the Father or Me. ⁴But I have shared all this with you, so that when the hour comes for them to do these things, you will remember what I told you. I did not tell you these things from the beginning, because I was with you. ⁵Now I am going to Him who sent Me; and none of you asks Me, 'Where are You going?' ⁶But because I have said these things to you, sorrow has filled your heart. ⁷But I am telling you the truth: it is to your advantage that I go away. Unless I go away, the Counselor will not come to you; but if I go, I will send Him to you. ⁸And when He comes, He will convict the world concerning sin, righteousness, and judgment. ⁹Concerning sin, because they do not believe in Me, ¹⁰Concerning righteousness, because I am going to the Father and you will not see Me anymore, ¹¹And concerning judgment, because the ruler of this world has been judged. ¹²I have many more things to say to you, but you cannot bear them now. ¹³But when He, the Spirit of Truth comes, He will guide you into all truth; for He will not speak on His own initiative, but whatever He hears; He will speak; and He will make known to you what is yet to come. ¹⁴He will glorify Me; for He will take what is Mine and make it known to you. ¹⁵All that belongs to the Father is Mine. This is why I said that the Spirit takes what is Mine and will make it known to you.

¹⁶"In a little while, you will not see Me anymore; and then, after a little while, you will see Me again." ¹⁷His disciples therefore said to one another, "What does this mean, 'In a little while, you will not see Me anymore; and then, after a little while, you will see Me again' and, 'Because I am going to the Father'?" ¹⁸And so they kept saying, "What does He mean by 'a little while'? We don't understand what He is talking about." ¹⁹Jesus knew that they wanted to ask Him questions about this, so He said to them, "Are you asking one another what I meant when I said, 'In a little while, you will not see Me anymore; and then, after a little while, you will see Me again'? ²⁰I am telling you the truth: you will cry and mourn, but the world will be glad; you will be full of sorrow, but your sorrow will be turned into joy. ²¹When a woman is giving birth to a child she has pain because her time has come; but when her baby is born she no longer remembers the anguish because of her joy that a child has been born into the world. ²²Even so it is with you: now is your time of sorrow, but I will see you again and your heart will be glad, and no one will take your joy away from you. ²³And on that day, you will need to ask Me no questions. I am telling you the truth: if you will ask the Father for anything, He will give it to you in My name. ²⁴Until now you have not asked for anything in My name; ask, and you will receive, that your joy may be complete.

²⁵"I have shared these things with you using figurative language; an hour is coming when I will no longer speak to you in figurative language, but will tell you plainly of the Father. ²⁶On that day you will ask in My name. I am not saying that I will ask the Father on your behalf. ²⁷For the Father Himself loves you because you have loved Me and have believed that I came from the Father. ²⁸I came from the Father and entered the world; now I am leaving the world again and returning to the Father." ²⁹His disciples said, "Now you are speaking plainly, and not using a figure of speech. ³⁰Now we realize that You know all things and You do not even need anyone to ask you any questions. This makes us believe that you came from God. ³¹Jesus answered them, "Do you believe now? Look, the hour is coming and has now come, for you to be scattered, each to his own home, and I will be left alone. But I am not alone, because the Father is with Me. ³²I have shared these things with you, so that in Me you may have peace. In this world you will have tough times, but take courage; I have overcome the world!"

17 Jesus shared these things; then lifted His eyes to heaven, and said, "Father, the hour as come; glorify Your Son, that the Son may glorify You. ²You gave Him authority over all mankind, that He may give eternal life to all those You have given Him. ³This is eternal life: that they may know You, the only true God, and Jesus Christ, whom You have sent. ⁴I have glorified You on the earth, by completing the work You gave Me to do. ⁵And now, Father, glorify Me in Your presence with the glory which I had with You before the world was made.

⁶"I have revealed You to the men whom You gave Me out of the world. They were Yours, and You gave them to Me, and they have obeyed Your Word. ⁷Now they have come to know that everything You have given Me comes from You. ⁸For I gave them the words You gave Me and they accepted them and truly understood that I came from You, and they believed that You sent Me. ⁹I ask on their behalf; I am not asking on behalf of the world, but of those when You have given Me, for they are Yours. ¹⁰All I have is Yours, and all You have is Mine. And I have been glorified in them. ¹¹And I am no longer in the world, but they are in the world, and I am coming to You, Holy Father, keep them in Your name, which You gave Me, that they may be one as We are one. ¹²While I was with them, I kept them in Your name, which You gave Me, and I protected them, and not one of them was lost except the son of rebellion, in order that the Scripture might be fulfilled. ¹³Now I am coming to You, but I say these things in the world, so that they may have My joy made complete in themselves. ¹⁴I have given them Your Word and the world has hated them, because they are not of the world, just as I am not of the world. ¹⁵I do not ask that You take them out of the world, but that You protect them from evil. ¹⁶They are not of the world, just as I am not of the world. ¹⁷Set them apart in the truth; Your Word is truth. ¹⁸As You have sent Me into the world, I have sent them into the world. ¹⁹For their sakes I have been set apart, that they themselves may also be set apart in truth.

²⁰"I do not ask on behalf of these alone, but also for those who will believe in Me through their message; ²¹That they may be one, Father, just as You are in Me and I am in You. May they also be in Us, that the world may believe that You sent Me. ²²I have given them the glory You gave Me, that they may be one as We are one. ²³I in them and You in Me, that they may be completely one, so that the world will know that You sent Me and have loved them as You have loved Me. ²⁴Father, I want those You have given Me to be with Me where I am, and to see My glory, which You gave Me, because You loved Me before the creation of the world. ²⁵O Righteous Father, though the world does not know You, I know You; and these have realized that You have sent Me. ²⁶I made Your name known to them, and will continue to make it known, so that the love You have for Me may be in them, and that I Myself may be in them."

18 Having said these things, Jesus left with His disciples and went across the Kidron Valley. There was a garden there, which He and His disciples entered. ²Now Judas, who was betraying Him, also knew the place; for Jesus had often met there with His disciples. ³Then Judas, guiding a detachment of soldiers and officers from the chief priests and Pharisees, arrived there with lanterns, torches, and weapons. ⁴At this point, Jesus, knowing all that was going to happen to Him, went to them and said, "Who are you looking for?" ⁵They

answered Him, "Jesus of Nazareth." He said to them, "I am." Now Judas, who was betraying Him, was also standing with them. ⁶When Jesus said to them, "I am," they drew back and fell to the ground. ⁷Again, he asked them, "Who are you looking for?" And they replied, "Jesus of Nazareth." ⁸"I told you that I am," Jesus answered, "If you are looking for Me, then let these men go," ⁹In order that the statement He had made might be fulfilled: "I have not lost one of those You gave Me." ¹⁰Then Simon Peter, having a sword, drew it, and struck the high priest's servant, cutting off his right ear. The servant's name was Malchus. ¹¹Jesus therefore said to Peter, "Put your sword into its sheath! Shall I not drink the cup which the Father has given Me?"

¹²So the soldiers, their commander, and the Jewish officers arrested Jesus. They bound Him, ¹³and led Him first to Annas, who was the father-in-law of Caiaphas, the high priest that year. ¹⁴Now Caiaphas was the one who had advised the Jews that it was better for one man to die on behalf of the people.

¹⁵Simon Peter and another disciple followed Jesus. The other disciple was known to the high priest, so he entered into the courtyard of the high priest with Jesus, ¹⁶But Peter had to wait outside at the door. So the other disciple, who was known to the high priest, came back and talked to the girl at the gate, and brought Peter inside. ¹⁷The girl at the gate then asked Peter, "You are not one of His disciples, are you?" He replied, "I am not." ¹⁸It was cold, and the servants and officers were standing around a fire they had made to warm themselves. Peter also was standing with them, warming himself.

¹⁹Meanwhile, the high priest questioned Jesus about His disciples and about His teaching. ²⁰Jesus answered him, "I have spoken openly to the world. I always taught in synagogues and in the temple where all the Jews come together, and I spoke nothing in secret. ²¹Why, then, do you question Me? Ask those who heard what I shared with them. Surely they know what I said." ²²When Jesus said this, one of the officers standing nearby struck Him in the face. "Is that the way You answer the high priest?" ²³Jesus answered him, "If I have spoken wrongly, testify as to what is wrong; but if I have spoken truthfully, why did you strike Me?" ²⁴With this, Annas sent Him, still bound, to Caiaphas the high priest.

²⁵Now as Simon Peter stood warming himself, they said to him, "You are not one of His disciples, are you?" He denied it, and said, "I am not." ²⁶One of the high priest's servants, a relative of the man whose ear Peter had cut off, said, "Didn't I see you with Him in the garden?" ²⁷Peter again denied it, and at that moment, the cock crowed.

²⁸Early in the morning, the Jews led Jesus from Caiaphas into the governor's palace. However, they themselves did not enter into the palace, so that they might not be defiled, but might eat the Passover meal. ²⁹So Pilate went out to them and asked, "What charge do you bring against this man?" ³⁰"If He was not a criminal," they replied, "we would not have handed Him over to you." ³¹Pilate therefore said to them, "Take Him yourselves, and judge Him according to your law." The Jews objected, saying, "But, we are not permitted to execute anyone." ³²So that the statement Jesus made, regarding the kind of death He was going to die, might be fulfilled.

³³At this point, Pilate came back inside the palace, summoned Jesus, and said to Him, "Are You the King of the Jews?" ³⁴Jesus answered, "Are you saying this on your own initiative, or did others tell you about Me?" ³⁵Pilate replied, "I am not a Jew, am I? Your own

people and the chief priests handed You over to me. What have You done?" ³⁶Jesus answered, "My kingdom is not of this world. If My kingdom were of this world, then My servants would fight to keep Me from being handed over to the Jews, but My kingdom is not of this world." ³⁷Pilate therefore said to Him, "So You are a king?" Jesus answered, "You say that I am a king. In fact, for this I was born and for this I came into the world, to testify to the truth. Everyone who is of the truth hears My voice." ³⁸Pilate asked Him, "What is truth?" After he had said this, he went back out to the Jews, and said to them, "I find no fault in Him.

³⁹"But you have a custom that I should release someone to you at the Passover. Do you want me to release 'the King of the Jews'?" ⁴⁰Then they cried out again, saying, "Not this Man, but Barabbas!" Now Barabbas was a robber.

19 Pilate therefore took Jesus and had Him whipped. ²And the soldiers made a crown of thorns and put it on His head, and clothed Him in a purple robe, ³then they went up to Him again and again, saying, "Hail, King of the Jews." And they struck Him in the face. ⁴Again Pilate went out, and said to them, "Look, I am bringing Him out to you, so that you may know that I find no fault in Him." ⁵So Jesus came out, wearing the crown of thorns and the purple robe, and Pilate said, "Here is the man!" ⁶When the chief priests and officers saw Him, they cried out saying, "Crucify! Crucify!" Pilate said to them, "You take Him, and crucify Him yourselves, for I find no fault in Him." ⁷The Jews answered Him, "We have a law, and according to that law He ought to die, because He claimed to be the Son of God." ⁸When Pilate heard this statement, he was even more afraid; ⁹And he entered into the palace again, and said to Jesus, "Where are You from?" But Jesus did not answer him. ¹⁰So Pilate said to Him, "You won't talk to me? Don't You realize that I have the power to set You free. And the power to crucify You." ¹¹Jesus answered, "You would have no power over Me, unless it had been given to you from above; therefore, the one who handed Me over to you has a greater sin." ¹²From that point on, Pilate tried to set Jesus free, but the Jews cried out, saying, "If you let this Man go you are no friend of Caesar. Anyone who claims to be a king opposes Caesar." ¹³When Pilate heard these words, he brought Jesus out and sat down on the judge's seat in a place called the Stone Pavement or Gabbatha in Hebrew. ¹⁴Now it was the day of Preparation for the Passover, at about the sixth hour. And Pilate said to the Jews, "Here is your King!" ¹⁵Then they cried out, "Away with Him! Away with Him! Crucify Him!" Pilate said to them, "Crucify your King?" The chief priests answered, "We have no king but Caesar." ¹⁶Finally, Pilate handed Him over to them to be crucified. So they took Jesus and let Him away.

¹⁷Bearing His own cross, He went out to the place called the Skull. In Hebrew it is called Golgotha. ¹⁸There they crucified Him, and with Him two other men – one on each side and Jesus in the middle. ¹⁹And Pilate also wrote an inscription and put it on the cross, and it read: "Jesus of Nazareth, The King of the Jews." ²⁰Many of the Jews read this inscription, for the place where Jesus was crucified was near the city, and it was written in Hebrew, Latin and Greek. ²¹And so the chief priests of the Jews protested to Pilate, "Do not Write, 'The King of the Jews,' but that 'He said, I am the King of the Jews,'" ²²Pilate answered, "What I have written, I have written." ²³Then the soldiers, when they had crucified Jesus, took His outer garments and divided them up into four parts, one part for each soldier. They also took His

robe, which was seamless, woven in one piece. ²⁴Therefore they said to one another, "Let's not tear it, but cast lots to see who will get it"; in order that the Scripture might be fulfilled, "They divided My garments among them, and for My robe they cast lots." ²⁵So these are the things the soldiers did. Near the cross of Jesus stood His mother, His mother's sister, Mary the wife of Cleopas, and Mary Magdalene. ²⁶When Jesus saw His mother there and the disciple whom He loved standing nearby, He said to His mother, "Woman, here is your son!" ²⁷Then He said to the disciple, "Here is your mother!" From that time on, this disciple took her into his home.
²⁸After this, Jesus, knowing that all things had been accomplished, in order that the Scripture might be fulfilled, said, "I am thirsty." ²⁹A jar of sour wine was there, so they put a sponge soaked with sour wine on a hyssop branch, and lifted it up to His mouth. ³⁰When He had received the drink, Jesus said, "It is finished!" And He bowed His head and gave up His spirit.
³¹Since it was the day of Preparation, in order to prevent the bodies from remaining on the cross on the Sabbath (for that Sabbath was special), the Jews asked Pilate that their legs might be broken, and that they might be taken away. ³²The soldiers therefore came and broke the legs of the first man who had been crucified with Jesus, and then the legs of the other man. ³³But when they came to Jesus and saw that He was already dead, they did not break His legs. ³⁴One of the soldiers, however, pierced His side with a spear, and immediately blood and water poured out. ³⁵And the one who saw this has given testimony, and his testimony is true. He knows that he is telling the truth, so that you also may believe. ³⁶For these things happened so that the Scripture might be fulfilled, "Not one of His bones will be broken." ³⁷And, as another Scripture says, "They will look on Him whom they pierced." ³⁸Later, Joseph of Arimathea, asked Pilate for permission to take away the body of Jesus. (Now Joseph was a disciple of Jesus, but secretly because he feared the Jews.) Pilate granted his request, so he came and took away Jesus' body. ³⁹And Nicodemus, the man who had first come to Jesus at night, also came with Joseph bringing a mixture of about 100 pounds of myrrh and aloes. ⁴⁰And so they took the body of Jesus, and wrapped it with the spices in strips of linen, according to the burial custom of the Jews. ⁴¹Now there was a garden in the place where Jesus was crucified, and in the garden a new tomb, in which no one had ever been laid. ⁴²So because of the Jewish day of Preparation, and since the tomb was nearby, they laid Jesus there.

**20** Now on the first day of the week, Mary Magdalene came to the tomb early, while it was still dark, and saw that the stone had been removed from the entrance. ²So she ran and went to Simon Peter and the other disciple, the one whom Jesus loved, and said to them, "They have taken the Lord out of the tomb, and we don't know where they have laid Him." ³Right away Peter and the other disciple went to the tomb. ⁴And the two were running together, but the other disciple went to the tomb. 4And the two were running together, but the other disciple outran Peter and reached the tomb first. ⁵Stooping down to look in, he saw the linen wrappings lying there, but he did not go in. ⁶Then Simon Peter, who was following him, arrived and went into the tomb. He noticed the linen wrappings lying there, ⁷and the cloth that had been around Jesus' head was not lying with the linen wrappings, but was rolled up in a place by itself. ⁸Then the other disciple, who had reached the tomb first, also went inside; and he saw and believed. ⁹For they still did not understand from Scripture that Jesus had to rise from the dead. ¹⁰Then the disciples went back to their homes.

¹¹But Mary stood outside the tomb crying. As she wept, she stooped down and looked into the tomb. ¹²She saw two angels in white, sitting where the body of Jesus had been lying – one at the head, and one at the feet. ¹³They asked her, "Woman, why are you crying?" She said to them. "Because they have taken my Lord away, and I don't know where they have laid Him." ¹⁴After saying this, she turned around and saw Jesus standing there, but she didn't realize that it was Jesus. ¹⁵"Woman, why are you crying?" Jesus asked her. "Who are you looking for?" Thinking He was the gardener, she said to Him, "Sir, if You have carried Him away, tell me where you have laid Him, and I will take Him away." ¹⁶Jesus said to her, "Mary." She turned toward Him said to Him in Hebrew, "Rabboni!" which translated means Teacher. ¹⁷Jesus said to her, "Stop holding on to Me, for I have not yet ascended to the Father. Instead, go to My brothers and tell them, 'I am ascending to My Father and your Father, and to My God and your God." ¹⁸Mary Magdalene went to the disciples, exclaiming, "I have seen the Lord!" And she told them that He had said these things to her.

¹⁹That evening, on the first day of the week, though the disciples were together behind locked doors for fear of the Jews, Jesus came and stood in their midst, and said to them, "Peace be with you." ²⁰After saying this, He showed them His hands and His side. The disciples were filled with joy at seeing the Lord. ²¹Then Jesus said to them again, "Peace be with you. As the Father has sent Me, so I am sending you." ²²At that point, He breathed on them and said to them, "Receive the Holy Spirit. ²³If you forgive the sins of anyone, they have already been forgiven; those whose sins you do not forgive, they have not been forgiven."

²⁴Now Thomas, one of the twelve, who is called the Twin, was not with them when Jesus came. ²⁵So the other disciples kept saying to him, "We have seen the Lord!" But Thomas said to them, "Unless I see the nail marks in His hands, and put my finger in the place where the nails were, and put my hand into His side, I will not believe."

²⁶A week later, His disciples were inside again, and Thomas was with them. Though the doors were locked, Jesus came and stood among them and said, "Peace be with you." ²⁷Then He said to Thomas, "Put your finger here, and look at My hands; reach out your hand, and put it into My side. Stop doubting and believe." ²⁸Thomas said to Him, "My Lord and my God!" ²⁹Jesus said to him, "Because you have seen Me, you have believed; blessed are those who have not seen and yet have believed."

³⁰Now Jesus performed many other miraculous signs in the presence of the disciples which are not recorded in this book; ³¹but these are written in order that you may believe that Jesus is the Christ, the Son of God; and that believing you may have life in His name.

21 After these things, Jesus revealed Himself again to His disciples by the Sea of Tiberias. He did it in this way. ²Simon Peter, Thomas called the Twin, and Nathanael of Cana in Galilee, the sons of Zebedee, and two others of His disciples were all together. ³Simon Peter said to them, "I am going fishing." They said to him, "We'll go with you." So they went out, and got into the boat and they caught nothing all night. ⁴As the day was breaking, Jesus stood on the beach; but the disciples didn't realize that it was Jesus. ⁵So Jesus said to them, "Children, you do not have any fish, do you?" They answered Him, "No."

⁶And He said to them, "Throw the net on the right side of the boat, and you will find some." When they did, they were unable to haul it in because of the great number of fish. ⁷That disciple whom Jesus loved then said to Peter, "It is the Lord!" When Peter heard him say, "It is the Lord," he put his outer garment on for he had taken it off and jumped into the sea. ⁸The other disciples came in the boat, towing the net full of fish, for they were not far from the shore, only about one hundred yards away. ⁹When they stepped ashore, they saw a fire had been made with fish placed on it and some bread. ¹⁰Jesus said to them, "Bring some of the fish you have just caught." ¹¹Simon Peter climbed aboard and dragged the net ashore. It was full of big fish, 153 of them, and although there were so many, the net was not torn. ¹²Jesus said to them, "Come, have breakfast." None of the disciples dared ask Him, "Who are You?" knowing that it was the Lord. ¹³Jesus came and took the bread and also the fish and gave it to them. ¹⁴This was now the third time that Jesus revealed Himself to the disciples after He was raised from the dead.

¹⁵When they had finished breakfast, Jesus said to Simon Peter, "Simon, son of John, do you truly love Me more than these others do?" He said to Him, "Yes, Lord, You know that I love You." Jesus said to him, "Feed My lambs." ¹⁶He said to him again a second time, "Simon, son of John, do you truly love Me?" He answered, "Yes, Lord, You know that I love You." Jesus said, "Shepherd My sheep." ¹⁷A third time, Jesus said to him, "Simon, son of John, do you love Me?" Peter was hurt because Jesus asked him the third time, "Do you love Me?" So he said to Him, "Lord, You know all things; You know that I love You." Jesus said to him, "Feed My sheep. ¹⁸I am telling you the truth: when you were younger, you girded yourself and went where you wanted to go; but when you grow old, you will stretch out your hands, and someone else will put a girdle around you, and carry you where you don't want to go." ¹⁹Jesus said this to indicate the kind of death by which Peter would glorify God. After saying this, Jesus said to him, "Follow Me!" ²⁰Peter turned around and saw the disciple whom Jesus loved following them. This was the one who also had leaned back against Jesus at the supper and had said, "Lord, who is going to betray You?" ²¹When Peter saw him, he asked Jesus, "Lord, what about this man?" ²²Jesus said to him, "If I want him to live until I come, what is that to you? You follow Me! ²³Because of this, the word spread among the brothers that this disciple would not die. But Jesus did not say that to him that he would not die, He said, "If I want him to live until I come, what is that to you?"

²⁴This is the disciple who testifies to these things and also wrote them down, and we know that his testimony is true. ²⁵Now there are also many other things which Jesus did. If every one of them were recorded in detail. I imagine that even the whole world would not have room for the books that would be written.

# THE ACTS
## *of the Apostles*

1 Indeed the first record I made, O Theophilus, concerning everything which Jesus began both to do and to teach ²until the day in which He was taken up, having given injunctions to the apostles whom He chose through the Holy Spirit; ³to whom also He presented Himself living after He suffered by many irrefutable proofs, throughout forty days being seen by them and speaking the facts concerning the kingdom of God. ⁴And coming together with them to eat, He instructed them not to depart from Jerusalem, but to wait for the promise of the Father "which He said you heard from Me; ⁵because John indeed immersed in water, but you shall be immersed in the Holy Spirit after not many days."

⁶Indeed then they coming together with Him were asking Him, saying, "Lord, is it at this time you are going to restore the kingdom to Israel?" ⁷But He said to them, "It is not for you to know the general time or the exact period which the Father has placed in His own authority; ⁸but you shall receive power, with the Holy Spirit coming upon you, and you shall be My witnesses, both in Jerusalem and in all Judea and Samaria and until the end of the earth." ⁹And having spoken these words, as they were watching He was taken up, and a cloud took Him up from their eyes. ¹⁰And as they were gazing intently into the heaven as He was going, behold two men being clothed in white stood beside them, ¹¹and they said, "Men, Galileans, why have you stood up from you into heaven? This same Jesus having been received up from you into heaven, thus shall come in the same way as you viewed Him going into heaven."

¹²Then they returned into Jerusalem from the mount being called Olivet, which is near Jerusalem a Sabbath day's journey. ¹³And when they came into it, they went up into an upper room where they were staying, both Peter and John and James and Andrew, Philip and Thomas, Bartholomew and Matthew, James son of Alpheus and Simon the Zealot and Judas son of James. ¹⁴These all were continuing diligently with one spirit in prayer with the women and Mary, the mother of Jesus and His brothers.

¹⁵And in these days Peter standing up in the midst of the brethren said, the crowd numbered together about 120. ¹⁶"Men, brethren, it is necessary that the Scripture be fulfilled which the Holy Spirit spoke before through the mouth of David concerning the one becoming guide to the ones capturing Jesus, ¹⁷because he was counted among us and obtained a place in this ministry. ¹⁸This one indeed purchased a field out of the reward of his unrighteousness, and falling headlong burst in the middle, and all his bowels spilled out. ¹⁹And it became known to all those dwelling in Jerusalem, so that that field was called in their own dialect 'Akeldema' this is, 'Field of Blood.' ²⁰For it has been written in the book of Psalms, 'Let his habitation become desolate and let no one dwell in it.' And 'let another take his position of oversight.' ²¹It is necessary of the men having accompanied us in all the time the Lord Jesus went in and out among us, ²²beginning from the immersion of John until the day in which He was taken up from us, that one of these become a witness of His resurrection with us." ²³And they selected two, Joseph the one being called Barsabbas, who was surnamed Justus, and Matthias. ²⁴And praying they said, "You Lord, heart knower of all men, point out whom You have chosen of

these two, one ²⁵to take the place of this ministry and apostleship, from which Judas defected to go to his own place." ²⁶And they gave lots to them, and the lot fell upon Matthias and he was added with the eleven apostles.

2 And when the Day of Pentecost arrived, they all were together in one place. ²And suddenly a sound came out of heaven as a blowing of a violent wind and it filled the whole house where they were sitting; ³and there appeared to them tongues like as fire being divided, and one sat upon each of them, ⁴and all were filled with the Holy Spirit, and began to speak in other tongues even as the Spirit was given to them to speak eloquently.
⁵And there were dwelling in Jerusalem Jews, devout men from every nation under heaven. ⁶And this sound having happened, the multitude came together and were confused because each one heard them speaking in his own dialect. ⁷And they were amazed and were marveling saying, "Behold are not all these speaking Galileans? ⁸And how do we each hear our own dialect in which we were born? ⁹Parthians and Medes and Elamites and the ones living in Mesopotamia, both Judeans and Cappadocians, Pontus and Asia, ¹⁰Phyrgia and Pamphylia, Egypt and the parts of Libya around Cyrene and the Roman visitors, ¹¹both Jews and proselytes, Cretes and Arabs, we hear them speaking in our own tongues concerning the great works of God." ¹²And all were amazed and were perplexed, saying to one another, "what would this be?" ¹³But others of a different nature were making a joke of it saying that, "They are drunk on sweet wine."
¹⁴But Peter having stood up with the eleven raised his voice and spoke eloquently, "Men, Judeans and all those dwelling in Jerusalem, let this be known to you and listen carefully to my words, ¹⁵for these are not drunken as you suppose, for it is just the third hour of the day, ¹⁶but this is that having been spoken through the prophet Joel, ¹⁷and it shall be in the last days, God says I will pour out from My Spirit upon all flesh, and your sons and your daughters shall prophesy and your young men shall see visions and your elder men shall dream dreams. ¹⁸And even on My male slaves and upon My female slaves in those days I shall pour out from My Spirit, and they shall prophesy that ¹⁹I shall give wonders in the heaven above and signs upon the earth below, blood and fire and vapor of smoke; ²⁰the sun shall be turned into darkness and the moon into blood before that great and glorious day of the Lord comes. ²¹And it shall be that all whoever shall call on the name of the Lord shall be saved.' ²²Men, Israelites, you hear these words, Jesus the Nazarene, a man affirmed from God to you by miracles and signs and wonders which also God did through Him in the midst of you, even as you know; ²³this One in the determined purpose and foreknowledge of God being delivered up through the hands of lawless men, having nailed to a cross, you killed; ²⁴Whom God raised up, loosing the torment of death since it was not possible for Him to be held by it. ²⁵For David says of Him, 'I forsee the Lord always before me because He is on my right hand in order that I not be shaken. ²⁶On account of this my heart rejoiced and my tongue was made glad and still also my flesh will dwell in hope; ²⁷because You will not abandon my soul in Hades neither give Your Holy One to see corruption. ²⁸You made known to me the ways of life, You will fill me with gladness.'
²⁹Men, brethren, let me speak to you with boldness about the patriarch David, that he also died and was buried and his tomb is among us until this day. ³⁰Therefore, being a prophet and knowing that God swore to him with an oath that out of the fruit of his loin One would sit

upon his throne, ³¹forseeing this, he spoke concerning the resurrection of Christ, that neither was He abandoned in Hades nor His flesh see corruption. ³²This Jesus God raised up of which we all are witnesses. ³³Therefore, being exalted on the right hand of God and having received from the Father the promise of the Holy Spirit He poured out this which you see and hear. ³⁴For David did not ascend into the heavens, but he says, 'The Lord said to My Lord, sit upon My right hand ³⁵until whenever I make your enemies the footstool of your feet.' ³⁶Therefore, let all the house of Israel know assuredly that God made Him both Lord and Christ, this Jesus Whom you crucified."

³⁷Hearing this they were convicted in their heart and said to Peter and the remainder of the apostles, "What shall we do, men, brethren?" ³⁸And Peter said to them, "You repent and let each of you be immersed upon the name of Jesus Christ for the forgiveness of your sins and you will receive the gift of the Holy Spirit; ³⁹for to you is the promise and to your children and to all those far away, whoever the Lord God may call." ⁴⁰And with many other words he witnessed thoroughly, and was pleasing with them saying, "Be saved from this perverse generation." ⁴¹Indeed, therefore, the ones readily accepting his word were immersed, and in that day about three thousand souls were added to them.

⁴²And they were continuing diligently in the teaching of the apostles and the fellowship and the breaking of the bread and the prayers. ⁴³And great fear came on every soul, and many wonders and signs were being done by the apostles. ⁴⁴And all the ones believing were together and were having all things in common. ⁴⁵And they were selling their properties and possessions, and distributing them to all according as anyone might have need. ⁴⁶And from day to day they were continuing diligently with one accord in the temple, and breaking bread from house to house, and were partaking of food with gladness and simplicity of heart, ⁴⁷praising God and having favor with all the people. And the Lord was adding together day by day those being saved.

3 And Peter and John were going up into the temple at the ninth hour for prayer. ²And a certain man being lame from his mother's womb was being carried whom they were placing daily at the gate of the temple being called Beautiful to ask for gifts of mercy from those going into the temple; ³who seeing Peter and John being about to enter into the temple was requesting to receive gifts of mercy. ⁴But Peter, with John, gazing intently on him said, "Look at us." ⁵And the man was paying attention to them, expecting to receive something from them. ⁶But Peter said, "I do not have silver or gold, but what I have, this I give to you; in the name of Jesus Christ of Nazareth, rise and walk." ⁷And having seized him by his right hand, he raised him; and instantly his feet and ankle bones were strengthened, ⁸and leaping up, he stood and was walking, and entered with them into the temple, walking and leaping and praising God. ⁹And all the people saw him walking and praising God, ¹⁰and recognizing him that he was the one sitting and asking for gifts of mercy at the Beautiful Gate of the temple and they were filled with amazement and excitement at what had happened to him. ¹¹As he was clinging on to Peter and John, all the people ran to them at the portico being called Solomon's, out of amazement.

¹²And Peter beholding, answered to the people, "Men, Israelites, why do you marvel at this, or why do you gaze upon us as if by our own power or godliness we have made him to

walk? ¹³The God of Abraham and Isaac and Jacob, the God of our fathers, glorified His Servant Jesus, Whom you indeed delivered up and denied in the presence of Pilate, when that one was judging to release Him; ¹⁴but you denied the holy and just One, and asked for a man who was a murderer to be granted to you, ¹⁵but you killed the Prince of Life, Whom God raised up out of the dead, of which we are witnesses. ¹⁶And upon faith in His name this one whom you behold and you know was strengthened through His name, and the faith which was through Him gave to him this wholeness of body before all of you.

¹⁷"And know brothers, I know that through ignorance you acted, even as also your rulers. ¹⁸But what God previously announced through the mouth of all the prophets that His Christ would suffer He thus fulfilled. ¹⁹Repent therefore and turn around in order for your sins to be wiped out, ²⁰so that the times of refreshing may come from the presence of the Lord, and He may send to you the Christ having been before appointed even Jesus, ²¹Whom indeed it is necessary that heaven receive until the times of restoration of all which God spoke through the mouth of His holy prophets from the ages. ²²Moses indeed said that, 'The Lord your God will raise up a prophet out of your brethren like me; you listen to Him according to everything whatever He may say to you. ²³And it shall be that every soul whoever does not listen to that prophet shall be completely cut off out of the people.' ²⁴And all the prophets from Samuel and the ones following whoever spoke also proclaimed this day. ²⁵You yourselves are the sons of the prophets and the covenant which God covenanted with your fathers, saying to Abraham, 'And in your seed all the nations of the earth shall be exceedingly blessed.' ²⁶To you first God having raised up His Child, sent Him to bless you by turning each one from your wicked ways."

4 As they were speaking to the people, the priests and the captain of the temple guard and the Sadducees stood over them suddenly, ²being very disturbed because they were teaching the people and proclaiming the resurrection of the dead in the name of Jesus. ³And laying hands on them, they put them in custody until the morrow, for it was already evening. ⁴But many of those having heard the Word believed, and the number of men became about five thousand.

⁵And it happened on the morrow that the rulers and the elders and the scribes in Jerusalem gathered together. ⁶And Annas the high priest and Caiaphas and John and Alexander were there and whoever was of the family of the high priest. ⁷And standing them in the midst, they were inquiring, "By what power or in what name did you this?" ⁸Then Peter, having been filled with the Holy Spirit, said to them "Rulers of the people and elders, ⁹if we this day are being examined about a good deed done to an infirm man, in what this one was healed, ¹⁰let it be known to all of you and to all the people of Israel that in the name of Jesus Christ of Nazareth, whom you crucified, whom God raised out of the dead, in this One, this man has stood before you healthy. ¹¹This One is 'the stone rejected by you the builders, the One becoming the head of the corner.' ¹²And salvation is not in any other for no other name has been given among men in which it is necessary for us to be saved."

¹³And beholding the boldness of Peter and John and considering that they were unlearned and ordinary men, they were marveling, realizing that they had been with Jesus; ¹⁴and seeing the man having been healed standing there with them, they had nothing to say against them.

¹⁵But having commanded them to go outside of the Sanhedrin they were discussing with one another; ¹⁶saying, "What shall we do with these men? For indeed that a remarkable miraculous sign has been done through them is manifest to all those dwelling in Jerusalem, and we are not able to deny it. ¹⁷But in order that it may not be further circulated among the people let us strictly warn them no longer to speak about this name to any men." ¹⁸And having called them, they charged them not to discourse about nor teach at all in the name of Jesus. ¹⁹But Peter and John answering said to them, "If it is right in the sight of God to listen to you rather than God, you judge, ²⁰for we are not able to stop speaking about what we saw and heard." ²¹And having threatened them more, they released them, not finding anything on which to punish them, on account of the people, because all were glorifying God upon what had happened; ²²for the man upon whom this sign of healing was done was more than forty years of age.
²³And being released they went to their own group and announced whatever the chief priests and the elders said. ²⁴And the ones having heard with one accord raised a voice to God and said, "Sovereign Lord, you are 'the One making the heaven and the earth and the sea and all that is in them,' ²⁵our Father through the Holy Spirit by the mouth of Your servant David having said, 'Why did the Gentiles rave and the people contrive vanities? ²⁶The kings of the earth stood against, and the rulers gathered together against the Lord and against His Christ.' ²⁷For of a truth in this city Herod and Pontius Pilate with the Gentiles and the people of Israel gathered together against Your holy Servant Jesus Whom You anointed, ²⁸to do whatever Your hand and Your will foreordained to happen. ²⁹And now, Lord, look upon their threats, and give to Your slaves to speak with all boldness Your Word, ³⁰when You extend Your hand for healing and signs and wonders happen through the name of Your holy Servant Jesus." ³¹And they having offered petition, the place in which they were gathered was shaken, and all were filled with the Holy Spirit, and were speaking the Word of God with boldness.
³²And the multitude of those believing were of one heart and soul, and no one was saying that his possessions were his own, but all things were common to them. ³³And with great power the apostles were giving witness of the resurrection of the Lord Jesus, and great grace was upon all of them. ³⁴For no one was needy among them; for as many owners as were possessors of lands or houses were selling them, and bringing the proceeds of that being sold, ³⁵and placing at the feet of the apostles; and it was being distributed to each according to whoever was having need. ³⁶And Joseph, the one having been surnamed Barnabas by the apostles, which is being interpreted son of Comfort, a Levite, a Cyprian by birth, ³⁷possessing a field, having sold it, brought the sum of money and placed at the feet of the apostles.

5 A certain man named Ananias with Sapphira his wife sold property, ²and held back for himself from the price of it, his wife having knowledge also of this, and having brought a certain part, laid it at the feet of the apostles. ³But Peter said, "Ananias, why did Satan fill your heart to lie to the Holy Spirit and hold back for yourself from the price of the land? ⁴Remaining unsold was it not remaining to your hands? And having been sold was it not in your authority? Why then did you put this deed in your heart? You have not lied to man but to God." ⁵And Ananias hearing these words died, and great fear came upon all hearing of this. ⁶And the young men arising wrapped him, and carrying him out buried him. ⁷And it happened

at about a three hour interim, his wife also entered, not knowing what had happened; ⁸and Peter said to her, "Tell me if for so much as you gave up the land? And she said, "Yes, for so much." ⁹Peter said to her, "Why have you agreed together to test the Spirit of the Lord? Behold, the feet of those having buried your husband are at the door and they will take you out also." ¹⁰And she fell instantly at his feet and died, and carrying her out they buried here next to her husband. ¹¹And great fear came upon the whole church and upon all those hearing these events.

¹²And many miraculous signs and wonders were being done through the hands of the apostles among the people. And they all were with one accord in Solomon's Portico. ¹³And none of the remainder dared to join them, but the people were magnifying them. ¹⁴And more believers in the Lord were being added to them, a multitude of both men and women, ¹⁵so that they even were carrying out the sick into the streets and placing them on cots and pallets in order that when Peter was coming if even his shadow might overshadow some of them. ¹⁶And the multitude was coming together also from the cities around Jerusalem, bearing the sick and those being defiled by unclean spirits, who were all being healed.

¹⁷And arising the high priest and all the ones with him, being of the sect of the Sadducees, were filled with jealousy, ¹⁸and laid hands on the apostles and placed them in public custody. ¹⁹But an angel of the Lord by night opened the doors of the prison, and leading them out said, ²⁰"You go and standing in the temple, speak to the people all the words of this life." ²¹And having heard they went into the temple at dawn and were teaching. But the high priest and those with him having come, they called together the Sanhedrin, even all the elder leaders of the sons of Israel and sent to the jail to have them brought. ²²But the officers going did not find them in the prison, and having returned they declared ²³saying that, "We found the jail having been closed in all security and the guards standing by the doors, but having opened the doors, we found no one within. ²⁴And when the captain of the temple guard and the chief priests heard these words they were perplexed concerning them, what this would become. ²⁵And someone coming announced to them, "Behold, the men whom you placed in the prison are standing in the temple and teaching the people.

²⁶Then departing, the captain with the officers brought them, not with force, for they were fearing the people that they might be stoned. ²⁷And leading them in they stood them in the Sanhedrin, and the high priest questioned them ²⁸saying, "We commanded you with a command not to preach in this name, and behold you have filled Jerusalem with your teaching, and desire to bring upon us the blood of this man." ²⁹And Peter and the apostles answering said, "It is necessary to obey God rather than man. ³⁰The God of our fathers raised Jesus Whom you killed, hanging Him on a tree. ³¹God exalted this One as Prince and Savior to His right hand to give repentance to Israel and forgiveness of sins. ³²And we are witnessed of these words and the Holy Spirit which God gave to those obeying Him." ³³And those having heard this were enraged and were determining to kill them. ³⁴But a certain one in the Sanhedrin, a Pharisee by name Gamaliel, a teacher of the Law, honored among all the people, commanded that they be put outside for a little while. ³⁵And he said to them "Men, Israelites, take heed to yourselves what you are about to do to these men. ³⁶For before these days Theudas rose up saying he himself was somebody, to whom a number of men were enlisted, about four thousand, and all whoever were persuaded by him were destroyed and they came to nothing.

⁣³⁷After this Judas the Galilean rose up in the days of the census and people followed after him; and that one also was destroyed, and all whoever were persuaded by him were scattered. ³⁸And now I say this to you, withstand from these men and leave them alone; because if this purpose or this work be of men, it will be overcome. ³⁹But if it is of God we will not be able to overcome them, lest also we be found fighters of God." And they were persuaded by him. ⁴⁰And having called the apostles in, beating them, they commanded them not to speak I the name of Jesus and released them. ⁴¹Indeed, therefore, they were going from the Sanhedrin rejoicing that they were considered worthy to suffer disgrace on behalf of the Name. ⁴²And every day in the temple and from house to house they did not cease teaching and preaching good news of Christ Jesus.

**6** And in these days as the disciples were multiplying, a grumbling arose among the Hellenists toward the Hebrews, that their widows were being overlooked in the daily ministry of food. ²And the apostles calling together the multitude of the disciples said, "It is not proper for us to neglect the Word of God to serve tables. ³So brethren, you select from among you seven men being witnessed they are full of the Spirit and wisdom whom we may appoint over this need; ⁴and we will continue diligently in prayer and the ministry of the Word." ⁵And the word was acceptable before all the multitude, and they chose Stephen, a man full of faith and the Holy Spirit, and Philip and Prochorus and Nicanor and Timon and Parmenas and Nicholas, a proselyte of Antioch. ⁶And they set them before the apostles, and having prayed, they laid hands upon them. ⁷And the Word of God was increasing and the number of the disciples in Jerusalem was multiplying exceedingly, and a great crowd of priests were obeying the faith.
⁸And Stephen being full of grace and power was doing wonders and great signs among the people. ⁹But there rose up certain men of the synagogue being called Freedman and of Cyrenians and Alexandrians and the ones from Cilicia and Asia, disputing with Stephen, ¹⁰and they were not able to stand against the wisdom and Spirit with which he was speaking. ¹¹Then they suborned men saying that, "We heard him saying blasphemous words about Moses and God." ¹²And they stirred up the people and the elders and the scribes, and coming upon him, they seized him and led him into the Sanhedrin. ¹³And false witnesses stood up saying, "This man does not cease speaking words against this holy place and the Law; ¹⁴for we heard him saying that Jesus the Nazarene will destroy this place and will change the customs which Moses handed down to us." ¹⁵And all the ones sitting in the Sanhedrin, gazing intently on him, saw his face as the face of an angel.

**7** The high priest said, "Are these things so?" ²But he said, "Men, brethren and fathers, listen, the God of glory appeared to our father Abraham being in Mesopotamia before he dwelt in Haran, ³and He said to him, 'Go out of your land and your relatives, and go into the land which I will show you.' ⁴Then having gone out of the land of Chaldea he dwelt in Haran. And from there after his father died, He removed him into this land in which you now dwell, ⁵and He did not give him an inheritance in it, not even a place to set a foot, yet He promised to give him it as a possession and to his seed after him, even though he had no child. ⁶But God spoke thus that his seed shall be aliens in another land, and they shall be made slaves and be evilly treated four hundred years; ⁷and God said, 'I will judge whatever nation in which they are enslaved, and after these things they shall be freed and they shall worship Me in this place.' ⁸And he gave to him a covenant of circumcision; and thus he begat Isaac and circumcised him on the eighth day, and Isaac begat Jacob, and Jacob the twelve patriarchs.

⁹"And the patriarchs having been jealous of Joseph sold him into Egypt; and God was with him, ¹⁰and rescued him from all his tribulation, and gave him grace and wisdom before Pharaoh king of Egypt, and he established him Joseph governor over Egypt and his whole household. ¹¹And a famine came over the whole Egypt and Canaan, and great tribulation, and our fathers were not finding sustenance. ¹²And Jacob hearing that there was grain in Egypt sent fourth first our fathers; ¹³and on the second visit Joseph was made known to his brothers, and the family of Joseph became manifest to Pharaoh. ¹⁴And Joseph having sent, invited his father Jacob and all his relatives to come to him, seventy-five souls. ¹⁵And Jacob came down into Egypt, and he and our fathers died, ¹⁶and they were removed to Shechem and were placed in the tomb which Abraham purchased for a price of silver from the sons of Hamor in Shechem.

¹⁷"But even as the time of the promise was drawing near which God had declared to Abraham, the people increased and were multiplied in Egypt, ¹⁸until another king arose over Egypt who did not know Joseph. ¹⁹This one having treated our race deceitfully did evil toward our fathers by making them expose their infants so that they would not survive. ²⁰In which time Moses was born, and he was very splendid to God; and he was nourished in his father's house for three months. ²¹And he having been exposed to die, Pharaoh's daughter took him and reared him as her own son. ²²And Moses was educated in all the wisdom of Egypt, and he was powerful in his words and deeds.

²³"And when he was fulfilling forty years of age, it came upon his heart to visit his brethren, the sons of Israel. ²⁴And beholding a certain one being treated harmfully, he defended him, and avenged the one being afflicted, striking the Egyptian. ²⁵And he was supposing that his brethren understood that God by his hand was giving them deliverance; but they did not understand. ²⁶And on the following day he saw them fighting and tried to reconcile them to peace saying, 'Men you are brothers; why do you harm one another?' ²⁷But the one harming his neighbor shoved him away, saying, 'Who appointed you a ruler and judge over us? ²⁸Do you want to kill me in the same manner you killed the Egyptian?' ²⁹So Moses fled at this remark, and became an alien in the land of Midian where he begat two sons.

³⁰"And forty years having been fulfilled, there appeared to him in the wilderness of mount Sinai an angel in flaming fire of a bramble-bush. ³¹And Moses beholding it, was marveling at the sight; and as he was approaching to consider it closely, the voice of the Lord came. ³²'I am the God of your fathers, the God of Abraham and Isaac and Jacob.' And Moses was trembling, not daring to consider it closely. ³³And the Lord said to him, 'Loose your sandals from your feet, for this place on which you have been standing is holy ground. ³⁴Beholding I saw the bad treatment of My people in Egypt, and heard their groanings, and I have come down to deliver them; come now, I will send you into Egypt.'

³⁵"This Moses whom they denied saying 'Who appointed you a ruler and judge?' This one God has sent as a ruler and redeemer with the hand of the angel appearing to him in the bramble-bush. ³⁶This one led them out having done wonders and signs in the land of Egypt

and in the Red Sea and forty years in the wilderness. ³⁷This is the Moses, the one having said to the sons of Israel, 'God shall raise up a prophet like me out of your brethren.' ³⁸This is Moses, the one being in the congregation in the wilderness with the angel speaking to him in mount Sinai, and with our fathers, who received the living oracles to give to you, ³⁹to whom our fathers would not become obedient but also rejected him, and turned back their hearts to Egypt, ⁴⁰having said to Aaron, 'Make for us gods who will go before us, for this Moses, who led us out of the land of Egypt, we do not know what became of him.' ⁴¹And in those days they made a calf and offered up sacrifices to the idol and rejoiced in the works of their hands.

⁴²"And God turned away and gave them up to worship the hosts of heaven, even as it has been written in the book of the Prophets, 'You did not offer to Me victims and sacrifices forty years in the wilderness, did you, house of Israel? ⁴³And you took up the tabernacle of Moloch and the star of your god Rephan, the images which you made to worship them; and I will transfer you beyond Babylon.' ⁴⁴The tabernacle of witness was with our fathers in the wilderness, even as the One speaking to Moses commanded it to be made according to the pattern which he had seen, ⁴⁵which also our fathers having received, brought it with Joshua into the land possessed by the Gentiles, whom God drove out from before our face until the days of David, ⁴⁶who found favor before God and asked to build a dwelling place for the God of Jacob. ⁴⁷But Solomon erected a house for Him. ⁴⁸But the Most High does not dwell in handmade places, even as the prophet says, ⁴⁹'The heaven is My throne, and the earth the footstool of My feet; what kind of house will you erect for Me, says the Lord, or what place for My relaxation? ⁵⁰Did not My hand make all these?'

⁵¹"Stiffnecked and uncircumcised in hearts and ears, you always resist the Holy Spirit, as your fathers did you also do. ⁵²Which of the prophets did not your fathers persecute? And you killed those proclaiming beforehand the coming of the Righteous One Whom you betrayed and became murderers, ⁵³who received the Law in ordinances of angels, and you did not keep it."

⁵⁴And having heard these words, they were cut in their hearts and gnashed their teeth upon him. ⁵⁵And being full of the Holy Spirit, gazing intently into heaven, he saw the glory of God and Jesus standing on the right hand of God, ⁵⁶and he said, "Behold, I see the heavens having been opened and the Son of Man standing on the right hand of God." ⁵⁷And crying out with a great voice they rushed upon him with one accord. ⁵⁸And casting him out of the city, they were stoning him. And the witnesses place their garments at the feet of a young man being called Saul. ⁵⁹And as they were stoning Stephen he calling upon the Lord, saying, "Lord Jesus, receive my spirit." ⁶⁰And kneeling he cried out with a great voice. "Lord, do not place this sin against them" And saying this he fell asleep.

8 And Saul was consenting to the slaying of him. And on that day a great persecution came upon the church in Jerusalem; and all were dispersed, except the apostles, throughout the countries of Judea and Samaria. ²And devout men buried Stephen and made great lamentation over him. ³And Saul was ravaging the church, entering house after house, and dragging the men and women, committed them into prison.

⁴Indeed, therefore, the ones having been dispersed went everywhere, preaching the good news of the Word. ⁵But Philip, having gone down to the city of Samaria, was preaching Christ

to them. ⁶And the crowd was paying attention with one accord to what was being spoken by Philip when they were hearing, and were seeing the miraculous signs which he was doing. ⁷For many of the ones having unclean spirits – they were going out, crying with a great voice, and many being paralyzed and lame were being healed. ⁸And great joy came upon that city.

⁹And a certain man named Simon was previously performing sorcery in the city and amazing the nation of Samaria saying that he himself was some great one, ¹⁰to whom all from the smallest to the greatest were paying attention saying, "This is the power of God being called Great." ¹¹And they were paying attention to him because for a long time he had been amazing them with his sorceries. ¹²But when they believed Philip preaching good news about the kingdom of God and the name of Jesus Christ, they were being immersed both men and women. ¹³And also Simon himself believed, and having been immersed was continuing diligently with Philip, viewing the signs and great miracles being done, he was amazed.

¹⁴And the apostles in Jerusalem, having heard that Samaria had received the Word of God, sent to them Peter and John ¹⁵who, having come down, prayed concerning them that they might receive the Holy Spirit; ¹⁶for He not yet had fallen upon anyone, but only having been immersed in the name of the Lord Jesus, they were possessing Him. ¹⁷Then they laid hands on them, and they were receiving the Holy Spirit. ¹⁸And Simon beholding that through the laying on of the hands of the apostles the Spirit was given, offered them money ¹⁹saying, "Give to me this authority in order that upon whomever I lay my hands they may receive the Holy Spirit." ²⁰But Peter said to him, "May your silver be with you in destruction, because you supposed to obtain the free gift of God through money. ²¹You do not have part nor place in this word for your heart is not proper before God. ²²Repent therefore of this evil of you, and petition the Lord if then the schemes of your heart shall be forgiven to you. ²³For I see that you are in the gall of bitterness and the bond of unrighteousness." ²⁴And Simon answering said, "You petition the Lord on my behalf, so that nothing which you have aid may come upon me." ²⁵Then indeed they, having witnessed thoroughly, and having spoken the Word of the Lord, were returning to Jerusalem, preaching the good news in many villages of the Samaritans.

²⁶And an angel of the Lord spoke to Philip saying, "Arise and go down south upon the road going down from Jerusalem to Gaza." This is wilderness. ²⁷And arising, he went; and behold a man of Ethiopia, a eunuch, an official of Queen Candace of Ethiopia who was over all her treasury, who had come worshipping in Jerusalem. ²⁸And was returning and sitting in his chariot and reading the prophet Isaiah. ²⁹And the Spirit said to Philip, "Go to this chariot and join company with it." ³⁰And running forward Philip heard him reading Isaiah the prophet and said, "Indeed, then, do you understand what you are reading?" ³¹And he said, "For how would I be able unless someone will guide me?" And he invited Philip to come up and sit with him. ³²And the passage of Scripture which he was reading was this: "He was led as a sheep to slaughter and as a lamb before his shearer is silent, thus He did not open His mouth. ³³In His humiliation His justice was taken away; who can declare His generation because His life was taken from Him." ³⁴And the eunuch answering Philip said, "I beg you to tell me concerning whom does the prophet say this?" ³⁵And Philip opening his mouth and beginning from this Scripture preached to him Jesus. ³⁶And as they were going down the road, they came upon some water, and the eunuch said to him, "Behold, water; what prevents me to be immersed?" ³⁷And Philip said to him, "If you believe out of your whole heart, it is right to do so." And

answering he said, "I believe Jesus Christ to be the Son of God." ³⁸And he commanded the chariot to stand, and they went down into the water, both Philip and the eunuch, and he immersed him. ³⁹And when they came up out of the water, the Spirit of the Lord carried away Philip and the eunuch did not see him any more; for he was going on his way rejoicing. ⁴⁰And Philip was found in Azotus, and going through, he was preaching the good news in all the cities until he came to Caesarea.

**9** But Saul still breathing out threat and murder upon the disciples of the Lord, having gone to the high priest, ²asked from him letters to the synagogues in Damascus, so that if he might find any being of the Way, both men and women, binding them, he might bring them to Jerusalem. ³And it happened that as he was going, he drew near to Damascus, and suddenly a light out of heaven flashed brightly round about him, ⁴and falling upon the ground, he heard a voice saying to him, "Saul, Saul, why do you persecute Me?" ⁵And he said, "Who are you Lord?" And He said, "I am Jesus Whom you are persecuting. ⁶But arise and go into the city, and it shall be told to you what it is necessary for you to do." ⁷But the men traveling with him had stood speechless, hearing indeed the voice, but seeing no one. ⁸And Saul rose up from the ground and having opened his eyes, was seeing nothing; and leading him by the hand, they brought him into Damascus. ⁹And he was three days not seeing, and he did not eat nor drink anything.
¹⁰And there was in Damascus a certain disciple named Ananias, and the Lord said to him in a vision, "Ananias." And he said, "Behold, I am here, Lord." ¹¹And the Lord said to him, "Ananias, go to the street being called Straight and seek in
the home of Judas, a man named Saul of Tarsus; for behold he is praying, ¹²and he saw in a vision a man named Ananias coming in and laying hands on him so that he might recover sight." ¹³And Ananias answered, "Lord, I have heard from many concerning this man how much evil he did to your saints in Jerusalem. ¹⁴And he was come here with authority from the chief priests to bind all those calling upon Your name." ¹⁵And the Lord said to him, "Go, because this one is a chosen agent to Me to bear My name before both Gentiles and kings and to sons of Israel; ¹⁶for I will demonstrate to him how much it is necessary for him to suffer on behalf of my name." ¹⁷And Ananias sent and entered into the home, and laying his hands upon him, said, "Brother Saul, the Lord Jesus Who appeared to you on the road by which you were coming, has sent me, so that you might recover sight and be filled with the Holy Spirit." ¹⁸And immediately there fell from his eyes as scales and he recovered sight, and arising was immersed, ¹⁹and having taken food, he was strengthened. And he was with the disciples in Damascus several days. ²⁰And immediately in the synagogues he was preaching Jesus that He was the Son of God. ²¹And all those hearing him were amazed and were saying, "Is not this the one making havoc of the ones calling on this Name in Jerusalem, and he had come here in order that he might bind them and bring them to the chief priests?" ²²But Saul was becoming more able and was confusing the Jews dwelling in Damascus, systematically proving that this Jesus is the Christ.
²³And as considerable days were fulfilled, the Jews plotted together to kill him. ²⁴But their plot was known to Saul. And they also were guarding closely the gates of the city both day and night so that they might destroy him. ²⁵But his disciples taking him at night, let him

down through the city wall, lowering him in a basket. ²⁶And arriving in Jerusalem he attempted to join with the disciples; and all were fearful of him, not believing that he is a disciple. ²⁷But Barnabas taking it upon himself, led him to the apostles and related fully to them how he saw the Lord on the road, and that He spoke to him, and how in Damascus he boldly spoke out for the name of Jesus. ²⁸And he was with them going in and out of Jerusalem boldly speaking out for the name of the Lord, ²⁹both speaking to and disputing with the Hellenists; but they were attempting to kill him. ³⁰But the brethren learning about this took him to Caesarea and sent him off to Tarsus. ³¹Indeed therefore the church was having peace throughout all Judea and Galilee and Samaria, and being built up, was going forward in the fear of the Lord and comforted by the Holy Spirit, it was multiplying.

³⁶And in Joppa there was a certain disciple named Tabitha, which being interpreted is saying Dorcas; she was full of good works and charity which she was doing. ³⁷And it happened in those days she became sick and died; and washing her they placed her in an upper room. ³⁸Joppa being near Lydda, the disciples having heard that Peter is in it, sent two men to him, pleading, "Do not hesitate to come to us." ³⁹And Peter having arisen went with them, whom when he arrived, they brought into the upper room, and all the widows stood by him, crying and showing him tunics and garments Dorcas was making being with them. ⁴⁰But Peter sent all out and falling on his knees, prayed, and turning to the body said, "Tabitha, arise." And she opened her eyes and having seen Peter she sat up. ⁴¹And giving her a hand he raised her, and calling the saints and widows presented her living. ⁴²And it became known throughout the whole of Joppa, and many believed on the Lord. ⁴³And it happened he remained several days in Joppa with a certain Simon, a tanner.

**10** And there was in Caesarea a man named Cornelius, a centurion of the regiment being called Italian, ²a devout man and fearing God with all his house, doing much charity to the people and petitioning God constantly. ³He saw in a vision plainly around the ninth hour an angel of God coming to him and saying to him, "Cornelius!" ⁴And gazing intently on him and becoming frightened, he said, "What is it, Lord?" And he said to him, "Your prayers and your charity have come up as a memorial before God. ⁵And now send men to Joppa and summon a certain Simon, the one being surnamed Peter; ⁶this one is lodging with a certain Simon the Tanner, whose home is beside the sea." ⁷And when the angel speaking to him departed, calling two of the household servants and a devout soldier of those continuing diligently with him, ⁸and having explained everything to them, he sent them to Joppa.

⁹And on the morrow as those men were traveling on the road and were coming near the city, Peter went up upon the housetop to pray about the sixth hour. ¹⁰And he became hungry and was wanting to eat; but as they were preparing a meal a trance came upon him, ¹¹and he views the heaven having been opened and an object coming down like a great sheet being lowered by four corners to the earth, ¹²in which were all the four footed animals and reptiles of the earth and birds of heaven. ¹³And a voice came to him, "Arise Peter, slay and eat." ¹⁴But Peter said, "May it not be so, Lord, because I never yet ate anything unholy or unclean." ¹⁵And a voice again the second time said to him, "What God cleansed you should not call unholy." ¹⁶This happened three times, and immediately the object was taken into heaven. ¹⁷And as Peter was perplexed within himself as to what this vision might be which he saw, behold, the men

having been sent by Cornelius, having asked around for Simon's home, stood at the door. ¹⁸And calling out they inquired if Simon the one Surnamed Peter was a guest there.

¹⁹And while Peter was deliberating thoroughly concerning the vision, the Spirit said to him, "Behold, three men are seeking you. ²⁰But arising go down and go with them, doubting nothing because I sent them." ²¹And going down Peter said to the men, "Behold, I am whom you are seeking. What is the reason for which you came?" ²²And they said, "Cornelius, a centurion, a righteous man and fearing God as being witnessed by the whole nation of Jews, was instructed by a holy angel to summon you to his house and to hear words from you. ²³Then he invited them to be his guests. And on the morrow arising, he went forth with them, and certain of the brethren from Joppa went with him. ²⁴And on the morrow he entered into Caesarea and Cornelius was expecting them, having called together his relatives and close friends. ²⁵And it happened when Peter entered, Cornelius, meeting him, falling at his feet worshipped him. ²⁶But Peter raised him up, saying, "Stand up, I myself am also a man." ²⁷And conversing with him, he entered and finds many having come together. ²⁸And he said to them, "You yourselves will know how it is unlawful for a man, a Jew, to join with or to keep company with a foreigner; and God showed me not to call any man unholy or unclean. ²⁹Wherefore then without objection I came being summoned. I inquired therefore for what reason did you summon me?" ³⁰And Cornelius said, "From four days ago until this hour, I was at the ninth hour praying in my house, and behold, a man stood before me in bright apparel, ³¹and he says, 'Cornelius, your prayer was heard and your charity remembered before God. ³²Send therefore to Joppa and call for Simon who is surnamed Peter; this one is a guest in the home of Simon a tanner beside the sea.' ³³At once therefore I sent to you, and you did well being here present. Now therefore we all are here present before God to hear everything having been commanded to you by the Lord."

³⁴And opening his mouth Peter said, "Upon a truth I perceive that God does not show partiality to anyone ³⁵but in every nation the one fearing Him and working righteousness is acceptable to Him. ³⁶The Word which He sent to the sons of Israel preaching good news of peace through Jesus Christ, this One is Lord of all ³⁷you yourselves know, the Word having come throughout the whole of Judea, beginning from Galilee after the immersion which John proclaimed, ³⁸Jesus from Nazareth, how God anointed Him with the Holy Spirit and power, Who went about doing good and healing all the ones being subjected by the power of the devil, because God was with Him. ³⁹And we are witnesses of all which He did in the country of the Jews and Jerusalem, Whom also they killed, hanging Him on a tree. ⁴⁰This One God raised up on the third day, and granted Him to become manifest, ⁴¹not to all people but to witnesses having been chosen beforehand to God, to us, who ate with and drank with Him after He from the dead. ⁴²And He commanded us to preach to the people and to witness thoroughly that this is the One having been ordained by God as judge of the living and the dead. ⁴³To this all the prophets witness that all the ones believing in Him, through His name, receive forgiveness of sins."

⁴⁴While Peter was still speaking these words the Holy Spirit fell upon all those hearing the Word, ⁴⁵and the believers, out of circumcision, who came with Peter were amazed that even upon Gentiles the gift of the Holy Spirit was poured out; ⁴⁶for they were hearing them speaking in tongues and magnifying God. Then Peter asked, ⁴⁷"No one is able to forbid water

that these be not immersed who received the Holy Spirit even as we, can one?" ⁴⁸And he directed them to be immersed in the name of Jesus Christ. Then they requested him to remain certain days.

**11** But the apostles and the brethren being at Jerusalem heard that the Gentiles also received the Word of God. ²And when Peter went up to Jerusalem, those out of circumcision censured him, ³saying that, "You went in with uncircumcised men and ate with them." ⁴But Peter began explaining to them in order saying, ⁵"I was in the city of Joppa praying and saw a vision in a trance, a certain object coming down like a great sheet, being lowered out of heaven by four corners, and it came till reaching me. ⁶Gazing intently I was considering it closely and saw four-footed animals of the earth and wild beasts and reptiles and birds of heaven. ⁷And I heard also a voice saying to me, 'Arise, Peter lay and eat.' ⁸But I said, 'May it not be so, Lord, because never has anything unholy or unclean entered my mouth.' ⁹But a voice answered the second time out of heaven, 'What God cleansed you should not call unholy.' ¹⁰And this happened three times and everything was again pulled up into heaven. ¹¹And behold at once three men arrived at the home in which I was, having been sent from Caesarea to me. ¹²And the Spirit said to me, 'Go with them nothing doubting.' And these six brethren went with me and we went into the man's house. ¹³And he declared to us how he saw the angel in his house standing and saying, 'Send to Joppa and summon Simon the one being surnamed Peter, ¹⁴who will speak words to you by which you shall be saved and all your household.' ¹⁵And as I began to speak the Holy Spirit fell upon them as also upon us in the beginning. ¹⁶And I remembered the Word of the Lord as He was saying, 'John indeed immersed in water, but you yourselves shall be immersed in the Holy Spirit.' ¹⁷If therefore God gave the same gift to them as also to us having believed upon the Lord Jesus Christ, how was I able to thwart God?" ¹⁸And having heard this, they were silent and glorified God, saying, "Therefore, God also has given repentance to life to the Gentiles."

¹⁹Therefore, indeed, the ones being dispersed from the tribulation coming upon Stephen went abroad as far as Phoenicia and Cyprus and Antioch, speaking the Word to no one except Jews only. ²⁰But there were certain men of Cyprus and Cyrene, and going to Antioch, were speaking also to the Greeks, preaching the good news about the Lord Jesus. ²¹And the hand of the Lord was with them, and a great number believing turned to the Lord. ²²And the Word concerning them was heard in the ears of the church being in Jerusalem, and they sent out Barnabas to Antioch; ²³who arriving and beholding the grace of God, rejoiced, and was encouraging all with determination of heart to remain steadfast to the Lord, ²⁴because he was a good man and full of the Holy Spirit and faith and a considerable crowd was added to the Lord. ²⁵And he went out to Tarsus to seek for Saul, ²⁶and finding him, brought him to Antioch. And it happened that they were gathered together with them a whole year in the church and taught a considerable crowd and called the disciples Christians first in Antioch.

²⁷And in these days prophets went down from Jerusalem to Antioch; ²⁸and one of them named Agabus arising signified through the Spirit a great famine was about to come upon the whole inhabited earth; which happened during the reign of Claudius. ²⁹And any of the disciples as were prosperous, each of them determined to send for the ministration of the brethren dwelling in Jerusalem; ³⁰which also they did having sent forth to the elders by the hands of Barnabas and Saul.

12 And about that time Herod the King laid hands on certain ones from the church to do them evil. ²And he killed James the brother of John with a sword. ³And seeing that this was pleasing to the Jews, he proceeded to capture also Peter, but it was the days of Unleavened Bread, ⁴whom having captured, he placed in prison, delivering him to four quaternions of soldiers to guard him, determining after Passover to bring him out before the people. ⁵Therefore, indeed, Peter was kept in prison; but prayer was being made earnestly by the church to God for him. ⁶But when Herod was about to bring him out, that night Peter was sleeping between two soldiers being bound with two chains, and guards before the doors were keeping the prison. ⁷And behold an angel of the Lord appeared suddenly and a light shown in the building; and striking Peter's side, raised him, saying, "Arise in haste," and his chains fell off his hands. ⁸And the angel said to him, "Clothe yourself and put on your sandals." And he did thus. And he says, "Put your cloak about you and follow me." ⁹And having gone out, he was following and he did not know that what was being done by the angel was true, but was supposing that he was seeing a vision. ¹⁰But having gone through the first and second guard, they came to the iron gate bringing into the city, which opened automatically to them, and having gone out they went by one street, and immediately the angel departed from him. ¹¹And Peter, coming to himself, said, "Now I know truly that the Lord sent forth His angel and delivered me out of the hand of Herod and all the expectations of the people of the Jews." ¹²And realizing this he went to the home of Mary the mother of John, the one being surnamed Mark, where many were gathered together and were praying. ¹³And when he knocked on the door of the gate, a maidservant named Rhoda came to it to answer; ¹⁴and recognizing Peter's voice from joy, she did not open the gate, but running declared that Peter stood before the gate. ¹⁵But they said to her, "You are speaking madness." But she continued definitely asserting that it was so. But they were saying "It is his angel." ¹⁶But Peter continued knocking; and having opened, they saw him and were amazed. ¹⁷And motioning with his hand to be silent he declared in full to them how the Lord led him out of the prison and said, "Report to James and the brethren these events." And having gone out, he went to another place. ¹⁸And when day came there was no little disturbance among the soldiers as to what happened to Peter. ¹⁹And Herod having searched for him and not finding him having examined the guards, commended that they be led away to be killed; and having gone down from Judea to Caesarea, he stayed there.

²⁰And he was furiously angry with those of Tyre and Sidon; but with one accord they came to him and having persuaded Blastus the chamberlain of the king to assist them, they were seeking peace because their country was fed by the king's. ²¹And on an appointed day Herod, having been clothed in royal apparel and sitting upon the judgment seat was delivering a public oration to them. ²²And the mob continued calling out, "It is a voice of God not man." ²³And instantly an angel of the Lord struck him since he did not give glory to God, and being eaten by worms, he died. ²⁴But the Word of God was increasing and multiplying. ²⁵And Barnabas and Saul returned from Jerusalem, having completed their ministry, taking with them John being surnamed Mark.

**13** And there was throughout the church being in Antioch prophets and teachers: both Barnabas and Simeon the one being called Niger, and Lucius the Cyrenian, and Manean, brought up with Herod the tetrarch, and Saul. ²And as they were serving the Lord and fasting, the Holy Spirit said, "Separate now to Me Barnabas and Saul for the work to which I have called them." ³Then fasting and praying and laying hands on them they sent them away.

⁴So then, having been sent out by the Holy Spirit, they went down to Seleucia, and from there sailed to Cyprus. ⁵And being in Salamis, they were proclaiming the Word of God in the synagogues of the Jews; and they had John Mark as a menial servant. ⁶And having gone through the whole island as far as Paphos, they found a certain magician, a Jewish false prophet, whose name was Bar-Jesus, ⁷who was with the proconsul, Sergius Paulus, a rational man. This one, summoning Barnabas and Saul, was seeking to hear the Word of God; ⁸but Elymas the magician, for such was the interpretation of his name, was opposing them, seeking to turn away, the proconsul from the faith. ⁹But Saul, who is also Paul, being full of the Holy Spirit, gazing intently on him ¹⁰said, "O you full of every deceit and every villainy, son of the devil, enemy of all righteousness, will you not stop turning away from the right ways of the Lord? ¹¹And now behold the hand of the Lord is upon you and you shall be blind, not seeing the sun for a time." And instantly a mist and darkness fell upon him, and he was going around seeking someone to lead him by the hand. ¹²Then the proconsul seeing what had happened believed, being astonished by the teaching of the Lord. ¹³Those accompanying Paul having set sail at Paphos, came to Perga in Pamphylia; and John Mark departing from them, returned to Jerusalem.

¹⁴And they, going through from Perga arrived at Antioch of Pisidia, and entering into the synagogue on the Sabbath day, sat down. ¹⁵And after the reading of the Law and the prophets, the synagogue ruler sent to them, saying, "Men, brethren, if any among you has a word of exhortation for the people, you speak." ¹⁶And Paul arising and motioning with his hand said, "Men, Israelites, and those fearing God, listen. ¹⁷The God of this people, Israel, chose our fathers, and lifted up the people during their sojourn in Egypt, and with an uplifted arm led them out of it, ¹⁸and about forty years He endured their conduct in the wilderness. ¹⁹And having destroyed seven nations in the land of Canaan, He divided the land as an inheritance for them, ²⁰as about four hundred and fifty years. And after these events He gave them judges until Samuel the prophet. ²¹And then they asked for a king, and God gave to them Saul, son of Kish, a man of the tribe of Benjamin, for forty years. ²²And having removed him, He raised up David for them as king, to whom also having witnessed, He said, 'I found David, the son of Jesse, a man after my heart who will do all My will.' ²³From the seed of this one, according to the promise, God brought to Israel a Savior, Jesus. ²⁴John having previously proclaimed before the fact of His entrance, an immersion of repentance to all the people of Israel. ²⁵And as John completed his course, he was saying, 'What do you consider me to be? I am not He; but behold, He comes after me of Whom I am not worthy to loosen the sandals of His feet.'
²⁶Men, brethren, sons of the family of Abraham and the ones fearing God among you, to you the Word of this salvation was sent out. ²⁷For those dwelling in Jerusalem and their rulers not knowing, and not hearing the voices of the prophets being read every Sabbath after Sabbath, condemning Him, fulfilled them, ²⁸and finding not one reason for death, they asked Pilate to

destroy Him; ²⁹And when they finished all the things having been written concerning Him, taking Him down from the tree, they laid Him in a tomb. ³⁰But God raised Him up out of the dead; ³¹Who was seen many days by those having gone down with Him from Galilee to Jerusalem, who now are His witnesses to the people. ³²And we preach good news to you, the promise having come to the fathers, ³³that God fulfilled this promise to us, their children, having raised up Jesus, as also it has been in the second Psalm, 'You are My Son, this day I have begotten you.' ³⁴That He raised Him out of the dead, no more being about to return to corruption, thus He has spoken that, 'I will give to you the holy and faithful mercies of David.' ³⁵Wherefore also in another Psalm it says, 'You will not give Your Holy One to see corruption.' ³⁶For David indeed, having served his own generation for the purpose of God, fell asleep and was buried with his fathers and saw corruption. ³⁷But Whom God raised from the dead did not see corruption. ³⁸Therefore, be it known to you, men, brethren, that by this One forgiveness of sins is proclaimed to you, ³⁹and from all shortcomings of which you were not able by the Law to be justified; in this One everyone who believes is justified. ⁴⁰Take heed, therefore that everything having been spoken in the prophets does not come upon you. ⁴¹'Behold, you the ones despising, and marvel and vanish because I work a work in your days, a work which you will absolutely not believe, even if someone declare it to you.'"

⁴²And when they were leaving, they were pleading with them to speak these words to them on the following Sabbath. ⁴³The synagogue being dismissed; many of the Jews and the worshipping proselytes followed Paul and Barnabas, who speaking to them, were persuading them to continue in the grace of God. ⁴⁴And on the coming Sabbath almost all the city were gathered together to hear the Word of the Lord. ⁴⁵But the Jews seeing the crowds were filled with jealousy and were contradicting the words being spoken by Paul, and were slandering him. ⁴⁶Both Paul and Barnabas, speaking boldly, said, "It was necessary that the Word of God first be spoken to you; since you reject it and do not judge yourselves worthy of eternal life, behold we turn to the Gentiles. ⁴⁷For thus the Lord has commanded us, 'I have placed you as a light for the Gentiles that you be for salvation to the end of the earth.'" ⁴⁸And the Gentiles hearing, were rejoicing and glorifying the Word of the Lord, and as many as had determined themselves for eternal life believed. ⁴⁹And the Word of the Lord spread throughout the whole country. ⁵⁰But the Jews agitated the worshipping, well respected women and the leading men of the city, and stirred up a persecution against Paul and Barnabas and cast them out of their boundaries. ⁵¹But they, shaking off the dust of their feet on them came to Iconium. ⁵²And the disciples were being filled with joy and the Holy Spirit.

14 And it happened in Iconium that as usual they entered into the synagogue of the Jews and spoke thus so that a large multitude of both Jews and Greeks believed. ²But the Jews being unpersuaded stirred up and made evil the souls of the Gentiles against the brethren. ³Indeed, therefore they continued a considerable time speaking boldly with the Lord witnessing to the Word by His grace, giving miraculous signs and wonders to be done through their hands. ⁴But the multitude of the city was divided, and some were indeed with the Jews but others with the apostles. ⁵And when a project was made by both the Gentiles and the Jews with their rulers to treat them shamefully and to stone them, ⁶they became aware of it, and fled into the cities of Lycaonia, Lystra and Derbe and the surrounding country. ⁷And there they were preaching the gospel.

⁸And in Lystra a certain man sat unable to use his feet, lame from his mother's womb, who had never walked. ⁹This one heard Paul speaking, who gazed intently on him seeing that he has faith to be saved, ¹⁰said with a great voice, "Stand up erect on your feet." And he leaped up and started walking. ¹¹And the crowds seeing what Paul did raised their voice, saying in the Lycaonian language, "The gods having become like men have come down to us." ¹²And they were calling Barnabas, Zeus and Paul, Hermes since he was the leading speaker. ¹³And the priest of Zeus, the temple being before the city gates, brought bulls and garlands to the gates, with the crowds he was desiring to offer sacrifice to them. ¹⁴But the apostles Barnabas and Paul having heard, tearing their garments, rushed out into the crowd, crying out ¹⁵and saying, "Men, why are you doing these acts? We are men of like passions as you and preach the gospel to you that you might turn from these futilities to the living God. Who made the heaven and the earth and the sea and everything that is in them; ¹⁶who in the preceding generations allowed all nations to go their own ways; ¹⁷even so He did not leave Himself without a witness by doing good, giving to you rain from heaven and times of fruitbearing, filling your hearts with food and gladness. ¹⁸Even saying these words they scarcely restrained the crowds to not offer sacrifice to them.

¹⁹But Jews came from Antioch and Iconium and having persuaded the crowds and having stoned Paul, they were dragging him outside the city, supposing him to be dead. ²⁰But the disciples having gathered around him, arising he went into the city. And on the morrow he went with Barnabas to Derbe. ²¹And preaching the gospel in that city, and making considerable number of disciples, they returned to Lystra and to Iconium and to Antioch, ²²strengthening the souls of the disciples, encouraging them to remain in the faith and that through much tribulation it is necessary for us to enter into the kingdom of God. ²³And in every church they were having elders chosen for them, and with prayer and fasting set them apart to the Lord in whom they had believed. ²⁴And going through Pisidia they came to Pamphylia, ²⁵and having spoken the Word in Perga, they went down to Attalia. ²⁶And from there they sailed to Antioch, where they had been committed by the grace of God to the work which they fulfilled. ²⁷And having arrived and gathering the church together they reported whatever God did with them and that He opened the door of faith to the Gentiles. ²⁸And they stayed no little time with the disciples.

15 And certain ones coming down from Judea were teaching that except you be circumcised in the custom of Moses, you are not able to be saved. ²And no little opposition and dispute happening with Paul and Barnabas, it was determined for Paul and Barnabas and certain others of them to go up to the apostles and elders in Jerusalem concerning this disputation. ³They indeed therefore being sent forth by the church were going through both Phoenicia and Samaria, reporting fully the conversion of the Gentiles and were bringing great joy to all the brethren. ⁴And having arrived in Jerusalem, they were welcomed by the church and the apostles and the elders, and they reported whatever God did with them. ⁵But certain ones of the sect of the Pharisees having been believers, stood forth saying that it is necessary to circumcise them and to command them to keep the Law of Moses.

⁷And after much dispute was happening, Peter arising said to them, "Men, brethren, you know exactly that from earlier days among you God chose through my mouth for the Gentiles

to hear the Word of the gospel and believe. ⁸And God the heart-knower witnessed to them, giving the Holy Spirit even as also to us, ⁹and was not discriminating any way between us and them. ¹⁰Now therefore why do you test God, placing a yoke upon the neck of the disciples which neither our father nor we were able to bear? ¹¹But we believe that through the grace of the Lord Jesus we are saved even as those also in the same manner." ¹²And the multitude was silent, and were hearing Barnabas and Paul relating whatever miraculous signs and wonders God did among the Gentiles through them. ¹³And after they were finished, James answered saying, "Men, brethren, hear me, ¹⁴Simeon related how God first visited to take out of the Gentiles a people for His name. ¹⁵And the words of the prophets agree with this, even as it has been written, ¹⁶'After these days I will return, and will rebuild the fallen tabernacle of David, and I will rebuild the ruins of it and I will restore it, ¹⁷so that the rest of men may seek the Lord, and all the Gentiles who are called by My name, says the Lord doing these deeds, ¹⁸being known from the ages.' ¹⁹Wherefore I judge that we do not disturb those from among the Gentiles turning to God, ²⁰but write to them that they should abstain from pollutions of idols and fornication and from what is strangled and from blood. ²¹For Moses from ancient generations has in city after city those preaching him in the synagogues, being read every Sabbath."

²²Then it was pleasing to the apostles and the elders and to the whole church, choosing men out of them to send to Antioch with Paul and Barnabas, Judas being called Barsabbas and Silas, leading men among the brethren, ²³having written by their hand, "The apostles and the elder brethren to the brethren among the Gentiles in Antioch and Syria and Cilicia, greetings. ²⁴Since we heard that certain ones out of us having come, troubled you with words upsetting your souls, to whom we did not give commandment, ²⁵it seemed pleasing to us, being of one accord, having chosen men to send to you with our beloved Barnabas and Paul, ²⁶men having given up their lives on behalf of the name of our Lord Jesus Christ. ²⁷We have sent therefore Judas and Silas, and they will declare the same by word of mouth. ²⁸For it seemed pleasing to the Holy Spirit and us to place upon you no more burden than these necessities, ²⁹abstain from sacrifices to idols and blood and things strangled and fornication; from which keeping yourselves away, you will do well. Farewell." ³⁰Indeed therefore, having been dismissed, they went down to Antioch and gathering together the multitude they delivered the epistle; ³¹and reading it they rejoiced upon the exhortation. ³²Both Judas and Silas, also being themselves prophets, through much speech exhorted and strengthened the brethren. ³³And having spent some time here, they were dismissed with peace from the brethren to go to those having sent them. ³⁴But it seemed good for Silas to remain there. ³⁵But Paul and Barnabas were staying in Antioch teaching and preaching the Word of the Lord, also with many others.

³⁶And after certain days Paul said to Barnabas, "Returning then, let us visit the brethren at every city in which we proclaimed the Word of the Lord, to see how they have done." ³⁷But Barnabas was wanting to take with them also John, the one being called Mark; ³⁸but Paul was considering it not right to take with them this one, he having deserted from them from Pamphylia and not going on with them to the work. ³⁹And there came a sharp contention so that they separated from one another, and Barnabas taking Mark sailed off to Cyprus. ⁴⁰But Paul having chosen Silas went out, having been committed to the grace of the Lord by the brethren, ⁴¹and went through Syria and Cilicia strengthening the churches.

**16** And they arrived in Derbe and Lystra. And behold there was there a certain disciple named Timothy, a son of a Jewish woman of faith and a Greek father, ²who was witnessed to by the brethren in Lystra and Iconium. ³Paul desired this one to go with him and taking, circumcised him on account of the Jews being in those places, for everyone knew that his father was Greek. ⁴And as they were going through the cities, they were delivering to them the degrees to be kept having been determined by the apostles and elders in Jerusalem. ⁵Indeed therefore, the churches were being strengthened in the faith, and were increasing in number day after day.

⁶And they went through the country of Phrygia and Galatia, having been forbidden by the Holy Spirit to speak the Word in Asia. ⁷And having come near Mysia, they were trying to go into Bithynia and the Spirit of Jesus did not allow them. ⁸And passing by Mysia they went down to Troas. ⁹And a vision during the night appeared to Paul, a certain man of Macedonia was standing and pleading with him, saying, "Come over into Macedonia and help us." ¹⁰And when he saw the vision, immediately we sought to go out into Macedonia, concluding that God had called to us to evangelize them. ¹¹And having set sail from Troas, we ran a straight course to Samothrace, and the next day to Neapolis, ¹²and from there to Philippi, which is the first city of the district of Macedonia, a Roman colony. And we were staying in this city certain days. ¹³And on the Sabbath day we went out of the gate beside the river where we supposed there was a place of prayer, and having sat down we spoke to the women having come together there. ¹⁴And a certain woman named Lydia, a seller of purple dyed garments from the city of Thyatira, being a worshipper of God, was listening, whose heart the Lord opened to take heed to that being spoken by Paul. ¹⁵And when she was immersed and her household she pleaded, saying, "If you have judged me to be faithful to the Lord, come into my house to abide." And she persuaded us.

¹⁶And it happened as they were going to the place of prayer a certain slave girl having the spirit of sorcery met us, who brought much business to her masters by fortune telling. ¹⁷Following after Paul and us, she was crying out, saying, "These men are slaves of the Most High God, who are proclaiming to you a way of salvation." ¹⁸And this she was doing for many days. And Paul being greatly disturbed and turning upon the spirit said, "I command you in the name of Jesus Christ to come out of her." And it came out that same hour. ¹⁹And her masters seeing that the hope of their business had gone out, grasping Paul and Silas, dragged them into the market place before the rulers. ²⁰And having led them to the magistrates said, "These men being Jews are seriously upsetting our city, ²¹and proclaim customs which it is not lawful for us to either accept or practice being Romans." ²²And the crowd rose up together against them and the magistrates tearing their garments, commanded them to be beaten with rods. ²³And having laid many blows upon them, they cast them in prison commanding the jailor to keep them securely; ²⁴who having received such a command as this cast them into the inner prison and secured their feet in stocks.

²⁵And about midnight Paul and Silas were praying, singing hymns to God, and the other prisoners were paying close attention to them. ²⁶And suddenly there came a great earthquake so that the foundation of the jailhouse was shaken, and instantly all the doors were opened, and everyone's bonds were unfastened. ²⁷And the jailor being awakened and seeing the doors

of the prison having been opened, having drawn his sword was about to kill himself, supposing the prisoners had fled. ²⁸But Paul called with a loud voice saying, "Do not do to yourself any evil, for we are all here." ²⁹And asking for a light, he rushed in, and trembling he fell before Paul and Silas, ³⁰and bringing them out, he said, "Sirs, what is it necessary that I do in order to be saved?" ³¹And they said, "Believe on the Lord Jesus and you may be saved and your household." ³²And they spoke to him the Word of the Lord with everyone in his home. ³³And taking them in that hour of the night, he washed their stripes, and he was immersed and all of his household instantly. ³⁴And bringing them into the house, he set a table before them, and rejoiced with all his house, having believed in God.

³⁵And having become day the magistrates sent the officers saying, "Release those men." ³⁶And the jailor declared the words to Paul that, "The magistrates have sent in order that you be released; now therefore coming out, go in peace." ³⁷But Paul said to them, "Having beaten us publicly without trial, men being Romans, they cast us into prison and now privately they cast us out? No indeed! But let them come themselves and lead us out." ³⁸And the officers reported to the magistrates these words and they were frightened hearing that they are Romans, ³⁹and coming pleaded with them and leading them out was asking them to leave the city. ⁴⁰And going out from the prison they went to the house of Lydia, and seeing the brethren, encouraged them, and they departed.

17 And traveling through Amphipolis and Apollonia they came to Thessalonica where there was a synagogue of Jews. ²And according to Paul's custom he went to them, and upon three sabbaths reasoned with them from the Scriptures, ³explaining and setting before them that it was necessary for Christ to suffer and rise out of the dead and that this Jesus is the Christ Whom I proclaim to you. ⁴And certain of them were persuaded and threw in their lot with Paul and Silas, and of the worshipping Greeks a large group of women and of leading men not a few. ⁵And the Jews being jealous and taking certain wicked men of the marketplace, and forming a mob, they were agitating the city; and attacking the home of Jason, they were seeking for them to bring them to the mob. ⁶Not finding them they were dragging Jason and certain brethren to the city rulers, crying that, "These men who have turned over the inhabited earth have arrived here also, ⁷whom Jason has welcomed; and these all act against the decrees of Caesar saying there is another king, Jesus." ⁸And they troubled the crowd and the city rulers hearing these words. ⁹And taking bond from Jason and the others they released them.

¹⁰And the brethren immediately during the night sent Paul and Silas out to Berea, who having arrived, went into the synagogue of the Jews. ¹¹And these were more noble than those in Thessalonica who received the Word with enthusiasm, daily examining the Scriptures to see if these words were so. ¹²Indeed many therefore of them believed of the honorable Greek women and men not a few. ¹³But when the Jews from Thessalonica knew that also in Berea the Word of God was proclaimed by Paul, they went there stirring and troubling the crowds. ¹⁴And immediately then the brethren sent Paul out to go by the sea; but Silas and Timothy remained there. ¹⁵And the ones who accompanied Paul went as far as Athens, and receiving commandment from Silas and Timothy that they come quickly to him, they left.

¹⁶And as Paul was waiting for them in Athens, his spirit was irritated in him, beholding

the collection of idols being in the city. ¹⁷Indeed therefore, he was reasoning in the synagogue with the Jews and those worshipping God; and in the marketplace every day to those happening to be there. ¹⁸And certain also of the Epicureans and Stoic philosophers encountered him, and certain were saying, "What would this charlatan desire to say?" But others said, "He seems to be a proclaimer of strange demons", because he was preaching the good news about Jesus and the resurrection. ¹⁹Then taking him up they brought him upon the Areopagus, saying, "May we be able to know what this new teaching being spoken by you is? ²⁰For you bring strange words to our ears, therefore we want to know what these teachings mean to be." ²¹Now all Athenians and strangers sojourning there were spending time in nothing other than speaking or hearing something novel.

²²And Paul standing in the midst of the Areopagus said, "Men, Athenians, I see that in every way you are very religious; ²³for going around and observing your objects of worship, I found even an altar on which was inscribed, 'To an unknown god.' Therefore, what you worship being without knowledge, this I proclaim to you. ²⁴The God making the world and everything in it, this One being Lord of heaven and earth, does not dwell in handmade sanctuaries; ²⁵neither is He served by hands of men, having need of anything, He himself giving to all life and breath and all blessings. ²⁶And He made out of one every nation of men to dwell on the face of the earth, having predetermined exact times and boundaries of their dwelling places, ²⁷to seek God if then they might touch Him and find Him, since He is not far from each one of us; ²⁸for in Him we live and move and exist as even certain of the poets among you have said, 'For we also are of His generation.' ²⁹Being therefore the generation of God we ought not to suppose deity to be like gold or silver or stone, an engraved word of art of man's imagination. ³⁰Indeed therefore, God having overlooked the times of ignorance, now commands all men everywhere to repent, ³¹because He set a day in which He is about to judge the inhabited earth in righteousness by a Man whom He designated, providing assurance to all, raising Him out of the dead."

³²And having heard of the resurrection of dead, some were sneering but some said, "We will hear you concerning this also again." ³³So Paul went out from the midst of them. ³⁴But certain men having joined with him, believed, among whom was Dionysis the Areopagite, and a woman named Damaris, and others with them.

18 After these events he departed out of Athens, and went to Corinth. ²And finding a certain Jew named Aquila, a native of Pontus and his wife Priscilla, having come recently from Italy because Claudius ordered all Jews to depart from Rome, he Paul came to them, ³and because he was of the same trade, he remained with them and was working for they were tentmakers by trade. ⁴And he was reasoning in the synagogue every sabbath, and was persuading both Jews and Greeks. ⁵But when both Silas and Timothy came down from Macedonia, Paul was holding himself exclusively to the Word, strongly witnessing to the Jews that Jesus was the Christ. ⁶But when they were setting themselves against him and blaspheming him, shaking off his garments, he said to them, "Your blood be upon your head; I am clean; from now on I go to the Gentiles."

⁷And having departed from there he went into the home of a certain man named Titius Justus, a worshipper of God whose home was joined next to the synagogue. ⁸And Crispus the

ruler of the synagogue believed with his whole household, and many of the Corinthians hearing, believed and were being immersed. ⁹And the Lord spoke in the night through a vision to Paul, "Do not be afraid, but continue to speak and do not be silent, ¹⁰because I am with you and no one will assault you to do you evil, because I have many people in this city." ¹¹And he stayed there a year and six months teaching to them the Word of God.

¹²But Gallio being proconsul of Achaia, the Jews with one accord rose up against Paul, and brought him before the judgment seat, ¹³saying that, "This one persuades men to worship God contrary to the law." ¹⁴And as Paul was about to open his mouth, Gallio said, to the Jews, "If indeed this were a matter of injustice or violent wickedness, O Jews, according to reason I would put up with you; ¹⁵but if it is questions concerning a word or names and your own law, see to it yourselves; I myself am not willing to be a judge of these." ¹⁶And he expelled them from the judgment seat. ¹⁷And taking hold of Sosthenes the synagogue ruler, they were beating him before the judgment seat; and Gallio was not concerned about any of these acts.

¹⁸But Paul having remained yet considerable days, taking leave of the brethren, set sail for Syria, and with him Priscilla and Aquila, having his hair cut off in Cenchrea for he had a vow. ¹⁹And arriving at Ephesus he left them there. He himself going into the synagogue, reasoned with the Jews. ²⁰And when they were asking him to remain a longer time, he did not consent, ²¹but taking leave and saying, "I will come back to you again, God willing," he sailed from Ephesus. ²²And having landed in Caesarea, he went up and having greeted the church, went down to Antioch. ²³And having spent some time there, he went out passing through in order the country of Galatia and Phrygia strengthening all the disciples.

²⁴And a certain Jew named Apollos an Alexandrian by birth, an educated man, arrived in Ephesus, being mighty in the Scriptures. ²⁵This one was instructed in the way of the Lord, and being fervent in spirit was speaking and teaching accurately the things concerning Jesus, though being aware of only the immersion of John. ²⁶And this one began speaking boldly in the synagogue; but Priscilla and Aquila having heard him, took him to themselves, and explained to him more accurately the way of God. ²⁷And when he wanted to go to Achaia, the brethren being encouraging, wrote to the brethren to welcome him, who arriving helped much those having believed through grace, ²⁸for he forcefully was refuting the Jews with reasoning publicly, demonstrating through the Scriptures that Jesus was the Christ.

19 And it happened when Apollos was in Corinth, Paul going through the upper country came to Ephesus and found some disciples. ²And said to them, "Having believed, did you receive the Holy Spirit?" And they said to him, "But we have not heard that there is a Holy Spirit." ³And he said, "Into what then were you immersed?" And they said, "Into the immersion of John." ⁴And Paul said, "John immersed an immersion of repentance, saying to the people that they should believe on the One coming after him, that is Jesus." ⁵And having heard, they were immersed in the name of the Lord Jesus; ⁶And Paul having laid hands on them, the Holy Spirit came upon them, and they were speaking with tongues and were prophesying. ⁷And all were about twelve men.

⁸And going into the synagogue, he was speaking boldly for about three months, reasoning and persuading concerning the kingdom of God. ⁹And as certain ones were being hardened and unpersuaded, speaking evil of the Way before the multitude, he separated from them with

the disciples, reasoning daily in the school Tyrannus. ¹⁰And this happened for two years, so that all those dwelling in Asia heard the Word of the Lord, both Jews and Greeks. ¹¹And God was doing out of the ordinary miracles through the hands of Paul, ¹²so that handkerchiefs and aprons from his body were brought away for the sick, and they were released from their diseases, and evil spirits went out from them.

¹³But certain wandering exorcists attempted to name over those having evil spirits the name of Jesus, saying, "I adjure you by the name of Jesus whom Paul preaches." ¹⁴And there were seven sons of a certain Sceva, a Jewish chief priest, who were doing this. ¹⁵But the evil spirit answered and said to them, "Jesus I know, and I am aware of Paul, but who are you?" ¹⁶And the man in whom the evil spirit was, leaping on them mastering both, overpowered them, so that they fled out of that house naked, and having been wounded. ¹⁷And this became known to all those dwelling in Ephesus, they were magnifying the name of the Lord Jesus. ¹⁸And many of those having believed were coming, making confession and declaring their practices. ¹⁹And a considerable number of those practicing necromancy having brought their books together were burning them before everyone; and counted together the value of them, and found it to be fifty thousand silver pieces. ²⁰Thus according to the might of the Lord, the Word was increasing and growing strong.

²¹And when all these events were fulfilled, Paul planned in the Spirit going throughout Macedonia and Achaia, to go to Jerusalem, saying that, "After I go there, it is necessary for me to see Rome also." ²²And having sent into Macedonia two of those serving him, Timothy and Erastus, he spent some time in Asia. ²³And about that time no little disturbance happened concerning the Way. ²⁴For a certain one, Demetrius by name, a silversmith, making silver shrines of Artemis, was bringing in no little business for the craftsmen; ²⁵Whom having gathered together, and workmen of such trades as this, he said, "Men, you are aware that our prosperity is out of this business, ²⁶and you behold and hear that not only in Ephesus but in almost all of Asia, this Paul having persuaded them, has turned away a considerable crowd, saying that what is being made by hands are not gods. ²⁷And not only is there this danger to us that our part comes into disrespect, but also the temple of the great goddess Artemis will be considered nothing, and also she herself is about to be deprived of her magnificence whom the whole of Asia and the inhabited world worships." ²⁸And having heard and being filled with anger, they cried out saying, "Great is Artemis of the Ephesians." ²⁹And the city was filled with the turmoil as with one accord they rushed into the theater having seized Gaius and Aristarchus of Macedonia, travel companions of Paul. ³⁰And when Paul wanted to go into the mob of people in the theater, the disciples would not allow him. ³¹And certain of the Asiarch, being friends with him, having sent to him, were pleading that he not venture into the theater. ³²Indeed therefore, some were crying out one thing and others another, for the assembly was being confused, and the majority did not know for what reason they had come together. ³³And out of the crowd they urged forward Alexander, the Jews pressing him forth; and Alexander, waving his hand, was desiring to make a defense to the mob of people. ³⁴But recognizing that he was a Jew, one voice came from all as for two hours they were crying out, "Great is Artemis of the Ephesians." ³⁵And having quieted the crowd, the town clerk said, "Men, Ephesians, for what man is there who does not know the city of Ephesus is the temple guardian of the great Artemis, and the image fallen from heaven. ³⁶Therefore these facts being

undeniable, it is needful for you to be quiet and to do nothing reckless. [37]For you brought these men here who are neither temple robbers nor blasphemers of our goddess. [38]Indeed therefore, if Demetrius and the craftsmen with him have any accusation against anyone, court days are going on, and there are proconsuls available, let them bring charges on one another. [39]But if you seek anything further, it shall be settled in the lawful assembly. [40]For we are even in danger of being charged of rioting concerning this day, being no cause for it, concerning which we will not be able to give an account for this disturbance." [41]And having said these words he dismissed the assembly.

20 And after the tumult ceased, Paul sent for the disciples, exhorting them, bidding farewell, he departed to go into Macedonia. [2]And having gone through those parts and exhorting them with many words, he came into Greece, [3]and having spent three months, a plot arose against him by the Jews as he was about to set sail for Syria, so he decided to return through Macedonia. [4]And there he was accompanied by Sopater of Berea, the son of Pyrrhus; and by Aristarchus and Secundus of Thessalonica; and by Gaius of Derbe, and Timothy; and by Tychicus and Trophimus of Asia. [5]And these having gone on ahead, were waiting for us at Troas. [6]And we ourselves sailed from Philippi after the days of Unleavened Bread, and we came to them in Troas after five days, where we stayed seven days.

[7]And on the first day of the week, having been gathered together to break bread, Paul reasoned with them, intending to depart on the morrow, and he prolonged the word until midnight. [8]And there were many lamps in the upper room where we were assembled; [9]and a certain young man named Eutychus sitting upon the window-sill being borne down with a deep sleep, as Paul was reasoning yet longer, being overcome with sleep, he fell down from the third floor, and was taken up dead. [10]But Paul going down fell upon him, and having embraced him said, "Stop being troubled, for his life is in him." [11]And going up and breaking bread and eating, and for a considerable time conversing with them until daybreak, thus he departed. [12]And they took the young man alive, and were greatly comforted.

[13]And having gone ahead by boat we sailed to Assos, intending to take Paul aboard there, for thus it was arranged as he was intending to walk overland. [14]And when he met us at Assos, taking him aboard we came to Mitylene. [15]And sailing from there, the following day, we arrived opposite Chios, and the next day we crossed over at Samos, and the coming day we came to Miletus. [16]For Paul had determined to sail past Ephesus, so that he would not spend time in Asia, for he was hurrying if possible that he might be in Jerusalem by the day of Pentecost.

[17]And from Miletus, having sent to Ephesus, he called to him the elders of the church. [18]And when they came to him, he said to them, "You yourselves are aware that from the first day in which I set foot in Asia how I was with you all the time, [19]serving the Lord with all humility of mind and tears, and trials coming upon me by the plots of the Jews; [20]how I did not ever draw back from declaring to you anything beneficial and to teach you publicly and from house to house, [21]witnessing thoroughly both to Jews and Greeks the repentance toward God and faith in our Lord Jesus. [22]And now, behold, I am going to Jerusalem being bound in the Spirit not knowing the things that will happen to me in it, [23]except that the Holy Spirit witnesses thoroughly too me saying that bonds and tribulations await me. [24]But I do not

myself make my life of any account worthy to myself so I may finish my race, witnessing thoroughly to the gospel of the grace of God. ²⁵And now, behold, I myself know that all you among whom I went about preaching the kingdom will see my face no more; ²⁶wherefore, I witness to you this very day that I am clean from the blood of all men, ²⁷for I did not draw back to not declare to you all the will of God. ²⁸Take heed to yourselves and all the flock over which the Holy Spirit has placed you overseers to shepherd the church of God, which He secured through His own blood. ²⁹For I know that after my departure vicious wolves will come in among you not sparing the flock, ³⁰and men will rise up out of you yourselves speaking perversions in order to draw away the disciples after them. ³¹Wherefore be watchful, remembering that for three years night and day I did not cease admonishing each one of you with tears. ³²And now I commit you to God and to the Word of His grace being able to build you up, and to give you the inheritance to all those being sanctified. ³³I did not covet silver or gold or garments of anyone. ³⁴You yourselves know that these hands served to meet my needs and those being with me. ³⁵I demonstrated all ways to you that thus laboring it is necessary to assist those being weak, and to remember the works of the Lord Jesus that He said, 'It is more blessed to give than to receive.'"

³⁶And having said these words, bowing his knees, he prayed with all them. ³⁷And all were weeping considerable, and embracing Paul, were kissing him, ³⁸being distressed mostly by his word in which he said that they were about to see his face no more. And they accompanied him to the boat.

**21** And it happened that having departed from them, we set sail, running a straight course, we came to Kos, and the next day to Rhodes, and from there to Patara; ²and having found a boat crossing over to Phoenicia, going aboard we set sail. ³And sighting Cyprus, leaving it on the left, we were sailing to Syria, and landed at Tyre, for there the boat was unloading the cargo. ⁴And finding disciples there, we remained with them for seven days, who were telling Paul through the Spirit not to set foot in Jerusalem. ⁵And it happened that when we completed the days there, going out we were proceeding on our journey, all the disciples with women and children accompanying us until outside the city, and kneeling on the shore, praying, ⁶we bid one another farewell, and embarked on the boat, and they returned to their own homes. ⁷And we, having finished the voyage from Tyre, arrived at Ptolemais, and greeting the brethren, remained one day with them.

⁸And on the morrow, having gone out, we came to Caesarea, and going into the house of Philip the evangelist being one of the seven, we stayed with him. ⁹And this one had four virgin daughters who prophesied. ¹⁰And as we were stopping over there several days, a certain prophet named Agabus from Judea came down. ¹¹And coming to us, taking Paul's belt, binding his own feet and hands, said, "Here is what the Holy Spirit says, 'The man whose belt this is, the Jews will bind thus in Jerusalem and deliver over into the hands of Gentiles.'"

¹²And as we heard these words, both we and the local people were pleading with him not to go up to Jerusalem. ¹³Then Paul answered, "What are you doing, weeping and breaking my heart? For I am not only ready to be bound but also to die in Jerusalem on behalf of the name of the Lord Jesus." ¹⁴And as he would not be persuaded we kept silent, saying, "The will of the Lord be done."

¹⁵And after these days, having prepared ourselves with necessary equipment, we went up to Jerusalem; ¹⁶And also disciples from Caesarea went with us taking us to Mnason of Cyprus, an early disciple, with whom we would be guests. ¹⁷And we having come into Jerusalem, the brethren welcomed us gladly. ¹⁸And on the following day Paul went in with us to James, and all the elders were present. ¹⁹And greeting them Paul was recounting to them one by one each accomplishment which God did among the Gentiles through his ministry. ²⁰And the ones having heard were glorifying God, and said to him, "You see, brother, how many thousand of the ones believing are among the Jews, and all have zeal for the Law. ²¹And they were informed about you that you teach all Jews among the Gentiles to turn away from Moses, saying not to circumcise their children nor to maintain the customs. ²²Therefore, what is it? They certainly will hear that you have come. ²³Therefore, you do this which we tell you; we have four men having a vow upon themselves. ²⁴You take these, be purified with them, and meet the expenses for them in order that they may shave their head and all will know that there is nothing to what was informed about you, but you yourself also walk orderly and keep the Law. ²⁵But concerning the Gentiles having believed, we wrote having judge that they guard themselves from both that offered to idols and blood and that strangled and fornication." ²⁶Then Paul taking the men the next day, having been purified with them, went into the temple, declaring the fulfillment of the days of the purification until the offering on behalf of each of them would be presented.

²⁷And as the seven days were about to be completed, the Jews from Asia seeing him in the temple were stirring up all the crowd, and laid hands on him, ²⁸crying out, "Men, Israelites, come help; this is the man teaching everyone everywhere against the people and the Law and this place, and even also has brought in Greeks into the temple and has defiled this holy place." ²⁹For they had previously seen Trophimus the Ephesian in the city with him whom they were supposing Paul had brought into the temple. ³⁰And the whole city was incited and the people were running together, and grabbing Paul, they dragged him out of the temple; and immediately the doors were shut. ³¹And as they were seeking to kill him, information came up to the commander of the regiment that all Jerusalem was in turmoil, ³²who at once, taking along soldiers and centurions ran down upon them; and they seeing the commander and the soldiers stopped beating Paul. ³³Then the commander drawing near took hold of him and commanded him to be bound with two chains, and was questioning who he was and what he had done. ³⁴But some in the crowd shouted one thing and others another; and not being able to know of a certainty on account of the tumult, he commanded him to be brought into the barracks. ³⁵And when they came to the stairs, it so happened he was carried by the soldiers on account of the violence of the crowd, ³⁶for the multitude of the people was following, crying out, "Away with him!" ³⁷And as they were about to go into the barracks, Paul says to the commander, "Is it permissible for me to say something to you?" And he said, "Do you know Greek? ³⁸Then you are not the Egyptian who before these days made an insurrection and led out into the wilderness four thousand men of the Sikarii?" ³⁹And Paul said, "I am indeed a Jewish man, of Tarsus of Cilicia, a citizen of no insignificant city; and I beg of you, permit me to speak to the people." ⁴⁰And as he granted permission, Paul, standing on the stairs, gestured to the people with his hand; and much silence ensuing, he addressed them in the Hebrew dialect, saying,

**22** "Men, brethren and fathers, hear now my defense to you." ²And having heard that he was addressing them in the Hebrew dialect they became more silent. And he said,

³"I am a Jewish man, having been born in Tarsus of Cilicia but brought up in this city at the feet of Gamaliel, being instructed according to the strictness of the Law of our fathers, being a zealot of God even as you are today; ⁴who persecuted this Way until death, binding both men and women and delivering them into prison, ⁵as also the high priest and all the elders can witness for me, from whom also having received letters to the brethren in Damascus, I was going in order to also bring those being there, having been bound, to Jerusalem that they might be punished. ⁶And it happened to me going and nearing Damascus about noon, suddenly a very bright light out of heaven flashed around me, ⁷and I fell to the ground and heard a voice saying to me, 'Saul, Saul, why do you persecute me?' ⁸And I answered, 'Who are you, Lord?' And he said to me, 'I am Jesus the Nazarene, Whom, you are persecuting.' ⁹Those being with me indeed saw the light, but did not understand the voice speaking to me. ¹⁰And I said, 'What shall I do, Lord?' And the Lord said to me, 'Arising, go into Damascus, and there it will be told to you all concerning which it has been appointed for you to do.' ¹¹And as I could not see from the glory of that light, being led by the hand by those being with me, I went into Damascus. ¹²And a certain Ananias, a devout man according to the Law, being witnessed by all the Jews dwelling there, ¹³coming to me and standing by, said to me, 'Brother Saul receive sight'; and at this hour I looked up at him. ¹⁴And he said, 'The God of our Fathers has appointed you to know His will and to see the Righteous One and to hear a message out of His mouth, ¹⁵that you may be a witness to Him before all men of what you have seen and heard. ¹⁶And now, why do you hesitate? Arising, be immersed and wash away your sins, calling on His name.' ¹⁷And it happened to me, having returned to Jerusalem and as I was praying in the temple, I was in a trance, ¹⁸and I saw Him speaking to me, 'Make haste and leave quickly out of Jerusalem, because they will not accept your witness concerning Me.' ¹⁹And I said, 'Lord, they themselves are aware that I was in the past imprisoning and beating from synagogue to synagogue those believing in You; ²⁰and when the blood of Your witness Stephen was being shed, I myself also was standing and approving and guarding the garments of those killing him.' ²¹And He said to me, 'Go, because I will send you out far away to the Gentiles.'"

²²And they were listening to him until this statement, and then they raised their voice saying, "Away from the earth with such a one as this, for it is not fit for him to live." ²³And as they were crying out and throwing off their garments and casting dust into the air, ²⁴the commander ordered him to be brought into the barracks, having said to examine him by flogging, in order that he might discover what reason they were shouting thus at him. ²⁵And as they were stretching him out for the thongs, Paul said to the centurion standing by, "Is it lawful for you to flog a Roman, and legally uncondemned?" ²⁶And the centurion having heard this, having gone to the commander, declared saying, "What are you about to do? For this man is a Roman." ²⁷And the commander coming to him said, "Tell me, are you a Roman?" And he said, "Yes." ²⁸And the commander answered, "I obtained this citizenship with a large sum of money." And Paul said, "But I was born a citizen." ²⁹Immediately therefore, those being about to examine him, unhanded him; and the commander was also afraid, having discovered that he was a Roman and that he had bound him. ³⁰And on the morrow, determining to know the

certainty of why he had been accused by the Jews, he released him; and ordered the chief priests and all the Sanhedrin to come together, and having brought Paul down, set him before them.

**23** And Paul, gazing intently on the Sanhedrin said, "Men, brethren, I have in all good conscience conducted my life before God until this day." ²And the high priest Ananias commended the ones standing by him to strike him on the mouth. ³Then Paul said to him, "God is going to strike you, you whitened wall! Do you sit judging me according to the Law, and contrary to the Law command me to be struck?" ⁴And the ones standing by said, "Do you revile the high priest of God?" ⁵And Paul said, "I did not know, brethren, that it is the high priest; for it has been written that 'You shall not speak evilly of the ruler of your people.'"

⁶And Paul, knowing that one party in the Sanhedrin was Sadducees and the other Pharisees, was crying out, "Men, brethren, I am a Pharisee, a son of a Pharisee; concerning the hope and resurrection of the dead I am being judged." ⁷And he having said this, a disagreement arose, and the group was divided. ⁸For Saducees say there is no resurrection, nor angels nor spirits, but Pharisees confess them all. ⁹And there was a great quarrel, certain of the scribes arising of the party of the Pharisees were arguing fiercely saying, "We find no evil in this man, and if a spirit or an angel spoke to him…" ¹⁰And as a great disagreement arose, the commander, fearing that Paul might be torn to pieces by them commanded the soldiers to come down to take him by force out of their midst, and to take him into the barracks. ¹¹But on the following night the Lord standing beside him, said, "Take courage, for as you witnessed thoroughly to the facts concerning Me in Jerusalem, it is necessary that thus you will witness also in Rome."

¹²When it became day, the Jews having made a plot, put themselves under an oath, saying not to eat nor drink until when they would kill Paul. ¹³There were more than forty having made this conspiracy; ¹⁴who, having come to the chief priests and to the elders said, "We have put ourselves under an oath with an oath to taste nothing until when we kill Paul. ¹⁵Now therefore you along with the Sanhedrin enlighten the commander so that he may bring him down to you, as though you were about to determine more accurately the charges concerning him; and we before he comes near are prepared to kill him." ¹⁶But the son of Paul's sister having heard about the ambush, having gone and entering into the barracks informed Paul. ¹⁷And Paul, having called one of the centurions, said, "Take this young man to the commanded for he has something to declare to him." ¹⁸Indeed then, having taken him, he brought him to the commander and said, "Paul, the prisoner, having called to me, asked me to bring this young man to you; he has something to tell you." ¹⁹The commander, taking him by his hand, and going aside privately, questioned him, "What is it you have to declare to me?" ²⁰And he said that, "The Jews have agreed to ask you that tomorrow you bring Paul into the Sanhedrin so as to inquire more accurately concerning him. ²¹Therefore, you should not be persuaded by them, for more than forty men of them plan to ambush him, who have put themselves under an oath not to eat or drink until when they destroy him, and now they are ready, waiting for the promise from you." ²²Then the commander dismissed the young man, charging him not to speak out to anyone that, "you have enlightened me about this." ²³And

calling to him certain two of the centurions, said, "You prepare two hundred soldiers and seventy horsemen and two hundred spearmen to proceed to Caesarea at the third hour of the night," [24]and to provide beasts so that, mounting Paul, they might bring him through safely to Felix. [25]And he wrote a letter having this form: [26]"Claudius Lysias to the most excellent governor Felix, greetings. [27]This man having been captured by the Jews, and being about to be killed by them, I rescued, having stood upon them with a detachment of soldiers, having learned that he is a Roman; [28]and wanting to discover the reason for which they were accusing him, I brought him down into their Sanhedrin; [29]whom I found being accused concerning questions of their law, not having any charge worthy of death or bonds. [30]And having been shown to me that there would be a plot against the man by them, I sent him to you at once, and charging the accusers to speak against him before you." [31]Indeed, then the soldiers according to the instructions to them, taking Paul brought him by night to Antipatris. [32]And on the morrow, leaving the horsemen to go on from there, they returned to the barracks; [33]which ones, having come into Caesarea, and delivering the letter to the governor, also presented Paul to him. [34]And having read it, and asking from what province he is, and learning that he was from Cilicia, [35]he said, "I will give you an audience when your accusers also arrive" commanding him to be placed under guard in Herod's Praetorium.

**24** And after five days the high priest Ananias came down with some elders and a certain orator named Tertullus, who informed the governor against Paul. [2]Paul having been called, Tertullus began to accuse him saying, "Much peace being obtained through you and reforms coming to this nation through your foresight, [3]both in every way and in every place, we acknowledge with all thankfulness, most excellent Felix. [4]But in order not to bother you more, I beg you to hear us briefly by your forbearance. [5]For having found this man to be a pest, and stirring up insurrection everywhere among the Jews and around the inhabited earth, and ringleader of the sect of the Nazarenes, [6]who also attempted to desecrate the temple, whom also we laid hold of, and determined to judge according to our Law. [7]But Lysias the commander having come, grasped him with much force out of our hands, [8]having commanded his accusers to come before you from whom you yourself will be able, having examined him concerning all these circumstances, to recognize of what we accuse him." [9]And the Jews also joined in, affirming these incidents were thus.

[10]The governor having motioned to him to speak, Paul answered, "Being aware of the many years you have been judge of this nation, I gladly present my defense of myself, [11]you being able to ascertain that not more than twelve days ago I went up to Jerusalem to worship, [12]and they neither found me in the temple reasoning with anyone nor causing a dissension of the crowd, neither in the synagogue or the city, [13]nor are they able to prove to you concerning what they now accuse me. [14]But I confess this to you that according to the Way which they call a sect, thus I serve our ancestral God, believing everything having been written according to the Law and the prophets, [15]having hope in God, which also these themselves accept, there shall be a resurrection of the dead, both of the righteous and the unrighteous, [16]in this also I myself strive always to have a conscience without offense toward God and man. [17]And after many years I arrived bringing gifts of mercy and offering to my nation, [18]in which they found me having been purified in the temple, not with a crowd or tumult. [19]But certain Jews from

Asia, who ought to be present before you and to accuse me if they have anything against me. [20]Or let these men themselves tell what unrighteousness they found in me standing before the Sanhedrin, [21]except for this one statement which I cried out when standing among them, 'Concerning the resurrection of the dead I am being judged this day by you.'" [22]And Felix dismissed them, knowing the matters concerning the Way more accurately said, "Whenever Lysias the commander comes down I will decide on the matters against you." [23]Having given orders to the centurion to keep him under guard, but to have relaxation of bonds, and not to prevent any of his own people to minister to him. [24]But after some days, Felix, arriving with Drusilla, his own wife, being a Jewess, sent for Paul and heard him concerning his faith in Christ Jesus. [25]And as he was reasoning concerning righteousness and temperance and the coming judgment, Felix becoming fearful answered, "Go for the present, receiving later an opportune time, I will send for you." [26]At the same time also he was hoping that money might be given to him by Paul; wherefore also sending for him more frequently, he was conversing with him. [27]But two years having been fulfilled, Felix received a successor, Portius Festus; and wishing to furnish the Jews a favor Felix left Paul in bonds.

25 Festus therefore arriving in the province, after three days went up to Jerusalem from Caesarea. [2]And the chief priests and the leaders of the Jews enlightened him about Paul; and were pleading with him, [3]asking a favor against him, that he might have him sent to Jerusalem, for they were preparing an ambush to kill him along the way. [4]Indeed therefore Festus answered that Paul was being kept under guard in Caesarea, and he himself was about to journey there shortly; [5]therefore, he said, "The powerful men among you, coming down, let them accuse him if there is in the man anything out of place." [6]And having spent not more than eight or ten days among them, having gone down to Caesarea, on the morrow sitting on the judgment seat, he commanded Paul to be brought. [7]He having arrived, the Jews having come down from Jerusalem, stood around him and brought down against him many serious charges, which they were not able to prove. [8]Paul making defense for himself, said that, "I have not sinned, neither against the Law nor against the temple nor against Caesar." [9]But Festus, willing to furnish a favor to the Jews, answering Paul, said, "Are you willing, going down to Jerusalem, there to be judged by me concerning these matters?" [10]And Paul said, "I am standing before the judgment seat of Caesar, where it is necessary for me to be judged. I have done no wrong to the Jews as you very well realize. [11]If indeed I have done wrong and practiced anything worthy of death, I do not refuse to die; but if none of these are so of which these men accuse me, no one is able to grant me to them. I appeal to Caesar." [12]Then Festus having conferred with the counsel, answered "You have appealed to Caesar, you shall go to Caesar."

[13]After certain days transpired, Agrippa the king and Bernice arrived at Caesarea greeting Festus. [14]And as they stayed there many days, Festus presented to the king the matters about Paul saying, "A certain man has been left here a prisoner by Felix, [15]concerning whom when I went to Jerusalem the chief priests and the elders of the Jews enlightened me, asking a sentence of condemnation against him; [16]to whom I answered that it is not the custom of Romans to hand over any man before the one being accused has the accusers face to face and receives an opportunity of defense concerning the charges. [17]Therefore, they having come

here, making not any delay on the next day, sitting on the judgment seat I commanded the man to be brought; ¹⁸about whom the accusers, having stood up were bringing not one reason of wicked acts which I was expecting, ¹⁹but had some questions with him concerning their own religion; and concerning a certain Jesus having died, whom Paul affirmed was alive. ²⁰And being perplexed as to the investigation of these matters, I was asking if he was willing to go to Jerusalem and there be judged concerning these matters. ²¹But Paul having appealed to be kept under guard for the decision of the Emperor, I commanded him to be kept under guard until when I might send him to Caesar." ²²And Agrippa said to Festus, "I myself also would desire to hear this man." "On the morrow," he said, "you will hear him." ²³Then on the morrow, Agrippa having come and Bernice with great display, and having entered the auditorium with the commanders and the outstanding men of the city, and Festus having commanded, Paul was brought in. ²⁴And Festus said, "King Agrippa, and all men here present with you, behold this one concerning whom all the multitude of the Jews petitioned me both in Jerusalem and here, crying out that he should no live any longer. ²⁵But I perceived that he had committed nothing worthy death, and this one himself appealed to the Emperor, so I decided to send him, ²⁶concerning whom I have nothing certain to write to my lord; wherefore, I am bringing him before you, and especially before you, King Agrippa, so that having made examination, I might have something to write; ²⁷for it seems unreasonable to be sending a prisoner and not signifying the charge against him."

**26** And Agrippa said to Paul, "It is permissible for you to speak for yourself," then Paul, stretching out his hand, began making his defenses. ²"Concerning all of which I am being accused by Jews, O King Agrippa, I consider myself blessed by you, being about to make my defense before you this day, ³especially you being knowledgeable concerning both all the customs and controversies; wherefore I beg you to hear me patiently. ⁴Indeed therefore, all the Jews know the manner of my life since my youth, from the beginning being in my nation and in Jerusalem, ⁵having known me previously from the first, if they are willing to witness that according to the strictest sect of our religion I lived as a Pharisee. ⁶And now for the hope of the promise having been made to our fathers by God, I stand here being judged, ⁷for which promise our twelve tribes hope to arrive, serving with earnestness night and day; concerning which hope I am accused by the Jews, O King. ⁸Why is it judged unbelievable by you if God raised the dead? ⁹Indeed, then I thought in myself it to be necessary to do many things against the name of Jesus of Nazareth; ¹⁰which I also did in Jerusalem, and I locked up many of the saints in prison, having received authority from the chief priests, and they being killed, I cast my vote against them; ¹¹and punishing them often in all the synagogues, I was trying to make them blaspheme, and being excessively enraged against them I persecuted them even until in outlying cities.

¹²"In which activities, going to Damascus with authority and commission of the chief priests, ¹³I saw during the way at midday, O king, a heavenly light above the brightness of the sun, shining around me and those traveling with me; ¹⁴and all of us falling to the ground, I heard a voice saying to me in the Hebrew dialect, 'Saul, Saul, why do you persecute Me? It is difficult for you to continue kicking against the goads.' ¹⁵And I said, 'Who are you Lord?' and the Lord said, 'I am Jesus whom you are persecuting. ¹⁶But arise and stand upon your feet; for

I have appeared to you for this purpose, to appoint you a servant and a witness both of the fact you have seen Me and of that in which I shall appear to you, [17]delivering you from the people and from the Gentiles, to whom I am sending you, [18]to open their eyes that they may turn from darkness to light and the authority of Satan to God, that they may receive forgiveness of sins and an inheritance among the ones having been sanctified by faith that is in Me.'
[19]Accordingly, O king Agrippa, I was not disobedient to the heavenly vision, [20]but both in Damascus first and in Jerusalem, in both all the country of Judea and to the Gentiles I was declaring to repent and to return to God, practicing works worthy of repentance. [21]On account of these activities, the Jews having captured me being in the temple were trying to kill me. [22]Having therefore obtained assistance from God, until this day I have stood having witnessed to both small and great, saying nothing except what both the prophets and Moses said were about to happen, [23]that the Christ would suffer; that He would be first arising from the dead, being about to announce light both to the people and to the Gentiles."
[24]And as Paul was saying these words in his defense, Festus said with a great voice, "Paul, you are a maniac; your much learning is turning you into mania." [25]But Paul said, "I am not a maniac, most excellent Festus, but am speaking sensible words of truth and soberness. [26]For the King is aware of these matters to whom also I am speaking being bold, for I am persuaded that none of these matters are hidden from him, for this has not occurred in a corner. [27]Do you believe, O king Agrippa, the prophets? I know you believe." [28]But Agrippa said to Paul, "In such little time do you persuade me to become a Christian?" [29]And Paul said, "I would to God whether in little or great, not only you but also all those hearing me this day might become such as I am, except for these bonds." [30]Both the king and the governor and Bernice arose and those being seated with them, [31]and having drawn aside, they were speaking to one another saying that, "This man is not doing anything worthy of bonds." [32]And Agrippa said to Festus, "It would be possible to release this man, if he had not appealed to Caesar."

# 27

And when it was decided for us to sail to Italy both Paul and certain other prisoners were delivered over to a centurion named Julius of the Augustan regiment. [2]Embarking on an Adramyttium boat being about to sail for the places along Asia, we put out to sea, Aristarchus a Macedonian of Thessalonica being with us. [3]And on the next day we landed at Sidon, Julius treating Paul with benevolence, permitted him to go to his friends to receive personal attention. [4]From there putting to sea, we sailed under the lee of Cyprus, because the winds were against us, [5]and having sailed the sea against Cilicia and Pamphylia we came to Myra of Lycia. [6]And there the centurion found an Alexandrian boat sailing for Italy, and boarded us on it. [7]And proceeding slowly for considerable days, and with difficulty coming against Cnidus, the wind not allowing us, we sailed under the lee of Crete against Salmone, [8]and with difficulty coasting along we came to a certain place being called Fair Havens, which was near the city of Lasea. [9]And considerable time having passed and the voyage being dangerous already, because even the Fast already had gone by, Paul advised, [10]saying to them, "Men, I see that the voyage is about to be with damage and much loss, not only to the cargo and the boat, but also to our lives." [11]But the centurion was persuaded more by the pilot and the captain than the words being said by Paul.
[12]The harbor being unsuitable for going through the winter the majority made the

decision to sail on from there, if somehow they might be able, arriving at Phoenix, to pass the winter there, being a harbor of Crete facing southwest and northwest. [13]And when a south wind started blowing gently, supposing they had obtained their purpose, raising anchor, they were coasting along Crete. [14]But after not much time a typhoon wind being called Euraquilon beat down from it; [15]the boat having been forcibly caught with the wind, and not being able to face against the wind, giving way, we were carried along by it. [16]And running under the lee of a certain small island being called Cauda, we were able with difficulty to secure the lifeboat, [17]which having hoisted up, they were using helps for undergirding the boat; and fearing lest they be run aground into the Syrtis, lowering the gear, thus they were being driven along. [18]And as we were being exceedingly tossed about by the storm, the next day they began throwing overboard the cargo. [19]And on the third day with their own hands they threw overboard the boat's tackle. [20]And neither sun nor stars appearing for many days, and no small tempest enveloping us, now all hope for us to be saved was being forsaken.

[21]And there being much abstinence from food, Paul standing in the midst of them, said, "It was indeed necessary, O men, to have been persuaded by me not to sail from Crete, so not to obtain this damage and loss. [22]and now I advise you to keep in good spirit, for there will be no loss of any life among you except the boat; [23]for there stood by me this night an angel of the God whom I serve [24]saying, 'Do not fear, Paul; it is necessary for you to stand before Caesar, and behold, God has granted to you all those sailing with you.' [25]wherefore, keep in good spirit men, for I believe God, that thus it will be in the manner in which He has spoken to me. [26]But it is necessary that we run aground on a certain island." [27]But as the fourteenth night came, we were being driven about in the Adria, about midnight the sailors were suspecting that land was coming near to them. [28]And having taken soundings and found it twenty fathoms, and having moved a little farther, having sounded again found it fifteen fathoms; [29]And fearing that somewhere we might run aground against rocks, throwing overboard from the stern four anchors, they were praying for it to become day. [30]And as sailors were seeking to flee from the boat, and had lowered the lifeboat into the sea as a pretense for being about to let down anchors from the prow, [31]Paul said to the centurion and to the soldiers, "If these do not remain in the boat, you yourselves will not be able to be saved." [32]Then the soldiers cut away the ropes of the lifeboat and let it fall away. [33]And until day was about to come, Paul was encouraging all them to partake of food saying, "This day is the fourteenth day and you have continued waiting having taken nothing to eat; [34]wherefore I plead with you partake of food, for this is for your safety, for not one hair from your head will perish." [35]And having said these words, and having taken bread, he gave thanks to God before everyone, and breaking it, he began to eat. [36]And all became in good spirits, and they themselves also took food. [37]And all we in the boat were two hundred seventy-six souls. [38]And having been satisfied with enough food, they were lightening the boat, casting the wheat into the sea. [39]And when the day came, they were not recognizing the land; but they were considering a certain bay having a beach on which they were determining if it were possible, to ground the boat. [40]And having cast off the anchors, leaving them in the sea, as the same time having loosed the fastening of the rudders and having raised up the foresail to the wind, they held the boat toward the beach. [41]And running upon to a place where two seas meet, they drove the vessel and the prow having run aground remained immovable; and the stern was being broken by the

force of the waves from two currents. ⁴²And the will of the soldiers was that the prisoners might be killed, so that anyone swimming out might not escape. ⁴³But the centurion, willing to save Paul, hindered them of their intention, and commanded the ones being able to swim, casting themselves overboard, to go first out to the land. ⁴⁴And the rest, some upon planks and others upon some of the things from the boat might follow; and thus it happened that all were saved upon the land.

**28** And when they were brought safely through, we discovered that the island was called Melita. ²And the natives were showing to us no ordinary kindness for they received us all, having kindled a fire on account of the rain having settled in and on account of the cold. ³And Paul having gathered many dry sticks and having laid them on the fire, a viper having come out from the heat, fastened down on his hand. ⁴And when the natives saw the little beast hanging on to his hand, they were saying to one another, "Certainly this man is a murderer whom though having been saved out of the sea, yet Justice does not permit him to live. ⁵Indeed therefore, having shaken the little beast into the fire, he suffered no evil. ⁶But they were expecting him to be about to swell up or suddenly to fall down dead, but after they were waiting a long time; and beholding nothing out of place happening to him, changing their minds, were saying that he is a god. ⁷And in the areas around that place were lands belonging to the First man of the island by name Publius, who having welcomed us, treated us as guests sociably for three days. ⁸And it happened that the father of Publius was lying in bed suffering from intermittent fevers and dysentery; Paul entering in to him, having prayed, laying hands on him cured him. ⁹And this having happened, the rest of the people on the island having sicknesses were coming to Paul; and they were being healed. ¹⁰Also they honored us with many honors and when we sailed they put on board the supplies needed.

¹¹And after three months we set sail on a boat having passed the winter on the island, an Alexandrian boat having an insignia of the Twin Sons. ¹²And having put down at Syracuse we remained three days. ¹³From there sailing in a circuit, we arrived at Rhegium. And after one day, a south wind coming up, we came to Puteoli. ¹⁴Finding brethren there, we were invited by them to stay seven days, and thus we came on to Rome. ¹⁵And the brethren there having heard the reports about us, came to meet us as far as Appium Forum and Three Taverns, whom Paul having seen, gave thanks to God and took courage. ¹⁶And when we came to Rome, Paul was permitted to remain by himself, with the soldier guarding him.

¹⁷And it happened after three days that he called together the ones being leaders of the Jews; and they having come, he was saying to them, "Men, brethren, I did nothing against our people or the customs of our fathers, yet I was delivered over in Jerusalem into the hands of the Romans, ¹⁸who examining me, were willing to release me because there was no reason in me deserving of death. ¹⁹But when the Jews protested, I was compelled to appeal to Caesar, not as though I had any accusation of my nation. ²⁰On account of this reason I pleaded to see and speak to you, for it is for the sake of the hope of Israel I am bound with this chain." ²¹And they said to him, "We have neither received letters concerning you from the Jews, nor any of the brethren arriving related or spoke any wickedness concerning you. ²²But we think it fair to hear from you what your views are, for indeed concerning this sect it is known to us that it is everywhere spoken against."

²³And having appointed with him a day, many came to him in his dwelling, to whom he set forth the kingdom of God witnessing thoroughly, and persuading them concerning Jesus both from the Law of Moses and the prophets from morning till evening. ²⁴And some were being persuaded by what was being spoken, but others were not believing. ²⁵And being without agreement with one another, they were beginning to leave, Paul having said one word that, "Well the Holy Spirit spoke through Isaiah the prophet to your fathers, ²⁶saying, 'You go to this people and say, "In hearing you will hear, and you absolutely will not understand and seeing you will see and absolutely not perceive. ²⁷For the heart of this people was calloused, and with their ears that hardly hear, and their eyes they have closed that they may not at anytime see with their eyes and hear with their ears and understand with their heart and be converted and I will heal them."' ²⁸Let it be known therefore to you that this salvation of God has been sent to the Gentiles, and they will listen." *[²⁹Omitted in older manuscripts]*

³⁰And he remained two whole years in his own rented dwelling, and was welcoming all those coming to him, ³¹Preaching the kingdom of God and teaching the truths concerning the Lord Jesus Christ with all boldness, unhindered.

## *The Letter of Paul the Apostle to the*
# ROMANS

1 ¹Paul, a servant of Jesus Christ, a called apostle, separated unto good news of God, ²which He had told before through His prophets in holy Scriptures, ³about His Son Who came out of the seed of David as of the flesh, ⁴set forth as Son of God in power, by the Spirit of Holiness, by rising from the dead, - Jesus Christ our Lord; ⁵by Whom we received grace and the office of an apostle unto obedience of faith in all the nations for His name, ⁶among Whom are you also, called of Jesus Christ; ⁷to all who are in Rome, beloved of God, called holy ones. Grace to you and peace from God our Father, and from the Lord Jesus Christ.

⁸First, I thank my God through Jesus Christ for you all, that your faith is told in the whole world. ⁹For God is my witness, Whom I serve in my spirit in the good news of His Son, that without stopping I make mention of you ¹⁰always in my prayers begging if somehow now at last I shall be given favor in the will of God to come to you. ¹¹For I long to see you, that I may give you some spiritual gift, that you may be strengthened, ¹²that is, to be comforted among you through the faith of each other, both yours and mine. ¹³But I do not want you not to know, brothers, that many times I planned to come to you, and I was hindered until now, that I might have some fruit also among you, even as also among the rest of the nations. ¹⁴I am a debtor both to Greeks and barbarians, both to wise and to foolish. ¹⁵So as for me, I am ready to tell the good news also to you in Rome.

¹⁶For I am not ashamed of the good news of Christ; for it is the power of God unto salvation to everyone who believes, both to Jew first, and to non-Jew. ¹⁷For in it is uncovered the righteousness of God out of faith unto faith, even as it has been written, "The just shall live out of faith." ¹⁸For the anger of God is uncovered from Heaven upon all ungodliness and injustice of men, who hold the truth in injustice.

¹⁹Because what is known of God is shown in them, for God showed it to them. ²⁰For the unseen things of Him from the creation of the world are seen, being made clear to the mind by the things made, both His eternal power and that He is God, so that they are without excuse. ²¹Because, having known God, they did not give Him glory as God, nor were they thankful, but became proud in their discussions, and their foolish hearts were darkened. ²²Saying that they were wise, they became feeble-minded, ²³and changed the glory of the God Who cannot decay into a likeness of an image of man who can decay, and of birds and four-footed animals, and creeping things – reptiles. ²⁴And so God gave them over in the longings of their hearts unto uncleanness, to dishonor their bodies among themselves. ²⁵who changed the truth of God into a lie, and worshiped and served the created thing along with the Creator, Who is blessed forever. Amen. ²⁶Because of this God gave them over to desires of dishonor. For even the females changed the natural use into that which is against nature. ²⁷And likewise also the males, having left the natural use of the female, were fired up in their evil desire unto each other, males among males working shameful acts, and receiving in themselves the evil result which their error deserved. ²⁸And even as they did not see fit to have God in their

knowledge, God gave them over to an unfit mind, to do what is not right, [29]being filled with all injustice, immorality, evil, greed, malice, full of envy, murder, strife, deceit, bad thoughts, whisperers, [30]speaking evil, God-haters, insulting, proud, boasting, inventors of evil, disobedient to parents, [31]without understanding, truce-breakers, without natural affection, unmerciful, [32]who, having known the right judgment of God, that those doing such things are worthy of death, not only keep doing them, but also are well pleased with those who do them.

**2** Therefore, O man, everyone who is judging, you are without excuse, for in what you judge another, you are condemning yourself, for you who are judging are doing the same things. [2]But we know that the sentence of God is according to truth upon those who are doing such things. [3]But do you reason this, O man, who judges those doing such thing, and are doing them yourself that you may run away from the judgment of God? [4]Or do you look down on the riches of His kindness and forbearance and long-suffering, not knowing that the kindness of God is leading you to repentance? [5]But according to your hardness and impenitent heart are you treasuring up to yourself anger in a day of anger and of unveiling of the righteous judgment of God? [6]Who will give to each person according to his works [7]– to those who with continuing in good work are seeking glory and honor and incorruption, – life eternal. [8]But to those who strive, and disobey the truth, but obey injustice, – ire and anger, [9]trouble and difficulty, on every soul of man who works evil, both of the Jew first and the non-Jew, [10]but glory, and honor, and peace to everyone who works good, both to the Jew first and to the non-Jew: [11]for there is no favoritism with God. [12]For as many as without Law sinned, without Law also they shall perish, and as many as in the Law sinned, shall be judged by the Law, [13]for it is not the hearers of the Law that are just with God, but the doers of the Law shall be counted just. [14]For when nations which do not have the Law, by nature do the Law, these, not having the Law, are a law unto themselves. [15]who show the work of the Law written in their hearts, their consciences bearing witness, and between each other their thoughts accusing or defending, [16]in a day when God will judge the secrets of men, according to my good news, by Jesus Christ.
[17]Lo, you are called a Jew, and you rest upon the Law, and boast in God, [18]and you know His will, and you approve the better things, being taught out of the Law; [19]and you have been persuaded that you yourself are a guide of the blind, a light of those in darkness, [20]a corrector of the foolish, a teacher of babies, having the form of knowledge and of the truth in the Law; [21]you then who are teaching another, are you not teaching yourself? Preaching not to steal, do you steal? [22]Saying not to commit adultery, do you commit adultery? You who hate idols, do you rob what is holy? [23]You who boast in the Law, through departing from the Law, do you dishonor the Law of God? [24]For the name of God through you is evil spoken of among the nations, even as it has been written. [25]For indeed circumcision profits if you do the Law, but if you should depart from the Law, your circumcision has become uncircumcision. [26]So if the uncircumision keeps the justice of the Law, will not his uncircumcision be counted as circumcision? [27]And will the uncircumcision by nature judge you when it fulfills the Law, you who living by the letter and circumcision are a breaker of the Law? [28]For he is not a Jew who is one in appearance, nor is circumcision in the show in flesh, [29]but he is a Jew, who is one in the secret man, and circumcision is of the heart, in the spirit, not in the letter, whose praise is not of men, but of God.

3 What then is the benefit of the Jew? Or what is the profit of circumcision? ²Much in every way. For first that they were entrusted with the sayings of God. ³For what if some did not believe? Their unbelief will not make the faith of God not work, will it? ⁴Let it not be; but let God be true, though every man a liar, even as it has been written, "That You may be counted just in Your words, and may win in Your being judged." ⁵But if our unjustness confirms the justness of God, what will we say? Is God unjust Who retains anger? – I speak as a man. ⁶Let it not be; for how then will God judge the world? ⁷For if the truth of God in my lie has abounded unto His glory, why am I also yet judged as a sinner? ⁸And not as we are evil spoken of, and as some declare that we say, "Let us do evil, that good may come" – whose condemnation is just.

⁹What then? Do we come out ahead? Not at all, for we have before proved both Jews and non-Jews all are under sin. ¹⁰As it has been written, "There is not a just one, not one." ¹¹There is not one who understands, not one seeking out God. ¹²All have gone out of the way, together they became unprofitable. There is not a man doing good, there is not even one. ¹³Their throat is an open tomb, their tongues deceived; poison of asps is under their lips. ¹⁴Their mouths are full of curses and bitterness. ¹⁵Their feet are swift to shed blood. ¹⁶Ruin and misery are in their ways. ¹⁷And the way of peace they have not known. ¹⁸The fear of God is not before their eyes. ¹⁹But we know that whatever the Law says, it speaks to those in the Law, that every mouth may be stopped, and that all the world may become under the justice of God. ²⁰Because of this not any people will be accounted just before Him from works of Law, for through law is knowledge of sin.

²¹But now apart from Law the justice of God has been shown, witnessed to by the Law and the prophets. ²²But the justice of God, through faith in Jesus Christ is unto all and upon all those who believe, for there is no difference. ²³For all have sinned, and come short of the glory of God, ²⁴being accounted just as a gift of His grace, through the ransom that is in Christ Jesus, ²⁵Whom God set forth as a mercy seat through faith in His blood, to show His justice through the passing by of the sins that had taken place before, in the forbearance of God, ²⁶for showing His justice now in the present time, unto His being just, and justifying the one who is of faith in Jesus. ²⁷Where then is boasting? It is shut out. Through what law? Of works? No indeed, but through a Law of faith. ²⁸We reason then that a man is to be justified by faith apart from works of Law. ²⁹Is He the God only of Jews and not of non-Jews also? Yes, also of non-Jews, ³⁰since it is one God, Who will justify the circumcision Jews by faith, and uncircumcision non-Jews through faith. ³¹Do we then make the Law not to work through faith? Let it not be, but we confirm the Law.

4 What then shall we say that Abraham our father has found according to the flesh? ²For if Abraham was made just by works, he has reason to boast, but not towards God. ³For what does the Scripture say? Abraham believed God, and it was counted to him unto righteousness. ⁴But to him who works the reward is not counted according to grace, but according to debt. ⁵But to him who does not work, but is believing on Him Who counts just the ungodly, his faith is counted unto righteousness. ⁶Even as David speaks of the blessed state of the man to whom God counts righteousness apart from works, – ⁷"Blessed are those whose law-breakings are forgiven, whose sins are covered. ⁸Blessed is the man to whom the

Lord will not account sin." ⁹Is this blessed state for the circumcision Jews, or also for the uncircumcision non-Jews? For we say that it was counted to Abraham – faith unto righteousness. ¹⁰How then was it counted? When it was in circumcision, or in uncircumcision? Not in circumcision, but in uncircumcision. ¹¹And he received the sign of circumcision, a seal of the righteousness of the faith which he had in the uncircumcision, that he might be father of all who believe while in uncircumcision, that the righteousness might be counted also to them, ¹²and father of circumcision to those not of circumcision only, but also to those who walk in the steps of the uncircumcision faith of our father Abraham.

¹³For it was not by Law, the promise to Abraham or to his seed that he was to be heir of the world, but by the righteousness of faith. ¹⁴For if those of the Law are heirs, faith has been made empty, and the promise is not working. ¹⁵For the Law causes anger, for where there is no Law, there is also no sin. ¹⁶Because of this it is of faith, in order that it might be according to grace, so the promise is made sure to all the seed, not to that of the Law only, but also to those of the faith of Abraham, who is father of us all. ¹⁷Even as it has been written, "A father of many nations I have made you," before Whom he believed, God, Who makes the dead alive, and calls the things that are not as though they are. ¹⁸Who against hope believed in hope, that he might become father of many nations, even as it had been said, "So shall your seed be." ¹⁹And not being weak in the faith, not thinking about his own body already having become dead, being about a hundred years old, and the deadness of the womb of Sarah. ²⁰But he did not doubt the promise of God in unbelief, but was made powerful in faith, giving glory to God. ²¹And being fully assured that what He has promised, He is able also to do. ²²Because of this also it was counted to him for righteousness. ²³But it was not written because of him only, that it was counted to him, ²⁴but also because of us, to whom it is going to be counted, – to those who believe on Him Who raised Jesus our Lord from the dead, ²⁵Who was given over for our sins, and was raised for our justification.

5 Having been made just then by faith, we have peace toward God through our Lord Jesus Christ. ²Through Whom also we have a way to draw near by faith into this grace in which we stand. And we may boast in hope of the glory of God. ³But not only so, but also we may boast in great troubles, knowing that trouble works endurance, ⁴and endurance works approval, and approval, hope, ⁵and the hope does not bring shame; because the love of God is poured out in our hearts by the Holy Spirit Who was given to us. ⁶For when we were yet without strength, in due time Christ died for the ungodly. ⁷For scarcely for a just man someone will die, – for the good man maybe someone might even dare to die. ⁸But God strongly confirms His own love for us, that while we still were sinners, Christ died for us. ⁹Much more, then, having been made just now in His blood, we shall be saved b y Him from anger. ¹⁰For if, being enemies, we were brought back to God through the death of His Son, much more, having been brought back, we shall be saved by His life. ¹¹But not only so, but also, boasting in God through our Lord Jesus Christ, we received now through Him the restoration.

¹²Because of this, as through one man sin came into the world, and death through sin, and so death passed through unto all men, upon all who sinned, ¹³– for until the Law sin was in the world, but sin is not counted, there not being Law. ¹⁴But death ruled from Adam

until Moses also on those who had not sinned in the like manner of the sin of Adam, who is a type of the Coming One. [15]But not like the sin is the gift of grace. For if by the sin of one, the many died, much more the grace of God, and the gift of grace, which of the one Man Jesus Christ, overflowed to the many. [16]And the gift is not like by the one who sinned, – for indeed the judgment was from one man unto condemnation, but the gift of grace is of many sins to justification. [17]For if by the one sin, death reigned by the one, much more those receiving the overflow of grace and the gift of righteousness, shall reign in life by the One, Jesus Christ. [18]Now then as by one sin, condemnation came to all men, so also by one performance of righteousness, there came to all men justification of life. [19]For even as by the disobedience of the one man, many were made sinners, so also by the obedience of the One, the many shall be made righteous. [20]But Law came in, that the sin might increase. But where sin increased, grace overflowed more. [21]So that even as sin reigned in death, so also might grace reign through righteousness unto eternal life, by Jesus Christ our Lord.

**6** What then shall we say? Shall we remain in sin, that grace may overflow? [2]Let it not be. We who died to sin, how yet shall we live in it? [3]Or do you not know that as many as were immersed into Christ Jesus, into His death we were immersed. [4]So we were buried with Him through immersing into death, that as Christ was raised from the dead through the glory of the Father, so also we should walk in newness of life. [5]For if we have become united in the likeness of His death, so also we shall be of His rising. [6]Knowing this, that our old man died on the cross with Him, that the body of sin might be made inactive, that no longer we are to serve sin. [7]For he who has died has been justified from sin. [8]But if we died with Christ, we believe that also we shall live with Him, [9]knowing that Christ raised from the dead, dies no more, – death no more is lord over Him. [10]For when He died, He died to sin once for all, but as He lives, – He lives to God. [11]So also you, count yourselves to be dead indeed to sin, but living to God in Christ Jesus our Lord. [12]Do not then let sin be king in your mortal body, to obey it in its desires. [13]And do not allow your limbs to be means of unrighteousness unto sin, but allow yourselves to be unto God as alive from the dead, and your limbs means of righteousness to God. [14]For sin shall not be your lord, for you are not under law, but under grace. [15]What then? Shall we sin because we are not under law, but under grace? Let it not be! [16]Do you not know that to whom you let yourselves be slaves unto obedience, you are slaves to whom you obey, whether of sin unto death, or of obedience unto righteousness. [17]But thanks be unto God, that though you were servants of sin, yet you obeyed from the heart the pattern of teaching which was given to you. [18]Then being set free from sin, you were made servants of righteousness. [19]I am speaking like a man because of the weakness of your flesh. For as you allowed your limbs to be in slavery to uncleanness and to unlawful acts unto an unlawful state, so now let your limbs be in slavery to righteousness leading to holiness. [20]For when you were slaves of sin, you were free of righteousness. [21]So what fruit did you have then, from the things of which now you are ashamed? For the end result of those things, – death! [22]But now, being set free from sin, and being made servants to God, you have your fruit unto holiness, and the end result, life eternal. [23]For the wages of sin is death, but the gift of God is life eternal in Christ Jesus our Lord.

7 Do you not know, brothers, for I am speaking to those knowing the Law, that the Law rules over a man as long a time as he may live? ²For the married woman is tied by Law to the living husband, but if the husband should die, she is loosed from the Law of the husband. ³So then while her husband is living, she will be called an adulteress if she becomes a wife to another man. But if the husband should die, she is free from the Law, so she would not be an adulteress, in becoming a wife to another man. ⁴And so, my brothers, you also were made dead to the Law by the body of Christ, to be wed to another, Who was raised from the dead, that we should bear fruit to God. ⁵For when we were in the flesh, the longings of sin, which were through the Law, worked in our limbs unto bringing forth fruit unto death. ⁶But now we have been removed from the Law, having died in regard to that in which we were subjected, so that we should serve in newness of spirit, and not in oldness of the letter.

⁷What shall we say, then? Is the Law sin? Let it not be! But I did not know sin except by Law, for I would not have known evil desire if the Law did not say, "You shall not have evil desire." ⁸But sin, having received an opportunity through the command, worked in me every kind of evil desire. For apart from the Law sin was dead. ⁹But I was alive apart from the Law at one time, but when the command came, sin revived, but I died. ¹⁰And the command, which was unto life, was found to be death unto me. ¹¹For sin took an opportunity through the command and deceived me, and by it killed me. ¹²So the Law indeed is holy, and the command is holy, and just and good. ¹³Did that which is good, then, become death to me? Let it not be. But sin, that it might appear to be sin, through the good was working death toward me, that sin by the command might become sinful beyond measure.

¹⁴For we know that the Law is spiritual, but I am fleshly, having been sold under sin. ¹⁵For I do not know what I am doing. For I keep doing what I do not desire, but what I hate, this I am doing. ¹⁶But if I am doing this which I do not desire, I am agreeing to the Law, that it is good. ¹⁷Now then no longer I am doing it, but sin that is making its home in me. ¹⁸For I know that good is not making a home in me, that is, in my flesh. For to desire is present with me, but I do not find that the good is worked out. ¹⁹For the good which I desire is not what I keep doing, but the evil which I do not desire, this I keep doing. ²⁰But if I keep doing this which I do not desire, it is not longer I who am doing it, but sin, which is making a home in me. ²¹I find then a law of my desiring to keep doing the good, but that the evil is present with me. ²²For I am happy with the Law of God in the inner man. ²³But I see another law in my limbs making war against the law of my mind, and making me captive to the law of sin which is in my limbs. ²⁴I am an unhappy man. Who shall rescue me from the body of this death? ²⁵I than God, – through Jesus Christ our Lord! So then with my mind I indeed serve the Law of God, but with the flesh the law of sin.

8 So nothing now is a condemnation to those in Christ Jesus, – they do not walk according to the flesh, but according to the Spirit. ²For the Law of the Spirit of life in Christ Jesus frees me from the law of sin and death. ³For what the Law was without power to do, in that it is weak through the flesh, God did, having sent His own Son in the likeness of the flesh of sin, and concerning sin, and condemned sin in the flesh, ⁴that the just state of the Law might be fulfilled in us, who walk not according to the flesh, but according to the Spirit. ⁵For they who are fleshly mind the things of the flesh. But those who are spiritual

mind the things of the Spirit. ⁶For the mind of the Spirit is life and peace. ⁷Because the mind of the flesh is enmity unto God, for it is not put under the Law of God, for it cannot be. ⁸So those who are in the flesh cannot please God. ⁹But you are not in the flesh, but in the Spirit, if indeed the Spirit of God is making His home in you. But if someone does not have the Spirit of Christ, he is not of Him. ¹⁰But if Christ is in you, the body is dead through sin, but the Spirit is life through righteousness. ¹¹But if the Spirit of Him Who raised Jesus from the dead lives in you, He Who raised Christ from the dead will make alive also your mortal bodies through His Spirit Who is living in you. ¹²So then, brothers, we are debtors not to the flesh, to live according to the flesh. ¹³For if you live according to the flesh, you are going to die, but if you by the Spirit put to death the deeds of the body, you will live. ¹⁴For as many as are led by the Spirit of God, these are sons of God. ¹⁵For you did not receive a spirit of slavery again to fear, but you received a spirit of son-ship, in which we cry out, "Papa, the Father." ¹⁶The Spirit Himself witnesses with our spirit, that we are children of God. ¹⁷But if children, also heirs, – heirs indeed of God, heirs together with Christ, if so it is that we suffer together, that also we may be made glorious together.

¹⁸For I account that the sufferings of the present time are not worthy to be compared with the glory which is going to be revealed unto us. ¹⁹For the looking ahead of the creation is waiting for the revealing of the sons of God. ²⁰For the creation was made subject to foolishness, not willingly, but through Him Who made it subject in hope, ²¹that the creation itself shall be set free from the slavery of rottenness unto the freedom of the glory of the children of God. ²²For we know that all of the creation is groaning together and is in the pains of birth together until now. ²³And not only so, but also ourselves having the first-fruit of the Spirit, we also ourselves groan in ourselves, waiting for son-ship, the ransom of our bodies. ²⁴For we may be saved by hope, but hope seen is not hope. For that which someone sees, why does he also hope for? ²⁵But if we hope for that which we do not see, we wait for it through endurance. ²⁶And so also the Spirit takes hold opposite our weaknesses; for we do not know what we ought to pray for, but the Spirit Himself moves for us with groanings which cannot be spoken. ²⁷But He Who searches the hearts knows what is the mind of the Spirit, because according to God He moves for the saints. ²⁸And we know that to those loving God, all things He is working together unto good, to those who are called according to His purpose. ²⁹Because those whom He knew before, also He determined ahead of time to be made like the image of His Son, that He should be the first-born of many brothers. ³⁰But whom He determined ahead of time, these also He called. And whom He called, these also He justified. And whom He justified, these also He glorified.

³¹What then shall we say to these things? If God is for us, who is against us? ³²He Who indeed did not spare His own Son, but gave Him up for us all, how shall He not also with Him give us all things? ³³Who shall call out against the chosen ones of God? It is God Who is justifying. ³⁴Who is he who is condemning? Christ it is Who died, Who rather also is risen, Who also is at the right hand of God, Who also moves for us. ³⁵Who shall separate us from the love of Christ? Shall trouble, or a narrow place, or mistreatment, or famine, or nakedness, or danger, or sword? ³⁶As it is written, "For Your sake we are put to death all the day. We are accounted like sheep about to be butchered." ³⁷But in all these things we may be more than victorious through the One Who loved us. ³⁸For I have been persuaded that neither death, nor

life, nor angels, nor rulers, nor forces, nor things present, nor things about to be, [39]nor height, nor depth, nor any other created thing, shall be able to separate us from the love of God which is in Christ Jesus our Lord.

**9**[ ]I am saying the truth in Christ, I am not lying, my conscience witnessing with me in the Holy Spirit, [2]that my grief is great, and continual sorrow is in my heart, [3]for I might pray that I myself to be accursed from Christ for my brothers, my relatives according to the flesh, [4]who are Israelites, of whom is the sonship and the glory, and the contracts, and the giving of the Law, and the worship, and the promises. [5]Of whom are the fathers, and out of whom also is Christ according to the flesh, Who is over all, God, well-spoken of unto the ages, amen.

[6]But not as if that the Word of God has fallen down, for not all who are of Israel, are Israel. [7]Nor because they are seed of Abraham, are all children, but, "In Isaac your seed shall be called." [8]That is, not the children of the flesh are the children of God, but the children of the promise are counted as seed. [9]For this is the Word of promise, "At this time I will come, and Sarah will have a son." [10]And not only so, but also Rebecca having conceived by one man, our father Isaac, [11]for they had not yet been born, nor had done anything good or evil, that the purpose of God according to election should remain, not of works, but to Him Who is calling, [12]it was said to her, "The greater shall serve the lesser." [13]Even as it was written, "Jacob I loved, but Esau I hated."

[14]What then shall we say? Is there injustice with God? Let it not be. [15]For to Moses He says, "I will have mercy on whom I may have mercy, and I will pity him whom I may pity." [16]So then it is not of the willing one, or of the running one, but of God having mercy. [17]For the Scripture says to Pharaoh, "For this same thing I raised you up, so that I might show in you My power, and so that My name should be declared in all the earth." [18]So then on whom He wills He has mercy, but whom He wills He hardens.

[19]You will say then to me, "Why does He yet blame anyone? For who has stood against His will?" [20]Indeed then, O man, who are you who is answering against God? Shall the thing formed say to Him who formed it, "Why did You make me like this?" [21]Or has not the potter a right over the clay to make out of the same lump an object unto honor, and another unto dishonor? [22]So if God, willing to show His anger, and to make known His power, endured with much longsuffering objects of anger suited to ruin, [23]and that He might make known the riches of His glory upon objects of mercy, which He made ready ahead of time unto glory, [24]even us, whom He called, not only out of the Jews, but also out of the non-Jew nations. [25]As also He says in Hosea, "I will call the ones who are not My people, – My people, and the ones not beloved, – beloved. [26]And it shall be, in the place where it was said to them, 'You are not My people,' there they shall be called, 'sons of the living God.'" [27]But Isaiah cries out about Israel, "If the number of the sons of Israel is like the sand of the sea, only what is left shall be saved. [28]For He is lending and cutting short His Word in righteousness; because the Lord will do a short work on the earth." [29]And even as Isaiah said before, "If the Lord of armies had not left us a seed, we would have become like Sodom, and we would have been made like Gomorrah."

[30]What shall we say then? That non-Jew nations who do not follow righteousness,

attained righteousness, but righteousness that comes by faith; ³¹but Israel, following a Law of righteousness, did not attain. ³²Why? Because it was not of faith, but as by works of Law. For they stumbled at the stone of stumbling. ³³Even as it has been written, "Lo. I set in Zion a stone of stumbling and a rock of offense. And everyone who believes on Him shall not be made ashamed."

10 Brothers, indeed the good pleasure of my heart, and my petition to God in behalf of Israel is for their salvation. ²For I witness about them that they have a zeal for God, but not according to full knowledge. ³For not knowing the righteousness of God, and seeking to set up their own righteousness, they have not submitted to the righteousness of God. ⁴For Christ is the end of the Law unto righteousness to everyone who believes. ⁵For Moses writes about the righteousness which is of the Law, that the man who keeps doing those things shall live by them. ⁶But the righteousness of faith speaks like this, "Do not say in your hearts, Who shall go up into heaven?" That is, to bring Christ down? ⁷ Or "Who shall go down into the depths?" That is, to bring Christ up from the dead? ⁸But what does it say? "The Word is near to you, in your mouth, and in your heart." This is the Word of faith which we preach: ⁹That if you will confess with your mouth the Lord Jesus, and will believe in your heart that God raised Him from the dead, you will be saved. ¹⁰For in the heart is faith unto righteousness, and by the mouth declaration is made unto salvation. ¹¹For the Scripture says, "Everyone who believes on Him shall not be made ashamed."
¹²For there is not any difference between a Jew and a non-Jew, for the same Lord of all is rich unto all those calling upon Him. ¹³For everyone who shall call on the name of the Lord shall be saved. ¹⁴How then shall they call on Whom they have not believed? But how shall they believe on Whom they have not heard? But how shall they hear without preaching? ¹⁵But how shall they preach, unless they shall be sent? Even as it has been written, "How beautiful are the feet of those reporting the good news of peace, of those reporting the good news of good things!" ¹⁶But not all obeyed the good news. For Isaiah says, "Lord, who believed our report?" ¹⁷So faith is by hearing, but the hearing is through the Word of God. ¹⁸But I say, "Did they not hear?" Indeed so, – their voice went out into all the earth, and their words into the ends of the world." ¹⁹But I say, "Did not Israel know?" First, Moses says, "I will make you jealous by those not a nation, by a nation without understanding I will make you angry." ²⁰But Isaiah is very bold, and says, "I was found by those who did not seek Me; I was revealed to those who did not ask about Me." ²¹But to Israel He says, "All the day I stretched out My hands to a disobedient and contradicting people."

11 I say, then, "God did not put away His people, did He?" Let it not be. For I also am an Israelite, of the seed of Abraham, of the tribe of Benjamin. ²God did not put away His people, whom He knew ahead of time. Do you not know what the Scripture says in the time of Elijah, as he is pleading with God about Israel, saying, ³"Lord, they killed Your prophets, and dug down Your altars, and I am left alone, and they seek my life." ⁴But what says the reply to him? "I've left for Myself seven thousand men who did not bow a knee to Baal." ⁵So then also in the present time there has been a remnant according to the choice of grace. ⁶But if of grace, no more of works. Else grace is no more grace. But if of

works, it is no more grace. Else work is no more work.

⁷What then? What Israel is seeking, this he did not obtain, but the chosen ones obtained it, but the rest were hardened. ⁸As it has been written, "God has given to them a spirit of stupor, – eyes but not to see, and ears but not to hear, even to today. ⁹And David says, "Let their table be a snare to them, and a trap, and a stumbling-block, and a punishment to them. ¹⁰Let their eyes be made dark, that they not see, bow down their backs always."

¹¹I say, then, did they stumble in order that they might fall? Let it not be. But by their falling aside, salvation has come to the non-Jews, to make them jealous. ¹²But if their falling aside be the riches of the world, and their loss the riches of non-Jews, how much rather their fullness? ¹³For I speak to you, the non-Jews. Since I am the apostle of the non-Jews, I make glorious my ministry, ¹⁴if somehow I may make those of my own flesh jealous, and may save some of them. ¹⁵For if the throwing away of them be the reconciliation – bringing back again, of the world, what will the receiving be, if not life from the dead?

¹⁶But if the beginning fruit is holy, so also is the rest, and if the root is holy, so also are the branches. ¹⁷But if some of the branches are broken off, and you, being a wild olive tree, were grafted in among them, and became a sharer of the root and fatness of the olive tree, ¹⁸do not boast against the branches. But if you boast, you are not carrying the root, but the root is carrying you. ¹⁹You will say, then, "The branches were broken off, that I might be grafted in." ²⁰Well, – they were broken off by unbelief, and you are standing by faith. Be not high-minded, but fear. ²¹For if God did not spare the natural branches. He may not spare you, either. ²²See then, the gentleness and cutting off from God. Upon those indeed who fell, cutting away, but upon you, gentleness, if you remain in His gentleness. Or else you also will be cut out. ²³And they, also, if they should not remain in unbelief, may be grafted in. For God is able to graft them in again. ²⁴For if you were cut out of the olive tree which is wild by nature, and contrary to nature were grafted into a good olive tree, how much more may these who are natural branches, be grafted into their own olive tree. ²⁵For I do not want you not to know brothers, this mystery, that you may not be wise in yourselves, that hardness in part has happened to Israel, until the fullness of the non-Jews be come in. ²⁶And so all Israel will be saved, even as it has been written, "The Rescuer will come out of Zion, and He will turn away ungodliness from Jacob. ²⁷And this is the contract to them from Me, when I have taken away their sins."

²⁸In regard to the good news, they are your enemies, but in regard to the election, they are beloved because of the fathers. ²⁹For the gifts and the calling of God are not subject to a change of mind. ³⁰For as you also at one time were not obedient to God, but now have been given mercy by the disobedience of these Jews, ³¹so also these now were disobedient, unto receiving mercy from you, that they may be given mercy. ³²For God has locked up all men together in unbelief, that He might give mercy to all.

³³O depth of riches both of the wisdom and knowledge of God! How beyond inquiry are His judgments, and how beyond tracking are His paths! ³⁴For who knew the mind of the Lord? Or who became His co-planner? ³⁵Or who first has given to Him, and it will be given back to him? ³⁶Because out of Him, and through Him, and unto Him are all things. To Him be the glory unto the ages. Amen

**12** ¹I beg you then, brothers, by the mercies of God, to give your bodies as a living offering, – holy, well-pleasing to God, – your logical service. ²And do not make yourselves like this age, but be changed in form by the renewing of your minds, to test what is the good, and well-pleasing, and perfect will of God. ³For I say through the grace which is given to me, to everyone who is among you, not to be high-minded beyond what you ought to think, but to think seriously, as God has given to each one a measure of faith. ⁴For even as in one body we have many parts, but the parts do not all have the same action. ⁵So we are many, – one body in Christ, – and each one part of one another. ⁶Having, then, different gifts according to the grace which is given to us, whether prophecy, let it be according to the amount of faith; ⁷or hard work, let us work hard; or he who is teaching, in teaching; ⁸or he who calls to action, in his pleading; he who gives, in simple humility; he who is the leader, with diligence; he who has mercy, in a happy spirit. ⁹Let love be not faked, – hating evil and holding to the good. ¹⁰In brotherly love to each other, have loving-kindness, eager to honor one another, ¹¹not lazy in effort, warm in spirit, serving at the right time, ¹²rejoicing in hope, enduring trouble, keeping constantly in prayer, ¹³meeting the needs of the saints, continuing to love strangers, ¹⁴Bless those who mistreat you, bless and do not curse. ¹⁵Rejoice with the rejoicing, and weep with the weeping. ¹⁶Be in agreement with each other. Do not be proud, but go along with the humble. Do not be wise in your own eyes. ¹⁷Give no one evil for evil, planning good things in the sight of all men. ¹⁸If possible, for your part, be at peace with all men. ¹⁹Do not avenge yourselves, beloved, but give place to anger, for it has been written, "Vengeance is Mine, I will repay, says the Lord." ²⁰So if your enemy should be hungry, feed him. If he should be thirsty, give him a drink. For in doing this, you will heap coals of fire on his head. ²¹Do not be overcome by the evil, but overcome the evil by the good.

**13** ¹Let every person be subject to authorities which are over him. For there is no authority except from God, and those authorities that are, have been appointed by God. ²So that he who sets himself against the authority, is standing against the appointment of God. Then they who resist shall receive judgment unto themselves. ³For the rulers are not a terror to the good works, but to the evil ones. So do you wish not to be afraid of the authority? Do the good, and you will have praise out of it. ⁴For he is a servant of God to you unto the good, but if you do evil, fear. For he does not carry the sword in vain. For he is a servant of God, an avenger unto anger to him who is doing evil. ⁵So it is necessary to be subject, not only because of anger, but also because of conscience. ⁶For because of this also pay tribute. For they are servants of God, taking care of this very thing.

⁷So give dues to all, the tribute to whom the tribute is due, custom to whom custom, fear to whom fear, honor to whom honor. ⁸Do not owe anything to anyone, except to love one another. For he who loves the other has fully kept the Law. ⁹That is, "You shall not commit adultery, you shall not murder, you shall not steal, you shall not give false witness, you shall not have evil desire," and if there is any other command, in this word it is headed up, "You shall love your neighbor as yourself." ¹⁰Love does not work evil to the neighbor, so love is the fullness of the Law.

¹¹Also this, knowing the time, that it is the hour we should be raised from sleep. For now is our salvation nearer, than when we believed. ¹²The night is far gone, and the day has

come near. Let us then put away the works of darkness, and let us put on the armor of light. [13]As in the day, let us walk in a right manner, not in over-eating and drunkenness, not in immorality and excess, not in strife and envy. [14]But put on the Lord Jesus Christ, and do not plan ahead of the flesh, to do its evil desires.

**14** Receive him who is weak in the faith, but not to judging of debates. [2]One person indeed believes it right to eat all things, but the weak one eats plant life. [3]He who eats meat, let him not belittle him who does not eat. And he who does not eat meat, let him not judge him who eats, for God has received him. [4]Who are you, judging another man's servant? To his own Lord he stands or falls. And he shall be made to stand. For God is able to make him stand. [5]Indeed one man judges a day above another day, but another man judges every day to be alike. Let each man be fully persuaded in his own mind. [6]He who observes the day, to the Lord he observes it. And he who does not observe the day, to the Lord he does not observe it. He who eats, eats to the Lord, for he gives thanks to God. And he who does not eat, to the Lord he does not eat, and gives thanks to God. [7]For no one of us lives to himself, and no one dies to himself. [8]For if we should live, we should live unto the Lord, or if we should die, we should die unto the Lord. So if we should live or if we should die, we are of the Lord. [9]For unto this purpose Christ both died and rose and lived again, that He might rule over both the dead and the living. [10]But why do you judge your brother? Or why do you make your brother to be nothing? For we all shall stand at the judgment seat of Christ. [11]For it has been written, "I live, says the Lord, that every knee shall bow to Me, and every tongue shall confess to God." [12]So then each of us shall give account about himself to God. [13]No longer, then, should we judge each other, but rather judge this, not to put a stumbling-block or hindrance to his brother. [14]I know and I am persuaded in the Lord Jesus, that nothing is unclean through itself. But if anything is thought to be unclean, it is unclean to that person. [15]But if your brother is grieved because of meat, you are not walking any longer according to love. Do not destroy with your meat that man for whom Christ died. [16]So do not let your good be evil spoken of. [17]For the kingdom of God is not food and drink, but righteousness and peace and joy in the Holy Spirit. [18]For he who in these things serves Christ is well-pleasing to God, and is approved by men. [19]Now then let us follow the things of peace, and the things that build up one another. [20]Do not because of meat destroy the work of God. All things indeed are pure, but it is evil to the man who is eating and stumbling. [21]It is good not to eat flesh, nor to drink wine, and not to do what makes your brother stumble, or be offended, or made weak. [22]Do you have faith? Have it to yourself before God. Blessed is he who does not condemn himself in what he approves. [23]But he who is in doubt, if he eats, has condemned himself, because it is not of faith. Any everything which is not of faith is sin.

**15** But we who are strong ought to bear the weaknesses of those who are not strong, and not to please ourselves. [2]For let each of us please our neighbor unto good, for building him up. [3]For Christ also did not please Himself; but as it has been written, "The reproaches of those reproaching You fell on Me." [4]For those things which were written before were written before for our learning, that through the support and the comfort of the Scriptures, we might have hope.

⁵So may the God of patience and comfort give to you to think the same thing among each other according to Christ Jesus, ⁶that you may glorify the God and Father of our Lord Jesus Christ with one accord and one mouth.

⁷Because of this, be receptive toward each other, as also Christ received us unto the glory of God. ⁸Now I say that Jesus Christ has become a servant of the circumcision for the glory of God, to confirm the promises made to the fathers, ⁹and that the non-Jewish nations might glorify God for His mercy, even as it has been written, "Because of this I will confess You among the non-Jewish nations, and I will sing praise to Your name." ¹⁰And again it says, "Rejoice, nations, with His people." ¹¹And again, "Praise the Lord, all the nations, and praise Him, all the peoples." ¹²And again, Isaiah says, "There shall be the Root of Jesse, and One arising to rule nations, – nations shall put their hope on Him."

¹³Now the God of hope fill you with all joy and peace in believing, that you may abound in hope, in the power of the Holy Spirit.

¹⁴Now I am persuaded, my brothers, even I myself about you, that you are yourselves even full of goodness, filled with all knowledge, able to counsel one another. ¹⁵But I wrote to you more boldly, brothers, partly as reminding you, because of the grace given to me from God, ¹⁶that I should be a minister of Jesus Christ to the nations, in the holy work of the good news of God, that the offering up of the nations might become acceptable, made holy in the Holy Spirit.

¹⁷So I have a boasting in Christ Jesus of the things moving toward God. ¹⁸For I will not dare to speak of anything which Christ did not do through me, unto obedience of the nations, by word and by work, ¹⁹in the power of signs and wonders, in the power of the Spirit of God. So as for me, from Jerusalem and in a circle unto Illyricum, I have fully preached the good news of Christ. ²⁰And so, I am loving the honor of telling the good news, not where Christ was named, that I might not build on the foundation of another man. ²¹But as it is written, "To whom it was not told about Him, they shall see, and those who have not heard shall understand."

²²Because of this ministry I was kept many times from coming to you. ²³But now, no longer having a place in these areas, but having great desire to come to you for many years, ²⁴when I may go to Spain, I will come to you. For I hope in going through, to see you, and to be sent forward on my way there by you, when first I may be in part satisfied with you. ²⁵But now I am going to Jerusalem, serving the saints. ²⁶For some from Macedonia and Achaia were pleased to make a fellowship gift for the poor saints who are in Jerusalem. ²⁷For they were pleased, and they are their debtors, for if the non-Jewish nations shared in their spiritual things, they ought to serve them in material things. ²⁸So then after finishing this, and sealing this fruit to them, I will come by you into Spain. ²⁹Now I know that coming to you, I shall come in the fullness of the blessing of the good news of Christ.

³⁰But I beg you, brothers, by our Lord Jesus Christ, and by the love of the Spirit, to strive together with me in prayers for me to God, ³¹that I may be rescued from the unbelievers in Judea, and that my service which is for Jerusalem may be well received by the saints, ³²that I may come to you in joy by the will of God, and have a pleasant stay with you. ³³Now the God of peace be with you all. Amen – Truly.

16 ¹Now I commend to you Phoebe our sister, who is a servant of the church in Cenchrea, ²that you may receive her in the Lord as is worthy of the saints, and that you may help her in whatever action she may have need of you, for she has become a supporter of many people, and of me myself. ³Greet Priscilla and Aquila my co-workers in Christ Jesus, ⁴who for my life have lain down their own necks. Not only do I thank them, but also all the churches of the non-Jewish nations, ⁵and the church at their house. Greet Epenetus my beloved, who is a firstfruit of Achaia unto Christ. ⁶Greet Mary, who labored much for us. ⁷Greet Andronicus and Junia my relatives, my fellow-prisoners, who are notable among the apostles, who also were before me in Christ. ⁸Greet Amplias my beloved in the Lord. ⁹Greet Urbanus our co-worker in Christ, and Stachys my beloved. ¹⁰Greet Apelles, approved in Christ. Greet the family of Aristobulus. ¹¹Greet Herodion my relative. Greet the family of Narcissus, who are in the Lord. ¹²Green Tryphena and Tryphosa, laborers in the Lord. Greet Persis the beloved, who labored much in the Lord. ¹³Greet Rufus, chosen in the Lord; and his mother and mine. ¹⁴Greet Asyncritus, Phlegon, Hermas, Patrobus, Hermes and the brothers with them. ¹⁵Greet Philologus and Julia, Nereus and his sister, and Olympas, and all the saints with them. ¹⁶Greet each other with a holy kiss. The churches of Christ greet you.

¹⁷Now I beg you, brothers, to notice those who make divisions and offenses, contrary to the teaching you have learned, and turn away from them. ¹⁸For such persons do not serve our Lord Jesus Christ, but their own belly, and by nice words and flattery lead astray the hearts of the innocent. ¹⁹For your obedience has reached to all men. So I rejoice over you. But I wish you indeed to be wise unto the good, but simple unto the evil, ²⁰but the God of peace will bruise Satan under your feet shortly. The grace of our Lord Jesus Christ be with you.

²¹Timothy my co-worker greets you, and Lucius, and Jason, and Sosipater, my relatives. ²²I, Tertius, who wrote the epistle, greet you in the Lord. ²³Gaius my host, and of the whole church, greets you. Erastus the steward of the city greets you, and brother Quartus. ²⁴The grace of our Lord Jesus Christ be with you all. Amen.

²⁵Now to Him Who is able to strengthen you by my good news, and the preaching of Jesus Christ, according to the unveiling of the mystery kept silent in ancient times, ²⁶but now revealed through the prophetic Scriptures, according to the command of the eternal God, unto obedience of faith, made known to all the nations, ²⁷to the only wise God, through Jesus Christ, to Whom be glory unto the ages. Amen.

## *The First Epistle of Paul the Apostle to the*
# CORINTHIANS

1 ¹Paul, a called apostle of Jesus Christ, by the will of God, and Sosthenes our brother, ²unto the church of God which is in Corinth, to those who have been made holy in Christ Jesus, called saints, with all those calling on the name of our Lord Jesus Christ in every place, both theirs and ours. ³Grace to you and peace from God our Father, and the Lord Jesus Christ. ⁴I thank my God always about you, for the grace of God given to you in Christ Jesus, ⁵that in every thing you were made rich in Him, in all speaking, and all knowledge, ⁶even as the witness of Christ was confirmed in you. ⁷So that you are not behind in any gift, waiting for the revealing of our Lord Jesus Christ, ⁸Who also will confirm you unto the end, without blame in the day of our Lord Jesus Christ. ⁹Faithful. Is God, by Whom you were called into the fellowship of His Son Jesus Christ our Lord.

¹⁰Now I beg you, brothers, by the name of our Lord Jesus Christ, that you all say the same thing, and that there not be divisions among you, but that you may be molded together in the same mind and in the same opinion. ¹¹For it was shown to me about you, my brothers, by those of the family of Chloe, that there are strifes among you. ¹²But I say this, that each of you says, "I am of Paul, and I of Apollos, and I of Peter, and I of Christ." ¹³Is Christ divided? Was Paul crucified for you? Or were you immersed unto the name of Paul?

¹⁴I thank God that I immersed none of you, except Crispus and Gaius, ¹⁵so that no one might say that I immersed in my own name. ¹⁶And I immersed the family of Stephanus. Of the rest, I do not know if I immersed any other.

¹⁷For Christ did not send me to immerse, but to tell the good news, not in wisdom of words, that the cross of Christ be made in vain. ¹⁸For the message of the cross is foolishness to those who are lost, but to us who are saved it is the power of God. ¹⁹For it was written, "I will destroy the wisdom of the wise, and the knowledge of the knowing ones I will set aside." ²⁰Where is the wise? Where the scribe? Where the inquirer of this age? Has not God made foolish the wisdom of this world? ²¹For since in the wisdom of God, the world did not know God by wisdom, God was pleased by the foolishness of the preaching to save those who believe. ²²And although Jews ask for a sign, and Greeks seek wisdom, ²³we, however, preach Christ crucified, to Jews an offence, and to Greeks foolishness, ²⁴but to those called, both Jews and Greeks, Christ the power of God, and the wisdom of God. ²⁵Because the "foolishness" of God is wiser than men, and the "weakness" of God is stronger than men. ²⁶For you see your calling, brothers, that there are not many wise after the flesh, not many powerful, not many well-born. ²⁷But God has chosen the foolish things of the world, that the wise might be shamed. And weak things of the world God chose, that He might shame the strong things. ²⁸And the not well born of the world and the nothing people God chose, and the things that are not, that the things that are He may not work through, ²⁹so that all flesh might not boast before Him. ³⁰But of Him are you in Christ Jesus, Who was made to us wisdom from God and righteousness, and holiness, and ransom, ³¹that, even as it has been written, "He who is boasting, let him boast in the Lord."

2 And when I came to you, brothers, I came not with fine words or wisdom, telling you the witness of God. ²For I judged it best not to know anything among you, but Jesus Christ, and Him crucified died on the cross. ³And I was with you in weakness, and in fear, and in much trembling. ⁴And my message and my preaching was not in persuasive words of human wisdom, but in showing forth of the Spirit and of power, ⁵so that your faith should not be in the wisdom of men, but in the power of God.
⁶But we speak wisdom among the mature; but not the wisdom of this age, nor of the rulers of this age, who are being brought to nothing. ⁷But we speak the wisdom of God in a mystery, the hidden wisdom which God determined before the ages unto our glory, ⁸which none of the rulers of this age has known. For if they had known, they would not have crucified the Lord of glory. ⁹But as it has been written, "What the eye did not see, and the ear did not hear, and what did not come into the heart of man, God prepared for those loving Him." ¹⁰But God revealed them to us by His Spirit, for the Spirit searches all things, even the deep things of God. ¹¹For who of men knows the things of man, if not the spirit of man that is in him? So also no one knows the things of God, if not the Spirit of God. ¹²But we have not received the spirit of the world, but the Spirit Who is from God, that we might know the things given to us by the favor of God. ¹³Which things also we speak, not in words taught of human wisdom, but in what is taught by the Holy Spirit, judging spiritual things with spiritual means. ¹⁴But the natural man does not receive the things of the Spirit of God, for they are foolishness to him, and he can not know them, because they are spiritually understood. ¹⁵But the spiritual man understands all things, but he is understood by no one. ¹⁶For who has known the mind of the Lord, who will instruct Him? But we have the mind of Christ.

3 And I, brothers could not speak to you as to spiritual persons, but as to fleshly, as to babes in Christ. ²I gave you milk to drink, and not meat. For you were not yet able to eat it, and you still are not able now. ³For you are yet fleshly. For where there is envy, and strife, and divisions among you, are you not carnal, and walk according to man? ⁴For you are yet fleshly. For where someone says, "I am of Paul", but another, "I of Apollos", are you not carnal? ⁵Who then is Paul, and who Apollos, but the servants through whom you believed, and as the Lord gave to each one?
⁶I planted, Apollos watered, but God made the increase. ⁷So neither he who is planting is anything, nor he who is watering, but God Who increases. ⁸He who is planting and he who is watering are one, but each shall receive his own reward according to his own labor. ⁹For we are workers with God. You are God's farming, God's building. ¹⁰According to the grace of God which was given to me, as a wise architect I have laid the foundation, and another builds upon it. But let each one watch how he builds upon it. ¹¹For other foundation no one can lay besides that which is laid, which is Jesus the Christ. ¹²But if anyone builds on this foundation, gold, silver, precious stones, wood, grass, reeds, ¹³the word of each one will become apparent, for the Day will declare it, because it is revealed in fire, and the fire will test the work of each man, what it is like. ¹⁴If the work of man remains which he built, he will receive a reward. ¹⁵If the work of any man shall be burned down, he shall suffer loss, but he him self shall be saved, but so as through fire. ¹⁶Do you not know that you are a temple of God, and that the Spirit of God lives in you? ¹⁷If anyone defiles the temple of God, God shall

defile him. For the temple of God is holy, which you are. ¹⁸Let no one deceive himself. If anyone among you thinks he is wise in this age, let him become foolish, that he may become wise. ¹⁹For the wisdom of this world is foolishness with God. For it has been written, "He takes the wise in all of their schemes." ²⁰And again, "The Lord knows the ideas of the wise, that they are vain." ²¹So let no one boast in men, for all things are yours; ²²whether Paul, or Apollos, or Peter, or the world, or life, or death, or present things, or coming things, all are yours, ²³and you are Christ's and Christ is God's.

4 So let a man think of us as workers under Christ, and stewards of the mysteries of God. ²But for the rest, it is sought in stewards that one be found faithful. ³But to me it is a very little thing that I should be judged by you, or by a human day. Neither do I judge myself. ⁴For I know nothing of myself, but I am not justified by this. But He Who judges me is the Lord. ⁵So do not judge anything before the time, until the Lord comes, Who will light up the hidden things of darkness, and will make plain the thoughts of the hearts. And then praise will be to everyone from God. ⁶But these things, brothers, I applied to myself and Apollos for your sakes, that you may learn in regard to us not to think above what has been written. So that not one of you should be puffed up for one and against the other.

⁷For who makes you to be different? And what do you have that you did not receive? But if you received it, why do you boast as if not having received it? ⁸Already you are filled, already made rich, made kings apart from us. And I wish indeed that you were made kings, so that we also might reign with you. ⁹For I think that God displayed us the apostles last as dying men, so that we were made a spectacle to the world, and to angels, and to men. ¹⁰We are fools because of Christ, but you are wise in Christ. We are weak, but you are strong, you are praised, but we are not honored. ¹¹Until the present hour we are both hungry and thirsty and without clothes, and beaten, and we do not have a home. ¹²And we labor, working with our hands. Being ridiculed, we bless; mistreated, we bear it. ¹³Being evil spoken of, we plead. We are become as the dirt of the world, as scum of all things until now.

¹⁴I am writing these things not to shame you, but as beloved children I remind you. ¹⁵For if you should have ten thousand teachers in Christ, yet you do not have many fathers. For in Christ Jesus, through the good news, I have given you birth. ¹⁶I beg you, then, become imitators of me.

¹⁷Because of this I sent Timothy to you, who is my beloved and faithful child in the Lord, who will bring again to your memories my ways in Christ, even as every where in every church I teach. ¹⁸But as I am not coming to you, some were puffed up. ¹⁹But I shall come to you soon, if the Lord should wish it, and I shall learn, not the word of those who have been puffed up, but the power. ²⁰For the kingdom of God is not in word, but in power. ²¹What do you wish? I should come to you with a rod, or in the love of the Spirit, and meekness?

5 All report among you immorality, and such immorality that is not mentioned even among the non Jews, that someone has the wife of his father as a sex mate. ²And you are puffed up, and not rather grieved, that he who did this deed might be taken out of your midst. ³For I as being absent in the body, but being present in spirit, already have judged as being present, him who has so done this deed, ⁴in the name of our Lord Jesus Christ,

you and my spirit being gathered together, with the power of our Lord Jesus Christ, ⁵to give over such a person to Satan unto the destruction of the flesh, that the spirit may be saved in the day of the Lord Jesus. ⁶Your boasting is not good. Do you not know that a little leaven leavens the whole lump?
⁷Purge out then the old leaven, that you may be a new lump, even as you are unleavened. For Christ our Passover was sacrificed for us, ⁸so that we might keep the feast, not in the old leaven, nor in the leaven of evil and wickedness, but in the unleavened bread of clear judgment and of truth.
⁹I wrote to you in the letter not to be mingled together with immoral persons. ¹⁰And not altogether with the immoral ones of this world, or with the greedy, or grasping, or idolaters, for then you ought to go out of the world. ¹¹But now I wrote to you not to mingle with any brother who is called either immoral, or greedy, or an idolater, or a railer, or a drunkard, or grasping, with such a one not even to eat. ¹²For what is it to me to judge those who are outside? Do you not judge those who are inside? ¹³But those outside God judges. And so take out the wicked one from your selves.

**6** Do any of you dare, having a matter against the other, to be judged by the unjust, and not before the saints? ²Do you not know that the saints will judge the world? And if the world is judged by you, are you unworthy of judgments of the smallest things? ³Do you not know that we shall judge angels? And not then things of this life? ⁴Things of this life indeed then, if you have judgment, put those who are nobodies in the church over these. ⁵I speak to your shame. Is there not even one wise man among you, who can decide between his brothers? ⁶But brother goes to judgment against brother, and this before unbelievers. ⁷Already then it is wholly a fault among you, that you have law suits among your selves. Why not rather be unjustly treated? Why not rather be cheated? ⁸But you do wrong and cheat, and do these things to brothers.
⁹Do you not know that the unjust shall not inherit the kingdom of God? Do not be led astray. Neither immoral people, nor idolaters, nor adulterers, nor effeminate, nor homosexuals, ¹⁰nor thieves, nor greedy ones, nor drunkards, nor railers, nor grasping persons shall inherit the kingdom of God. ¹¹And some of you may have been these things, but you were washed, but you were made holy, but you were made just, in the name of the Lord Jesus, and in the Spirit of our God.
¹²All things are lawful, for me, but not all things are profitable. All things are lawful, but I will not be brought under the power of any. ¹³Food for the belly, and the belly for food, but God will bring them both to nothing. But the body is not for immorality, but for the Lord, and the Lord for the body. ¹⁴And God both raised up the Lord, and He will raise us up by His power. ¹⁵Do you not know that our bodies are parts of Christ? Having become then a part of Christ, shall I make myself a part of a whore? Let it not be! ¹⁶Do you not know that he who is joined to the whore is one body? For the two, He says, shall be one flesh. ¹⁷But he who is joined to the Lord is one spirit. ¹⁸Flee from immorality. Every sin which a man may keep doing is out side his body. But he who is immoral sins against his own body. ¹⁹Or do you not know that your body is a temple of the Holy Spirit, Who is in you, which you have from God, and you are not your own? ²⁰For you were bought for a price, so glorify God in your body, and in your spirit, which are God's.

**7** But about the things that you wrote to me, it is good for a man not to touch a woman. ²But because of immorality, let each man have his own wife, and let each woman have her own husband. ³Let the husband give due good will to the wife, and likewise the wife to the husband. ⁴The wife does not have rule over her own body, but the husband does, and likewise also the husband does not have rule over his own body, but the wife does. ⁵Do not deprive one another, except by agreement for a time, that you may be free for fasting and for prayer, and come together again as one, that Satan may not tempt you because of your not mating. ⁶But I am saying this as advice, not as a command. ⁷For I wish that all men were as I myself am. But each man has his gift from God, one like this, one like that. ⁸But I say to the unmarried and to the widows, that it is good for them if they would stay as I. ⁹But is they cannot refrain, let them marry, for it is better to marry than to burn.

¹⁰But to those who have been married, I charge, not I, but the Lord, that wife is not to be separated from husband. ¹¹But even if she may be separated, let her stay unmarried, or be brought back to the husband. And the husband is not to go away from his wife. ¹²But to the rest I myself say, not the Lord, if any brother has an unbelieving wife, and it seems good to her to live with him, let him not go away from her. ¹³And a woman who has an unbelieving husband, and he is well pleased to live with her, let her not leave him. ¹⁴For the unbelieving husband is made holy in the wife, and the unbelieving wife is made holy in the husband; or else your children would be unclean, but now they are holy. ¹⁵But if the unbeliever goes away, let him go away. The brother or the sister is not bound in such cases. But God has called us to peace. ¹⁶For what do you know, wife, if you will save your husband? Or what do you know, husband, if you will save your wife?

¹⁷Just let each one walk as God has given his part, each one as the Lord has called. And so I order in all the churches. ¹⁸Is someone called after being circumcised? Let him not be uncircumcised. Is someone called in uncircumcision? Let him not be circumcised. ¹⁹Circumcision is nothing, and uncircumcision is nothing, but keeping of the commands of God. ²⁰Let each one stay in the calling in which he was called. ²¹Were you called as a servant? Do not let it worry you. But if you are able to become free, rather, make use of it. ²²For he who is called in the Lord as a servant is a freed man of the Lord. So also a free man who is called is a servant of Christ. ²³You were bought with a price, do not become servants of men. 24Each one, brothers, let him stay in the calling in which he was called, with God.

²⁵But I do not have a command about virgins, though I give an opinion, as one who has received mercy from the Lord to be faithful. ²⁶So I think then that this is good because of the present need that it is good for a man to be like this. ²⁷Have you been tied to a wife? Do not seek to be loosed. Have you been loosed from a wife? Do not seek a wife. ²⁸But if you may be married, you did not sin. And if the virgin may marry, she did not sin. But such persons will have trouble in the flesh, but I spare you. ²⁹But this I say, brothers, the time is short. The rest is, that also those having wives should be as not having them. ³⁰And those weeping, as not weeping, and those rejoicing, as not rejoicing, and those buying, as not having. ³¹And those using this world, as those not overly using it. For the pattern of this world is passing away. ³²But I wish you to be without worry. The unmarried person is concerned for the things of the Lord, how he will please the Lord. ³³But the married person is concerned for the things of the world, how he will please his wife. ³⁴The wife and the virgin are different.

The unmarried woman is concerned for the things of the Lord, that she may be holy both in body and in spirit. But she who is married is concerned for the things of the world, how she will please her husband. ³⁵But I say this for your own profit, not that I may throw a lasso over you, but for what seems good and for your steadily serving the Lord with no distraction.

³⁶But if someone thinks that he is not acting right about his virgin, if he may be past his peak, and it ought to be so, let him do what he wishes, he is not sinning, let them marry. ³⁷But he who stands firm in heart, not having a need, but has control over his own will, and has decided in him heart to keep himself a virgin, does well. ³⁸So even he who gives in marriage does well, but he who does not give in marriage does better.

³⁹A wife is bound by law for so long a time her husband may live. But if her husband should have fallen asleep, she is free to be married to whom she wishes, only in the Lord. ⁴⁰But she is more happy if she remains so, according to my opinion, and I think also that I have the Spirit of God.

8 Now about idol offerings, we know all of us have knowledge. Knowledge puffs up but love builds up. ²But if someone thinks he knows something, he has known nothing yet as he needs to know. ³But if someone should love God, He is known by him.

⁴So about the eating of things offered to idols we know that an idol is nothing in the world, and that there is no other God but One. ⁵For even if they are spoken of as gods, whether in heaven or on the earth, as, "they are many gods and many lords." ⁶but to us, one God, the Father, from Whom are all things, and we are His, and one Lord, Jesus Christ, by Whom are all things, and we are by Him.

⁷But this knowledge is not in all people, but some eat with a conscience about the idol until now, as an idol offering, and consciences, being weak, are defiled. ⁸But food does not commend us to God. For we are neither greater if we should eat, nor lesser if we should not eat. ⁹But see to it that this right of yours does not become a stumbling block to those who are weak. ¹⁰For if someone should see you, who have knowledge, at an idol temple, lying there to eat, will not the conscience of him who is weak be encouraged to eat as of idol offerings? ¹¹And the weak brother will die over your knowledge, he for whom Christ died. ¹²In so sinning against the brothers, and hurting their weak conscience, you are sinning against Christ. ¹³Because of this, if meat makes my brother stumble, I should not eat meat at all forever, in order that I may not make my brother stumble.

9 Am I not an apostle? Am I not free? Have I not seen Jesus Christ my Lord? Are you not my work in the Lord? ²If I am not an apostle to others, yet I am indeed to you. For you are the seal in the Lord of my being an apostle.

³My reply to those who are judging me is this. ⁴Do we not have a right to eat and to drink? ⁵Do we not have a right to lead around a sister, a wife, as also do the rest of the apostles, and the brothers of the Lord, and Peter? ⁶Or only I and Barnabas, do we not have a right not to work? ⁷Who ever serves as a soldier at his own expenses? Who plants a vineyard, and does not eat of the fruit of it? Or who shepherds a flock, and does not drink of the milk of the flock? ⁸Am I saying these things as a man? Or does not also the Law say these things? ⁹For in the Law of Moses it is written, "You may not muzzle an ox that is treading out grain." Is

God concerned about the oxen? [10]Or is He saying this entirely because of us? It was written because of us, that he who is plowing ought to plow in hope, and he who treads out grain, ought to have his share in hope. [11]If we sowed to you the spiritual things, is it a great thing if we shall reap your material things? [12]If brothers have a share of rule over you, should we not, rather? But we did not use this rule, but we cover all expenses, in order that we should give no hindrance to the good news of Christ. [13]Do you not know, that those who are serving the holy things, eat of the temple, and those attending the altar, have their share with the altar? [14]So also the Lord ordered to those telling the good news, that they should live of the good news.
 [15]But I have used none of these things. And I have not written these things that it should be so with me. For it would be good for me rather to die, than someone should make my boasting empty. [16]For if I tell the good news, boasting is not for me, for necessity is laid upon me. Woe is unto me if I do not tell the good news. [17]For if I do this willingly, I have a reward. But if unwillingly, I am entrusted with a stewardship. [18]What then is my reward? That in telling the good news I may make the good news of Christ without cost, to not use wrongly my authority in the good news.
 [19]For being free from all people, I became a servant to all, that I might gain the more. [20]So I became like a Jew to the Jews, that I might gain Jews, to those under Law as under Law, that I might gain those under Law. [21]To those without Law as without Law, not being without Law to God, but within Law to Christ, that I might gain those without Law. [22]I became to the weak, as weak, that I might gain the weak. I have become all things to all, that by all ways I might save some. [23]And this I do because of the good news, that I might be a partner with it.
 [24]Do you not know that all who are running in a racing arena run, but only one receives the prize? So run, that you may receive it. [25]But every one who is contesting, strengthens himself in every way, they indeed that they may receive a perishable crown, but we an imperishable. [26]Truly now I am so running, not as uncertainly, so I am fighting, not like one beating the air. [27]But I hold my body under, and bring it into the place of a servant, so that in no way, having preached to others, I myself might become disapproved.

**10** But I do not want you to be uninformed, brothers, that our fathers all were under a cloud, and all passed thru the sea, [2]and all were immersed unto Moses in the cloud and in the sea, [3]and all ate the same spiritual food, [4]and all drank the same spiritual drink. For they drank of a spiritual Rock following them, and the Rock was Christ. [5]But God was not well pleased with most of them, for they were struck down in the desert.
 [6]Now these things became patterns for us, that we should not be longing for evil things, as they also desired. [7]And do you not become idolaters, as some of them did. As it is written, "The people sat down to eat and drink, and stood up to play." [8]And let us not do immoral acts as some of them did, and fell dead, twenty three thousand in one day. [9]And let us not tempt Christ, as also some of them did, and were killed by snakes. [10]Nor do you murmur, as some of them also did, and were killed by the destroyer. [11]Now all these things happened to them as patterns, and were written for our learning, unto whom the end of the ages has come. [12]So he who seems to stand let him see that he may not fall. [13]Testing has not taken you except what is common to man. But God is faithful, Who will not let you be tested above what you

are able, but He will make, with the testing, also a way out, so you will be able to bear it. ¹⁴Because of this, flee away from idol worship.

¹⁵I speak as to wise people, you judge what I am saying. ¹⁶The cup of praise in which we praise, is it not the fellowship of the body of Christ? ¹⁷Because, we, the many, are one loaf, for we all have part of one loaf. ¹⁸Look at Israel according to the flesh. Are not those eating the offerings in fellowship with the altar? ¹⁹What am I saying, then? That an idol is anything? Or that an idol offering is anything? ²⁰But what the non-Jews offer, they offer to demons, and not to God. I do not want you to become in fellowship with demons. ²¹You cannot drink a cup of the Lord, and a cup of demons. You cannot have part of a table of the Lord and a table of demons. ²²Or should we stir up the anger of the Lord? Are we stronger than He?

²³All things are lawful for me, but not all things are helpful. All things are lawful for me, but not all things are constructive. ²⁴Let no one seek his own things, but each one that of the other. ²⁵All that is sold in a market, eat, not passing judgment because of conscience, ²⁶for the earth is the Lord's, and its fullness. ²⁷So if someone of the unbelievers calls you to eat, and you wish to go, eat all that is set before you, not passing judgment because of conscience. ²⁸But if someone should say to you, "This is offered to an idol," do not eat, because of that one who showed you, and for conscience. For the earth is the Lord's, and its fullness. ²⁹Conscience, I say, not yours, but that of the other person. But why is my freedom judged by another person's conscience? ³⁰And if I partake with thanks, why am I evil spoken of, for what I give thanks? ³¹Well, whether you eat, or drink, or what you do, do all unto God's glory. ³²Do not cause to stumble either Jews, or Greek, or the church of God, even as I also please all people in all things, not seeking my own profit, but that of the many, that they may be saved.

11 Become imitators of me, even as I also am of Christ. ²Now I praise you, brothers, that you have remembered things from me, and as I gave to you, you keep the instructions. ³But I want you to know that Christ is the head of every man, but the head of the woman is the man, and the head of Christ, God. ⁴Every man, praying or speaking forth, having a covering on the head, shames his head. ⁵But every woman praying or speaking forth, with her head not covered, shames her head, for it is one and the same with being shaved. ⁶For if a woman is not covered, let her also be shorn. But if it is a shame for a woman to be shorn or shaved, let her be covered. ⁷For a man indeed ought not to have the head covered, being the image and glory of God, but a woman is the glory of man. ⁸For man is not of woman, but woman of man. ⁹For also man was not created because of the woman, but woman because of the man. ¹⁰Because of this the woman ought to have authority on her head, because of the angels. ¹¹Neither, however, is man apart from woman, nor woman apart from man, in the Lord. ¹²For as the woman is out of the man, so also is the man by the woman, but all things are of God. ¹³Judge in yourselves; is it fitting for a woman to pray to God not covered? ¹⁴Or does not even nature it self teach you that if a man has long hair, it is a dishonor to him? ¹⁵But if a woman has long hair, it is a glory to her, because the long hair is given to her instead of a shawl. ¹⁶But if anyone seems to be contentious, we have no such custom, nor do the churches of God.

¹⁷Now as to this which I am telling you, I should not praise you, that you are come

together not for the better, but for the worse. ¹⁸For, first, in your coming together in the church, I hear that there are divisions among you, which I believe in part. ¹⁹For there must be heresies also among you, that the approved among you may become apparent. ²⁰So your coming together in one place is not to eat the Lord's supper. ²¹For each one takes first his own supper in the course of eating, so one is hungry, and one is drunk! ²²Do you not have houses for eating and drinking? Or do you look down on the church of God, and shame those who do not have anything? What should I say to you? Shall I praise you in this? I should not praise! ²³For I received from the Lord what I also gave to you, that the Lord Jesus in the night in which He was betrayed, took bread, ²⁴and having given thanks, He broke it and said, "Take, eat, this My body, broken for you. This do in remembrance of Me." ²⁵So also the cup, after the supper, saying, "This cup is the new pact in My blood. This do, as often as you may drink it, in remembrance of Me." ²⁶For as often as you may eat this bread, and drink this cup, you tell of the death of the Lord, until He should come. ²⁷So that whoever should eat this bread, or drink the cup of the Lord unworthily, shall be guilty of the body and of the blood of the Lord. ²⁸But let a man test himself, and so let him eat of the bread and let him drink of the cup. ²⁹For he who is eating and drinking unworthily, eats and drinks judgment to himself, not discerning the body of the Lord. ³⁰Because of this many among you are weak and sick, and a good number are fallen asleep. ³¹For if we judged our selves, we should not be judged. ³²But, being judged, we are trained as children by the Lord, that we should not be condemned with the world. ³³So, my brothers, in coming together to eat, wait for each other. ³⁴But if someone should be hungry, let him eat at home, that you are not come together unto judgment. But the rest, when I may come I will set in order.

**12** Now about the affairs of the Spirit, brothers, I do not want you to be uninformed. ²You know that you were non-Jews, being led away unto dumb idols, as you were led. ³So I am letting you know, that no one speaking in the Spirit of God says that Jesus is accursed. And no one can say, "Lord Jesus," except in the Holy Spirit. ⁴But there are differences of gifts, but the same Spirit. ⁵And there are differences of services, and the same Lord. ⁶And there are differences of workings, but it is the same God Who works all things in all. ⁷But to each is given the showing forth of the Spirit for profit. ⁸For indeed to one is given through the Spirit of a word of wisdom, but to another a word of knowledge, according to the same Spirit. ⁹But to another, faith, in the same Spirit. And to another, gifts of healing, in the same Spirit. ¹⁰And to another, works of power, and to another, speaking forth from God, and to another, discerning of spirits, and to another, kinds of tongues, and to another, interpretation of tongues. ¹¹But all these things, one and the same Spirit works, dividing to each person his own as He wills.

¹²For even as the body is one, and has many parts, but all the parts of the one body, being many, are one body, so also is Christ. ¹³For also in one Spirit we all into one body were immersed, whether Jews or Greeks, whether slaves or free. And we all were caused to drink into one Spirit. ¹⁴For the body also is not one part, but many. ¹⁵If the foot shall say, "Because I am not a hand, I am not of the body" because of this is it not of the body? ¹⁶And if the ear should say, "Because I am not an eye, I am not of the body," because of this is it not of the body? ¹⁷If the whole body were an eye, where would the hearing be? If the whole were

hearing, where would the smelling be? ¹⁸But now God set the parts, each one of them, in the body, even as He desired. ¹⁹But if all were one part, where would the body be? ²⁰But now indeed there are many parts, but one body. ²¹And an eye cannot say to the hand, "I have no need of you." Or again, the head to the feet, "I have no need of you." ²²But much rather the parts seeming to be weaker are needed, ²³and those of the body that we think to be less honored, these we encircle with more abundant honor, and our homely parts have more abundant beauty. ²⁴But our beautiful parts have no such need. But God joined the body together, having given more honor to the part which lacked, ²⁵that there might not be a division in the body, but that the parts might have the same concern for each other. ²⁶And if one part suffers, all the parts suffer together. If one part is glorified, all the parts rejoice together. 27Now you are Christ's body, and individually members of it. ²⁸And God has set these in the church: first, the apostles; secondly, prophets; thirdly, teachers; then, works of power; then, gifts of healing; skills; governments; kinds of tongues. ²⁹Are all apostles? Are all prophets? Are all teachers? Are all workers of power? ³⁰Do all have gifts of healing? Do all speak in tongues? Do all interpret? ³¹But be eager for the better gifts. And yet I show you a much higher way.

**13** If I should speak in the tongues of men and of angels, but have not love, I have become echoing brass, or a noisy cymbal. ²And if I have prophecy, and I should know all mysteries and all knowledge, and if I have all faith, so as to remove mountains, but I do not have love, I am nothing. ³And if I should feed people with all my property, and if I should give up my body to be burned, but I do not have love, I am profited nothing.

⁴Love suffers greatly, and is kind; love is not envious; love does not boast, is not puffed up, ⁵is not disorderly, does not seek the things of itself, not irritated, does not think evil, ⁶does not rejoice at injustices, but rejoices with the truth; ⁷covers all things, believes all things, hopes all things, endures all things.

⁸Love never falls out. But whether there are prophecies, they shall stop working, or tongues, they shall cease, or knowledge, it shall stop working. ⁹For we know in part, and we prophesy in part. ¹⁰But when the perfect comes, then that which is in part shall stop working. ¹¹When I was a young child, I spoke like a young child, I thought like a young child, I reasoned like a young child. But when I became a man, I did away with the things of the young child. ¹²For we see now through a mirror, in a puzzle, but then face to face. Now I know in part, but then I shall know even as also I am known. ¹³So now remain faith, hope, love, these three things, but the greatest of these love.

**14** Follow after love. Desire the spiritual gifts, but rather that you may prophesy. ²For the one speaking in a tongue does not speak to men, but to God. For no one gives ear, but in spirit he speaks mysteries. ³But he who is preaching speaks to men, building up, and help, and comfort. ⁴He who is speaking in a tongue, edifies himself. But he who is preaching edifies the church. ⁵So I wish all of you to speak in tongues, but rather that you might preach. For greater is he who preaches than he who is speaking in tongues, except if he should interpret, that the church may receive edification.

⁶But now, brothers, if I come to you speaking in tongues, what shall I profit you, except I shall speak to you either in revelation, or in knowledge, or in prophecy, or in teaching? ⁷Even the lifeless things giving a sound, whether a flute or a harp, if they do not give a distinction to the sounds, how shall it be known what is being blown or harped? ⁸For also if a trumpet should give an uncertain sound, who will get ready for a battle? ⁹So also you, except you should give by the tongue an easily understood message, how shall it be known what is being spoken? For you will be speaking into the air. ¹⁰There are, it may be, so many kinds of sounds in the world, and none of them without meaning. ¹¹If then I do not know the meaning of the sound, I shall be a barbarian to him who is speaking. And he who is speaking will be a barbarian to me. ¹²So also you, since you are zealous of spiritual matters, seek that you may abound to the building up of the church. ¹³Wherefore he who is speaking in a tongue, let him pray that he may interpret. ¹⁴For if I pray in a tongue, my spirit prays, but my mind is not fruitful.

¹⁵What is it, then? I will pray with the spirit, but also I will pray with the mind. I will sing with the spirit, but also with the mind. ¹⁶Else if you bless with the spirit, he who fills the place of the uninformed, how will he say, "Amen", upon your thanks giving, since he does not know what you are saying? ¹⁷For you indeed give thanks well, but the other person is not built up. ¹⁸I thank my God, speaking in tongues more than all of you. ¹⁹But in the church I would rather speak five words with my mind, that I might teach others also, than ten thousand words in a tongue. ²⁰Brothers, do not become children in understanding, but in evil be little children, but in understanding become mature.

²¹In the Law it has been written, "In other tongues, and other lips I will speak to this people, and not even for this will they give heed to Me, says the Lord." ²²So tongues are for a sign, not to those who believe, but to the non-believers. But the prophecy, not to the non-believers, but to those who believe. ²³If then the whole church should come together at one place, and all should speak in tongues, and uninformed ones or non-believers should come in, will they not say that you have become crazy? ²⁴But if all preach, and some non-believer or uninformed should come in, he is convicted by all, he is judged by all, ²⁵and so the secrets of his heart become clear, and so, falling upon his face, he will worship God, declaring that God really is among you.

²⁶What is it, then, brothers? When you come together, each of you has a psalm, has a teaching, has a revelation, has an interpretation. Let all things be done for building up. ²⁷And if someone speaks in a tongue let it be by two or at the most three, and in turn, and let one interpret. ²⁸But if there should not be an interpreter, let him be silent in a church, but let him speak to himself and to God. ²⁹But let two or three preachers speak, and let the others judge. ³⁰But if there should be a revelation to another sitting by, let the first be silent. ³¹For you can all preach, one at a time, that all may learn, and all may be helped. ³²And the spirits of preachers are under the command of preachers. ³³For God is not the source of disharmony, but of peace, as in all the churches of the saints.

³⁴Let your women be silent in the churches, for it is not allowed for them to speak, but to be subjected, even as the Law says also. ³⁵But if they desire to learn something, let them ask at home from their own husbands. For it is a shame to women to speak in church. ³⁶Or did the Word of God go out from you? Or did it come to you only? ³⁷If someone thinks that he is a

preacher or spiritual, let him fully know the things I am writing to you, that they are commands of the Lord. ³⁸But if someone is ignorant, let him be ignorant! ³⁹So, brothers, be eager to preach and do not forbid to speak in tongues. ⁴⁰Let all things be done in a good manner and according to order.

**15** Now I make known to you, brothers, the good news which I told you, which you also received, and in which you stand, ²through which also you are saved, if you hold on to that message I told you, unless you believed vainly. ³For I gave to you in the first place, which also I received, that Christ died for our sins, according to the Scriptures, ⁴and that He was buried, and that He was raised the third day, according to the Scriptures, ⁵and that He was seen by Cephas, then by the twelve. ⁶Then He was seen by more than five hundred brothers at once, of whom the greater part remain until now, but some also are fallen asleep. ⁷Then He was seen by James, then by all the apostles. ⁸And last of all, as to one born out of due time, He was seen by me also. ⁹For I am the least of the apostles, who am not fit to be called an apostle, because I mistreated the church of God. ¹⁰But by the grace of God I am what I am, and His grace unto me has not been in vain, but I labored more abundantly that they all, but not I, but the grace of God which was with me. ¹¹Whether, then, I or they, so we preach, and so you believed.

¹²But if Christ is preached, that He has been raised from the dead, how do some among you say that there is not a resurrection of the dead? ¹³But if there is not a resurrection of the dead, Christ has not been raised. ¹⁴But if Christ has not been raised, then our preaching is vain, and also your faith is vain. ¹⁵But also we have been found false witnesses of God, because we witnessed about God that He raised Christ, Whom He did not raise, if indeed the dead are not raised. ¹⁶For if the dead are not raised, even Christ has not been raised. ¹⁷But if Christ has not been raised, your faith is vain, you are yet in your sins. ¹⁸Then also those who have fallen asleep in Christ are destroyed. ¹⁹If in this life only, we have hope in Christ, we are more miserable than all men.

²⁰But now Christ has been raised from the dead, He became a first fruit of those who have fallen asleep. ²¹For since through man came death, also through man came the resurrection of the dead. ²²For as in Adam all die, so also in Christ, all shall be made alive. ²³But each in his own rank, Christ the first fruit, then those of Christ in His coming. ²⁴Then the end, when He will give the kingdom of God, even the Father, when He shall have done away with all rule and all authority and power. ²⁵For He must reign, until He has set all the enemies under His feet. ²⁶The last enemy done away with is death. ²⁷For all things He has put in subjection under His feet. But when it is said that all things have been subjected, it is evident that He is excepted who subjected all things to Him. ²⁸But when all things shall be subjected to Him, then also the Son Himself will be subjected to Him Who subjected all things to Him, that God may be all in all. ²⁹Now what will they do who are immersed for the dead if the dead are not raised at all? Why are they immersed for the dead? ³⁰Why also are we in danger every hour? ³¹I die daily, I attest by our boasting, which I have in Christ Jesus our Lord. ³²If as men do, I fought with wild animals in Ephesus, what profit is it to me, if the dead are not raised? Let us eat and let us drink, for tomorrow we die. ³³Do not be misled. Rotten morals make good company evil. ³⁴Awake unto righteousness, and do not sin, for some people have no knowledge of God. I speak to your shame.

³⁵But some will say, "How are the dead raised? And with what body do they come? ³⁶Unthinking person, what you sow is not made alive unless it should die. ³⁷And what you sow, you do not sow the body which it will become, but a bare grain, it may be wheat or some of the rest of the grains. ³⁸But God gives it a body as He wishes, and to each of the seeds its own body. ³⁹Not all flesh is the same flesh. But one flesh of men, and another flesh of animals, and another of fishes, and another of birds. ⁴⁰Also heavenly bodies, and earthly bodies; but the glory of the heavenly is one, and that of the earthly is another. ⁴¹One glory of the sun, and another of the moon, and another of the stars, for a star is different from another star in glory. ⁴²So also the resurrection from the dead. It is sown in corruption, it is raised in incorruption. ⁴³It is sown in dishonor, it is raised in glory. It is sown in weakness, it is raised in power. ⁴⁴It is sown a physical body, it is raised a spiritual body. There is a physical body, and there is a spiritual body. ⁴⁵So also it is written, "The first man, Adam, became a living soul, the last Adam, a life-giving Spirit. ⁴⁶But the spiritual was not first, but the physical, then the spiritual. ⁴⁷The first man was out of the earth, of dust. The second man, the Lord of Heaven. ⁴⁸Even as he who was made of dust, such also are those of dust. And even as the heavenly One, such also are the heavenly ones. ⁴⁹And according as we carried the image of the one made of dust, we shall carry also the image of the heavenly One. ⁵⁰But this I say, brothers, that flesh and blood cannot inherit the kingdom of God, nor corruption inherit incorruption.

⁵¹Lo, I tell you a mystery. We indeed shall not all sleep, but we shall all be made different. ⁵²In an instant, in a blink of an eye, at the last trumpet: for the trumpet shall sound, and the dead shall be raised incorruptible, and we shall be made different. ⁵³For this corruption must put on incorruption, and this mortal shall have put on immortality. ⁵⁴But when this corruption shall have put on incorruption, and this mortal shall have put on immortality, then shall come to pass the saying that has been written, "Death is swallowed up in victory." ⁵⁵O death, where is your sting? O Hell, where is your victory? ⁵⁶Now the sting of death is sin. And the power of sin is the Law. ⁵⁷But thanks be to God, Who is giving to us the victory through our Lord, Jesus Christ. ⁵⁸So, my beloved brothers, become steady, unmovable, abounding in the work of the Lord always, knowing that your labor is not empty in the Lord.

**16** Now about the collection which is for the saints, even as I ordered the churches of Galatia, so also you do. ²On the first day of the week, let each of you set by him, storing up what good way he has been led, that then there should not be collections when I should come. ³Then when I shall have come by, those whom you may approve by letters, these I will send to take away your kind gift to Jerusalem. ⁴But if it should be proper for me to go also, they shall go with me.

⁵But I shall come to you when I have gone through Macedonia, for I am going through Macedonia. ⁶Then it may be I shall stay with you, or even spend the winter, that you may send me forward whenever I should go. ⁷For I do not want to see you now in going by, but I hope to remain with you for some time, if the Lord should permit. ⁸But I shall remain in Ephesus until Pentecost. ⁹For a great and effectual door has been opened to me, and there are many opponents.

¹⁰Now if Timothy should come, see that he may be without fear among you, for he is doing the work of the Lord, even as I. ¹¹So let not anyone belittle him, but send him forward in

peace, that he may come to me, for I am waiting for him with the brothers. [12]About brother Apollos, I pled with him much that he should come to you with the brothers, and it was not at all his will that he should come now, but he will come when it may be the right time. [13]Watch, stand fast in the faith, act like men, be strong. [14]Let all your affairs be done in love. [15]Now I exhort you, brothers, you know the family of Stephanas, that it is a first fruit of Achaia, and they devoted them selves to service to the saints, [16]that you also be subject to such people and to every one who is working and laboring with us. [17]And I rejoice over the coming of Stephanas and Fortunatus and Achaicus, because they filled up your lack of service. [18]For they refreshed my spirit and yours; so give recognition to such people. [19]The churches of Asia greet you. Aquila and Priscilla greet you heartily in the Lord, with the church that is in their house. [20]All the brothers greet you. Greet one another with a holy kiss. [21]The greeting of my hand, Paul. [22]If anyone does not love the Lord Jesus Christ, let him be accursed. Our Lord is coming. [23]The grace of our Lord Jesus Christ be with you. [24]My love be with all of you in Christ Jesus. Amen.

## *The Second Epistle of Paul the Apostle to the*
# CORINTHIANS

1 Paul, an apostle of Jesus Christ through the will of God, and Timothy the brother, to the church of God which is in Corinth, with all the saints who are in all Achaia. [2]Grace to you and peace from God our Father and the Lord Jesus Christ. [3]Blessed be the God and Father of our Lord Jesus Christ, the Father of mercies and God of all comfort; [4]Who comforts us in all our trouble, through the comfort of which we ourselves are comforted by God. [5]Because even as the sufferings of Christ abound unto us, so through Christ also our comfort abounds. [6]But whether we are troubled, it is for your comfort and salvation, which is brought about in the endurance of the same sufferings which we also suffer, or whether we are comforted, it is for your comfort and salvation.
    [7]And our hope for you is sure, knowing that as you are sharers of the sufferings, so also of the comfort. [8]For we do not want you to be uninformed, brothers, about our trouble which came to us in the province of Asia, that we were weighed down to the extreme, beyond strength, so as not to have any way out even of life. [9]But we had the sentence of death in ourselves, that we should not be trusting in ourselves, but in God, Who raises the dead; [10]Who rescued us from so great a death, and does rescue, in Whom we have hope that also yet He will rescue; [11]You also working together for us by prayer, that from many people, the gift unto us through many, may thanks be given for us.
    [12]For our boasting is this, the witness of our conscience, that in simple words and the clear judgment of God, we behaved in the world, and more abundantly toward you. [13]For we do not write other things to you but what you read or even fully know, and I hope that you will fully know even unto the end. [14]Even as you did fully know us in part, that we are your boasting, even as also you are ours in the day of the Lord Jesus.
    [15]And in this persuasion I planned to come to you before this, that you might have a second favor. [16]And to come through by you into Macedonia, and again from Macedonia to come to you, and to be sent forth by you into Judea. [17]Planning this, then, did I indeed at all use lightness? Or what I plan, do I plan according to the flesh, that there should be with me the yes, yes and the no, no? [18]But God is faithful, that our message to you was not yes and no. [19]For the Son of God, Jesus Christ, Who was preached among you by us, by me and Silas and Timothy, was not yes and no, but has been yes in Him. [20]For how many promises of God in Him are yes, and in Him true, unto glory to God through us! [21]Now He Who confirms us with you unto Christ, and anointed us, is God. [22]Who also sealed us, and gave the down payment of the Spirit in our hearts. [23]But I call upon God as witness, that sparing you, I did not yet come to Corinth. [24]Not that we lord it over your faith, but we are workers together of your joy, for you stand by faith.

2 But I decided this in myself; not to come again in grief to you. [2]For if I grieve you, who is it who makes me glad, if not he who is grieved by me? [3]And I wrote to you this same thing, that I might not have grief from those of whom I ought to rejoice,

having trusted upon all of you, that my joy is of all of you. ⁴For out of much trouble and distress of heart I wrote to you through many tears, not that you might be grieved, but that you might know the love which I have more abundantly unto you.

⁵But if someone has grieved, he has not grieved me, but in part, that I may not burden all of you. ⁶Enough to such a one is the rebuke which is by the majority. ⁷So that on the contrary rather you should be forgiving and comfort him, so that such a man not be swallowed up by more abundant grief. ⁸Because of this I beg you to confirm your love to him. ⁹For unto this purpose also I wrote, that I might know the proof of you, if you are obedient in all things. ¹⁰And to whom you forgive anything, I do also. For if I have forgiven anything, to whom I forgave, it is in the person of Christ; ¹¹so that we may not be over matched by Satan, – for we are not uninformed of his thoughts.

¹²Now when I came to Troas for the good news of Christ, also a door was opened to me in the Lord. ¹³I had no rest in my spirit when I did not find Titus my brother, but having decided to leave them, I went out to Macedonia. ¹⁴But thanks be to God, Who always leads us to triumph in Christ, and causes the fragrance of the knowledge of Him to appear through us in every place. ¹⁵Because we are a fine fragrance of Christ to God in those who are saved, and in those who are lost. ¹⁶Indeed, to those, a fragrance of death unto death, but to the others a fragrance of life unto life. And who is sufficient for these things? ¹⁷For we are not like many, making money by the Word of God, but as out of clear judgment, but as out of God, before God, we speak in Christ.

3 Do we begin again to commend ourselves? If we do not need, like some, letters of commendation to you, or commendation from you? ²You are our letter, which has been written in our hearts, known and read by all men, ³shown that you are a letter of Christ, through our ministry; written not in ink, but in the Spirit of the living God, not on tablets of stone, but on fleshly tablets of the heart. ⁴And we have such confidence through Christ towards God. ⁵Not that we are sufficient to account from ourselves anything as out of ourselves; but our sufficiency is of God.

⁶Who also has made us able ministers of the new covenant; not of the letter, but of the spirit; for the letter kills, but the spirit makes alive. ⁷But if the ministry of death in letters, carved in stones, was brought into being in glory, so that the sons of Israel could not gaze into the face of Moses, because of the glory of his face, which is being made no longer in force, ⁸how shall not rather the ministry of the Spirit be in Glory? ⁹For if the ministry of condemnation has glory, much rather abounds the ministry of righteousness in glory. ¹⁰For even what has been glorious is not glorious in this way, on account of the glory which exceeds it. ¹¹For if that which is no longer working was glorious, much rather that which remains is glorious.

¹²Having then such hope, we use much boldness. ¹³And not like Moses, who put a veil on his own face, that the sons of Israel should not gaze into the end of that which was being done away. ¹⁴But their minds were hardened, for until today the same veil remains upon the reading of the old covenant, not unveiled, which veil is done away with in Christ. ¹⁵But unto this day, when Moses is read, a veil lies upon their hearts. ¹⁶When, however, they shall turn to the Lord, the veil will be taken away. ¹⁷Now the Lord is the Spirit, and where the Spirit

of the Lord is, there is freedom. ⁱ⁸But we all, with open faces seeing as in a mirror the glory of the Lord, are being changed into the same image, from glory unto glory, even as from the Spirit of the Lord.

4 Because of this, having this ministry, even as we have received mercy, we do not despair. ²But we have not spoken the hidden things of shame, not walking in clever ways, nor deceiving by the Word of God. ³But if our good news is covered up, it is covered up to those who are lost, ⁴in whom the god of this age has blinded the minds of the unbelieving, so the bright light should not shine into them, of the good news of the glory of Christ, Who is the image of God. ⁵For we do not preach ourselves, but Christ Jesus our Lord, and ourselves your servants through Jesus. ⁶Because God, Who spoke forth light to shine out of darkness, has shined in our hearts, for the bright light of the knowledge of the glory of God in the face of Jesus Christ. ⁷But we have this treasure in pottery containers, that the exceeding greatness of the power may be of God, and not out of us. ⁸Troubled, but not restricted, puzzled, but not out of measure, ⁹mistreated, but not left down and out, thrown down, but not destroyed, ¹⁰always carrying around the dying of the Lord Jesus in the body, that also the life of Jesus may be made to appear. ¹¹For we who are living are always given over to death through Jesus, that also the life of Jesus may be made to appear in our mortal flesh. ¹²So that death works in us, but life in you. ¹³And having the same spirit of faith, as it has been written, "I believed, because of which I spoke," and we believe, because of which we also speak, ¹⁴knowing that He Who raised up the Lord Jesus, also will raise us up through Jesus, and will stand alongside of us with you. ¹⁵For all things are for your sakes, that the grace abounding through the thanksgiving of many, may overflow unto the glory of God. ¹⁶Because of this we do not despair, but if indeed our outer man is decaying, yet the inner one is being renewed day by day. ¹⁷For our temporary light trouble is working for us a most exceeding eternal weight of glory,¹⁸as we are not looking at the things which are seen, but at the things not seen; for the things seen are but for a time, but the things not seen are eternal.

5 For we know that if our tent house on earth should be destroyed, we have a building from God, a house not made by hands, eternal in the heavens. ²For indeed in this we groan, longing to be clothed with our house which is from heaven, ³if indeed also being clothed, we shall not be found naked. ⁴For indeed we who are in this tent groan, being weighed down, since we do not wish to be unclothed, but to be clothed upon, that death may be swallowed up by life. ⁵Now He Who has worked out this same is God, Who also gave to us the down payment of the Spirit. ⁶So we are confident always, knowing that being at home in the body, we are away from home from the Lord. ⁷For we walk by faith, not by sight. ⁸But we are confident, and are pleased rather to be away from home from the body, and to be at home with the Lord. ⁹Because of this we are desiring the honor, whether being at home, or away from home, to be well pleasing to Him. ¹⁰For we must all appear before the judgment seat of Christ, that each may receive the things done in the body, according to what he did, whether good or evil. ¹¹Knowing then the fear of the Lord, we persuade men, but we have been made apparent unto God, and I hope also to have been made apparent in your consciences.

¹²For we are not commending ourselves to you again, but are giving to you an occasion of boasting in behalf of us, that you may have a reply to those boasting in face, and not in heart. ¹³For whether we might be beside ourselves, it is to God, or be serious minded, it is for you. ¹⁴For the love of God moves us, having judged this, that if One died for all, then all had died; ¹⁵And He died for all, that they who are living should no longer live for themselves, but for Him Who died for them and was raised.

¹⁶So that we now know no one according to the flesh, and even if we have known Christ according to the flesh, yet now no longer we know Him so. ¹⁷So that if anyone is in Christ, there is a new creation; the old things have gone away, lo, all things have become new. ¹⁸And all things are of God, Who reconciled us to Himself through Christ, giving to us the ministry of reconciliation. ¹⁹How that God was in Christ reconciling the world to Himself, not accounting to them their sins, and having given to us the ministry of reconciliation. ²⁰So we are ambassadors for Christ, as God is calling through us, we beg for Christ, be reconciled to God. ²¹For He made Him Who did not know sin, to be a sin offering for us, that we might become the righteousness of God in Him.

6 Now we beg you, working together, not to receive the grace of God in vain. ²For He says, "In an accepted time I gave ear to you, and in a day of salvation I rescued you. Lo, now is the time for acceptance, lo, now the day of salvation." ³Let no one give offence in anything, that the ministry be not blamed, ⁴but in everything let us prove ourselves as servants of God, in much endurance, in troubles, in needs, in difficulties. ⁵in stripes, in imprisonments, in tumults, in labors, in sleeplessness, in hunger, ⁶in purity, in knowledge, in longsuffering, in kindness, in the Holy Spirit, in genuine love, ⁷in the Word of truth, in the power of God, through the armor of righteousness on the right and the left, ⁸through glory and dishonor, through evil report and good report, as deceivers, and ⁹as being not known, and fully known, as dying, and lo, we live, as treated like a child, and not put to death, ¹⁰as sorrowing, but always rejoicing, as poor, but enriching many, as having nothing, and owning all things.

¹¹Our mouth is open to you, Corinthians, our heart has been wide open. ¹²You are not restricted in us, but you are restricted in your compassions. ¹³But in the same way, for a reward, I am speaking as to children, also be made wide open. ¹⁴Do not become yoked with another kind, with unbelievers. For what sharing has righteousness and lawlessness? And what fellowship, light with darkness? ¹⁵And what harmony, Christ with Satan? Or what part, a believer with an unbeliever? ¹⁶And what agreement, a temple of God, with idols? For you are a temple of the living God, even as God said, "I will live in them, and I will walk around in them, and I will be their God, and they will be a people to Me." ¹⁷Because of this, come out from the midst of them, and be separated, says the Lord, and do not touch the unclean, and I will receive you. ¹⁸And I will be a Father unto you, and you will be to Me for sons and daughters, says the Lord Almighty.

7 Having these promises, then, beloved, let us cleanse ourselves from every impurity of flesh and spirit, perfecting holiness in fear of God. ²Receive us. We did no one wrong; we corrupted no one; we were selfish with no one. ³I do not say this for

condemnation, for I have said before that you are in our hearts, to die with you and to live with you. ⁴Great is my boldness towards you, great is my boasting of you. I have been filled with comfort, I am overflowing with joy even during all our trouble.

⁵For when we had come into Macedonia, our flesh had no rest, but we were troubled in every way; outside, fightings; inside, fears. ⁶But He Who comforts those who are humbled, comforted us, that is, God, in the coming of Titus, ⁷and not only in his coming, but also in the comfort with which he was comforted over you, telling us of your longing, your mourning, your zeal for me, so as to make me to rejoice the more. ⁸For if I grieved you in the letter, I am not changing my mind, even if I did change my mind. For I see that that letter grieved, even if only for an hour. ⁹Now I rejoice, not because you were grieved, but because you were grieved unto repentance. For you were grieved according to God, that in nothing you might receive loss from us. ¹⁰For grief from God works repentance unto salvation, not to be regretted! But the grief of the world works death. ¹¹For lo, this very thing, for you to have been grieved from God, how much earnestness it worked in you, but also apology, indignation, fear, longing, zeal, revenge; in everything you proved yourselves to be pure in the thing that was done.

¹²Now if I wrote to you, it was not because of him who acted unjustly nor because of him who was treated unjustly, but because we wanted your earnestness to be shown, which is for us towards you before God. ¹³Because of this we have been comforted over your comfort, and more abundantly rather we rejoiced over the joy of Titus, because his spirit has been refreshed from all of you. ¹⁴For if I have boasted anything to him over you, I was not ashamed, but as we spoke all things in truth to you, so also our boasting to Titus came to be truth. ¹⁵And his loving concern is more abundant unto you, remembering again the obedience of all of you, as with fear and trembling you received him. ¹⁶I rejoice that in everything I am confident in you.

8 But we make known to you, brothers, the grace of God which has been given in the churches of Macedonia; ²that in much testing of trouble, the overflow of their joy and their deep poverty overflowed unto the riches of their sincerity. ³Because according to their power, I witness, and beyond their power, they chose this themselves, ⁴with much pleading, begging us to receive the grace gift and the fellowship of the ministry which was unto the saints. ⁵And not as we hoped, but they gave themselves first to the Lord, and to us by the will of God, ⁶so we begged Titus, that as he had begun before, so also he might complete unto you also this grace.

⁷But even as in everything you overflow, in faith, and word, and knowledge, and all diligence, and in the love from you to us, that also in this grace you may overflow. ⁸I am not speaking according to a command, but through the zeal of others, and proving the sincerity of your love. ⁹For you know the grace of our Lord Jesus Christ, that for your sakes He became poor, though being rich, that you by that poverty might be made rich. ¹⁰And in this matter I give an opinion, for this is profitable to you who began a year ago to do this who did not only the action but also had the desire. ¹¹But now also complete the action, so that even as there was the desire of the will, so also you have the completion. ¹²For if the desire is present, it is accepted even as someone may have, not as he does not have. ¹³For it is not that to others there should be ease, but trouble for you. ¹⁴But an equality, in the present time, your overflow for

their lack, that also their overflow may be for your lack, so that there may be an equality. ¹⁵Even as it was written, "He who gathered much had nothing over, and he who gathered little did not lack."

¹⁶Now thanks to God, Who is giving the same diligence for you in the heart of Titus. ¹⁷Because he indeed received your appeal, but being more diligent, he went out to you of his own accord. ¹⁸And we went with him the brother whose praise is in the good news through all the churches; ¹⁹and not only this, but also he was chosen by the churches as our fellow traveler with this grace-gift, which is ministered by us to the glory of the Lord Himself and to your desire, ²⁰taking care in this, that no one should blame us in this large amount which is ministered by us, ²¹planning good things, not only before the Lord, but also before men. ²²And we sent with them our brother whom we proved in many things many times to be diligent, and now much more diligent by the great trust which is unto you. ²³As regards Titus, he is my partner and a co-worker unto you, or our brothers, they are sent by apostles of the churches, Christ's glory! ²⁴So show the proof of your love, and of our boasting about you, to them, and unto the face of the churches.

**9** For about the ministry to the saints, it is not necessary for me to write to you. ²For I know your desire of which I boast about you to Macedonia, that Achaia was ready a year ago, and your zeal aroused many more. ³But I sent the brothers, that our boasting about you should not be made in vain in this part, that even as I said, you may be ready, ⁴if somehow Macedonians might come with me, and find you not ready, we would be put to shame, we would not say you, in this confidence of boasting. ⁵So I thought it necessary to urge the brothers that they should go ahead to you, and arrange beforehand your gift, so this might be ready as a gift, and not affected by greed.

⁶But this I say, that he who sows a little bit, shall also reap a little bit, and he who sows for big blessings, also shall reap big blessings. ⁷Each man, even as he chooses ahead of time in the heart, not from grief, nor of necessity; for God loves a joyful giver. ⁸But God is able to cause every grace to overflow unto you, that in everything always having all self-needs, you may overflow unto every good work. ⁹Even as it is written, "He scattered abroad, He gave to the poor, His righteousness remains unto eternity." ¹⁰Now He Who supplies seed to the sower and bread for food, may He supply and multiply your sowing, and increase the effects of your righteousness, ¹¹in everything being enriched unto all generosity, which works through us thanksgiving to God. ¹²Because the ministry of this service not only is a complete filling of the needs of the saints, but also an overflow by many thanksgivings to God. ¹³Through the proof of this ministry they are glorifying God upon the submission, in your confession, unto the good news of Christ, and your generosity of fellowship unto them and unto all people; ¹⁴also in their prayer for you, longing for you because of the exceeding grace of God upon you. ¹⁵Now thanks be to God over His indescribable Gift.

**10** Now I myself, Paul, beg you by the meekness and gentleness of Christ, who in person am humble among you, but being away am brave unto you. ²But I beg you, that not being with you, I should be brave in the confidence with which I think to be daring over some who are thinking of us as walking according to the flesh. ³For, walking in the flesh, we do not make war according to the flesh. ⁴For the weapons of our warfare are not fleshly, but powerful through God to the taking down of strongholds. ⁵Taking down reasonings and every high thing being lifted up against the knowledge of God, and taking captive every thought unto the obedience of Christ, ⁶and having in readiness to avenge all disobedience, when your obedience should be fulfilled.

⁷Do you look at things according to the surface? If someone has been persuaded by himself that he is Christ's, let him reason again of himself, that even as he is Christ's, so also we are Christ's. ⁸For if I should boast even more somewhat about our authority, which the Lord gave to us unto building up and not for taking you down, I should not be put to shame, ⁹that I should not seem as if to make you afraid by letters. ¹⁰For indeed the letters, he says, are weighty and strong, but the bodily presence weak, and the message being really nothing. ¹¹Let such a person think this, that such as we are in the message through letters, being absent, such also we will be, being present, in the dead.

¹²For we should not dare adjudge or compare ourselves with some, who commend themselves, but they, measuring themselves among themselves, and comparing themselves to themselves, do not understand. ¹³But we will not boast about things not in measure, but according to the measure of the rule which God allotted to us, of a measure to reach also unto you. ¹⁴For we do not overstretch ourselves as if not reaching unto you. For we came even unto you in the good news of Christ. ¹⁵Not boasting of the things not in measure, in the labors of others, but having hope, increasing your faith, to be enlarged among you according to our rule unto an overflow, ¹⁶to tell the good news unto that area beyond you, not to boast in another's rule, unto things made ready. ¹⁷But he who boasts, let him boast in the Lord. 18For not he who commends himself, but whom the Lord commends, that man is approved.

11 I wish you to bear with me a little in foolishness, but even bear with me. ²For I am jealous over you with a jealousy of God. For I have married you to one man, to present a chaste virgin to Christ. ³But I fear somehow as the serpent deceived Eve in his clever way, so your minds should be corrupted away from the simplicity which belongs unto Christ. ⁴For if indeed he who comes preaches another Jesus whom we did not preach, or you receive another spirit which you did not receive, or another good news which you did not accept, you might well bear with it.

⁵For I think that I am not at all behind the very greatest apostles. ⁶But even if I am an amateur in speech, yet not in knowledge, but in everything made plain unto you in all things. ⁷Or did I commit a sin, humbling myself that you might be exalted, because I preached the good news of God as a gift? ⁸I robbed other churches, having received wages for the ministry to you. ⁹And being with you and being in need, I was not a burden to anyone. For my need the brothers from Macedonia filled completely. And in everything I kept myself not a burden to you, and I will keep it so. ¹⁰The truth of Christ is in me that this boasting will not be closed up unto me in the areas of Achaia. ¹¹Why, because I do not love you? God knows. ¹²But what I am doing, also I will do, that I may cut off the occasion of those wanting an occasion, that that in which they are boasting, they may be found even as we. ¹³For such are false apostles, deceitful workers, changing their form into apostles of Christ. ¹⁴And this is not wonderful, for Satan himself changes his form into an angel of light. ¹⁵So it is not a great thing if his servants

also change their form as servants of righteousness, whose end will be according to their works. ⁱ⁶Again, I say, not anyone should think me to be a fool. But if otherwise, receive me even as a fool, that I may boast a little. ¹⁷What I say, I do not say according to the Lord, but as in foolishness, in this confidence of boasting. ¹⁸Since many boast according to the flesh, I also will boast. ¹⁹For gladly you bear with fools, being wise. ²⁰For you bear with it, if someone brings you into slavery, if someone eats you up, if someone takes away from you, if someone lifts himself up, if someone hits you on the face. ²¹I speak as to dishonor, as that we were weak. But in which someone may be bold, I speak in foolishness, I am bold also.

²²Are they Hebrews? I am also. Are they Israelites? I am also. Are they the seed of Abraham? I am also. ²³Are they servants of Christ? I speak as being beside myself, I am more: in labors more abundant, in stripes above measure, in prisons more often, in deaths many times. ²⁴From Jews five times I received forty stripes minus one. ²⁵Three times I was beaten with rods, once I was stoned, three times I was shipwrecked, a night and a day I have spent in the deep sea. ²⁶Many times going on trips, in dangers of rivers, in dangers of robbers, in dangers from my own race, in dangers from the non-Jews, in dangers in the city, in dangers in the desert, in dangers in the sea, in dangers among false brothers, ²⁷in labor and toil, many times in watching, in hunger and thirst in fasting many times, in cold and nakedness, ²⁸besides the external things, that which crowds in on me daily, the care of all the churches. ²⁹Who is weak, and I am not weak? Who is offended, and I do not burn? ³⁰If I ought to boast, I will boast of my weaknesses. ³¹The God and Father of our Lord Jesus Christ know, He Who is blessed unto the ages, that I do not lie. ³²In Damascus, the ethnarch under Aretas the king was guarding the city of the Damascenes in order to seize me, ³³and through a window in a basket I was lowered near the wall, and escaped out of his hands.

## 12

Indeed, to boast is not profitable to me. Now I shall come to visions and revelations of the Lord. ²I know a man in Christ fourteen years ago, whether in the body I do not know, or out of the body I do not know. God knows. Such a one caught away unto the third heaven. ³And I know such a man, whether in the body or out of the body I do not know. God knows: ⁴that he was caught away into Paradise, and he heard words which could not be spoken, which is not permitted to a man to speak. ⁵For such a one I shall boast, but for myself I shall not boast except in my weaknesses. ⁶For if I should wish to boast, I shall not be a fool; for I shall tell the truth. But I refrain, lest someone should think about me above what sees in me, or hears about me. ⁷And that I might not be lifted up by the exceeding greatness of the revelation, there was given to me a thorn in the flesh, a messenger of Satan, that he might hit me, that I might not be lifted up. ⁸For this three times I begged the Lord, that it might go away from me. ⁹And He said to me, "My grace is enough for you; for My power is made perfect in weaknesses, that the power of Christ may dwell upon me. ¹⁰Because of this I take pleasure in weaknesses, in insults, in necessities, in ill treatment, in hard places, for Christ. For when I am weak, then I am strong.

¹¹I have become a fool, boasting. You have made it necessary; for I ought to have been commended by you; for in nothing I was behind the very highest apostles, even if I am nothing. ¹²Indeed the signs of the apostle worked among you in all endurance, in signs, and

wonders, and deeds of power. ¹³For what is it in which you were inferior to the rest of the churches, except that I myself did not burden you? Forgive me this injustice! ¹⁴Lo, a third time I am ready to come to you, and I will not burden you, for I do not seek your things, but you. For the children ought not to save up for the parents, but the parents for the children. ¹⁵And I will most gladly spend and be spent out for your souls, even if the more I am loving you, the less I am loved. ¹⁶But let it be so, I did not weigh you down, but being clever, I took you by "deceit". ¹⁷Did I act greedy to you, by any of whom I have sent to you? ¹⁸I called for Titus, and I sent a brother with him. Was Titus greedy toward you? Did we not walk in the same spirit? And in the same steps? ¹⁹Again, do you think that we are making a defense to you? We speak before God in Christ; and all things, beloved, for building you up. ²⁰For I am afraid, somehow, when I come, that I shall not find you such as I wish, and that I might be found by you such as you do not wish; if perhaps there are strifes, jealousies, anger, contentions, evil speakings, whisperings, puffed up pride, uprisings. ²¹If my God should humble me about you when I have come again, and I should mourn over many of those who have sinned before this, and have not repented over the uncleanness and immorality and unholiness which they have been doing.

**13** This third time I am coming to you. From the mouth of two and three witnesses every word shall be established. ²I have spoken before, and I say ahead of time, as being with you the second time, and being away now I write to those who have sinned before, and to all the rest, that if I come again, I shall not spare. ³Since you seek a proof of Christ speaking in me, Who is not weak unto you, but is powerful in you. ⁴For indeed He was crucified out of weakness, yet He lives from the power of God. For we also are weak in Him, but we shall live with Him from the power of God given toward you. ⁵Test yourselves, if you are in the faith, prove yourselves. Or do you not fully know yourselves, that Jesus Christ is in you? Unless you are what is disapproved! ⁶But I hope that you will know that we are not disapproved.

⁷Now I pray to God for you to do nothing evil; not that we may appear approved, but that you may do the good, though we should be as disapproved. ⁸For we do not have any power against the truth, but for the truth. ⁹For we rejoice when we may be weak, but you may be powerful. ¹⁰Because of this, being away I write these things, that being with you I should not use severity, according to the authority which the Lord gave to me, unto building up and not unto tearing down.

¹¹For the rest, brothers, rejoice, be fully completed, be comforted, think the same thing, be peaceable; and the God of love and peace will be with you. ¹²Greet one another with a holy kiss. All the saints greet you. ¹³The grace of the Lord Jesus Christ, and the love of God, and the fellowship of the Holy Spirit be with you all. Amen.

*The Epistle of Paul the Apostle to the*
# GALATIANS

**1** Paul, an apostle, not sent from men neither through a man, but through Jesus Christ and God the Father who raised Him from the dead ²and the brothers with me to the churches of Galatia. ³Grace to you and peace from God our Father and the Lord Jesus Christ ⁴who gave Himself for our sins so that He might deliver us out of the age of impending evil according to the will of God, even our Father, ⁵to whom be the glory into the ages of the ages. Amen.

⁶I continually marvel that you are so quickly deserting the One who called you in the grace of Christ into another Gospel, ⁷which is not another except there are some who are disturbing you and they are wishing to pervert the Gospel of Christ. ⁸But, even if we or an angel of heaven should preach to you a different Gospel from which we preached to you, let him be accursed! ⁹As we have told you before and now again I am saying if anyone is preaching different from that which you received let him be accursed.

¹⁰For am I now pleasing men or God? Or shall I seek to please men? If I were still pleasing men, I am not Christ's servant to you. ¹¹For I declare to you brothers the Gospel which was preached by me that is not according to men. ¹²For I neither received it from man, nor was I taught it, but I received it through a revelation of Jesus Christ. ¹³For you heard of my conduct when I was in Judaism that I was extremely against the Gospel and I was persecuting the church of God and I was harassing it. ¹⁴And I was advancing in Judaism above many of my Jewish contemporaries, being extremely zealous of my elders' traditions. ¹⁵But when He, Christ, the one who set me apart from my mother's womb, and having called me through His Grace ¹⁶was pleased to reveal His Son in me in order that I should preach Him in the nations, I did not immediately confer with people ¹⁷neither did I go up to Jerusalem to the ones who were apostles before me, but I went away to Arabia and I returned again to Damascus. ¹⁸Then after three years I went up to Jerusalem to visit with Cephas and I stayed with him fifteen days. ¹⁹I did not, however, see other apostles only James the brother of the Lord. ²⁰These things I am writing to you, before God, I am not lying. ²¹Then I went into the regions of Syria and Cilicia, ²²but I was unknown by sight to the churches of Judea which are in Christ. ²³They however were only hearing "the one who once was persecuting and harassing us, now preaching the faith," ²⁴and they glorified God, because of me.

**2** Then after fourteen years, again I went up to Jerusalem with Barnabas, also taking Titus along. ²But I went according to the revelation and I submitted to them, to those who were of reputation, the Gospel which I preached in the nations. But I did so privately for fear somehow I had or should run in vain. ³However not even Titus who was with me, a Greek, was compelled to be circumcised. ⁴But on account of the false brothers who had sneaked in to spy out our freedom, which we are having in Christ Jesus, in order to make us slaves. ⁵We did not yield in subordination to them for a moment in order that the truth of the Gospel might continue unchanged to you. ⁶But for the ones who seemed to be something, what they were makes no difference to me. A man's appearance is neutral to God. Those men contributed nothing to my message. [7]On the other hand however, they knew that I have been entrusted with the Gospel to the uncircumcision just as Peter with the Gospel to the circumcision. [8]For the one Christ who having worked with Peter in the apostleship to the uncircumcised also worked with me in the apostleship to the nations. [9]And having experienced the Grace which had been given to me, James and Cephas and John, the ones who seemed to be pillars, gave to me and Barnabas the right hand of fellowship in order that we might go to the nations and they might go to the circumcision. [10]They asked only that we should remember the poor which I also was eager to do this very thing.

[11]When Cephas came to Antioch, however, I opposed him to his face because he had been wrong. [12]For before certain men came from James, Peter was eating with the Gentiles. But when they came, men from James, he was drawing back and he was separating himself, because he was fearing those who belonged to the circumcision. [13]And they joined with him, Peter, and the rest of the Jews so that even Barnabas was carried away with their hypocrisy. [14]But when I saw that they were not walking correctly according to the truth of the Gospel, I said to Cephas before all of them, "If you a Jew are living after the lifestyle of Gentiles and you are not living as the Jews, how is it you compel the Gentiles to live like Jews?" [15]We are by nature Jews and not from Gentile heathenism. [16]But knowing that a man is not made righteous by works of Law except through faith in Christ Jesus and we in Christ Jesus have believed in order that we may be justified by faith in Christ and not by the works of Law because by the works of Law shall no flesh be justified. [17]But if seeking to be justified in Christ we ourselves also have been found sinners then is Christ the minister of sin? May it never be! [18]For if I have destroyed this old system of Law and I rebuild it again I prove myself a transgressor. [19]For through the Law I died to the Law so that I might live to God. [20]With Christ I have been crucified. And it is no longer I who live but Christ lives in me but now however I live in the flesh by faith in the Son of God, and the One who loved me and delivered Himself on my behalf. [21]I do not reject the grace of God, for if through Law there is righteousness then Christ died in vain.

3 You foolish Galatians who has bewitched you before whose eyes Jesus Christ was advertised as the crucified one? 2This only I am wishing to learn from you; did you receive the Spirit by the works of Law or by hearing with faith? [3]Are you so foolish? After having begun by the Spirit are you now completed by the flesh? [4]Such things did you suffer in vain if indeed it was in vain? [5]Therefore God, the One who is constantly supplying the Spirit for you and constantly working miracles in you, does He do it by the works of Law of by hearing with faith?

[6]Just as Abraham believed God and it was accounted to him as righteousness, [7]You must know then that those of faith, these are the sons of Abraham. [8]Because the Scripture foreseeing that by faith God justifies the Gentiles, preached the good news beforehand to Abraham That in you, Abraham, all the Gentiles shall be blessed. [9]So the ones who are of faith are being blessed with the faith of Abraham. [10]For as many as are under the works of Law are under a curse, for it has been written, "Cursed is everyone who is not persisting in everything which is written, in the book of the Law to keep them." [11]By Law,

however, no one is justified with God because it is clear the just shall live by faith. ¹²The Law is not however of faith. On the contrary the one who does these things, he shall live by them. ¹³Christ delivered us out of the curse of the Law by being a curse on our behalf, for it is written, cured is everyone who hangs upon a tree ¹⁴in order that to the Gentiles the blessing of Abraham might come in Jesus Christ in order that we might receive the promise of the Spirit through faith. ¹⁵I am speaking according to human agreements. Yet a man's covenant having been ratified, no one violates it or sets it aside. ¹⁶The promises were spoken to Abraham and to his descendant. He is not saying: "And to descendants" as referring to many people but rather to your seed who is Christ. ¹⁷And this is what I am saying: the Law which was given 430 years later does not disannul the covenant with Abraham previously established by God so as to cancel the promise. ¹⁸For is the inheritance is based on the Law it is no longer from a promise; but God has given it to Abraham through a promise.

¹⁹What then is the Law for? It was added because of transgressions until there should come the descendent to whom the promise referred had come. The Law was ordained through angels by the agency of a mediator. ²⁰However a mediator is not just for one party but God is one. ²¹Is Law then against the promises of God? May it never be. For if a law had been given which is being able to bring forth life, indeed righteousness would have been based on Law. ²²But the Scripture locked up all men under sin in order that the promise by faith in Jesus Christ might be given to those who are believing. ²³But before faith came we were kept under Law having been locked up until the faith should be revealed. ²⁴Wherefore the Law has become our schoolmaster to lead us to Christ in order that by faith we might be justified. ²⁵Now that the faith has come, we are no longer under a schoolmaster. ²⁶For all are sons of God through faith in Christ Jesus. ²⁷For as many as have been immersed into Christ did put on Christ. ²⁸There is neither Jew nor Greek. There is neither slave nor free, there is neither male nor female, for you are all one in Christ Jesus. ²⁹And if you are Christ's then you are of Abraham's seed and heirs according to promise.

4 Now I say as long as the heir is a minor he does not differ from a slave although he is owner of all. ²But he is under guardians and trustees until the date approved by the father. ³So also when we were children, we were in slavery under elemental principles of the universe. ⁴But when the fullness of time came, God sent forth His Son born of a woman, born under Law, ⁵in order that He might redeem the ones under Law so that we might receive the adoption as sons. ⁶And because you are sons, God has sent the Spirit of His Son into our hearts crying, "Abba Father." ⁷So that you are no longer a slave but a son and if a son then made an heir by God.

⁸But formerly when you did not know God, you were in bondage to beings which by nature are not gods. ⁹And now you have known God or rather having been known by God, how can you turn back again to the weak and basic elemental principles to which you wish to be slaves again? ¹⁰You observe days and months and seasons and years. ¹¹I am afraid for you lest somehow in vain I have labored over you.

¹²I am begging you keep on becoming as I am for I became like you brothers. You did not wrong me. ¹³And you know that because of bodily illness, I preached the Gospel to you the first time. ¹⁴And in your trial over my bodily illness, you did not scorn me neither did

you reject me but you received me as an angel of God, as Christ Jesus. ¹⁵Where then is your joy? For I bear witness to you that if possible you would have plucked your eyes out for me. ¹⁶So have I become your enemy by telling you the truth?

¹⁷They are showing affection for you to no good end. They want to shut you out in order that you might show affection for them. ¹⁸But it is good to always show affection for good things and not only when I am with you.

¹⁹My little children with whom again I am in labor pains until Christ is formed in you. ²⁰But I am wishing to be present with you now and to change my tone for I am perplexed about you.

²¹Tell me, you who want to be under Law, do you not hear the Law? ²²For it is written that Abraham had two sons one by the handmaid and one by the free woman. ²³But the son from the handmaid was born according to flesh. But the son from the free woman was born through the promise. ²⁴Which things are an allegory for these women are two covenants, one from Mt. Sinai, Hagar bearing children into bondage. ²⁵Now this Hagar is Mt. Sinai in Arabia and now corresponds to the present city of Jerusalem for she is in slavery with her children. ²⁶But the Jerusalem above is free which is our mother. ²⁷For it is written, rejoice you barren woman who does not bear; cry and break forth; you that do not labor, because more are the children of a desolate woman, more than the one who has a husband. ²⁸Now you brothers, like Isaac, are children of promise. ²⁹But then he that was born according to the flesh, persecuted him who was born according to the Spirit and so it is now. ³⁰But what says the Scripture? Cast out the handmaid and her son, for the son of the handmaid shall not inherit with the son of the free woman. ³¹Therefore brethren we are not a handmaid's children, but children born of a free woman.

5 Therefore it was for liberty that Christ made us free. Stand fast and do not be tangled again to a yoke of bondage. ²Behold, I Paul, am saying to you that if you should be circumcised, Christ shall profit you nothing. ³I testify and again to every man that the one circumcised is a debtor to do the whole Law. ⁴You have been cut off from Christ; if you are the ones who are justified by Law, you have fallen out of grace. ⁵For we through the Spirit by faith are waiting for the hope of righteousness. ⁶For in Christ Jesus neither circumcision means anything nor uncircumcision means anything, but faith working by love. ⁷You were running well; who cut in on you, and kept you from following the truth? ⁸This persuasion is not from the One calling you. ⁹A little leaven leavens the whole lump. ¹⁰I have confidence in you, in the Lord, that you will adopt no other view, but the one troubling you shall bear his judgment whoever he may be. ¹¹And I brethren, if I am still preaching circumcision, why am I still being persecuted? Then the stumbling of the cross has been abolished. ¹²I also wish the ones troubling you would be cut off.

¹³For you were called to liberty brethren only do not use the liberty for an occasion for the flesh, but through love you must serve one another. ¹⁴For all the Law has been fulfilled in this one statement, "you shall love your neighbor as yourself." ¹⁵And if you bite and devour one another, watch out, lest you should be consumed by one another. ¹⁶But I say you must walk in the Spirit and you will not carry out the lust of the flesh. ¹⁷For the flesh lusts against the Spirit and the Spirit against the flesh, for these are contrary to one another, so that you may

not do the things that you want. ¹⁸But if you are led by the Spirit you are not under Law. ¹⁹Now the works of the flesh are clear which are fornication, impurity, sensuality, ²⁰idolatry, sorcery, enmities, strife, jealousy, anger, factions, divisions, heresies, ²¹envying, drunkenness, partying and the like. I forewarned you, even as I said before, that the ones who practice such things they shall not inherit the kingdom of God. ²²But the fruit of the Spirit is love, joy, peace, patience, kindness, goodness, faithfulness, ²³meekness, self-control. Against such things there is no law. ²⁴And the ones belonging to Christ Jesus, have crucified the flesh with its passions and lusts. ²⁵If we are living by Spirit let us also walk by the Spirit. ²⁶Do not become vain, challenging and envying one another.

6 Brethren even though a man be overtaken in any fault, you who are spiritual restore such a one in a Spirit of gentleness looking to yourselves lest you also should be tempted. ²You must carry one another's burdens and so you shall fulfill the law of Christ. ³For if someone thinks he is someone but is not, he is deceiving himself. ⁴But let each test his own work and then he shall have satisfaction and not by comparing himself to the other brother. ⁵For each one shall bear his own burden. ⁶And the one being taught in the Word should share all good things with the one who teaches. ⁷Do not be deceived, God is not being mocked; for whatever a man should sow that also he shall reap. ⁸Because the one sowing into his own flesh, shall from the flesh reap corruption. But the one sowing into the Spirit shall from the Spirit reap life eternal. ⁹And let us not be weary doing good, for in one's own season, we shall reap if we do not quit. ¹⁰So therefore as we are having opportunity let us work the good work toward all men and especially toward the ones of the household of the faith.

¹¹See what large letters I have written to you with my hand. ¹²As many as are wishing to make a good show in the flesh, these are compelling you to be circumcised so that they may avoid persecution for the cross of Christ. ¹³For not even the ones who are receiving circumcision are keeping the Law. But they wish you to be circumcised so that they may boast about your flesh. ¹⁴Now as for me, may it never come to pass to boast except in the cross of our Lord Jesus Christ through whom the world has been crucified to me and I to the world. ¹⁵For neither is circumcision anything nor uncircumcision but a new creation. ¹⁶And as many as shall follow by this rule, peace and mercy be upon them and upon the Israel of God. ¹⁷Finally let no one give me trouble. For I bear the marks of Jesus on my body. ¹⁸The grace of our Lord Jesus Christ be with your Spirit brethren. Amen.

## *The Epistle of Paul the Apostle to the*
# EPHESIANS

1 Paul, an apostle of Christ Jesus by the will of God, to the saints at Ephesus who are also believers in Christ Jesus: [2]Grace to you and peace from God our Father and the Lord Jesus Christ.
[3]Blessed be the God and Father of our Lord Jesus Christ, who has blessed us in Christ with every spiritual blessing in the heavenly places. [4]It was in Him He chose us before the foundation of the world, constituting us holy and blameless before Him. [5]It was for Himself He predestined us in love to be His sons through Jesus Christ. He did this in accord with the good purpose of His will, [6]to the praise of His glorious grace, which He freely bestowed on us in the beloved. [7]In Him, according to the wealth of His grace, we continue to have redemption through His blood, the forgiveness of our trespasses. [8]This grace He lavished upon us with full wisdom and insight [9]as He showed us the mystery of His will, according to the good purpose which He set forth in Him. [10]He did this as a plan that in the fullness of time He might unite everything in Christ, things in heaven and things on earth. [11]It was in Him too that we were claimed as an inheritance, being marked out beforehand according to the design of Him who works out everything in conformity with the purpose of His will. [12]This was that we might be to the praise of His glory – those of us who first put our hope in Christ. [13]Being in Him, you also, when you heard the Word of truth, the gospel of your salvation, and believed in Him, were sealed with the promised Holy Spirit. [14]This, to the praise of His glory, is the guarantee of our inheritance until we acquire possession of it.
[15]Consequently, having heard of your faith in the Lord Jesus and your love toward all the saints, [16]I do not cease being thankful for you. I remember you in my prayers, [17]asking that the God of our Lord Jesus Christ, the Father of glory, may give you a spirit of wisdom and of revelation in the special knowledge of Him. [18]I ask that the eyes of your hearts may be enlightened so that you may know what is the expectation to which He has called you, what are the riches of His glorious inheritance in the saints, [19]and what is His surpassingly great power in us who believe. This power is according to the working of His mighty strength, [20]which He produced in Christ, having raised Him from the dead and having seated Him at His right hand in the heavenly places, [21]far above all rule and authority and power and dominion and every name that is named, not only in this age but also in that which is to come. [22]He also placed everything under His feet. As well He made Him head over all things for the Church, [23]which is His body, the fullness of Him who fills all in all.

2 And you! You were dead through your trespasses and sins. [2]You followed this world-age. You followed the prince of the power of the air, the spirit that is now at work in the sons of disobedience. [3]At one time we were all slaves to our physical passions, acting out the desires of both body and mind. So by nature we were children of wrath, just as all mankind. [4]Yet God, being rich in mercy, loving us with so great a love, [5]even though we were dead through our trespasses, made us alive together with Christ. By grace you have been

saved! ⁶He raised us up with Him. He made us sit with Him in the heavenly places in Christ Jesus. ⁷He did this that in the coming ages He might demonstrate the immeasurably kind riches of His grace toward us in Christ Jesus. ⁸For by grace you have been saved through faith, and especially it is not your own doing; it is the gift of God. ⁹It is not because of works, for fear that someone should brag. ¹⁰For we are His workmanship, created in Christ Jesus for good works. These God prepared in advance so that we might put them into practice.

¹¹For this reason, recall that at one time you Gentiles by earthly descent – the ones called The Uncircumcised by those calling themselves The Circumcision by a handmade operation in the flesh – ¹²you were at that time without Christ, excluded from the citizenship of Israel, and strangers to the covenants of promise, lacking hope and without God in the world. ¹³But now, in Christ Jesus, you who once were far off have been brought near through the blood of Christ. ¹⁴For He, who has made us both one, is our peace. He has broken down the hostile fence that separated. In His flesh ¹⁵He annulled the Law of the commandments and ordinances, in order that in Him He might create one new man out of the two, so making peace. ¹⁶Through the cross He reconciled both to God in one body, in Himself canceling the hostility. ¹⁷And He came and preached peace to you who were far off and peace to you who were near. ¹⁸Because of this, through Him we both together have access in one Spirit to the Father. ¹⁹Accordingly, you are no longer foreigners and aliens, but you are fellow citizens with the saints and members of God's household. ²⁰You are built upon the foundation of the apostles and prophets, the cornerstone being Christ Jesus Himself. ²¹In Him the whole structure, being neatly fitted together, is growing into a holy temple in the Lord. ²²In Him you too are being neatly fitted together for a dwelling place of God in the Spirit.

3 Because of this, I, Paul, a prisoner for Christ Jesus on behalf of you Gentiles – ²surely you have heard of the plan that was given me for you with reference to the grace of God! ³As I have written above, the mystery was made known to me by revelation. ⁴When you read this you will be able to understand my insight into this mystery of Christ, ⁵which was not made known to the sons of men in other generations in the way it has now been revealed to his holy apostles and prophets by the Spirit. ⁶This is that the Gentiles are heirs together, members of the same body, and sharers in the promise in Christ Jesus through the gospel. ⁷I was made a servant of the gospel through the gift of God's grace, which was given me through the manifestation of His power. ⁸To me, the very least among all the saints, this grace was given. It was to proclaim to the Gentiles the unsearchable wealth of Christ ⁹and to enlighten everyone regarding the plan of the mystery hidden from the beginning of time in God, the creator of everything. ¹⁰This plan was that through the church the many-sided wisdom of God might now be made known to the principalities and powers in the heavenly places. ¹¹This is the design of the ages which He effected in Christ Jesus our Lord. ¹²In Him and through our faith in Him, we can speak freely and have free access to Him. ¹³So I ask that you not despair over my tribulations for you. They are your splendor.

¹⁴For this reason I bow my knees before the Father ¹⁵from whom every family in heaven and on earth is named. ¹⁶I pray that according to the wealth of His glory He may grant that through His Spirit you might be powerfully strengthened within ¹⁷so that Christ may dwell in your hearts through faith with you rooted and grounded in love. ¹⁸I pray that you might be

strong enough to comprehend with all the saints what is the breadth and length and height and depth, [19]even to know the love of Christ which surpasses knowledge. This is in order that you may be filled with all the fullness of God.

[20]Now to the One who is able by the power at work within us to do infinitely beyond whatever we ask or think, [21]to Him be glory in the church and in Christ Jesus to all generations, for ever and ever. Amen.

**4** [1]I therefore, a prisoner for the Lord, urge that you conduct yourselves worthy of the calling to which you have been called, [2]doing so with all humility and courteous consideration, with patience, in love putting up with one another, [3]working hard to maintain the unity of the Spirit through the bond of peace. [4]There is one body and one Spirit, just as also you were called to the one expectation that belongs to your call. [5]There is one Lord, one faith, one immersion. [6]There is one God and father of us all, who is above all and through all and in all.

[7]But grace was given to each one of us according to the measure of Christ's gift. [8]For this reason Scripture says, "When He mounted up on high He led a multitude as captives; He gave gifts to men." [9]What is the meaning of, "He mounted up," unless it also means that He came down into the lower regions of the earth? [10]He who came down is the one who also mounted above all the heavens, so that He might fill all things. [11]On the one hand He gave some to be apostles, on the other some to be prophets, some to be evangelists, some to be shepherds and teachers. [12]He did this that the saints might be equipped for the work of ministry for building up the body of Christ. [13]His purpose was that we all might reach unity of the faith and of the knowledge of the Son of God, reach mature manhood, reach the measure of the stature of the fullness of Christ. [14]This is so that we may no longer be children, tossed by waves this way and that and carried about by every wind of doctrine cunningly and craftily devised by humans as methodically they plan error. [15]Rather, being truthful with love, we shall in every way be growing up toward Him who is the head, Christ. [16]From Him the whole body is fitted and held together by every supporting connection with which it is supplied. When each part is working properly, through love He enables the body to make its own growth.

[17]In the Lord I go on to say and insist this: you are no longer to live as the Gentiles do with their purposeless minds. [18]They are darkened in their understanding. They are alienated from the life of God because they are filled with ignorance, all due to their hardness of heart. [19]Becoming insensitive they have given themselves up to indecency for the greedy practice of every kind of impurity. [20]This is not the way you learned Christ [21]inasmuch as you have heard about Him and were taught in Him, because the truth is in Jesus. [22]You have put off your old person, which belongs to your former lifestyle and becomes corrupted through deceitful lusts, [23]to be renewed in the spirit of your minds [24]and to put on the new person, which has been created in God's likeness in true righteousness and holiness.

[25]Therefore, putting away the lie, let each one be speaking truth with his neighbor, for we are members one of another. [26]Should you be angry, do not sin. Do not let the sun go down on your angry mood, [27]neither be giving ground to the devil. [28]The thief should stop stealing. Rather let him be working hard, doing honest work with his hands, in order that he may be able to share with the destitute. [29]Do not ever allow foul language to come out of your

mouths, but only whatever builds up wherever there is need, in order that it may impart grace to those listening. ³⁰And do not ever grieve the Holy Spirit of God, in whom you were sealed for the day of redemption. ³¹Let all bitterness, wrath, rage, clamor, and abusive speech be taken away from you right now, with every kind of malice. ³²Continue to be good to one another, compassionate, forgiving one another, just as God in Christ forgave you.

5 So as beloved children you must follow God's example, ²practicing love, just as Christ loved us and on our behalf gave himself up, an offering and sacrifice to God as a satisfying odor. ³But sexual misconduct and every kind of sexual viciousness or greed must not even be named among you, as befits those who are saints – ⁴no obscene act, no foolish talk or smutty joking, things that are not fitting. Instead let there be thanksgiving. ⁵Know this for sure; no fornicator or impure person, or one who is greedy – in short, an idol-worshiper – has any inheritance in the kingdom of Christ and of God. ⁶Do not be deceived with empty words. It is on account of these very things that the anger of God is coming on the sons of disobedience. ⁷Therefore do not associate with them, ⁸for there was a time you were darkness, but now, united with the Lord, you are light. Behave as children of light – ⁹for the fruit of light consists of everything that is good and right and true. ¹⁰Find out by experience what is pleasing to the Lord. ¹¹Have nothing to do with the unfruitful works of darkness. Instead show your abhorrence of them, ¹²for the things those people do in secret are disgraceful, even to mention. ¹³When anything is illuminated, its real character is shown, for light makes everything visible. ¹⁴Hence the saying: "Rise, you who sleep; rise from the dead, and Christ will shine upon you."

¹⁵Pay close attention to the way you conduct yourselves. Let it not be as unwise men but as wise. ¹⁶Make the most of the time, because the days are evil. ¹⁷Hence, do not be foolish, but become wise by understanding the will of the Lord. ¹⁸And do not get drunk with wine, for that is debauchery; but be getting filled by the Spirit, ¹⁹as a consequence you will be speaking to one another through psalms and hymns and spiritual songs, voicing melodious songs to the Lord with all your heart, ²⁰always and for everything giving thanks in the name of our Lord Jesus Christ to God the Father, ²¹being subordinate to one another in awe of Christ.

²²Wives, be subordinate to your husbands, as to the Lord. ²³For the husband is the head of the wife as Christ is head of the church, His body, and is Himself its Savior. ²⁴But as the church is subordinate to Christ, so in everything wives also are to be subordinate to their husbands. ²⁵Husbands, continue to love your wives, just as Christ also loved the church and gave Himself up for her. ²⁶He gave Himself that He might sanctify her, having cleansed her by the washing of water in connection with the Word. ²⁷It was that He might present the church to Himself in unsullied array having no spot or wrinkle or any such thing, that she might be holy and blameless. ²⁸In the same way, husbands have an obligation to love their own wives as their own bodies. He who loves his wife loves himself. ²⁹For no one ever hates his own flesh, but nurtures and takes care of it. In the same way Christ cares for the church, ³⁰because we are His body. ³¹ "For this reason a man will leave his father and mother and shall be bonded to his wife; the two will become as one." ³²This is a great mystery, but I interpret it as relating to Christ and the church. ³³In sum, also your, each one of you, must continue loving his wife as himself, and the wife is to continue respecting her husband.

6 ¹Children, continue to give heed to your parents in the Lord, for this is right. ²"Honor your father and mother" (this is the first commandment accompanied by a promise, ³"that it may be well with you and that you will have a long life on the earth." ⁴Fathers, do not enrage your children, but bring them up in the training and instruction of the Lord.

⁵Slaves, continually heed those who are your human masters with fear and trembling. Do so wholeheartedly, as really serving Christ. ⁶You are not to be attracting attention simply as men-pleasers, but from your very souls you are to be doing the will of God as slaves of Christ. ⁷Serve enthusiastically, as to the Lord and not to men. ⁸You know that anyone, whether slave or free, in whatever respect he does good, this very thing will be repaid by the Lord. ⁹Masters, treat your slaves the same way. Stop threatening them, since you know that he who is both their Master and yours is in heaven and that there is no partiality with Him.

¹⁰Finally, be getting strong in the Lord and in the strength of His might. ¹¹Put on God's complete armor, so that you may be able to stand against the wiles of the devil. ¹²For we are not contending against flesh and blood, but against the principalities, against the powers, against the world rulers of this present darkness, against spiritual hosts of wickedness in the heavenly places. ¹³So take the whole armor of God, that you may be able to resist in the evil day, and having proven victorious over everything, to stand. ¹⁴Stand firm, therefore, by having fastened the belt of truth about your waists, by having put on the breastplate of righteousness, ¹⁵by having shod your feet with the firm footing of the gospel of peace, ¹⁶and above all by taking the shield of faith, with which you can extinguish all the flaming arrows of the evil one. ¹⁷Likewise, take in hand the helmet of salvation and the sword of the Spirit, which is the Word of God. ¹⁸Be continually praying with every kind of Spirit-directed prayer and entreaty. To that end, stay alert and persevere, interceding on behalf of all the saints. ¹⁹Pray especially on my behalf, that as I open my mouth words will be given me, always being plain in presenting the mystery, namely the Gospel. ²⁰On behalf of the Gospel I am an ambassador in chains! So pray that I may declare it boldly, speaking as I ought to.

²¹In order that you also may know how things are going with me, what is taking place, Tychicus, a beloved brother who is a faithful minister in the Lord, will tell you everything. ²²I am sending him to you for this very purpose, that you may know how we are and encourage your hearts.

²³Peace be to the brethren, and love with faith, from God the Father and the Lord Jesus Christ. 24Grace for immortality be with all who love our Lord Jesus Christ.

## *The Epistle of Paul the Apostle to the*
# PHILIPPIANS

1 Paul and Timothy, men completely committed to Jesus Christ, and at His immediate disposal, send this letter to the community of believers, their pastors, and leaders in God's work in Philippi who have been earmarked by God for His plan. ²We ask God our Father and our Lord Jesus Christ to give you grace and peace.
³With every thought of you, I thank God. ⁴With every prayer for you, I am ecstatic. ⁵I am ecstatic for how you have worked with us for Jesus' message of hope from the very day you heard it up until this very moment. ⁶I am ecstatic for the confidence I have that God, who began the amazing project of filling you with grace, will continue His work within you until everything is finished at Christ Jesus' return for us.
⁷I have such deep affection for you all. I have the right to feel this way about you since we share God's grace. This is true even when my prison chains separate us or when I am busy defending and reinforcing the message of Jesus snatching us from the jaws of death. ⁸God is my witness that from deep within Christ Jesus comes my intense desire to be with you.
⁹I not only pray that you will flood others with your love, but that you will in reality learn how to actually love. Love with a true grasp of understanding how to love. Love with moral and spiritual insight. ¹⁰With this love, you will be able to decide what is important and what is not. Also, no one will be able to accuse you of wrong and you will not cause others to stumble. ¹¹Living this way will reveal a life full of spiritual fruit supplied by Jesus Christ. Because of this, everyone will praise and honor God.
¹²Be assured brothers and sisters, that instead of restraining the message as intended, my imprisonment has caused its expansion. ¹³It is well known to everyone here, especially to each one of the elite guards, that I am chained here because of my bond with Christ. ¹⁴These chains have also injected increased confidence of faith in most of the family of God here. So much so that these fellow followers of Jesus fearlessly venture to keep on spreading the message of God. ¹⁵A small minority is preaching about Christ simply with a desire to deprive me of any profit from my work, but most share the message with good intent. ¹⁶The majority is driven solely by love. They are aware I am compelled to defend Christ's message of hope. ¹⁷The others are selfish. Arrogantly, they try to frustrate and discourage me by emphasizing I am here on the inside while they are not. They assume I am decaying in prison. ¹⁸So what. If their motives are corrupt, or even if they are blameless, at least people are hearing about Jesus. I made the decision from now on to applaud what is happening. ¹⁹I will revel in this because I am certain by way of your prayers and via the help of the Spirit of Jesus, God will vindicate me. ²⁰I firmly expect, with a deep hope, nothing will scandalize me before God. However, with the courage of an honest, free man, I realize what's important is for Christ to be the ultimate focus in my living or in my dying.
²¹I firmly believe living means doing so for Christ, and yet, dying will also accelerate the spreading of His message. ²²By living, I am able to continue the mission. If the choice were mine, I could not make up my mind. ²³I remain motionless. I cannot lean to either side. At times, I hunger for nothing more than to simply go home with Jesus. Is there anything

comparable? ²⁴I realize, though, the great need to persevere here along with you. ²⁵Unquestionably, this is why I will stick around. I will be here to help you grow in your walk with God and to help you grasp the true purpose of joy. ²⁶When I am released from this distant cell we will praise Christ together because of my return to you.
²⁷Think about this; live up to the high standards of Christ. It really does not matter where I am, here or there. I want to hear that you are banded together, as many strands make one rope strong, for your faith in Jesus. ²⁸Do not be bullied by those against you. God will use your unity to show them they have no chance of winning and that you will triumph in the end. ²⁹Faith in Jesus is not our only windfall, but also the chance to suffer for Jesus. ³⁰This hostility is the same as what I endured, and am still going up against.

2 If you ever have been comforted in your walk with Christ, if you ever have been encouraged by His love, if you have benefited from the community of the Spirit, if you have any warmth and compassion, ²then cheer me up by choosing to think and act together, by caring for each other. Strive together with one mind towards one goal. ³Don't fight for your ego or for hollow flattery. Let go of your pride. Promote others. ⁴Do not focus solely on your personal goals. Take care, also, of other peoples' needs. ⁵Adapt the same approach to life as Jesus Christ did. ⁶Despite being the full expression of God, Jesus did not feel He had to cling to that equality. ⁷Actually, He chose not to use His deity and preferred to become a slave, a man like us. ⁸He was selfless. He was humble. So much so, that He obeyed to the point of dying a degrading death on a cross. ⁹It was because of this obedience that God lifted Him to a place higher than anything created. His place is incomparable. ¹⁰Everything in creation will concede and worship Jesus. ¹¹Everyone and everything will affirm Jesus Christ is Lord, the One in charge. This will bring praise and glory to God the Father.
¹²In light of this, you whom I love, keep on obeying whether I am with you or not. With awe and respect before God, demonstrate you have a new life in God. ¹³Don't be concerned. You are not on your own in this. The desire and the power to live this new life in God comes from God Himself, for His own pleasure.
¹⁴Although it is hard, live this life without grumbling and quarreling. ¹⁵When the slanderous and self-obsessed society around you sees you, let them see genuinely clean-handed people who can lead them to the truth. Give them no reason to berate you. Leave no skeletons in your closet. ¹⁶We are in a race. Don't drop the baton, the complete message of this new life. I don't want my part of the race to be wasted. I want to celebrate with you on the winner's stand. ¹⁷I am prepared to go to the limit, to die for you. My death would only be added to your sacrificial life of faith. If this happens, I will rejoice with you. ¹⁸If this happens, I want you to rejoice with me. ¹⁹Lord willing, I expect to send Timothy to you as soon as possible. Getting an update on your will lift my spirits. ²⁰There is no one else with me, beside him, who sincerely cares for you like I do. ²¹The others focus on their personal goals, not the goals of Jesus. ²²Timothy is different, as you know. Like a father and son we worked together to spread the message of our hope in Jesus. ²³As soon as it is clear what is in store for me here, I will send him to you. ²⁴I am certain Jesus will send me soon after him. ²⁵Before Timothy and I can leave here, I will send to you my brother and partner Epaphroditus, whom you sent to take care of me. ²⁶I am sending him back since he deeply misses all of you. He has been

restless since he heard you knew how sick he was. ²⁷He came close to dying, but God had mercy on him. In fact, not only on him but on me also. If he had died, the heartache added to my present struggle would have been enormous. ²⁸This is why I am so glad he is returning to you. Once you see him face to face you will rejoice that he is okay and I can relax that he is safe back with you. ²⁹Celebrate his return! Men like him deserve your respect. ³⁰He exposed himself to danger in his effort to finish your work here for Christ and he almost died because of it.

**3** Well then, my family in Jesus, find your joy in our Lord. It is no big deal for me to remind you of the following. I only do it to protect you from error. ²Put some distance between you and those prowling dogs, those deceitful men who cut up the flesh to prove their faith. ³We are the true followers of Jesus. We have the Spirit of God who helps us serve and please God. Our conviction comes from Jesus; not from anything we do or achieve. ⁴Tell me, if our religious achievements meant anything, could anyone compare themselves to me? ⁵I was circumcised on the designated eighth day, born a Jew in the distinguished Benjamin family line. I am a Hebrew son of Hebrew parents. I studied and lived the Law so that it became my job. ⁶I was so passionate for my faith that I oppressed followers of Jesus. I actually knew and followed every requirement in the expansive Law given by God. ⁷My hope and life's purpose was based on these qualifications. I now realize they were more harmful to me than good. ⁸Nothing, not all the good things I have accomplished have any value when seen in the same light as personally knowing, and being known by, Jesus Christ, my Lord. When I chose to follow Him, I lost what to me was important. I see now how filthy as human waste it all was. I gave it all up, though, so I could daily deepen my relationship with Christ. ⁹I can't get right with God by keeping score with the Law. Trusting and following Jesus is God's way of making people right with Him. Being right with God comes from faith. ¹⁰All else is tossed aside so that I can know, and understand by experience, Jesus. Knowing Jesus is applying the life-giving power of God and the ability to endure suffering for Him in my day to day events. In this, I follow Christ's lead by leaving in the grave everything that ties me to my old way of living. ¹¹I am not sure of how death will come, but I anticipate leaving the grave behind and rising up to be in the presence of Christ. ¹²Don't think I have finished everything I have set out to do. I am far from being perfect, from being complete. Yet, I am pushing myself to the limit to seize that for which Jesus seized me. ¹³My family of God, I don't know all the answers. I am not comparable to how I will be. I have one goal, though. I refuse to look over my shoulder. Instead, I am straining and stretching forward, focused only on the finish line. ¹⁴As I turn the last corner, I am catching my second wind. I am running to win. I am running to be with Jesus. ¹⁵Let all of us that focus on being with Jesus keep moving forward. If your focus is altered, God will open your eyes. ¹⁶In any case, let us not lose what together we have worked so hard to gain. ¹⁷My family, follow us who are heading toward the true finish line. ¹⁸I have often warned you, and it pains me to do it again, about so many others who despise the cross of Christ. ¹⁹Their end is in sight. They follow their bodies' every urge. They pride themselves in what disgraces them. What they value will vanish. ²⁰Not us! We are citizens of heaven. From heaven will come the One who will save us. We look forward to the arrival of Jesus Christ, the One we serve. ²¹He is in control. Jesus has the power to compel anything and everything to sit at His feet. He will use this same power to completely remake our feeble bodies into glorious, undying bodies like His own.

**4** My love for all of you is so strong. You fill me with pride and joy. Be strong in your faith. Don't vacillate back and forth. ²Please, Euodia and Syntyche, I encourage you to clear the bad air between you two. Work together, as God wants you to. ³In fact, Syzygus, my faithful partner, work closely with them in resolving their conflict. These two, along with Clement and my other colleagues whose names are in the Book of Life, grappled along side me to spread the message of Jesus. ⁴I can't say this enough, rejoice and celebrate Jesus with every breath you take. ⁵Let others see you humbly trust God in spite of being treated unfairly and being ridiculed. Have hope. He will be here soon. ⁶Stop letting worry torment you. Pray instead. Go ahead, let Him know whatever is on your heart. Thank Him for how He has helped in the past and how He will help again now. ⁷At that moment of pouring out your heart, God will flood your heart and mind with a deep sense of His peace. You won't begin to be able to grasp the peace that surrounds all that have committed to follow Jesus Christ. ⁸Just a few more thoughts for you. Constantly control what is going on in your mind. Ignore the lies and pay attention to what is moral and real. Focus on things that are worthy of respect, on things that lift our minds above the cheap, simple things in life that bog us down. Concentrate on what is morally and ethically innocent. Meditate on what is pleasing, or on what makes us attractive to others in the family of God, things that give pleasure to all and distaste to no one. Picture in your mind what is worth talking about, and avoid bring offensive. Focus on what is good and will cause others to applaud. ⁹You have been watching and listening and learning from me as I have been teaching you these things. Now do them. When you do, the God of peace, God Himself, will be with you.

¹⁰God has made me glad because you have shown interest in me once again. I realize you were concerned for me before but you had no way to express it. ¹¹Not that I felt neglected. I have learned to be satisfied in any situation I find myself. ¹²I am at home with the extremes of poverty and with the provisions of wealth. I have adapted to the testing of hunger and of a full stomach. I know what it means to have more than enough and to have almost nothing. ¹³I am able to do all of this because of my relationship with Jesus and His nonstop power in my life. ¹⁴Don't get me wrong, though. I deeply appreciate how you shared with me in my difficult times. ¹⁵All of you from Philippi already know that you were the only ones who helped me when I left Macedonia to share the message of hope about Jesus. No other church understood as well as you what it means to give and to receive. ¹⁶You even gave me support a number of times while I was in the city of Thessalonica. ¹⁷The money is not as important to me as the dividends I know you will receive from God for your timely investments in me. ¹⁸I am doing well for I have everything that I need. Actually, more than I need thanks to the gifts you sent along with Epaphroditus. These gifts fill the air with a sweet essence as a hearty sacrifice that greatly pleases God. ¹⁹Out of the unlimited resources of His liberal generosity, my God will provide for your needs through Jesus Christ.

²⁰We praise our God and Father whose glory is revealed throughout endless time. ²¹Give my greetings to everyone in the family of God. The family here with me sends their greetings. ²²The entire family of God here, especially those working for Caesar, sends their greetings. ²³May your spirit be filled by the grace of Jesus Christ. Yes, let it be.

*The Epistle of Paul the Apostle to the*
# COLOSSIANS

1 Paul, sent by Jesus Christ according to the plan of God along with Timothy our fellow believer, ²to the special and loyal believers in the city of Colosse: Grace and peace to you from God our Father.
³We keep on giving thanks to God the Father of our Lord Jesus Christ and we are always praying for you. ⁴We have heard of your trust in Jesus Christ and the sacrificial love you have for all believers, ⁵because of your hope that is continuing to be secure for you in heaven, since the day you heard the good news through the message of truth. ⁶The good news that has come to you is always bearing fruit and is spreading, just as it is in the rest of the world. It is also happening among you, since the time that you heard and understood the reality of God's grace, ⁷which you had learned from Epaphras, our well-loved minister, who, for your benefit is a loyal servant of Jesus Christ. 8He has explained to us your sacrificial love empowered by the Holy Spirit.
⁹Therefore since the time we had heard about you, we have not stopped praying for you asking that you would have a deep understanding of God's plan by a supernatural discernment and a supernatural insight. ¹⁰Your correct actions are pleasing to the Lord Jesus Christ, as you do good actions that are always bearing fruit, and as you also increase your understanding of God, ¹¹and as you also are strengthened by an increase in power that comes from God's massive storehouse of power. That power will give you endurance and patience in difficult situations. Joyfully ¹²keep on giving thanks to your Father, who prepared you to share in the inheritance with the holy believers who live in the light; ¹³for God has delivered us from the control of darkness and placed us into the kingdom of Jesus Christ, the Son He loves. ¹⁴In Him we have freedom from the penalty of sin and pardon from the effect of sin. ¹⁵Jesus Christ is the very likeness of God, who cannot be seen. He is also the ruler of every created thing. ¹⁶Only by Jesus were all things created, whether in the heavens or on earth including those things that can be seen as well as those things that cannot be seen. All things came into existence through Jesus and exist for Jesus. ¹⁷Only Jesus is the ruler over all things and continues to hold all things together. ¹⁸Only Jesus is the ruler of the church, which acts as His body because He is the founder of the church. He also is the first conqueror from among the dead so that He was and is supreme in all things. ¹⁹For God the Father was delighted to have all of His qualities dwelling permanently in Jesus. ²⁰Through the blood of Jesus, shed on the cross, we were completely changed and came to peace with God. This peace will change all things on earth and in the heavens.
²¹Even you were in a continual state of belonging to your evil nature with a mind hostile toward God that produced evil actions. ²²But you were completely changed by the physical death of Christ on the cross. He did this so that one day he could present you to God as holy, perfect, and beyond reproach. ²³Therefore continue trusting in Jesus as you grow, firmly based upon a permanent foundation that cannot be moved. This is because of your hope in the good news. The good news was announced by the servant Paul, whom you have heard

from, along with all the created things under heaven. ²⁴At this time I am glad to share in physical sufferings for you, just as Jesus was afflicted in His physical body, so I follow His example in suffering for the church that is His spiritual body. ²⁵I was made a servant, appointed by God and was given an assignment to share with you the complete message of God. ²⁶This completed message contains a secret hidden from the past generations, but now has been revealed to the holy believers today. ²⁷To them God decided to reveal the great value and power that this secret can have upon all people. The hope of glory is Jesus living in you. ²⁸Therefore proclaim Jesus to everyone, correcting and teaching them with all discernment, with the goal of presenting them to God, perfect in Jesus. ²⁹To this end I grow weary in my labor, relying upon God's strength to work powerfully through me. 2 I want you to know about the great emotional struggle that I continually have for you and those in Laodicea, although many of you have never seen me physically. ²My desire is that your heart would be encouraged as all of you are united with a sacrificial love. This is of great value as you have complete confidence, insight and full understanding through Jesus, because all of God's secrets are found in Christ. ³Hidden only in Jesus is the storehouse of wisdom and knowledge. ⁴I say this so that you are not deceived by those with slick words. ⁵Though I am not with you physically, I am with you in spirit. I am glad to see you standing unified with others and firmly trusting together in Jesus Christ.

⁶As you began with Jesus Christ as your Lord, continue in your actions by submitting to Him. ⁷You began firmly rooted in Christ so continue to grow and gain strength in the teaching you trust as you overflow daily with thanksgiving. ⁸Watch out that no one takes control of you by using false wisdom that is empty and deceiving. This false wisdom is based upon the earthly traditions and the basic teachings of this evil world that goes against the true wisdom of Jesus Christ. ⁹Why? Because in Jesus' physical body dwells forever all the qualities of God's essence. ¹⁰Jesus also has fully equipped you and at the same time is the ruler of all kings and of those who think that they are in control. ¹¹In Jesus you received a one time spiritual circumcision of the heart not done by physical hands. This spiritual circumcision is done by the work of Jesus Christ, who has completely stripped off your sinful nature. ¹²We were buried with Christ in a spiritual immersion and were spiritually raised from the dead together with Him through your trust in the work of God, who raised Jesus from the dead. ¹³You were dead in your sins and dead in your uncircumcision, because of your sinful nature, but God made you alive with Jesus, on the basis of God having freely forgiven all of your sins. ¹⁴Having canceled the record of debt and the decrees which were against us and at war with us, Jesus took them away from us and nailed the record of debt permanently to the cross. ¹⁵Jesus made the kings and those in control powerless; He exposed them publicly in defeat having been victorious over them.

¹⁶Therefore, do not keep on judging one another concerning what you eat or drink. Likewise, it does not matter if you worship once a month or on a special day each week. ¹⁷These things are just the shadow of the coming reality that is found in Jesus Christ. ¹⁸Let no one judge your freedom in Christ and steal your heavenly prize. They try to do this with false humility and a false worship of angels. They take pride in what they experienced and out of their sinful nature grows even more pride. ¹⁹They will continually lack submission to the

Head, which is Jesus. He is the ruler of the church which means He holds its muscles and bones together in unity, resulting in God producing spiritual growth in the body.

[20]Since believers have died with Jesus Christ to the basic teachings of this world, why would you submit to living according to the commands of this world? [21]The world teaches do not handle, do not taste, do not touch. [22]These things that come from the commands and teachings of the world are going to perish with use and cannot be useful again. [23]These false teachers speak false works of wisdom, lead in false worship, and live with false humility which causes them to harshly treat their bodies, but this is of no value as the sinful nature continues to sin. 3 Since you have been spiritually raised together with Jesus Christ, continually pursue the pattern of heaven in your daily actions. Right now in heaven Jesus has the position of ultimate authority and power. [2]Therefore, keep on thinking upon the pattern of heaven and not thinking about the basic teachings of this world. [3]For believers have died to sin and have their lives locked together with Jesus and God the Father. [4]When Jesus, who is the very source and meaning of our life, is revealed, we also will be revealed with Him in power.

[5]Therefore, while living on this earth, put to death the sinful nature and its sins. This includes all sexual sins, sexual impurity, evil sexual thoughts, evil sexual desires, and the desire to have more than what belongs to you, which results in false worship. [6]The punishment of God will come because of these sins. [7]And in these sinful actions you once lived before salvation. [8]But now you must remove from yourself all sinful actions like anger, rage, malice, slander, and filthy words that can come out of your mouth. [9]Do not have the habit of lying to each other, since you have made powerless the old sinful nature and its evil actions. [10]Realize that you have put on the new nature which continues to be transformed with more and more understanding according to the very likeness of our creator. [11]For believers with the new nature, there are no divisions based upon social, cultural, or language differences, because Christ is all and is in all.

[12]Therefore, the new believer is special and will always be loved by God having been chosen by Him. So now clothe yourself with heartfelt compassion, kindness, humility, gentleness and patience. [13]Endure with and freely forgive each other. Even when someone else is at fault, forgive them just as your Lord Jesus Christ freely forgave you. [14]More importantly, clothe yourself with a sacrificial love, which will produce perfect unity. [15]The peace of Jesus Christ is to guide your heart in all decisions, just as you were called to be at peace in one body with other believers. Therefore, be continually thankful! [16]Let the message of Jesus Christ be abundantly at home in your life as you teach with all discernment, correct, sing psalms, hymns, and spiritual songs. Sing with thanksgiving in your hearts to God. [17]So no matter what you do either verbally or in action, do all in the name of Jesus Christ your Lord. Through Jesus keep on giving thanks to God your Father.

[18]Wives, voluntarily submit to your husbands as should be your duty to the Lord Jesus. [19]Husbands, keep on sacrificially loving your wives and do not be harsh toward them.

[20]Children, always be obedient to your parents in every area of life, for this is pleasing to the Lord Jesus. [21]Fathers, do not keep on nagging your children so that they become discouraged.

[22]Slaves, always be obedient in every area of work for your physical master and not

just when the master is looking or to please him so that you get a promotion. But work with a heart set on reverently pleasing the Lord Jesus. ²³No matter what you do, put every ounce of strength into your work as if you are working for the Lord Jesus Himself rather than working for your physical master. ²⁴You know that we will receive the reward of our inheritance from the Lord Jesus Christ, since it is really Him that we continue to work for. ²⁵But watch out. If you disobey your master, then you will receive discipline. Remember the Lord Jesus will

discipline the disobedient no matter who they are without prejudice. 4Masters, provide for your workers what is right and fair knowing that you have a master in heaven keeping an eye on you.

²Be persistent in your prayer-life. Always be active and thankful in your prayers, ³praying at the same time for us, so that God will give us an opportunity to preach the message – the secret which is Jesus Christ, which is why I am now in prison. ⁴I want to reveal Jesus Christ, continuing to use the best words possible in my preaching. ⁵With non-believers you need to have wise actions so that you continually make the most out of every opportunity that you have with them. ⁶Let your words always be sensitive to the situation and produce a positive effect upon each person, so that you may know how to respond to every discussion.

⁷As to all the things going on in my life, Tychicus will report them to you. He is a well-loved brother, loyal servant and fellow minister in the Lord. ⁸I have sent Tychicus to you with this assignment so that you will know my concern and so he can encourage your heart. ⁹With him I have sent Onesimus, who is a loyal servant and well-loved brother. He is a member of your church and will report all the things going on here.

¹⁰Welcome Aristarchus my fellow prisoner and Mark the cousin of Barnabas. If they come to your church, receive and welcome them according to my instructions. ¹¹Jesus who is called Justus is one of the few Jewish believers to be a co-worker with me for the kingdom of God. He is a continual source of comfort and encouragement to me. ¹²Epaphras also sends his greeting to you. He is a member of your church and is a slave for Jesus Christ. You need to know that he is always growing weary in his labor of prayer for you. He wants you to stand perfect and fully satisfied in the plan of God. ¹³I can testify to his deep concern for you and those who live in Laodicea and Hierapolis. ¹⁴Luke the well-loved doctor and Demas send their greetings to you. ¹⁵Send greetings to the fellow-believers in Laodicea and to the church that meets at Nympha's house. ¹⁶When you read this letter, remember to also have it read in the church of Laodicea. When you receive the letter to the Ephesians also have that letter read in your church. ¹⁷Tell Archippus to focus on his ministry which he received from the Lord, so that he will fulfill the calling.

¹⁸I also send my greeting to you. This is Paul. I am signing this letter with my own hand. Please remember me in your prayers, while I'm in prison. Grace be with you.

## *The First Epistle of Paul the Apostle to the*
# THESSALONIANS

**1** From Paul, Silas, and Timothy, to the church of the Thessalonians in God the Father and the Lord Jesus Christ: may God's unmerited favor and peace be yours. [2]We always give thanks to God for all of you, mentioning you in our prayers. [3]In the presence of our God and Father, we continually remember your work rooted in faith, your labor produced by love, and your perseverance of hope in our Lord Jesus Christ. [4]For we know, brothers beloved by God, that He chose you, [5]because our message of good news about Jesus Christ did not come to you merely in words, but also in power, and in the Holy Spirit and in full conviction as you observed how we lived among you for your sake.

[6]And you became imitators of us and of the Lord. Despite great hardship, you welcomed the Word with joy inspired by the Holy Spirit. [7]And so you became a model to all the believers in Macedonia and Achaia. [8]For from you, the message about the Lord rang out, not only in Macedonia and Achaia, but in everyplace your faith in God has become known. As a consequence, we do not need to say anything about it to anyone. [9]Indeed, they themselves report about us. They tell how you received us, and how you converted to God from the worship of false gods to serve the living and true God, [10]and are waiting for His Son from heaven, whom He raised from the dead – Jesus, who rescues us from the wrath that is coming.

**2** You know, brothers, that our visit to you was not wasted effort. [2]But as you yourselves know, even though we had already been abused and insulted in Philippi, with our God's help we had the courage to tell you God's good news amidst great opposition. [3]For our appeal does not spring from delusion or corrupt motives, and we are not trying to fool you. [4]Just the opposite! We speak as men endorsed by God to be entrusted with the good news. We are not trying to please anyone but God, who examines our hearts. [5]You know, too – as does God Himself – that we never used a word of flattery. We did not scheme to take your money. [6]And we were not pursuing praise from people – not from you or anyone else. And while we could have thrown our weight around as those sent by Christ to establish His church [7]we were instead nurturing among you, like a nursing mother would care for her little children. [8]We loved you so much that we were overjoyed to share with you not only God's good news but also our very own lives as well, because you had become so precious to us.

[9]For you remember, brothers, our labor and toil. We worked night and day so as not to impose on any one of you while we preached God's good news to you. [10]Both you and God are witnesses of how devout, scrupulous and irreproachable was our conduct among you believers. [11]You well know that we treated each of you as a father treats his own children, [12]while urging you, and counseling you, and appealing to you from our own experience, to lead your lives in a way that shows you belong to the God who calls you into His kingdom and glory.

[13]And another reason we constantly thank God is this: that when you received the Word of God you heard from us, you accepted it not as the mere word of men, but for what it really is – the very Word of God. And this Word of God is at work in you believers. [14]For you, brothers, became exactly like God's churches in Judea which are united in Christ Jesus. You

suffered from your fellow countrymen the same abuse those churches endured from the Jews, [15]who killed the Lord Jesus and the prophets and chased us out as well. They offend God and have become everyone's enemy [16]trying to keep us from speaking God's Word to those who are not Jewish so that they may be saved. Such people always sin to the fullest extent. But they have gained God's wrath to the utmost as well.

[17]And, brothers, after we were separated from you for a short while though only in body, never in our heart, we were desperately eager to see you again face-to-face. [18]We wanted so much to come to you – I Paul, on more than one occasion – but Satan stood in our way. [19]For what is our hope or joy or crown of glory when we stand before our Lord Jesus at His coming – except you. Yes indeed, you are our glory and our joy!

3 So when we could not stand it any longer, we willingly decided to remain alone in Athens. [2]And we sent Timothy, our brother and God's helper in spreading the good news about Christ, in order to reinforce your resolve and encourage you in your faith, [3]so that no one would be disturbed by these hardships. And you yourselves know that we cannot avoid them. [4]Even while we were with you, we repeatedly warned you that we would be persecuted. And that is exactly what has happened, as you well know. [5]Because of this, when I myself could not stand it any longer, I sent for news about your faith. I feared that somehow the Tempter might have tempted you and all our work would have been for nothing.

[6]But now, Timothy has just arrived from visiting you, bringing good news about your faith and love. He tells us that you always have good memories of us and that you yearn to see us, even as we, too, yearn to see you. [7]This is why, brothers, that even in the face of all our own distress and hardships, we were encouraged about you because of your faith. [8]For us, life cannot get any better than this, because you are standing resolutely in the Lord. [9]How can we possibly thank God enough for you in return for all of the joy we have as we rejoice in the presence of our God because of you? [10]Night and day we are praying fervently to see you again face-to-face and to supply whatever you may lack in your faith.

[11]May our God and Father Himself and our Lord Jesus provide a way for us to come to you. [12]And as for you, may the Lord make your love abound and overflow for each other and for everyone else, just as our love for you does. [13]In this way He will strengthen your hearts in holiness so that you will be faultless in the presence of our God and Father when our Lord Jesus comes with all His holy ones.

4 Finally, brothers, we ask you – we urge you in the Lord Jesus – to abound all the more in living as you do, in the way we taught you to behave – the way of life that is pleasing to God. [2]For you know the commandments we gave you in the name of the Lord Jesus. [3]This is God's will: that you should commit your life to His service. You must shun sexual immorality. [4]Each of you must learn to control his own body in a way that is holy and honorable, [5]not giving in to passionate lust like pagans who do not know God. [6]And in this matter no one should sin against his brother or victimize him. For, as we have already told you and warned you, the Lord will hold everyone accountable for all such sins. [7]For God did not call us to be immoral, but to lead a life committed to His purposes. [8]Therefore, whoever rejects this commandment does not reject human instruction but rejects the God who gives you His Holy Spirit.

⁹As to the subject of loving those of the faith, you do not need us to write anything to you, since you yourselves have been taught by God to love one another. ¹⁰For in fact, you do love all the faithful throughout Macedonia. Yet we urge you, brothers, to do so all the more. ¹¹Commit yourselves to living quietly, attending to your own affairs, and earning your own living, just as we directed you. ¹²In this way, your conduct will be proper toward those outside the faith and you will not need anything.

¹³Brothers, we do not want you to be uninformed about those who die, so that you will not grieve for them in the same manner as those who have no hope. ¹⁴For since we believe that Jesus died and rose again, so also we believe that God, through Jesus, will bring with Him those who have died. ¹⁵We tell you this by the Lord's own Word, that we who remain alive until the coming of the Lord will by no means precede those who have died. ¹⁶For the Lord Himself will come down from heaven, with a commanding word, with the archangel's voice, and with the call of God's trumpet, and the dead in Christ will rise first. ¹⁷Only then will we who remain alive be caught up into the clouds together with them to meet the Lord in the air. And so we will be with the Lord forever. ¹⁸Therefore comfort each other with these words.

5 Now, brothers, you do not need us to write to you about setting times and dates, ²for you yourselves know quite well that the Day of the Lord will come like a thief in the night. ³When people are saying, "Peace and safety," sudden destruction will come on them – just as labor pains come abruptly upon a pregnant woman – and they will not escape. ⁴But you, brothers, are not in the dark, that this Day should pounce upon you like a thief.

5All of you are Sons of the Light and Sons of the Day. We do not belong to the night nor to the darkness. 6So then, we must not be caught napping like those others, but must stay wide-awake and sober. 7For those who sleep, sleep at night, and those who get drunk are drunk at night. ⁸But since we belong to the Day, we must be sober, putting on a breastplate of faith and love, and a helmet that is the certain hope of salvation. ⁹For God did not destine us for wrath but to receive salvation through our Lord Jesus Christ, ¹⁰who died for us so that whether we are watching for His return or we have died, together we may live with Him.

¹¹Therefore comfort one another and build each other up, just as you are, indeed, already doing. ¹²Now we ask you, brothers, to appreciate those who work hard among you, who lead you in the Lord and direct you in His ways. ¹³In love, hold them in your highest esteem because of their work. Live at peace with one another. ¹⁴And we encourage you, brothers, caution the undisciplined, motivate the meek, fortify the weak, be patient with everyone. ¹⁵See to it that nobody repays one wrong with another wrong, instead, always pursue what is good for one another and for everyone else.

¹⁶Always rejoice. ¹⁷Never stop praying. ¹⁸In every circumstance give thanks. This is God's will for you in Christ Jesus. ¹⁹Do not suppress the Spirit. ²⁰Do not ridicule revelations. ²¹Do test everything. Keep what is good. ²²Keep away from every kind of evil.

²³And may the God of peace Himself completely set you aside for His purpose and keep you entirely blameless in your spirit, soul and body for the coming of our Lord Jesus Christ. ²⁴The One who calls you is faithful and He will, indeed, do this. ²⁵Brothers, pray for us. ²⁶Greet all the brothers with a holy kiss. ²⁷By the Lord's authority, I direct you to read this letter to all the brothers. ²⁸The unmerited favor of our Lord Jesus Christ be with you.

# *The Second Epistle of Paul the Apostle to the*
# THESSALONIANS

1 Paul and Silvanus and Timothy to the church of the Thessalonians in God our Father and the Lord Jesus Christ: ²Grace to you and peace from God our Father and the Lord Jesus Christ. ³We are bound to give thanks to God at all time concerning you, brothers, just as it is fitting, because your faith greatly increases and the love of each one of you all grows and grows toward one another; ⁴so as for us to boast ourselves in you among the churches of God on behalf of your patience and faith in all your persecutions, and tribulations ⁵which you are enduring as proof of the righteous judgment of God, that you be counted worthy of the Kingdom of God, on behalf of which you also suffer; ⁶since it is just for God to repay those afflicting you with affliction, ⁷and give relief to you who are troubled at the revelation of the Lord Jesus from Heaven with His mighty angels, in flaming fire ⁸giving vengeance to those not knowing God, and to those not obeying the Gospel of our Lord Jesus Christ, ⁹who incur punishment, eternal destruction from the face of the Lord and from the glory of His strength, ¹⁰when He comes to be glorified in His saints and to be adored in all those believing because our testimony to you was believed in that Day. ¹¹For which also we always pray concerning you, in order that our God may count you worthy of His call and may fulfill every good pleasure of goodness and work of faith in power, ¹²so that the name of our Lord Jesus Christ may be glorified in you, and you in Him, according to the grace of our God and the Lord Jesus Christ.

2 Now, on behalf of the coming of our Lord Jesus Christ and our being gathered together to Him, we beg you brothers, ²that you be not quickly shaken in your mind, nor be troubled, neither through spirit, nor through word, nor through letter, as through us, as that the Day of Christ has come. ³By no means let no one deceive you, because that day shall not be except the falling away comes first, and the man of sin be revealed, the son of destruction, ⁴who is opposing and is exalting himself above all, being called God, or object of worship, so as for him to sit as God in the temple of God, proclaiming that he himself is God. ⁵Do you not remember when yet being with you, I told you these things? ⁶And now you know what is restraining for him to be revealed in his time. ⁷For the mystery of lawlessness is already working, only he is restraining now until it comes out of the midst. ⁸And then the lawless One shall be revealed, whom the Lord shall consume by the breath of His mouth; and He shall destroy at the manifestation of His coming; ⁹whose coming is according to the working of Satan in every power and signs and lying wonders, ¹⁰and in every deception of unrighteousness in those being destroyed because they did not receive the love of the truth for them to be saved. ¹¹And because of this God shall send to them a working of error, ¹²for them to believe the lie, in order that all may be judged who have not believed the truth, but took pleasure in unrighteousness.
    ¹³But we are always bound to thank God concerning you, brothers beloved by the

Lord, because from the beginning God chose you for salvation in sanctification by the Spirit and belief of the truth; [14]to the One Who called you by our Gospel that you may gain the glory of our Lord Jesus Christ. [15]Therefore then, brothers, stand fast and hold to the teachings which you were taught, whether by word or by our letter. [16]And may our Lord Jesus Christ Himself, and our God and Father who loved us and gave us eternal comfort and good home in grace; [17]may He comfort your hearts and strengthen you in every good word and work.

3 As to the rest, brothers, pray concerning us, in order that the Word of the Lord may rapidly advance and be magnified, just as also with you [2]and in order that we may be rescued from wicked and evil men, for faith is not of all. [3]But the Lord is faithful, who shall strengthen you and shall guard you from evil. [4]And we are confident in the Lord concerning you, that what we command, you are both doing and shall do. [5]And may the Lord direct your hearts into the love of God and into the patience of Christ.
[6]But we command you, brothers, in the name of our Lord Jesus Christ that you withdraw from every brother walking disorderly and not according to the teaching which he received from us. [7]For you yourselves know how it is necessary to imitate us, because we were not disorderly among you; [8]neither did we eat bread with anyone without pay, but in labor and travail, working night and day in order not to burden anyone of you. [9]Not because we do not have authority, but in order that we ourselves may give a pattern to you for you to imitate us. [10]For even when we were with you, this we commanded you, that if anyone wishes not to work, do not let him eat. [11]For we are hearing that some among you are walking disorderly, not working, but are busybodies. [12]And to such we command and exhort through our Lord Jesus Christ in order that with quietness they work that they may eat their own bread. [13]But you, brothers, be not faith-hearted in well doing. [14]And if anyone does not obey our work through the letter, this one you note, and do not associate with him, in order that he may be ashamed; [15]and do not count him as an enemy, but warn him as a brother. [16]And may the Lord of peace Himself give you peace through everything and in every way. The Lord be with you all.
[17]The greeting of Paul by my hand which is a sign in every letter; thus I write. The grace of our Lord Jesus Christ be with you all. Amen

## *The First Epistle of Paul the Apostle to*
# TIMOTHY

1 Paul, an apostle of Jesus Christ by the order of God our Savior and of Christ Jesus our hope ²to Timothy, a true child in the faith: Grace, mercy, peace, from God our Father and Christ Jesus our Lord!
³Just as I urged you while on my way to Macedonia to stay in Ephesus, continue to command certain ones not to teach false doctrine ⁴nor to direct attention to endless myths and genealogies which only promote speculation rather than godly instruction in salvation which is by faith. ⁵Now the goal of this command is love that flows out of a clean heart and an upright conscience and an honest faith. ⁶Some people, having missed these, have wandered into meaningless chatter. ⁷They want to be teachers of the Law, yet they have no understanding of either the words they speak or the matters about which they make such bold affirmations.
⁸Now we know that the Law is a good thing, if someone uses it lawfully. ⁹We also know this, that the Law was not made for the righteous person. Rather, the Law is laid down for the lawless and disobedient, for the ungodly and the sinful, for the impious and the profane, for those who kill their fathers and mothers, for murderers, ¹⁰fornicators, homosexuals, kidnappers, liars, perjurers – and for anything else that is opposed to healthy teaching ¹¹conforming to the Gospel of the glory of the blessed God with which I was entrusted.
¹²I thank Christ Jesus our Lord who empowered me, because He deemed me faithful, commissioning me to the ministry, ¹³even though I was once a blasphemer and a persecutor and an insolent man. But I was treated with mercy because being ignorant I acted in unbelief. ¹⁴Moreover, the grace of our Lord abounded in company with the faith and love that is in Christ Jesus. ¹⁵This saying can be counted on and is worthy of acceptance by all: "Jesus Christ came into the world to save sinners" – of whom I myself am among the worst. ¹⁶Yet it is for this reason that I was treated with mercy, that in me as a prime example Jesus Christ could show all His patience as a model to those who are going to trust in Him for eternal life. ¹⁷Now to the King of eternity, immortal, invisible, the only God: honor and glory forever and ever. Amen!
¹⁸I commission you with this command, child Timothy, in accordance with the prophecies spoken concerning you, so that by their power you may campaign in the good warfare ¹⁹having faith and an upright conscience. Some have thrust aside their conscience and shipwrecked their faith, ²⁰among whom are Hymeneus and Alexander, whom I have delivered over to Satan so that they may be disciplined not to blaspheme.

2 I urge, then, first of all, petitions, prayers, intercessions, thanksgivings be made in behalf of all humanity, ²in behalf of kings and all who are in high office, so that we may lead a tranquil and quiet life in every kind of reverent conduct and virtue. ³This is good and acceptable before our Savior God, ⁴who desires all humanity to be saved and to come to full knowledge of the truth. ⁵For God is One, and the Mediator for God and human beings is One – a human being, Christ Jesus, ⁶the One who gave Himself as a ransom on behalf of all, the testimony given at its proper time. ⁷For this testimony I was appointed a

herald and apostle – I am speaking truth, not lying – a teacher of Gentiles in faith and in truth. [8]Therefore, I desire the men to do the praying in every place lifting up holy hands without wrath and argument. [9]In the same manner, I desire women to adorn themselves in adorning dress with modesty and discretion, not drawing attention with conspicuous hairdos and gold or pearls or expensive clothing, [10]but by good works, as suits women professing godly conduct. [11]Let a woman learn in quietness and respect. [12]And I do not permit a woman to teach nor to exercise authority over a man, but to be in quietness. [13]For Adam was formed first, then Eve. [14]And Adam was not beguiled, but the woman being completely deceived and fell into transgression. [15]But she will be saved in her role as child-bearer, if they continue in faith, and love, and holiness, and discretion.

3 This saying can be counted on: "If anyone aspires to the office of overseer he desires a noble work." [2]Therefore, it is necessary that an overseer be above reproach, a one-woman man, stable, discrete, orderly, hospitable, able to teach, [3]not a heavy drinker nor contentious, on the contrary, gentle, neither belligerent nor a money-grubber. [4]He must manage his own household well, with all dignity having his children behave respectfully [5]for if anyone does not know how to govern his own household, how will he care for God's church? [6]He must not be a recent convert, so that he not become conceited and fall under the same judgment as the devil. [7]It is also necessary for him to have a good reputation among those outside, so that he will not fall into disgrace and the devil's snare.

[8]In the same manner, deacons must be dignified, not double-tongued, not over indulgent in wine, not embezzlers, [9]possessing the mystery of faith with a clean conscience. [10]Moreover, let them first be closely observed, then because they are above reproach let them serve. [11]In the same way women must be dignified, not slanderers, stable, trustworthy in all things. [12]Let deacons be one-woman men who manage their children and their own households well. [13]Thus those who have served well earn for themselves great respect and much assurance to speak about matters of faith in Christ Jesus.

[14]I am writing these things to you even though I hope to come to you shortly, [15]so then in case I am delayed you may know how you must conduct yourself in the household of God, which is the church of the living God, the pillar and foundation of the truth. [16]And the great confession of what we believe is the revealed secret of godliness: He who appeared in the flesh, was justified in the Spirit, was seen by angels, was proclaimed among the nations, was believed in the world, was received up in glory.

4 Now the Spirit states clearly that in latter times some will depart from the faith. They will pay attention to deceiving spirits and demonic teachings, [2]which come through hypocritical liars whose own conscience has been seared. [3]They forbid people to marry and require them to abstain from foods, which things God has created to be received with thanksgiving by those who believe and comprehend the truth. [4]For every creation of God is good and nothing should be refused when it is received with thanksgiving, [5]for it is sanctified by God's Word and by prayer.

6By drawing the attention of the brothers to these things you will be a good minister of Christ Jesus, nourished by the words of the faith and the good teaching which you have been following. [7]And do not bother with godless myths and old wives' tales. Instead, continue training yourself in godliness. ⁸ "For physical training is profitable for a short time, but training in godliness is a long-term investment, yielding dividends both in this life now and in the life to come." ⁹This saying can be counted on and is worthy of acceptance by all. ¹⁰Yes, it is for this reason we toil and struggle because we have set our hope on the living God, who is Savior of all human beings, particularly of those who believe.

¹¹Insist on these things and teach! ¹²Let no one disregard you because you are young but continue to be an example for believers in speech, in behavior, in love, in faith, in purity. ¹³Until I come give close attention to the public reading of Scripture, to preaching, to teaching. ¹⁴Do not neglect your gift which was given to you by means of prophecy together with the laying on of hands by the elders. ¹⁵Continue to be diligent in these things. Give yourself completely over to them, so that your progress may be plain to all. ¹⁶Remain conscientious about yourself and the teaching. Continue to persevere in them for in so doing you will both save yourself and those who hear you.

5 Never speak harshly to an older man, rather reprove him as you would a father – reprove younger men as brothers, ²older women as mothers, and younger women as sisters, doing so in all purity.

³Recognize properly as widows those who are genuinely widows. ⁴But if any widow has children or grandchildren let them learn the priority of proper care of their own family and so fulfill their obligation to support their parents, for this is pleasing in the sight of God. ⁵However, a genuine widow, a woman who has no one left to care for her, has set her hope on God as she continues in her petitions and prayers night and day. ⁶But the widow who indulges herself though she remains alive has already died.

⁷These things also command in order that the people may be above reproach.

⁸Now if anyone does not provide for his own people and especially for his family he has denied the faith and is worse than an unbeliever. ⁹Enroll on the list of widows only she who is not less than sixty years of age, who was the woman of one man. ¹⁰She must also be known for her good works: Has she reared her children well? Has she shown hospitality to strangers? Has she washed the feet of the saints? Has she comforted the afflicted? Has she been diligent in every good work? ¹¹But refuse to enroll younger widows refuse to enroll, for whenever their natural desires overcome their devotion to Christ they desire to marry. ¹²They bring judgment upon themselves because they set aside the first faith, ¹³and at the same time they also learn to be idle as they wander around from house to house – not just idlers but gossips and busybodies talking about things best left unsaid. ¹⁴Accordingly, I desire the younger widows to marry, to bear children, to look after their homes, and to offer the adversary not even one opportunity for reproach. ¹⁵Sadly, some have already turned aside to follow Satan. ¹⁶If any woman who is a believer has widows dependant on her, let her assist them and do not let the church be burdened so that it may assist the genuine widows.

¹⁷The elders who are discharging their office well should be deemed worthy of double compensation, especially those who labor in the Word and teaching. ¹⁸For the Scripture says: "You shall not muzzle an ox while it is threshing," and "The worker deserves his pay." ¹⁹Do not even begin to regard an accusation against an elder unless it is supported by two or three witnesses. ²⁰Those that are sinning reprimand in the presence of all so that the rest may

also take warning. ²¹I solemnly testify in the presence of God and Christ Jesus and of the chosen angels that you perform these things without prejudice, and doing nothing out of favoritism. ²²Do not be quick to lay hands on anyone, nor participate in the sins of others. Keep yourself innocent.

²³No longer drink only water, but use a little wine on account of your stomach and your frequent bouts of illness.

²⁴The sins of some people are plain to see going ahead of them into judgment, but the sins of others indeed are only evident later. ²⁵In the same manner also, good deeds are plain to see, but even those that are not cannot remain hidden.

6 Let all who are under the yoke as slaves consider their own masters worthy of all honor so that the name of God and the doctrine may not be blasphemed. ²And let those whose masters are believers not despise them, for they are brothers. Rather let them more diligently perform their service because they are believers and beloved, who diligently occupy themselves in benevolences.

Continue to teach and urge these things. ³If anyone teaches differently and does not maintain the sound words of our Lord Jesus Christ and the teaching about godly behavior ⁴he is conceited and comprehends nothing, but has a morbid interest in challenging everything and wars of words. All that ever comes from this is jealousy, strife, sacrilege, evil recriminations, ⁵and unending quarrels among people whose minds have been corrupted and are devoid of truth, who imagine that spirituality is a way to wealth. ⁶But godly behavior accompanied by contentment is a path to great profit. ⁷For we brought nothing into the world, nor can we take anything out of it. ⁸But when we have food and clothing, with these we shall be content. ⁹But those who set their heart to be rich take the bait and are snared by many foolish and harmful lusts that plunge people into ruin and destruction. ¹⁰For a root of all sorts of evils is the love of money, which some, chasing after it have wandered away from the faith and inflicted themselves with many wounds.

¹¹But you, O man of God, ever flee these things! And keep pursuing righteousness, godly behavior, faith, love, patience, humility. ¹²Remain a contender in the noble struggle for the faith. Hold on to the eternal life into which you were called when you professed the noble confession before many witnesses. ¹³Before God who gives life to everything, and before Christ Jesus who testified before Pontius Pilate the noble confession, I command ¹⁴you to keep the commandment spotless, beyond reproach until the appearance of our Lord Jesus Christ, ¹⁵which in its own time He will show – the King of kings and Lord of lords, ¹⁶who alone is immortal, dwells in light unapproachable, whom no human has ever seen nor can see, to whom be honor and power forever. Amen.

¹⁷Continue to command those who are rich in this present world not to be arrogant nor to put their hope in untrustworthy wealth. Rather let them hope in God who provides us richly with everything we need to be happy. ¹⁸They are to do good deeds, to be rich in good works, to be willing donors, fellowshipping, ¹⁹who store up treasure for themselves as a noble investment for the future so that they may lay hold of genuine life. ²⁰O Timothy, guard what has been entrusted to your care. Turn away from profane blather and the contradictions of so-called knowledge, ²¹which by advocating some have strayed away concerning the faith.

Grace be with you.

## *The Second Epistle of Paul the Apostle to*
# TIMOTHY

1 Paul, an apostle of Christ Jesus, by the will of God, according to the promised life in Christ Jesus ²to Timothy, my beloved son: Grace, mercy, and peace from God the Father and Christ Jesus our Lord. ³I give thanks to God whom I serve, as my forefathers did, with a clear conscience when I constantly remember you in my prayers, night and day. ⁴I want very much to see you, as I remember your tears, so that I may be filled with joy. ⁵I remember your hypocrisy-free faith, which was first lived out in your grandmother, Lois, and your mother, Eunice. I am convinced that it lives also in you.

⁶For this reason, I remind you to rekindle the gift of God which is in you through the laying on of my hands ⁷for God did not give us a spirit of cowardice, but of power and love and self-control. ⁸So, do not be ashamed of the testimony of our Lord; neither be ashamed of me, His prisoner. But join with me in suffering for the Gospel, by the power of God, ⁹who has saved us and called us with a holy calling – not because of anything we have done but in keeping with His own purpose and grace. This grace was given to us in Christ Jesus before the beginning of time, ¹⁰but it has now been revealed through the appearing of our Savior, Christ Jesus, who has disarmed death and has brought life and immortality to light through the Gospel. ¹¹And of this Gospel, I was personally appointed a preacher and an apostle and a teacher. ¹²That is why I am suffering these things. But, I am not ashamed – because I know whom I have believed, and am convinced that He is able to guard what I have entrusted to Him for that day.

¹³Keep as the example of sound teaching what you heard from me – in the faith and love which are in Christ Jesus. ¹⁴Guard the treasure that was entrusted to you – do it with the help of the Holy Spirit who lives in us.

¹⁵You already know that everyone in the province of Asia deserted me, including Phygelus and Hermogenes. ¹⁶May the Lord give mercy to the household of Onesiphorus, because he often refreshed me and was not ashamed of my chains. ¹⁷On the contrary, when he was in Rome, he searched diligently for me until he found me. ¹⁸On that Day, may the Lord Himself enable him to receive mercy from the Lord! You know very well in how many ways he ministered to me in Ephesus.

2 You then, my son, be strong by the grace that is in Christ Jesus. 2And the things you have heard me say in the presence of many witnesses, these entrust to faithful men who will become able to teach others also. ³Endure hardship with me like a good soldier of Christ Jesus. ⁴An active duty soldier does not become entangled in the affairs of civilian life – he wants to please his commanding officer. ⁵Also, if anyone competes as an athlete, he does not receive the victor's crown unless he competes according to the rules. ⁶The hardworking farmer ought to receive the first share of the crops. ⁷Think seriously about what I am saying, for the Lord will enable you to understand all this.

⁸Remember Jesus Christ, raised from the dead, descended from David. This is my Gospel, ⁹for which I am suffering even to the point of being chained as a criminal. But the

Word of God is not chained. ¹⁰Therefore, I endure everything for the sake of those God will call, so that they too may obtain the salvation that is in Christ Jesus with eternal glory.

¹¹Here is a trustworthy saying: If we died with Him, we will also live with Him; ¹²if we endure, we will also reign with Him. If we ever deny Him, He will also deny us; ¹³if we are faithless, He will remain faithful, for He cannot disown Himself.

¹⁴Continuously remind them of these things. Solemnly warn them before God not to engage in useless word battles – they are catastrophes for those who listen. ¹⁵Be diligent to present yourself to God as one approved not ashamed, a workman who accurately communicates the Word of Truth. ¹⁶Avoid godless empty conversation for those who indulge in it only increase ungodliness. ¹⁷Their words consume flesh like gangrene. Hymenaeus and Philetus are among them ¹⁸who have departed from the truth. They say that the resurrection has already taken place, and they destroy the faith of some. ¹⁹Nevertheless, God's firm foundation stands, having this seal: "The Lord knows those who are His," and, "Everyone who confesses the name of the Lord must turn away from wickedness."

²⁰Even in a great mansion, there are dishes not only of gold and silver, but also wood and clay; some that are cherished and some that are not. ²¹Therefore, if anyone cleanses himself from such things, he is like an honored vessel, holy and useful to the Master, prepared for every good deed.

²²Run from youthful lust; instead, pursue righteousness, faith, love, and peace – along with all who call on the Lord out of a pure heart. ²³Refuse any foolish or uninformed debates, knowing that they give birth to conflicts. ²⁴Now, the servant of the Lord must not be quarrelsome; instead, be gentle towards all, apt to teach, not resentful, ²⁵in gentleness correcting his opponents, in the expectation that God will grant them repentance leading to the knowledge of the truth, ²⁶and come again to their senses and escape the snare of the evil one, who has taken them captive to do his will.

3 But realize this, in the last days terrible times will come. ²For people will be selfish, greedy, boastful, arrogant, blasphemers, rebellious towards parents, ungrateful, disrespectful, ³unloving, unforgiving, slanderous, out of control, violent, hating what is good. ⁴They will be traitors, reckless, puffed up, lovers of pleasure rather than lovers of God, ⁵having a form of godliness, but rejecting its power. So, turn away from these people. ⁶For from these people are some who go into homes and deceptively gain control of foolish women, weighed down by sin and led by evil desires, ⁷continually trying to learn but never empowered to acknowledge the truth. ⁸Just like Jannes and Jambres opposed Moses, so also these men are opposed to the truth, men of depraved minds, total failures concerning the faith. ⁹But, they will not get very far, for their foolishness will become evident to everyone, just like it happened to the others.

¹⁰You, however, have followed in my footsteps, in my teaching, conduct, purpose, faith, patience with people, love, and perseverance, ¹¹through many persecutions and suffering, like what happened to me at Antioch, Iconium, and at Lystra. You saw the persecutions I endured; and how the Lord delivered me out of them all! ¹²And yes, all who seek to live a godly life in Christ Jesus will be persecuted; ¹³but evil men and phonies will go from bad to worse, deceiving and being deceived. ¹⁴But as for you, continue in the things you

have learned and have believed, knowing from whom you learned them, ¹⁵and that from the time you were little you have known the sacred Scriptures, which are able to make you wise into salvation through faith in Jesus Christ. ¹⁶All Scripture is God-breathed and profitable for teaching, for confronting, for correcting, for training in righteousness ¹⁷so that the man of God may be fully equipped for every good work.

4 I solemnly charge you in the presence of God, even Jesus Christ, who will judge the living and the dead at His appearing and His kingdom, ²preach the Word! Be ready in season and out of season, reprove, rebuke, encourage, with much patience and careful instruction. ³For the time will come when men will not pay attention to sound teaching. Instead, wanting to follow their own desires, they will gather teachers to say what their itching ears want to hear and will turn away from listening to the truth ⁴and will give their attention to myths.
⁵But you be diligent in all things, suffer hardship, do the work of an evangelist, fulfill your ministry. ⁶For I am already being poured out as an offering, and the time of my departure has arrived. ⁷I have fought the good fight, I have finished the race, I have kept the faith. ⁸What remains for me is the crown of righteousness, which the Lord, the righteous Judge, will award me on the Day; but not only me, but also all those that long for His appearing.
⁹Do your best to come to me quickly ¹⁰for Demas deserted me because he loves this present world, and has gone off to Thessalonica. Crescens went to Galatia, and Titus to Dalmatia. ¹¹Only Luke is with me. Pick up Mark and bring him with you, for he is now helpful to me in ministry. ¹²I appointed Tychicus to go to Ephesus. ¹³When you come, bring the coat I left in Troas with Carpus, and the books especially the parchments. ¹⁴Alexander the metal smith did me great harm. The Lord will repay him for his misdeeds. ¹⁵Be on your guard against him yourself, because he strongly opposed our teaching.
¹⁶At my first defense, no one stood with me; instead, everyone deserted me. May God not count it against them. ¹⁷But the Lord was beside me and infused me with strength in order that through me the complete message might be proclaimed for all the Gentiles to hear, and I was delivered from the lion's mouth. ¹⁸The Lord will rescue me from every evil act, and deliver me safely into His heavenly kingdom. To Him be glory forever and ever. Amen!
¹⁹Greet Priscilla and Aquila, and the household of Onesiphorous. ²⁰Erastus stayed in Corinth and I left Trophimus in Miletus because he was sick. ²¹Do your best to come before winter. Eubulus sends greetings to you, as does Pudens, Linus, Claudia and all the brothers. ²²The Lord be with your spirit. Grace be with you all. Amen.

*The Epistle of Paul the Apostle to*
# TITUS

1 Paul, slave of God and apostle for Jesus Christ, true to the faith of God's elect and the true knowledge, which comes from godly living, 2based upon the hope for eternal life, which God – for whom falsehood is foreign to his person – promised before time, 3but revealed His Word at the right time by a proclamation, to which I was entrusted by the command of God our Savior, 4to Titus, a true child aligned with the common faith – may you have grace and peace from God the Father and Christ Jesus our Savior.
⁵I left you in Crete for this reason: that you might set in order what is lacking and ordain elders according to city, as I also commanded you – that is, ⁶whoever is above reproach, a one-woman man, having faithful children, not accused of wasteful spending or rebellion. ⁷For the overseer must be above reproach as God's house-manager: not self-willed, not given to anger nor drinking, not a bully, not a swindler, ⁸but a lover of strangers and good, self-controlled, just, holy, disciplined, ⁹holding onto the faithful teaching of the Word, that he may be able both to exhort by sound teaching and convict those who contradict.
¹⁰For there are many rebellious people, shallow-talkers, and liars – especially those of the circumcision group, ¹¹who must be muzzled because they are overturning whole house churches by teaching what they should not for dishonest gain. ¹²One of their own, a prophet, has said: "Cretans are always liars, evil beasts, lazy bellies." ¹³This witness is true. Therefore, reprove them severely that they might be sound in the faith – that is, ¹⁴not following Jewish myths and human commandments thereby rejecting the truth. ¹⁵To the clean, everything is clean; to the stained and non-believing, nothing is clean, but both their mind and conscience are defiled. ¹⁶They confess to know God but deny Him by their works, being detestable and disobedient and disqualified from every good work.

2 But you, Titus, are speaking what is appropriate for sound teaching. ²Elderly men must be sober, dignified, sensible, sound in faith, love, and endurance. ³Elderly women also must be like priests in their behavior, not devil-tongued, nor enslaved to excessive drinking. They must teach the good, ⁴that they may advise the younger women to be husband-lovers and children-lovers. ⁵The younger women must be sensible, pure, good homemakers, choosing to submit to their own husbands, that the Word of God may not be blasphemed.
⁶Likewise exhort the young men to be sensible ⁷about everything, showing yourself to be an example of good works, teaching from pure motives and with dignity ⁸a sound word beyond reproach, that the opponent might be shamed having nothing evil to say about us.
⁹Slaves must submit to their own masters in everything, to be pleasing, not argumentative, ¹⁰not stealing, but showing all good faith, that they may wear the teaching of our Savior God in everything.
¹¹For the grace of God, which brings salvation to every person, has appeared, ¹²instructing us to deny ungodliness and worldly lusts, that we might live moderately and

justly and godly in the present age, ¹³yearning for the blessed hope and appearing of the glory of our great God and Savior, Jesus Christ, ¹⁴who gave Himself up for us, that He might redeem us from all lawlessness and purify for Himself a chosen people, zealous for good works.

¹⁵These things speak and exhort and reprove with all authority; let no one disregard you.

3 Remind them to subject themselves to rulers and authorities, to be ready for every good work, ²to blaspheme no one, to be peaceable, gentle, showing humility to every person. ³For we also used to be senseless, disobedient, deceived, enslaved to lusts and various pleasures, living in ill will and envy – hated, hating one another. ⁴But when the kindness and the philanthropy of our Savior God appeared ⁵– not by works, which we have done in righteousness, but according to His mercy – He saved us through the washing of regeneration and renewal by the Holy Spirit, ⁶whom He abundantly poured out upon us, through Jesus Christ our Savior, ⁷that being justified by this grace we might become heirs according to the hope of eternal life. ⁸Faithful is the Word; and concerning these things I want you to speak confidently, so that those who have listened may practice good works as a profession. These things are good and useful for people. ⁹But step around stupid speculations and genealogies and strife and fights about the Law, because they are useless and empty. ¹⁰Avoid a divisive person after a first and second warning. ¹¹You know that such a one is twisted and is sinning, being self-condemned.

¹²When I send Artemas or Tychicus to you, make an effort to come to me, because I have decided to winter there. ¹³Make an effort also to send Zenas, an expert in the Law, and Apollos on their way, so that nothing is lacking for them. ¹⁴And also let our people learn to practice good works as a profession to meet necessary needs, that they may not be unfruitful.

¹⁵Everyone with me greets you. Greet those who love us in the faith. Grace be with you all.

## *The Epistle of Paul the Apostle to*
# PHILEMON

¹Paul, a prisoner of Christ Jesus, and Timothy our brother to Philemon our dear friend and fellow worker, ²and to Apphia our sister, and to Archippus our fellow soldier, and to the church in your house: ³Grace to you and peace from God our Father and the Lord Jesus Christ.

⁴I give thanks to my God every time I remember you in my prayers ⁵because I hear about your love and the faith which you have toward the Lord Jesus and for all the saints, ⁶so that the sharing of your faith may be energized in full awareness of every worthy thing that is in us in Christ. ⁷Indeed, I had great joy and encouragement from your love, because the hearts of the saints have been refreshed by you, brother.

⁸So, even though in Christ I am bold enough to order you to do the right thing, ⁹yet instead, for the sake of love I appeal to you – just me, an old man named Paul who is now also a prisoner for Christ Jesus. ¹⁰I appeal to you for my own child, whom I have fathered in my fetters, Onesimus, ¹¹who once was useless to you, but now, both to you and to me, has become useful.

¹²I am sending him back to you – he who is my very heart. ¹³I so wanted to keep him with me that he might serve me on your behalf during my imprisonment for the Gospel, ¹⁴but without your permission I decided to do nothing so that your goodness would not be coerced but voluntary.

¹⁵For perhaps for this very reason he was separated from you for a while, so that you might receive him back forever ¹⁶no longer just a slave, but more than a slave – a beloved brother – particularly to me, but even more so to you both as a human being and in the Lord. ¹⁷So if you consider me to be your partner, welcome him as you would welcome me. ¹⁸And if he has wronged you or owes you anything, charge it to my account. ¹⁹I, Paul, write with my own hand – I will repay it! – so that I do not say "charge it to you" since you owe me your very self. ²⁰Yes indeed, brother, I want to make some profit from you in the Lord. Refresh my heart in Christ.

²¹Trusting in your obedience I write to you, knowing that indeed you will do far more than I am asking. ²²While you are at it, get your guest room ready for me, because I hope that through your prayers I will be restored to you.

²³Epaphras, my fellow prisoner in Christ Jesus, sends you greetings, ²⁴as do Mark, Aristarchus, Demas and Luke, my fellow workers.

²⁵The grace of the Lord Jesus Christ be with your spirit.

*The Epistle to the*
# HEBREWS

1 God, having spoken in many places and in many ways in the past to the fathers by the prophets, ²in these last days has spoken to us by a Son, Whom He appointed heir of all creation, through Whom also He made the ages; ³Who being the effulgence of His glory and the exact reproduction of His substance and bearing all things by the Word of His power, having Himself made purification of sins, sat down on the right hand of the Majesty on high, ⁴such a One as this having been better than the angels by so much that He has inherited a more excellent name than they.
⁵For to which of the angels did He ever say, "You are my Son, this day I have begotten you?" and again, "I shall be to Him a Father, and He shall be to Me a Son?" ⁶And again whenever He brings the first born into the inhabited earth, He says, "Let all the angels of God worship Him." ⁷Indeed in regard to the angels He says, "The one making His angels spirits and His ministers flames of fire;" ⁸but to His Son He says, "Your throne, O God, is forever and ever, and the staff of uprightness is the staff of Your kingdom. ⁹You loved righteousness and hated lawlessness; on account of this God, your God, anointed You, with the oil of gladness above Your fellows." ¹⁰And, "You at the beginning, Lord, laid the foundations of the earth, the heavens are works of Your hands; ¹¹they will perish but You remain; and they all shall become old as a garment, ¹²as a mantle You shall roll them up, as a garment also they shall be changed; but You are the same and Your years shall not ever fail."
¹³And to which of the angels has He ever said, "You sit on My right hand until when I place your enemies the footstool of your feet?" ¹⁴Are not they all ministering spirits having been sent forth for ministry to those being about to inherit salvation?

2 On account of this it is necessary that we pay attention more carefully to the words having been heard, lest we drift away from salvation. ²For if the word having been spoken by angels was reliable and every transgression and disobedience received a just recompense, ³how can we escape neglecting so great a salvation as this? Which beginning to be spoken through the Lord, was confirmed to us by the ones having heard Him, ⁴God bearing witness to them with both signs and wonders and various miracles and distributions of the Holy Spirit according to His will.
⁵For He did not subject to angels the coming inhabited earth of which we speak. ⁶But somewhere someone has strongly witnessed saying, "What is man that You remember him, or the son of man that You look after him? ⁷You made him a little lower than angels, with glory and honor You crowned him, ⁸You subjected all things under his feet." For when He subjected all things unto him He left nothing unsubjected to him. But now we do not see all things subjected to him; ⁹but we see Jesus "having been made a little lower than angels" through the suffering of death "having been crowned," so that by the grace of God He might taste death on behalf of everyone.
¹⁰For it was proper for Him, on account of Whom are all things and through Whom

are all things, bringing many sons unto glory, to perfect the Author of their salvation through sufferings. ¹¹For both the One sanctifying and those being sanctified are all of one; on account of which reason He is not ashamed to call them brothers, ¹²saying, "I will announce Your name to My brethren; in the midst of the church I will sing You hymns." ¹³And again, "Behold I and the children which God gave to me."

¹⁴Since therefore the children have partaken of blood and of flesh, He Himself also in like manner shared with them in order that He might destroy through His death the one having the power of death, that is, the devil, ¹⁵and might deliver those who in fear of death through all of life were subjects of slavery. ¹⁶For of course He does not assist angels but He assists the seed of Abraham. ¹⁷So then He ought according to all things to be made like His brethren, in order that He might become a merciful and faithful high priest in regard to the things toward God, to make propitiation for the sins of the people; ¹⁸for in which He Himself suffered, being tempted, He is able to help those being tempted.

3 So then, holy brethren, sharers of a heavenly calling, consider closely Jesus, the Apostle and High Priest of our confession, ²He was faithful to the One making Him such as also Moses in his whole house. ³For this One has been considered worthy of more glory than Moses, even as the one constructing it has more honor than the house. ⁴For every house is constructed by someone, but the One constructing all things is God. ⁵And Moses indeed was faithful in his whole house as a noble servant for a witness of the words which shall be spoken. ⁶But Christ as a Son of His house of which are we, if we hold firmly to our confidence and the boast of hope.

⁷Wherefore, even as the Holy Spirit says, "This day if you hear His voice, ⁸harden not your hearts as in the provocation, as day after day of temptation in the wilderness, ⁹where your fathers tried Me by a testing, and saw My works for forty years; ¹⁰wherefore I was very displeased with this generation, and said, 'They always are deceived in their heart, and they do not know My ways'; ¹¹as I swore in My wrath, 'If they shall ever enter into My rest.'"
¹²Watch, brethren, lest there shall be in any of you a wicked heart of unbelief in falling away from the living God, ¹³but encourage one another each and every day while it is still called "This day," in order that any of you not be hardened by the deceitfulness of sin; ¹⁴for we have become sharers with Christ, if then we hold tight the beginning of our confidence firm until the end, ¹⁵when it is said, "This day if you hear His voice, harden not your hearts as in the day of provocation." ¹⁶For some provoked Him having heard, but not all those having come out of Egypt through Moses. ¹⁷But He was very displeased with some for forty years. Was it not with those sinning, whose bodies fell in the wilderness? ¹⁸And to whom He swore that they would not enter into His rest, if not to the ones disobeying? ¹⁹And we see that they did not enter in on account of unbelief.

4 Therefore, let us fear lest the promise being left to enter into His rest, some of you seem to fall short; ²for we then are having the Gospel preached as those also, but the Word of hearing did not profit those, not being thoroughly mixed with faith in those hearing it. ³For we, the ones having believed do enter into His rest, even as it has been said, "As I swore in My wrath, if they shall ever enter into My rest," even though His works were

finished from the foundation of the world. ⁴For where it has been said concerning the seventh day, thus, "And God rested on the seventh day from all His works;" ⁵and again in this place, "If they shall ever enter into My rest." ⁶Therefore, since it is left that some must enter into it, and those to whom it was first preached did not enter in on account of disobedience. ⁷Again He determined a certain day, "This day," in David saying, after such a time, even as He said before, "This day if you hear His voice, harden not your hearts." ⁸For if Joshua gave them rest He would not be speaking of another day after that. ⁹Therefore there is left a sabbath for the people of God. ¹⁰For the One coming into His rest also Himself has rested from His works, even as God from His own work.

¹¹Therefore, let us be diligent to enter into that rest, in order that no one may fall after the same example of disobedience. ¹²For the Word of God is living and powerful and sharper than a double-edged sword, and piercing until the dividing of soul and spirit, both the bones and marrow, and capable of judging the imaginations and attitudes of the heart; ¹³and there is no creature not manifested before Him, but all things are naked and laid bare to His eyes toward Whom we give account. ¹⁴Therefore, having a great High Priest having passed through the heavens, Jesus the Son of God, let us hold firmly our confession; ¹⁵for we do not have a high priest not being able to sympathize with our weaknesses, but having been tempted in all ways in like manner as we, without sin. ¹⁶Let us approach with boldness to the throne of grace, in order that we may receive mercy and find grace in time of need.

5 For every high priest having been taken out of men is appointed on behalf of men to the services toward God, in order that he might offer both gifts and sacrifices on behalf of sins, ²being able to use moderate feelings toward the ones being ignorant and being deceived, since he himself is set around with weaknesses; ³and on account of this he ought, even as for the people, thus to offer also for himself concerning sins. ⁴And no one takes to himself the honor, but being called by God, even as Aaron. ⁵Thus also Christ did not glorify Himself to become a high priest, but the One saying to Him, "You are My Son, this day I have begotten You." ⁶Even as also in another place He says, "You are a priest forever according to the order of Melchisedek." ⁷Who in the days of His flesh, having offered up both petitions and intercessions to the One being able to save Him out of death with strong cries and tears and having been heard because of His devoutness, ⁸even though being a Son He learned obedience from what He suffered; ⁹and having been made perfect, He became the reason for eternal salvation to all those obeying Him, ¹⁰having been designated by God a High Priest according to the order of Melchisedek. ¹¹Concerning which we have many words to say to you and difficult to explain, since you have become dull of hearing.

¹²For even when by this time you ought to be teachers, you have need for someone to teach you again the basic principles of the beginning of the oracles of God, and have become in need of having milk not solid food. ¹³For everyone partaking of milk is without experience in the Word of righteousness, for he is an infant; ¹⁴but solid food is for the mature, the ones having by use, their faculties having been exercised, the ability to discern between both good and evil.

6 Wherefore, leaving the first principles of the Word of Christ, let us carry on unto perfection, not laying again a foundation of repentance from dead works, and of

faith toward God, ²of teaching of immersions, and of laying on of hands, and of the resurrection of the dead, and of eternal judgment. ³And this we will do if God permits. ⁴For it is impossible for the ones having once been enlightened, and having tasted of the heavenly gift, and having become partakers of the Holy Spirit, ⁵and having tasted the good Word of God, and the powers of the coming age, ⁶then falling away, to renew them again unto repentance, they having crucified again to themselves the Son of God, and exposing Him to public shame. ⁷For the earth drinking in the rain coming often upon it and producing a crop useful to those by whom it is tilled, having received blessing from God; ⁸but bringing forth thorns and thistles it is unapproved and near to being cursed, whose end is for burning.

⁹But we are confident concerning you, beloved, of better things, and things having to do with salvation, even if thus we are speaking; ¹⁰for God is not unrighteous to be forgetful of your work and the love which you have demonstrated for His name, having served the saints and are serving. ¹¹But we desire each of you to demonstrate the same diligence for the full assurance of hope until the end, ¹²in order that you do not become dull, but imitators of the ones who through faith and patience are inheriting the promises. ¹³For God making promise to Abraham, since He had no one greater by whom to make an oath, made oath by Himself, ¹⁴saying, "If indeed blessing, I will bless you and multiplying I will multiply you." ¹⁵And thus having patiently waited he obtained the promise. ¹⁶For men make oaths by that which is greater, and the oath made as a confirmation is the end of all argument; ¹⁷in this way God, willing more abundantly to show to the heirs of the promise the unchangeableness of His will, confirmed it with an oath, ¹⁸in order that through two unchangeable practices, in which it was impossible for God to lie, we might have strong consolation, the ones having fled for refuge to lay hold of the hope having been set before us; ¹⁹which we have as an anchor of our soul, both safe and firm and entering into the inside of the curtain, ²⁰where Jesus the forerunner entered on behalf of us, becoming a High Priest after the order of Melchisedek forever.

7 For this Melchisedek, king of Salem, priest of the Most High God, the one having met Abraham returning from the slaughter of the kings and having blessed him, ²to whom also Abraham divided a tenth from all spoils, was indeed first, being interpreted, king of righteousness and then also king of Salem, which is king of peace, ³without father, without mother, without genealogy, having neither beginning of days nor end of life, and having been made like the Son of God, remains a priest permanently. ⁴Now behold how great this one was to whom Abraham the patriarch gave a tenth of the best of the plunder. ⁵And indeed the sons of Levi, receiving the priesthood, have a commandment to receive a tenth from the people according to the Law, that is from their brethren, through having come forth from the loins of Abraham; ⁶but the one not being of their genealogy received a tenth from Abraham, and blessed the one having the promises. ⁷Now without any controversy the lesser is blessed by the greater. ⁸And here, on the one hand, dying men receive tithes, but there, on the other hand, it is being witnessed that he continually lives. ⁹And as I so say, through Abraham, even Levi, the one who receives tithes, paid tithes, ¹⁰for he was still in the loins of his father Abraham when he met Melchisedek.

¹¹If indeed then perfection was through the Levitical priesthood, for the people under it had been furnished with the Law why still a need for another priest to be called

according to the order of Aaron? ¹²For when there is a change of the priesthood, also of necessity there becomes a change of law. ¹³For He of Whom these words are said had a part in a different tribe, from which no one served at the altar; ¹⁴for it is plainly evident that our Lord has arisen out of Judah of which tribe Moses never spoke concerning the priesthood. ¹⁵And it is still more abundantly plainly evident, if according to the order of Melchisedek arises another priest, ¹⁶Who has become a priest, not according to a law of physical commandment but according to the power of an indestructible life. ¹⁷For it has been witnessed that, "You are a priest forever after the order of Melchisedek." ¹⁸For indeed there comes about an elimination of the preceding commandment on account of its weakness and unprofitableness, ¹⁹for the Law made nothing perfect, but the bringing in of a better hope did, through which we draw near to God. ²⁰And inasmuch as it was not apart from taking an oath for indeed they were becoming priests apart from taking of an oath, ²¹but He with taking of an oath through the one saying to Him, "The Lord swore and will not regret, You are a priest forever"; ²²according to such as this then Jesus became the surety of a better covenant. ²³And they on the one hand are becoming more priests on account of death hindered them from continuing, ²⁴on the other hand on account of Him remaining forever He has His priesthood inviolate; ²⁵so also He is able to save completely those coming to God through Him, since He is always living to intercede on behalf of them. ²⁶For such a High Priest as this also was proper, holy, innocent, undefiled, having been separated from sinners, and being lifted higher than the heavens; ²⁷who does not have need day after day even as the high priests under the Law to offer up sacrifices first on behalf of His own sins, then for those of the people; for this He did once and for all when He offered up Himself. ²⁸For the Law appoints men high priests having weakness, but the word of the oath-taking after the Law appointed a Son having been perfected forever.

**8** Now the summary of what we are saying, we have such a High Priest as this, Who sat down on the right hand of the Majesty in the heavens, ²a religious Servant of the holies and of the true tabernacle, which the Lord pitched, not man. ³For every high priest is appointed to offer both gifts and sacrifices, hence it is necessary that this One also has something to offer. ⁴Indeed, therefore, if He were on earth, He would not be a priest, there being the ones offering the gifts according to the Law; ⁵these serve as an example and shadow of the heavenlies, even as Moses was warned by God being about to erect the tabernacle, for He said, "See that you make all things according to the pattern having been shown to you on the mount."

⁶But now He has obtained a more excellent service, in so much as also He is a mediator of a better covenant, which has been legislated on better promises. ⁷For if that first covenant was faultless, no place would have been sought for a second; ⁸for finding fault with them, he says, "Behold the days are coming, says the Lord, and I will establish upon the house of Israel and upon the house of Judah a new covenant; ⁹not according to the covenant which I made with their fathers in the day I took them by My hand to lead them out of Egypt, because they did not remain in my covenant, and I will not take care of them, says the Lord. ¹⁰Because this is the covenant which I will covenant with the house of Israel after those days, says the Lord, giving My Laws into their mind, and I will write them upon their hearts, and I shall be their God, and they shall be My people. ¹¹And each one shall absolutely not teach his fellow

citizens, and each his brother saying, 'Know the Lord,' because all shall know Me from the least unto the greatest of them. [12]Because I will be merciful to their iniquities and their sins I will absolutely not remember any longer." [13]When He said, "A new covenant," He made the first antiquated; but being antiquated and growing old it is near to vanishing away.

**9** Indeed, therefore, the first covenant had regulations of sacred service and an earthly holy place. [2]For the first tabernacle was prepared, in which was the lampstand and the table for the setting forth of the bread, which is called the Holy Place; [3]And after the second curtain the tabernacle being called Holy of Holies, [4]having a golden censer and the ark of the covenant having been covered all around with gold, in which was a golden jar having the manna, and the rod of Aaron which budded and the tablets of the covenant, [5]and above it cherubim of glory overshadowing the mercy seat concerning which there is not now time or space to speak in detail. [6]Now these thus having been prepared, the priests indeed are continually entering into the first tabernacle performing the sacred services, [7]but into the second the high priest only enters once a year, not without blood, which he offers on behalf of himself and the ignorances of the people, [8]the Holy Spirit declaring this, that the way of the holiest had not yet been manifested, the first tabernacle still having stood, [9]which is an illustration for the present time according to which both gifts and sacrifices being offered, they are not able to prefect the conscience of the worshiper, [10]only regarding food and drinks and various washings, regulations of the flesh being imposed until a time of reformation.
[11]But Christ having appeared a High Priest of the good things having come through a greater and more perfect tabernacle not made with hands, that is not of this creation, [12]neither through blood of goats and calves but through His own blood, He entered once and for all into the Holy of Holies, having secured eternal redemption. [13]For if the blood of goats and bulls and ashes of a heifer sprinkling those having been defiled sanctifies to cleansing of the flesh, [14]how much more the blood of Christ, Who through the eternal Spirit offered Himself unblemished to God, will cleanse our conscience from dead works to serve the living God.
[15]And on account of this He is the Mediator of a new covenant, so that, a death having occurred for the redemption of transgressions under the first covenant, those having been called might receive the promise of the eternal inheritance. [16]For where there is a testament, it is necessary for the death of the one making the testament to be offered; [17]for a testament is firm after death; since it never is in force while the testator lives. [18]So neither the first covenant was instituted without blood; [19]for every commandment according to the Law having been spoken by Moses to all the people, having taken the blood of calves and goats with water and scarlet wool and hyssop, he sprinkled both the book itself and all the people, [20]saying, "This is the blood of the covenant which God commanded to you"; [21]and both the tabernacle and all the vessels of the religious service were sprinkled in the same way. 22And according to the Law almost all things are cleansed with blood, and without the shedding of blood there comes no forgiveness.
[23]Therefore, it was necessary indeed that the examples of the things be cleansed in heaven by these sacrifices, but the heavenly things themselves by better sacrifices than these. [24]For Christ did not enter into man-made holy places, an antitype of the true but into heaven

itself, now to be manifested before the face of God on behalf of us; ²⁵nor in order that He might offer Himself many times, as the high priest enters into the Holy of Holies, year after year with the blood of another, ²⁶since then He would have needed to suffer many times from the foundation of the world; but now once at the end of the ages He has appeared for elimination of sin through His sacrifice. ²⁷And according to such it is appointed for men once to die, and after this, judgment, ²⁸thus also Christ, once having been offered to bear the sins of many, the second time He will be seen by the ones awaiting Him, apart from sin for salvation.

10 For the Law being a shadow of the coming good things, and not the image itself, being practiced year after year, offering up the same sacrifices continually, is not at all able to make perfect the ones drawing near. ²Otherwise would they not have ceased being offered, because the ones worshiping, having once been cleansed, would no longer have had a consciousness of sins? ³But in those sacrifices there is a reminder year after year of sins. ⁴For it is impossible for the blood of bulls and goats to take away sins. ⁵Wherefore coming into the world He says, "You did not desire sacrifice and offering, but you prepared for Me a body; ⁶also with whole burnt offerings concerning sin You were not well disposed."

⁷"Then I said, 'Behold, I have come (in the roll of the Book it has been written concerning Me) to do, O God, Your will.'" ⁸After saying above that "Sacrifices and offerings and whole burnt offerings concerning sins You do not desire nor are pleased," which according to Law are being brought ⁹then He said, "Behold, I have come to do Your will." He takes away the first in order that He may establish the second; ¹⁰by this will we are being sanctified through the offering of the body of Jesus Christ once and for all. ¹¹And indeed every priest has stood day after day doing religious services and offering many times the same sacrifices, which are never able to take away sins. ¹²But this One having offered one sacrifice for sins in perpetuity, He sat down on the right hand of God, ¹³henceforth waiting until His enemies are placed as a footstool of His feet; ¹⁴for with one offering He has perfected in perpetuity the ones being sanctified. ¹⁵And the Holy Spirit witnesses to us also; for after that He has said, ¹⁶"This is the covenant which I shall covenant with them after those days, says the Lord, giving My laws upon their hearts and upon their mind I will write them, ¹⁷and their sins and their lawlessnesses I will absolutely not remember any more." ¹⁸Now where there is forgiveness, there is no longer offering concerning sins.

¹⁹Having therefore, brethren, boldness for entrance into the Holiest by the blood of Jesus, ²⁰which He instituted to us, a fresh and living way through the veil, that is through His flesh, ²¹and having a great Priest over the house of God, ²²let us come near with a true heart in full assurance of faith, our hearts having been sprinkled from a wicked conscience and our bodies having been washed with clean water. ²³Let us hold firmly the confession of our hope without wavering, for the One having promised is faithful. ²⁴Let us consider one another to motivate for love and good works, ²⁵nor forsaking the assembling together of ourselves, even as is the custom of some, but encouraging one another, and so much the more as we see the Day drawing near. ²⁶For if we continue sinning willfully after we received the full knowledge of truth, there is no longer left a sacrifice for sins, ²⁷but a certain fearful expectation of judgment and a furious fire being about to consume the adversaries. ²⁸Anyone rejecting the

Law of Moses upon two or three witnesses dies without pities. ²⁹Of how much worse punishment do you suppose one will be counted worthy having trampled under foot the Son of God, and having considered common the blood of the covenant by which he was sanctified, and having insulted the Spirit of grace? ³⁰For we know the One having said, "Vengeance is Mine, I will repay"; and again, "The Lord will judge His people." ³¹It is fearful to fall into the hands of the living God. ³²Now recollect the former days in which, having been enlightened you endured much struggle of sufferings, ³³this on the one hand was in being made a public spectacle with reproaches and tribulations, and this on the other hand was in having become sharers of those being treated thus. ³⁴For also you sympathized with those in bonds and accepted with joy the seizure of your possessions, knowing you yourselves have better and abiding possessions. ³⁵Therefore, do not throw away your confidence, which has great recompense of reward, ³⁶for you have need of perseverance in order that having done the will of God you may obtain the promise. ³⁷For yet a very, very little while, the One coming will come and will not delay; ³⁸and My righteous one shall live by faith, and if he shall draw back, My soul shall not be well disposed in him. ³⁹But we are not of those shrinking back unto perdition, but of faith unto the preserving of our soul.

**11** Faith is the basis of that being hoped for, the proof of that not being seen. ²By this faith the elders received witness. ³By faith we understand the worlds were framed by the Word of God, so that the things being seen have not been made out of the things appearing.
⁴By faith Abel offered a better sacrifice to God than Cain, through which he was witnessed to be righteous, God bearing witness about his gifts, and through it being dead yet speaks. ⁵By faith Enoch was translated so that he did not see death, and he was not found because God had translated him; for before his translation it was witnessed that he was well pleasing to God. ⁶Now without faith it is impossible to be well pleasing to God, for it is necessary that the one coming to God to believe He is and He becomes the rewarder of those seeking Him. ⁷By faith Noah, having been warned by God concerning things not yet being seen, being devout, prepared an ark for the salvation of his house, by which he condemned the world, and became an heir of righteousness which is according to faith. ⁸By faith Abraham having been called, obeyed to go out into a place which he was about to receive for an inheritance, and he went out not comprehending where he was going. ⁹By faith he made his home in the land of promise as a stranger, dwelling in tents with Isaac and Jacob, fellow heirs of the same promise; ¹⁰for he was expecting the city having foundations, whose planner and builder is God. ¹¹By faith also Sarah herself being barren received power for conception of seed even beyond the proper time of age, since she considered faithful the One having promised; ¹²wherefore from one man, and him having been dead in this regard, has been born even as the stars of heaven in the multitude of descendants and as innumerable as the sand by the side of the sea. ¹³These all died according to faith, not obtaining the promises, but having seen them from afar off and having welcomed them, and having confessed that they are sojourners and pilgrims upon the earth. ¹⁴For the ones saying such things as these manifest that they are seeking a fatherland. ¹⁵And if indeed they were remembering that from which they had gone out, they would have had opportunity to return; ¹⁶but now they were longing for a

better country that is a heavenly one. Wherefore, God was not ashamed of them to be called their God, for He had prepared for them a city. [17]By faith Abraham being tested offered up Isaac, and the one having received the promises was offering his only begotten son, [18]to whom it was said that, "In Isaac your seed shall be called." [19]He reasoned that God was able even to raise him from the dead, from which also in a figure he obtained him. [20]By faith also concerning coming things he blessed Isaac, Jacob, and Esau. [21]By faith Jacob when he was dying blessed each of the sons of Joseph, leaning on the top of his staff. [22]By faith Joseph nearing his end reminded the sons of Israel concerning the exodus, and gave commandment concerning his bones. [23]By faith Moses having been born was hidden three months by his parents, because they saw he was a splendid child, and they were not afraid of the declaration of the king. [24]By faith Moses having become an adult denied to be called a son of Pharaoh's daughter, [25]choosing rather to suffer evil treatment with the people of God than to have the enjoyment of sin for a time, [26]considering the reproach of Christ greater riches than the treasures of Egypt, for he was looking ahead to the recompense of reward. [27]By faith he left Egypt, not fearing the anger of the king, for he endured as seeing the unseen. [28]By faith he had prepared the Passover and the sprinkling of the blood in order that the one destroying the firstborn ones might not touch them. [29]By faith they went through the Red Sea as through dry land, which the Egyptians attempting were swallowed up. [30]By faith the walls of Jericho fell, having been circled for seven days. [31]By faith Rahab the harlot did not perish with the ones disobeying, having received the spies with peace.

[32]And what more may I say; for time will leave me if I recount concerning Gideon, Barak, Samson, Jephthah, of both David and Samuel and the prophets, [33]who through faith defeated kingdoms, worked righteousness, obtained promises, shut the mouths of lions, [34]quenched the power of fire, fled from the mouth of the sword; for weakness were made powerful, became strong in war, routed foreign battle lines; [35]women received their dead out of resurrection; but others were beaten to death not accepting redemption, in order that they might obtain a better resurrection; [36]others received trial of mockings and floggings, and still others bonds and imprisonment; [37]they were stoned, they were sawed in two, they were tempted, they died by murder with the sword, they went around in sheepskins, in goats' skins, being destitute being afflicted, being evil treated, [38]these of whom the world was not worthy, wandering over wilderness places and mountains and in caves, and in the holes of the earth. [39]And these all having been witnessed through their faith did not obtain the promise, [40]God having provided something better for us in order that apart from us they might not be perfected.

12 Consequently then we, having lying around us such a cloud of witnesses as this, laying aside every encumbrance and the easily entangling sin, let us run the race being set before us with patience, [2]looking away to Jesus the Author and Finisher of our faith, Who instead of the joy having been set before Him endured a cross despising the shame, and has been seated on the right hand of the throne of God. [3]For consider such a One as this having endured the antagonism of sinners toward Himself, in order that you do not become weary and being dejected in your souls.

[4]You have not yet resisted until blood struggling against sin, [5]and you have forgotten

the exhortation which reasons with you as sons, "My son, do not take lightly discipline of the Lord, neither be dejected being reproved by Him; ⁶for whom the Lord loves He disciplines and scourges every son whom He accepts." ⁷Endure discipline as sons; God is treating you as sons; for what son is there whom a father does not discipline? ⁸But if you are without discipline of which all have become sharers, then you are illegitimate children and not sons. ⁹Furthermore, indeed, we have had our fathers of flesh for discipline and we respected them; but how much more shall we be subject to the Father of spirits and we shall live? ¹⁰For indeed they were disciplining us for a few days according to what seemed good to them, but He for our profit that we might receive His holiness. ¹¹Now on the one hand all discipline is for the present, and does not seem to be joyful but sorrowful, on the other hand, later it gives back peaceable fruit to the ones having been trained by it. ¹²Wherefore, straighten the hands hanging down and the knees having been paralyzed, ¹³and make straight tracks for your feet, in order that the lame be not turned aside, but rather be cured. ¹⁴Pursue peace with all people, and holiness without which no one shall see the Lord, ¹⁵overseeing others so that no one falls short from the grace of God, and no root of bitterness springing up distresses, and through it many be defiled, ¹⁶and no one be a fornicator or profane as Esau, who for one meal sold his right as first born. ¹⁷For you know that then afterwards, desiring to inherit the blessing he was rejected, for he did not find a place of repentance, even though he sought after it with tears.

¹⁸For you have not come to a tangible mountain and one having been burned with fire, to blackness, to gloom, and to tempest, ¹⁹and to the sound of a trumpet and to the voice of words, which the ones having heard pleaded that the word not be applied to them; ²⁰for they could not bear that being commanded, "Even if a beast touches the mountain, it shall be stoned"; ²¹and so fearful was that appearing that Moses said, "I am afraid and trembling."

²²But you have come to Mount Zion and to the city of the living God, the heavenly Jerusalem, and to myriads of angels, to a general assembly, ²³and to the church of the first-born ones having been enrolled in heaven, and to God the Judge of everyone, and to the spirits of the righteous having been perfected, ²⁴and to Jesus, the Mediator of a new covenant, and to the blood of sprinkling speaking better than the blood of Abel. ²⁵See that you do not refuse the One speaking; for if those were not escaping upon earth from the One warning them, how much more we, the ones turning away from the One speaking from heaven, not escape, ²⁶whose voice shook the earth then but now He has promised saying, "Yet once more I shall shake not only the earth but also the heaven." ²⁷And the phrase, "Yet once more," I shall shake not only the earth but also the heaven." ²⁸Wherefore, receiving an unshakeable kingdom, let us have thanks, through which we may serve well pleasing to God with reverence and piety. ²⁹For indeed our God is a consuming fire.

13 Let brotherly love continue. ²Do not be forgetful of strangers for through this some have entertained angels unknowingly. ³Remember those in bonds as being bound with them, and the ones being evil treated as you yourselves also being in their body. ⁴Let marriage be honorable by all the marriage bed undefiled, for God will judge fornicators and adulterers. ⁵Let your way of life be free of the love of money, being satisfied with things being present; for He Himself has said, "I will absolutely not leave you nor forsake you." ⁶So that being confident we say, "The Lord is a helper to me, and I will not be afraid

what man will do to me." ⁷Remember the ones having led you, who spoke the Word of the Lord, observing the result of their conduct, imitate their faith. ⁸Jesus Christ the same yesterday, today and forever. ⁹Do not be carried away by various and strange teachings; for it is good for the heart to be confirmed by grace, not by meats in which the ones walking were not profited. ¹⁰We have an altar of which the ones serving in the tabernacle have no right to eat. ¹¹For the blood of animals which concerning sin is brought into the Holy of Holies by the high priests, the bodies of these are buried outside the camp. ¹²Wherefore, also Jesus, in order that He might sanctify the people through His own blood, suffered outside the gate. ¹³So then, let us go out to Him outside the camp, bearing His reproach. ¹⁴For we do not have here a continuing city, but we are seeking the coming One. ¹⁵Therefore, through Him let us offer a sacrifice of praise continually to God, that is the fruit of our lips confessing His name. ¹⁶And do not be forgetful of the doing of good and sharing for with such sacrifices as these God is well pleased. ¹⁷Be obedient to those leading you and be submissive, for they keep watch on behalf of your souls as ones giving an account in order that they may do this with joy and not groaning for this would be a disadvantage to you.

¹⁸Pray concerning us, for we are confident that we have a good conscience, in everything desiring to conduct ourselves well. ¹⁹And I plead with you more abundantly to do this in order that I may be restored to you sooner. ²⁰Now the God of peace, the One having brought up out of the dead, the great Shepherd of the sheep by the blood of the eternal covenant, that is our Lord Jesus, ²¹prepare you in every good to do His will, working in us that which is well pleasing before Him through Jesus Christ, to whom be the glory for ever and ever. Amen. ²²And I plead with you, brethren, take hold of this word of exhortation, for I have written to you through a short letter. ²³Know that our brother Timothy has been released, with whom if he comes soon I shall see you. ²⁴Greet all the ones leading you and all the saints. Those from Italy salute you. ²⁵Grace be with all of you.

## *The Epistle of*
# JAMES

**1** From James, a servant of God and of the Lord Jesus Christ. Greetings to the twelve tribes scattered across the world. [2]Consider it all joy, my brothers, when you go through various trials. [3]You know that the testing of your faith produces perseverance. [4]Allow your perseverance to complete itself so that you may be perfect and complete, lacking nothing. [5]But if any of you lacks wisdom, let him ask God who gives freely to everyone and doesn't condemn, and it will be given to him. [6]He must believe when he asks and not doubt. Whoever doubts is like a wave of the sea that is driven and tossed by the wind. [7]That man should not think he will receive anything from the Lord. [8]He is a double-minded man, unstable in all his actions.

[9]But let the brother of modest circumstances give praise to God; [10]and let the brother who has much give praise because of his position in the Lord. Like the flowers he, too, will pass away. [11]For as the sun rises with its burning heat, it causes the grass to wither and the beauty of the flowers to fade away. Likewise, the rich man will fade away even as he goes about his business. [12]Blessed is the man who perseveres through his trials for as he passes the test of his faith, he'll receive the crown of life the Lord has promised to those who love him.

[13]No one who is being tempted should say, "I am being tempted by God." For God is not tempted by evil, and He himself tempts no one. [14]But each person is tempted as his own lust lures him away and traps him. [15]Then once lust conceives and gives birth to sin, sin grows up only to cause death.

[16]Don't be deceived my dear brothers! [17]Every good and perfect gift from above comes down from the Father of lights, who does not change as a shifting shadow does. [18]By His own will He brought us into being by His Word of truth, that we might be the first children among all His creatures.

[19]So, dear brothers, everyone should be quick to listen, slow to speak and slow to become angry. [20]For man's anger does not achieve the righteous purpose of God. [21]So then, get rid of all your filthy habits and unethical behavior; instead, be humble and accept the Word God plants in your hearts because it will save you.

[22]Then, be doers of the Word, not just hearers who merely fool themselves. [23]For if anyone is only a hearer of the Word and not a doer, he is like the man who looks at his face in the mirror; [24]once he has looked at himself and goes away, he immediately forgets what he looks like. [25]Yet whoever is absorbed in the perfect Law that gives freedom and continues to dwell in it, not becoming a forgetful hearer but putting it into practice – that person will be blessed in what he does.

[26]If anyone among you seems to be religious, but cannot control his tongue, he is deceived in his heart and his religion is self-serving. [27]Religion that our God and Father considers to be pure and genuine in this: to visit orphans and widows in their hardship and to keep oneself from being corrupted by the world.

2 My brothers, as believers in our Lord Jesus Christ, the Lord of glory, don't show favoritism toward people. ²Suppose a man in beautiful clothes and fine jewelry were to come into your meeting and a man in ragged clothes were also to come. ³If you give the man in the fine clothes special attention by saying, "Sit in the best seat," but then say to the poor man, "You stand over there or sit here on the floor at my feet," ⁴do you not show favoritism among yourselves by becoming judges with evil motives?

⁵Listen up, my beloved brothers! Didn't God choose the poor of this world to be rich in faith and to inherit the kingdom which He promised to those who love him? ⁶But you dishonor the poor man! Isn't it the rich who intimidate you by dragging you off to court? ⁷Aren't they the ones who speak evil of the good name you have been given?

⁸However, you will do well if you live according to God's commandment: "Love your neighbor as yourself." ⁹But if you show favor to some, you sin and are convicted by the Law as lawbreakers. ¹⁰And whoever breaks even one part of the Law is actually guilty of breaking all the Law. ¹¹For the same One who said, "Do not commit adultery," also said, "Do not murder." If you do not commit adultery, but do murder someone, you still break the Law. ¹²So speak and act as people being judged by the Law of freedom. ¹³For God's judgment will not show mercy to the one who has not shown mercy; but mercy wins over judgment.

¹⁴My brothers – what good is it for someone to say he has faith, but has no works to prove it? Can that kind of faith save him? ¹⁵For instance, if a brother or sister is without clothes and doesn't have food to eat each day, ¹⁶and someone among you says, "Peace be with you, and may you keep warm and eat well," but the person does doesn't give them what they need, what good is that? 17It's the same with faith – without actions behind it, it is dead my itself.

¹⁸But someone will say, "You have faith, and I have actions. Show me your faith without actions, and I will show you my faith by what I do." ¹⁹You believe there is one God, and that is good. But even the demons believe that and tremble! ²⁰Are you just foolish, or are you willing to see that faith without actions is worthless? ²¹For example, when our father Abraham offered his son Isaac on the altar, didn't his actions prove his faith in God? ²²You can see that his faith and actions worked together and through his actions, his faith was made complete. ²³And the Scripture came true which says, "Abraham believed God, and because of his faith God considered him blameless." So, Abraham was called God's friend. ²⁴All of you should see, then, how someone makes himself right with God by the actions of his faith, and not by faith alone.

²⁵In the same way the prostitute, Rahab, was put right with God by her actions when she welcomed the messengers, then helped them escape on another road. ²⁶Therefore, just as the body without the spirit is dead, faith without works is dead, also.

3 Now, beloved brothers, not many of you should become teachers since you know that we who teach will be judged more strictly. ²For we all stumble in many ways, and if anyone does not stumble in what he says, he is perfect, able to control his entire body as well. ³When we put bits into the mouths of horses in order to make them obey us, we are able to direct their whole body, too. ⁴Or think about ships. As big as they are being driven

by forceful winds, they are steered by a very small rudder to go wherever the captain wants to go. ⁵And so it is with the tongue – though it is a small part of the body, it can brag of great things! Think about how a huge forest can be set on fire by just a tiny flame. ⁶The tongue is like that tiny flame. It is a world of evil among the parts of the body and can spread evil through our entire being, setting on fire the course of our whole lives with a fire that comes from Hell itself. ⁷Man can tame and has tamed all creatures such as wild animals, birds, reptiles, and fish. ⁸But no man can tame the tongue. It is an uncontrollable evil, full of deadly poison. ⁹With it we thank our Lord and Father, and with it we also curse men, who are made in God's likeness. ¹⁰Out of the same mouth come blessing and cursing! My beloved brothers, this should not be! ¹¹Can one spring of water send out both fresh and bitter water from the same opening? ¹²Or is a fig tree able to bear olives, my beloved brothers? Neither can salty water produce fresh water.

¹³Who is wise and understanding among you? Let him show it by his good behavior seen in his works done in humility and wisdom. ¹⁴But if you have bitterness and jealousy in your heart, do not be proud and lie against the truth. ¹⁵This type of wisdom is not from heaven above; rather, it is from the world, making it unspiritual and demonic. ¹⁶For where there is jealousy and selfishness, there is also disorder and every kind of evil. ¹⁷But the wisdom from above is first of all pure. It is also peaceful, gentle, and reasonable, full of compassion producing good deeds. Finally, it is without hypocrisy and prejudice. ¹⁸And the fruit of righteousness is harvested in peace by those who plant in peace.

**4** What causes all the fights and quarrels among you? Aren't they caused by your demands for pleasure which is constantly your body's desire? ²You want something and cannot have it, so you murder and covet. When you don't get what you want, you quarrel and fight. You do not have what you want because you do not ask God. ³And when you ask you do not receive because your motives are wrong, desiring something only for your own pleasure. ⁴You adulterous people, don't you know that friendship with the world puts you in opposition with God? In other words, whoever wants to be a friend of the world makes himself an enemy of God. ⁵Do you think that the Scripture is meaningless that says, "The natural spirit that God placed in us tends toward envy"? ⁶But God's grace is even stronger. That is why Scripture says, "God resists the proud, but gives grace to the humble."

⁷For this reason, submit yourselves to God. Actively resist the devil, and he will flee from you. ⁸Come near to God, and He will come near to you. Wash your hands, you sinners! And purify your hearts, you double-minded. ⁹Be sorrowful, mourn, and weep. Turn your laughter into mourning and your joy to gloom. ¹⁰Humble yourselves before the Lord, and He will lift you up.

¹¹Beloved brothers, don't slander one another. If you slander and judge your brother, you also slander and judge the Law. And if you judge the Law, you are not obeying it, but being the judge of it. ¹²God is the only Lawgiver and Judge, the One who is able to save and destroy. But who are you to judge your neighbor?

¹³Now, some of you say, "Today or tomorrow, we will go to a certain city, stay there a year, go into business and make a lot of money." ¹⁴You don't know what will happen in your life tomorrow! Your life is like a thin fog: it is here momentarily, then it is gone. ¹⁵This prayer

of faith will heal the one who is sick, and the Lord will raise him up; if he has sinned, he will be forgiven. ¹⁶Therefore, confess your sins to one another and pray for one another so that all of you may be healed. The active prayer of a man of integrity is powerfully effective. ¹⁷Elijah was a man just like us. He prayed earnestly for it not to rain, and it didn't rain for three and a half years. ¹⁸When he prayed again it poured rain, and the earth produced its crops.

¹⁹My beloved brothers, if anyone among you strays from the truth, and another one brings him back again, ²⁰remember this: whoever turns a sinner from the error of his way will save him from death and cover a multitude of sins.

# *The First Epistle of* PETER

**1** This is being written by Jesus' apostle Peter, to God's people who are scattered throughout the countries of Pontus, Galatia, Cappadocia, Asia and Bithynia. ²These people have been specially selected, and their acceptance was pre-planned by God the Father, and they were set apart through the work of the Holy Spirit. This resulted in their obedience and sprinkling by the blood of Jesus Christ. May God's unearned favor and peace be continually upon you.

³God, the Father of our Lord Jesus Christ, is to be praised for being so merciful as to have given us a new birth, which provided for us a hope of never ending life through the means of Jesus Christ's return from the dead. ⁴Through Him we have an inheritance that cannot be corrupted or contaminated, and will never disappear; it is reserved in Heaven for you. ⁵Through God's power you are protected by your faith, so that you can expect to be saved in the end. ⁶Because of this you can be very joyous, even though it is necessary for you to have suffered many trials for a little while. ⁷But these will only test your faith, which is more valuable than gold which, though refined by fire, eventually perishes. Your faith, however will endure and eventually prove to be praiseworthy and honorable when Jesus returns. ⁸Although you have not seen Jesus, you still love Him and believe in Him, and this causes you to have an indescribable, glorious joy. ⁹Your faith will finally bring about the salvation of your souls.
¹⁰The prophets of old, who spoke of this salvation, asked about and searched diligently concerning the unearned favor God provided for you people. ¹¹They studied their own prophecies to learn what, or which, person or time the Holy Spirit in them pointed to, in predicting the sufferings of Christ and the glories yet to come. ¹²It was revealed to these prophets that you people, not they, were the ones being ministered to in the matters now being announced to you by those who preached the Gospel to you by the Holy Spirit, who was sent from Heaven. This message contained things which angels would like to look into.

¹³So, gather your thoughts together for action, take control of yourselves and focus your hope completely on God's unearned favor, which will be brought to you by Jesus Christ when He returns. ¹⁴As obedient children, do not pattern your lives after the evil desires you formerly had when you were ignorant, ¹⁵but according to the Holy One, who called you, God, you people also should become holy, separated for God's service in all your conduct, ¹⁶because it is written, "You shall be holy, separated from sin, even as I am holy." ¹⁷And if you call upon God as your Father, who judges each person's work impartially, then conduct yourselves during the time you spend in this life showing reverence to God. ¹⁸You should know that you were bought back from Satan, from your useless way of life, inherited from your forefathers, not with such perishable things as silver and gold, ¹⁹but with the precious blood of Christ, who represents an unblemished lamb, without defect. ²⁰For Christ was previously known by God, even before the world was created, yet was not fully revealed for your benefit until these final times. ²¹It is through Christ, whom God raised from the dead and honored, that you people have become believers in God, so that your faith and hope could rest in God.

[22]Since you have purified your souls by your obedience to the truth, the Gospel message, which produces a genuine love for your brothers, now you should have this kind of fervent, heartfelt love for one another. [23]You have experienced new birth, not from seed that can decay, but from seed than cannot decay, through the living and enduring Word of God. [24]For all forms of flesh are similar to grass, and all the splendor of a person's flesh is like the flower which blossoms from the grass. But as with grass, a person's flesh withers, and its flower, his splendor, falls off. [25]But the Word of the Lord continues to live on and on forever. And this Word is the good news that was preached to you people.

2 Therefore, you should put out of your lives all malice, bad attitudes, and all deceit and hypocrisy, and all envy and unwholesome talk. [2]So, like newly born babies, you should desire the genuine, spiritual mile, God's Word, so that by it you may grow toward final salvation, [3]since you have experienced the goodness of the Lord, that the Lord is good.

[4]You should come to Him, who is a living Stone, rejected by people, but chosen as precious in God's sight. [5]And you yourselves are also like living stones, being constructed into a spiritual house. For you are like holy priests who offer spiritual sacrifices that are acceptable to God through Jesus Christ. [6]For it says in the Scripture, "Look, I am placing a stone in the city of Zion, Jerusalem. It is a specially selected, very valuable cornerstone. And the person who trusts in Him, the One represented by this stone will never have to suffer shame because of unforgiven sin being brought up against him." [7]To those of you who believe in Him then, this "Stone" is very precious. But to those who do not believe, "The stone which those in charge of the building project have rejected has been made the principal stone for aligning the whole structure." [8]And it also says, that He would be "A stone that people would stumble over and a rock over which they would trip and fall." The way they stumble is by disobeying the Gospel message. They were destined though not forced to do this.

[9]But you people are especially chosen by God; you are a royal body of priests; you are a nation especially set apart for God's use; you are a people who belong exclusively to God, that you may express the virtues of the One who called you out of darkness, of sin and error, and into His marvelous light, righteousness and truth. [10]At one time you Gentiles were not a chosen people, but now you are God's special people. Once you had not received His mercy, but now you have received it.

[11]My dearly loved ones, I urge you, as a people who are foreigners and strangers in this world, do not give in to sinful desires, which wage war against the soul. [12]You should live such good lives before unconverted Gentiles, so that even though they accuse you of being evildoers, by seeing your good deeds, they will be led to honor God for you on the day He visits us again to bring judgment.

[13]Submit yourselves to every authority set up by people for the Lord's sake. Submit to a king as the highest authority, [14]or to governors who are appointed by him to punish wrongdoers, and to commend those who do right. [15]For it is God's will that, by doing good, you should put to silence the ignorant talk and actions of foolish people. [16]As servants of God, you should live as free people, but do not use this freedom to cover up your wrongdoing. [17]Show proper respect for everyone. Love your Christian brothers and sisters. Have an awe-

inspiring respect for God. Show honor to the king.

¹⁸Slaves, submit yourselves to your masters and show them respect, not just the ones who are good to you and treat you well, but also to those who are harsh toward you. ¹⁹For those of you who put up with such suffering unjustly, because of your close relationship to God, are to be commended. ²⁰But it is no credit to you if you put up with a beating you deserve. But if you patiently tolerate suffering for doing good, this is pleasing to God. ²¹After all this is what you were called to do, because Christ also suffered for you, leaving you an example, so that you would follow in His steps. ²²For He neither sinned nor used deceitful words. ²³When He was spoken to with harsh insults, He did not reply in the same way. When He was made to suffer, He did not threaten His tormentors, but instead entrusted Himself to God, whom He knew would make a righteous judgment in the matter. ²⁴Jesus took upon Himself our sins when His body was placed upon the cross so that we, through dying to, giving up, the sinful life, would live for righteousness. You were healed from your sins by His being brutally treated. ²⁵For you people were wandering away like sheep, but have now returned to the Shepherd and Overseer of your souls.

3 In the same way that Jesus was submissive, you wives should submit yourselves to your own husbands so that, even though they may not obey the Gospel message they have heard they may, without your talking to them about it, ²be won by observing your godly and respectful behavior. ³Do not let your adornment be the decorations of the physical body, such as elaborate hair-dos, the wearing of golden jewelry and the wearing of stunning outfits. ⁴But the kind of adornment you should display is that of the inner person, with its enduring qualities of a meek and calm spirit, which are extremely valuable in God's eyes. ⁵For this is the way holy women in ancient times decorated themselves. Their hope was in God and they were known for being in subjection to their own husbands. ⁶Sarah obeyed her husband Abraham, even referring to him in respectful terms such as "sir." You wives are her spiritual descendants if you also do what is right and are not fearful that things in life will turn out badly.

⁷You husbands, in the same way, should live with your wives in an understanding way, recognizing their feminine nature as being physically weaker than yours, and showing special honor to them because of it. Realize that sharing your lives together is a gracious gift from God. If you have the right relationship with them it will help avoid problems in your prayer lives.

⁸Now to summarize: All of you should think alike. Be sympathetically understanding toward one another. Be loving toward your brothers and sisters. Be tender-hearted and humble-minded. ⁹Do not repay a wrong action with another wrong action, nor abusive language with additional abuse, but rather be a blessing to one another. For the purpose of your being called by God was so that you could receive a blessing from Him eventually. ¹⁰"The person who loves his life and wants to have happy days, should avoid saying anything bad or deceptive. ¹¹He should turn away from wrong living and do what is good. He should desire peace and do whatever it takes to maintain it. ¹²For the Lord's eyes see what the righteous person does and He hears their earnest prayers, but the Lord looks with disapproval on the person who does wrong."

[13] And who do you think would try to hurt you if you become enthusiastic for doing what is right? [14] But even if you have to suffer for doing what was right, you still have God's blessing. So, do not be afraid of the threats of your persecutors, and do not let it worry you. [15] But instead, set aside a place in your hearts where Christ is in full control as Lord, and be prepared always to give a suitable reply to every person who asks you for a reason why you have an inner hope. But be sure you do it in a meek and respectful way, however. [16] May your conscience be able to so approve of your conduct that, even if you are ridiculed, those doing it will eventually have to be ashamed of themselves for criticizing your good Christian behavior. [17] For, if it is God's will that you should suffer, it is better for you that it be on account of doing right than doing wrong. [18] For Christ suffered once for people's sins to be forgiven. It was the case of a righteous Man suffering for unrighteous people, so that He could bring you or, "us" to God for salvation. Though He, Jesus, was put to death physically, He was brought back to life by the Holy Spirit. [19] It was by the Holy Spirit that He went to preach to the now departed spirits of pre-Flood people who are now in prison, Hades. [20] These people had disobeyed Noah's preaching, back when God's patience waited for them to repent, during the days of Noah, when the ship was being constructed. It was by that means, the ship floating them to safety through the Flood waters, that a few persons, eight of them, were saved from destruction through water. [21] This water prefigured immersion into Christ, which now also saves you, not by removing dirt from the physical body, but by serving as an appeal or "pledge" to God for a clear conscience through the raising of Jesus Christ from the dead. [22] He has now gone to heaven, and is seated at the right side of God, where the angels and other authorities and powers have been subjected to Him.

4 Therefore, since Christ has suffered physically, you people should fortify yourselves with the same attitude He had. For the person who has suffered physically, in standing for Christ, has quit sinning. [2] So then, you should no longer live the rest of your lives to satisfy the sinful desires of your body, but to do what God wants. [3] For the time you have already spent in the past as Gentile unbelievers was long enough to have practiced unrestrained, indecent conduct, improper sexual cravings, riotous living, wild parties, drunken orgies and disgusting idol worship. [4] Now, those people you used to run around with cannot understand why you have stopped living such wasteful lives, so they just "badmouth" you. [5] But, they will have to answer to God, who will judge both those who are now alive and those who have already died, for the way they have lived. [6] This is the purpose that the Gospel was preached to those who have died physically for the faith. It was so that, even though they had been judged physically by suffering death at the hands of men, they could still live spiritually in the presence of God.

[7] But the end of everything as far as your lives are concerned is near, so be sensible, and sober so as to be prayerful. [8] Above everything else, have a warm love for one another, for such a love keeps many sins from occurring between you. [9] Extend hospitality to one another without complaining that you have to. [10] As each of you has received a gift from God, you should make use of it in the body, so that you will be good caretakers of the many unearned ways that God favors you. [11] If someone's gift is speaking, he should be sure to say only what God wants him to. If a person's gift is serving, he should do so by the strength provided by

God who supplies all such gifts. This is so that, in using all gifts, God may be honored through Jesus Christ. To whom belongs honor and power forever and ever. May it be so.

[12]Loved ones, do not be surprised that you people are undergoing extremely difficult trials, as though something strange were happening to you, for it is only a test of your faith. [13]You should rejoice that you are sharing some of what Christ has suffered, so that you will get to rejoice all the more when He returns in His splendor. [14]If you are spoken against for being Christians, you have God's blessing, because His glorious Holy Spirit rests upon you to provide comfort. [15]However, you should not have to suffer for murdering, stealing, doing evil or interfering in the affairs of others. [16]But if a person should have to suffer because he is a Christian, he should not be ashamed of it, but instead, he should bring honor to God by wearing the name of Christ. [17]For the time has now come for the house of God the church, to begin receiving judgment by undergoing persecution, and if it starts with us Christians, what will be the ultimate end of people who do not obey the Gospel of God? [18]And if people who are trying to do right, Christians, are saved through suffering such difficulties, where will the ungodly and sinful person end up, if not in hell? [19]Therefore, those who are allowed to suffer in harmony with God's permissive will, should commit their should to a trustworthy Creator, who will take everything into account, while they go on trying to do what is right.

5 So, the elders in the various places where you live are to receive the following exhortation. I too, am an elder and have witnessed the sufferings of Christ, and am also assured of partaking of the glorious salvation, that will someday be revealed. [2]You should serve as shepherds of God's flock, the church, among whom you minister, providing careful oversight of the people, not because you feel forced to, but because you want to, as this is in accordance with the way God wants it to be. Do not serve as elders simply out of a desire for the income you receive, but because your heart is in it. [3]Do not act as dictators over the people you are assigned to care for, but rather serve as examples of how they ought to live. [4]And when the Supreme Shepherd, Jesus, comes back, you will receive for your effort a glorious crown of reward that will never fade away.

[5]And in the same way, you younger Christians should be respectfully submissive to the older ones. And all of you should be willing to humbly serve one another, for God stands opposed to the efforts of proud people, but extends His unearned favor to those who serve with humility. [6]Therefore, be humble in your actions before God's powerful authority, so that you may be exalted by Him at the proper time. [7]Place all your anxious cares upon God in prayer because He genuinely cares about you. [8]Be sensible and alert; your enemy the Devil is prowling around like a roaring, hungry lion looking for someone to kill and eat. [9]You should withstand his efforts by maintaining a strong faith in God, remembering that your Christian brothers in the rest of the world are experiencing and enduring suffering similar to yours.

[10]And the God who bestows every unearned favor upon His people, who invited you to partake of His eternal splendor through Christ Jesus, will restore, confirm, strengthen and stabilize you people in the faith, after you have gone through a brief time of suffering. [11]May God have total authority over everything including your circumstances forever. May it be so.

[12]This brief message is being inscribed or delivered by Silvanus, whom I consider to be a faithful brother. In it I am exhorting you and giving testimony that it is a message about

God's genuine unearned favor upon you. So, continue to follow and obey what it says. ¹³Your sister church here in Babylon, also chosen by God as you have been, sends her greetings along with my spiritual son Mark. ¹⁴Greet one another lovingly, expressing it with a kiss of brotherly affection.

May there be peace of heart to all those there who are in the fellowship of Christ.

## The Second Epistle of
# PETER

1 Simon Peter, a servant and Apostle of Jesus Christ. To those who have obtained a precious faith like ours through the righteousness of our God and Savior Jesus Christ. To those who have obtained a precious faith like ours through the righteousness of our God and Savior Jesus Christ. ²May grace and peace be multiplied to you through the knowledge of God and Jesus our Lord. ³All the things for life and godliness have been given to us by His divine power through the knowledge of the One who called us by His own glory and excellence. ⁴Through these He has given His precious and very great promises to us. In order that through them you might become partners of the divine nature, escaping the corruption in the world caused by lust.'

⁵For this reason, make every effort to provide your faith with moral excellence; and to moral excellence, knowledge; ⁶and to knowledge, self-control; and to self-control, patient endurance; and to patient endurance, godliness; ⁷and to godliness, brotherly kindness; and to brotherly kindness, love. ⁸For if these things are in your possession and are increasing, they will cause you to be neither useless nor fruitless in your knowledge of our Lord Jesus Christ. ⁹For if a person does not possess these things, he is blind and shortsighted forgetting that his past sins have been cleansed. ¹⁰Therefore, brothers, zealously make certain of your calling and election. For you will never stumble if you do these things. ¹¹Thus, an entrance into the eternal kingdom of our Lord and Savior Jesus Christ will be richly provided for you.

¹² Therefore, I intend to always remind you of these things although you know them and are established in the truth you currently have. ¹³I consider it right, as long as I am in this body, to stir you up by way of reminder, ¹⁴because I know that soon, my body will be removed, as our Lord Jesus Christ made clear to me. ¹⁵And I will be zealous to make sure you recall these things any time after my death.

¹⁶For we did not follow cleverly devised myths when we made known to you the power and coming of our Lord Jesus Christ, but we were eyewitnesses of His majesty. ¹⁷For when He received from God the Father honor and glory, a voice came to Him by the Majestic Glory: "This is my beloved Son with whom I am well pleased." ¹⁸And we heard this voice that came from Heaven with Him on the holy mountain.

¹⁹And we have the prophetic Word made certain, which you would do well to pay attention to, as to a light shining in a dark place, until the day shines and the morning star rises in your hearts. ²⁰First of all, you must know that no prophecy of Scripture happened by one's own interpretation, ²¹because no prophecy came about through the will of man, but men spoke from God as they were brought along by the Holy Spirit.

2 But false prophets arose among the people, just as there will be among you false teachers who will secretly introduce destructive heresies, even denying the Master who bought them, bringing on themselves swift destruction. ²And many will follow their depravity and because of them the way of the truth will be blasphemed.

³And in their greed they will take advantage of you with false words; for their judgment from long ago has not lingered, and their destruction has been asleep. ⁴For if God did not spare angels when they sinned, but sent them to Hell, keeping them in gloomy pits until the judgment; ⁵and if He did spare the ancient world, but preserved Noah, a preacher of righteousness, with seven others, when He brought a flood upon the world of the ungodly; ⁶and if He condemned and destroyed the cities of Sodom and Gomorrah by reducing them to ashes, He even made them an example for those who would be ungodly.

⁷And if He rescued righteous Lot, who was tormented by the sensual conduct of the lawless ⁸for what that righteous man saw and heard by living among them day after day, was tormented in his righteous soul by their godless deeds, ⁹then the Lord knows how to rescue the godly from temptation, and keep the unrighteous in punishment until the day of judgment, ¹⁰and especially those focusing in the corrupt desire of the flesh and scorn authority. Bold and arrogant, they are not afraid to blaspheme glorious angelic beings; ¹¹whereas angels, who are greater in strength and power, do not bring a slanderous judgment against them before the Lord. ¹²But these men, like irrational animals, creatures of instinct, born to be captured and destroyed, blaspheme in matters they do not understand, will be destroyed in the same destruction of them, ¹³suffering wrong as wages of doing wrong. They consider it pleasure to indulge in the daytime. They are stains and blemishes, reviling in their deceptions, feasting along with you. ¹⁴They have eyes full of adultery and never cease to sin. They entice weak souls. They have a heart trained in greed, and are accursed children. ¹⁵Forsaking the straight way, they have gone astray by following the way of Balaam, the son Beor, who loved the wages of wickedness, ¹⁶but was rebuked for his own evil doing; a donkey incapable of speech, spoke with a human voice and restrained the madness of the prophet. ¹⁷They are waterless springs and mists driven by a storm; for whom the gloom of darkness has been reserved. ¹⁸For, proclaiming arrogant and empty words, they, by the sensual desires of the flesh, entice those who have barely escaped from ones living in error. ¹⁹They promised them freedom, while they themselves are slaves of corruption; for by what a man succumbs to, to this he becomes a slave. ²⁰For if, after they have escaped the corruption of the world by the knowledge of the Lord and Savior Jesus Christ, they become entangled again by them and have been defeated, the last state has become worse for them than the first. ²¹For it would be better for them not to have known the way of righteousness, than having known it and then turning from the holy commandment delivered to them. ²²It has happened to them according to the true proverb: "The dog returns to his own vomit" and "The washed sow returns to rolling in the mud."

3 This now, beloved, the second letter I am writing to you, and in both of them I am stirring up your sincere mind by way of reminder: ²that you should remember the previously spoken words of the holy prophets and the commandment of the Lord and Savior spoken through your apostles.

³First of all, you must know this – that in the last days scoffers will come, scoffing and following their own desires ⁴and saying: "Where is the promise of His coming? For from the day when the fathers died, all things have remained the same from the beginning of creation." ⁵For they purposely forget that by the Word of God, the heavens existed long ago and the earth was formed by water and through water, ⁶through which the world then was

flooded with water and destroyed. ⁷By the same Word, the present heavens and earth have been stored up for fire, being kept until the day of judgment and destruction of ungodly men.

⁸But, beloved, do not forget this one thing: that with the Lord one day is as if a thousand years and a thousand years as one day.

⁹The Lord is not slow about His promise as some consider slowness, but is patient with you, not wanting any to perish but everyone to reach repentance. ¹⁰But the day of the Lord will come like a thief, in which the heavens will pass away with a roar, and the elements will be destroyed with fire, and the earth and its works will be laid bare.

¹¹Since all these things will be destroyed in this manner, what sort of people ought you to be in holy lives and godliness, ¹²waiting and speeding up the coming of the Day of God which on the account of that day will be destroyed by fire and the elements will melt in the burning? ¹³But according to His promise we look for a new heaven and a new earth in which righteousness dwell. ¹⁴Therefore, beloved, since you are looking for these things, make every effort to be found by Him spotless and blameless and in peace. ¹⁵And consider the patience of our Lord to be salvation; as also our beloved brother Paul wrote to you through the wisdom given to him, ¹⁶as also in all his letters speaking about these things in them, in which some things are hard to understand, which the ignorant and unstable twist, as they do with the rest of the Scriptures to their own destruction. ¹⁷You, therefore, beloved, knowing this in advance, be on your guard so that you will not be carried away by the deception of lawless men and fall from your own stableness. ¹⁸But grow in the grace and knowledge of our Lord and Savior Jesus Christ. To Him be the glory both now and forever. Amen.

## *The First Epistle of*
# JOHN

**1** That which was from the beginning, that which we have heard, that which we have seen with our eyes, that which we have beheld and our hands touched concerning the Word of Life. ²And the life was manifested and we have seen and testify and announce to you the eternal life that was with the Father and was manifested to us. ³That which we have seen and have heard we announce to you also in order that you also may have fellowship with us and yet our fellowship is with the Father and with His Son Jesus Christ. ⁴And these things we write in order that our joy may be made full.
⁵And this is the message which we have heard from Him and announce to you that God is light and in Him is not any darkness at all. ⁶If we say that we have fellowship with Him and walk in the darkness, we lie and do not the truth. ⁷But if we walk in the light as He is in the light, we have fellowship with one another and the blood of Jesus, His Son, cleanses us from every sin. ⁸If we say that we have no sin we deceive ourselves and the truth is not in us. ⁹If we confess our sins He is faithful and righteous with the result that He will forgive our sins and cleanse us from all unrighteousness. ¹⁰If we say that we have not sinned we make Him a liar and His Word is not in us.

**2** My little children, I am writing these things to you in order that you should not commit an act of sin. And if anyone commits an act of sin. We have an advocate with the Father, Jesus Christ, the righteous one. ²And He is the satisfaction for our sins, but not concerning ours only, but also concerning the sins of the whole world.
³And by this we know that we have known Him, if we go on keeping His commandments. ⁴The one who says, "I have known Him" and yet does not go on keeping His commandments, is a liar, and the truth is not in this one. ⁵But whoever keeps His Word, truly in this one the love of God has been made perfect. By this we know that we are in Him. ⁶He who says that he is abiding in Him ought, just as that one walked, also to walk himself.
⁷Beloved I am not writing a new commandment to you but an old commandment which you had from the beginning, the old commandment is the Word which you heard. ⁸Again I write to you a new commandment which is true in Him and in you because the darkness is passing away and the true light is already shining. ⁹The one who is saying that he is in the light and is hating his brother is in the darkness until now. ¹⁰The one who is loving his brother abides in the light and there is no cause of stumbling in him. ¹¹But the one who is hating his brother is in darkness and is walking in darkness and does not know where he is going because the darkness has blinded his eyes.
¹²I am writing to you little children because your sins have been forgiven to you through His name. ¹³I am writing to you fathers because you have known the One who is from the beginning. I am writing to you, young men, because you have conquered the evil one. ¹⁴I have written to you little children because you have known the Father. I have written to you fathers because you have known the One who is from the beginning. I have written to you

young men because you are strong and the Word of God remains in you and you have conquered the evil one. [15]Do not go on loving the world nor the things in the world. If anyone loves the world the love of the Father is not in him. [16]Because everything in the world the lust which is of the flesh and the lust of the eyes and the boast of life is not of the Father. But it is of the world. [17]And the world and its lust is passing away. But the one who is doing the will of God abides forever.

[18]Little children it is the last hour and just as you have heard that the antichrist is coming and now many antichrists have come to pass, wherefore we know that it is the last hour. [19]They went out from us but they were not really of us. For if they had been of us they would have remained with us but they went out in order that it might show that they are not of us.

[20]And you are having an anointing from the Holy One and you all know this. [21]I have not written to you because you do not know the truth but because you know it and every lie is not of the truth. [22]Who is the liar except the one who denies that Jesus is the Christ. This is the antichrist, the one who denies the Father and the Son. [23]Everyone denying the Son, has not the Father. The one who confesses the Son also has the Father. [24]Let that which you have heard from the beginning abide in you. If what you heard from the beginning abides in you; you also will abide in the Son and in the Father. [25]And this is the promise which He promised to us, eternal life. [26]These things I have written to you concerning the ones who are trying to lead you astray. [27]And the anointing which you received from Him abides in you and you do not have the need that anyone should teach you but as the same anointing teaches you about all things and is true and is not a lie and just as He has taught you, abide in Him.

[28]And now little children remain in Him in order that whenever He shall be made manifest we may have confidence and not be put to shame by Him at His coming. [29]If you know that He is righteous you know also that everyone who is doing righteousness has been born of Him.

3 See what kind of love the Father has given to us in that we may be called the children of God and we are. For this cause the world has not known us because it did not know Him. [2]Now beloved, we are children of God and it is not yet been manifested what we shall be. We know when He shall be made manifest, we shall be like Him, because we shall see Him just as He is. [3]And everyone who has this hope set on Him purifies himself just as that One is pure.

[4]And everyone who is practicing sin is also practicing lawlessness and sin is lawlessness. [5]And you know that One was manifested in order that He might take away sins and in Him there is no sin. [6]Everyone who goes on abiding in Him does not continually sin. Everyone who goes on sinning, has not seen Him nor known Him. [7]Little children do not let anyone go on deceiving you. The one who is doing righteousness is righteous just as that One is righteous. [8]The one who is habitually doing sin is of the devil because the devil habitually sins from the beginning. For this purpose the Son of God has been made manifest in order that he might destroy the work of the devil. [9]Everyone who has been begotten of God is not continually doing sin because His seed remains in Him and he is not able to go on sinning because he is begotten of God. [10]By this, the children of God are manifested and the children

of the devil, everyone who is not doing righteousness is not of God also the one is not loving his brother. ¹¹For this is the message which you heard from the beginning, that we should go on loving one another, ¹²not as Cain who was of the evil one and murdered his brother. And for what reason did he murder him? Because his deeds were evil, but those of his brother were righteous. ¹³And do not marvel brothers if the world hates you. ¹⁴We know that we have passed out of death into life because we love the brethren. He who does not continually love, abides in death. ¹⁵Everyone who is hating his brother is a murderer and you know that no murderer has eternal life abiding in him. ¹⁶By this we have known love because that One laid down His life for us and we ought to lay down our lives for the brethren. ¹⁷But whoever has the world's goods and observes his brother in need and closes his heart against him, how does the love of God abide in him. ¹⁸Little children let us not love by means of word neither by means of tongue, but in deed and in truth. ¹⁹By this we shall know that we are of the truth and our heart shall rest before Him. ²⁰Because if our heart condemns us; God is greater than our hearts and He knows all things. ²¹Beloved if our heart does not condemn us we are having confidence before God. ²²And whatever we might ask we will receive from Him because we keep His commandments and we do the things that are pleasing in His sight. ²³And this is His commandment, that we should believe in the name of His Son Jesus Christ and you love one another, just as He gave commandment to us. ²⁴And the one who continually keeps His commandments abides in Him and He in him. And we know by this that He is abiding in us, from the Spirit which He has given us.

**4** Beloved do not believe every spirit but test the spirits to see if they are of God because many false prophets have gone out into the world. ²By this you know the Spirit of God, every spirit who confesses Jesus Christ has come in flesh from God. ³And every spirit who does not confess Jesus is not from God and this is the spirit of antichrist of which you have heard that he is coming and now he is already in the world. ⁴You are from God little children and have overcome them because greater is the One in you than the one in the world. ⁵They are from the world, on account of this, they are speaking from the world and the world hears them. ⁶We are from God. He who knows God, hears us; He who is not from God doesn't hear us. Bu this we know the spirit of truth and the spirit of error. ⁷Beloved let us love one another, because this love is from God. And everyone who is loving has been begotten of God, and knows God. ⁸The one who is not loving has not known God because God is love. ⁹By this was manifested the love of God in us that one God has sent His only Son into the world in order that we might live through Him. ¹⁰In this is love, not that we have loved God but that He loved us and sent His Son a satisfaction for our sins. ¹¹Beloved if God so loved us, we ourselves ought to love one another. ¹²No one at any time has seen God. If we love one another God abides in us and His love is made perfect in us. ¹³By this we have known that we abide in Him and He in us because He has given to us out of His Spirit.

¹⁴And we have seen and witness that the Father has sent the Son as Savior of the world. ¹⁵Whoever confesses that Jesus is the Son of God; God abides in him and he in God. ¹⁶And we have known and have believed the love which God has in us. God is love and the one who is abiding in love abides in God and God abides in him. ¹⁷By this the love has been made perfect among us in order that we may have confidence in the day of judgment because just as that One is, we also are in this world. ¹⁸There is no fear in love but perfect love casts out fear because fear has a penalty, but the one who fears has not been perfected in love. ¹⁹We love because He first loved us. ²⁰If someone says "I love God" and hates his brother, he is a liar, for the one who does not love the brother whom he has seen; is not able to love God whom he has not seen. ²¹And this commandment we have from Him in order that the one who loves God should love his brother also.

5 Whoever believes that Jesus is the Christ has been born of God. And whoever loves God loves the one born of Him. ²In this we know that we love the children of God whenever we love God and we do His commandments. ³For this is the love of God that we keep His commandments and His commandments are not burdensome. ⁴Because all that has been born of God overcomes the world and this is the victory which overcomes the world, our faith. ⁵But who is the one who overcomes the world except the one believing that Jesus is the Son of God.
⁶This is the one who came through water and blood Jesus Christ not in water only but in water and in blood and the Spirit is the witness that the Spirit is true. ⁷Because there are three witnesses. ⁸The Spirit, and the water and the blood and the three are one. ⁹If we receive the witness of men, the witness of God is greater because this is the witness of God that he has testified concerning His Son.
¹⁰The one who is believing the Son of God has the witness in himself. The one who is not believing God has made Him a liar because He has not believed the witness which God has testified concerning His Son. ¹¹And the witness is this that eternal life God has given to us and this life is in His Son. ¹²The one having the Son of God has life and the one not having the Son of God does not have the life. ¹³These things I have written to you in order that you may know that you have eternal life, to those believing on the name of the Son of God.
¹⁴And this is the confidence which we are having toward Him that if we should ask anything according to His will, He is hearing us. ¹⁵And if we know that He hears us whatever we ask, we know that we have the requests which we asked from Him. ¹⁶If anyone sees his brother sinning a sin not leading to death, he shall ask and He shall give life to those who are not sinning to death. There is sin leading to death. I am not saying that he should pray about that one. ¹⁷All unrighteousness is sin and there is a sin not to death.
¹⁸We know that everyone who has been born of God is not continually sinning, but he who has been born of God, God keeps him and the evil one, Satan, is not touching him. ¹⁹We absolutely know that we are of God and the whole world is laying in control of the evil one. ²⁰And we know that the Son of God has come and He has given to us an understanding with the result that we know the true One and we are in the true One, in His Son, Jesus Christ. This is the true God and true life eternal. ²¹Little children keep yourselves from the idols.

# *The Second Epistle of* JOHN

¹The elder to the elect lady and her children, whom I love in the truth and not only I, but also all who know the truth. ²For the sake of the truth which remains in us and will be with us forever. ³Grace, mercy, and peace from God the Father and from Jesus Christ, the Father's Son, will be with us in truth and love. ⁴I was overjoyed when I learned that some of your children are living in the truth, just as we have been commanded to do by the Father.

⁵And now, dear lady, I am not writing you a new commandment but the one we have had from the beginning. I ask that we love one another. ⁶And this is love, that we live according to His commandments. This is the commandment, just as you have heard from the beginning, that you should live by it.

⁷For many deceivers have gone out into the world, those who do not confess that Jesus Christ has come in the flesh; this one is the deceiver and the antichrist. ⁸Pay close attention to yourselves so that you do not lose what we worked for so that you may receive a full reward. ⁹Everyone who does not remain in the teaching of Christ, but goes beyond it, does not have God; whoever remains in the teaching has both the Father and the Son.

¹⁰If anyone comes to you and does not bring this teaching, do not receive him into your house and do not give him a greeting. ¹¹For the one who welcomes him shares in his wicked work.

¹²I have many more things to write to you, but will not do so with paper and ink, since I hope to visit and speak to you in person, so that our joy may be complete. ¹³The children of your elect sister greet you.

## *The Third Epistle of*
# JOHN

¹The elder to the beloved, Gaius, whom I love in the truth. ²Beloved I wish in all things you may do well and you may be in health, even as it is well with your soul.

³For I exceedingly rejoiced after the coming of the brothers who testified to your being in the truth and also know you walk in the truth. ⁴I have no greater joy than these things that I hear of – my children walking in the truth. ⁵Beloved, you do a faithful thing whenever you do a work for the brothers, especially when they are strangers, ⁶who testify of your love before the church. You will do well to send them on their way in a manner worthy of God; ⁷for on behalf of Christ they went forth taking no support from the Gentiles. ⁸We therefore ought to support such men, that they may be co-workers with the truth.

⁹I wrote something to the church; but the one loving to be first in the church, Diotrephes, does not acknowledge us. ¹⁰Therefore, if I come, I will remember his works, speaking malicious words and talking nonsense about us, and not being satisfied with these actions only, he does not receive the brothers and he prevents the ones intending to do so and he puts them out of the church. ¹¹Beloved, do not imitate the bad but the good. The one doing good is of God. The one doing bad has not seen God.

¹²Testimony has been given about Demetrius by all and also by the truth itself; also we give testimony, and you know that our testimony is true. ¹³I had many things to write to you but I do not want to write with ink and pen to you. ¹⁴But I am hoping soon to see you and we will speak face to face. ¹⁵Peace to you. Our friends send you their greetings. Greet the friends there, each one by name.

# *The Epistle of* JUDE

¹I, Jude, a servant of Jesus Christ and a brother of James, send this message to the beloved who have been called by God the Father and watched over by Jesus Christ. ²May mercy, peace and love be yours in multiplied proportions.

³Dear ones, while I have been making every effort to write to you about our salvation that we have in common, I have written to you encouraging you to struggle for the faith that was handed over to the believing saints. ⁴For certain men have secretly slipped in, those who in the past have already been recognized and marked for judgment, godless men manipulating the grace of our God into the perverted excuses of excess and even denying our only Lord and Master Jesus Christ. ⁵Now, with this in mind, I want to remind you that after the Lord delivered the people out of the Land of Egypt, He destroyed the ones who did not believe. ⁶And, the angels, who did not keep to their heavenly domain but deserted their own dwelling, are kept in chains for the great Day of Judgment. ⁷In the same way, Sodom and Gomorrah and the cities around them, having given themselves over to sexual perversion, are an example of those who receive eternal punishment through suffering.

⁸Likewise, the fact is that these men, who cannot think about anything other than the flesh, defile the authority of the Lord and reject and slander angelic beings. ⁹And, even Michael, the archangel, when he was arguing with the devil about the body of Moses, did not dare to pronounce stern judgment, but all he said was "the Lord rebuke you." ¹⁰And these men blaspheme those things that they do not understand, and are led astray by what they do grasp as unreasoning animals. ¹¹Woe to these men. It is over for them because they were motivated just like Cain and they yielded to the same kind of error as Balaam and they perished in the rebellion of Korah. ¹²These people horribly distract from your love feasts, eating without fear of the consequences of their behavior. Like waterless clouds they are carried away. As unfruitful trees they are very dead and uprooted. ¹³They are like fierce winds of the sea forming on their own, driven by their shameful deeds, stars forever wandering in the gloom of darkness. ¹⁴But Enoch, who was the seventh generation from Adam, prophesied regarding these people saying, "Behold, the Lord shall come with His tens of thousands of holy ones ¹⁵to judge everyone and to convict all ungodly people of their ungodly works that they have done and all the harsh things the ungodly say about Him." ¹⁶Some of these people are grumblers, complaining passionately and acting and speaking immodestly, as they flatter people for their own selfish reasons.

¹⁷But you, dear ones, are to be reminded of what has been foretold by the apostles of our Lord Jesus Christ. ¹⁸They told you that in later days there will be mockers driven by their own passions and living for ungodliness. ¹⁹These are the ones who create walls between people. They are worldly, without the spirit. ²⁰But you dear brothers are to keep building each other up in your very holy faith by praying in the Spirit. ²¹Keep watch over

yourselves in God's love as you wait expectantly for the mercy of our Lord Jesus Christ unto eternal life. [22]and show mercy to those who are doubting. [23]Save others, snatching them out of the fire and show mercy along with fear all the while hating that their garments are defiled by the flesh.

[24]Now to the One who is able to guard you and keep you from falling into sin and to stand you directly in the presence of His sinless glory unblemished and with exceeding joy [25]to the only God our Savior through Jesus Christ our Lord be credited all glory, greatness, power and authority before all people, from all eternity, now and forever. Amen.

# *The* REVELATION
## *of Jesus Christ*

**1** ¹Jesus Christ unveiled! The message God gave Him to reveal to His servants concerning events which will rapidly unfold. He sent His angel with this sign-filled message to His servant John. ²John then testified to the Word of God, to the testimony of Jesus Christ, and to all that he saw.
³Rich blessedness belongs to he who reads, as well as to those who both hear and keep the words of this message from God, because this time will unfold rapidly. ⁴John, to the seven churches which are in Asia: grace to you and peace from the One who is and who was and who is coming, and from the sevenfold Spirit before His throne, ⁵and from Jesus Christ; the Faithful Witness, the Firstborn from the dead, and the Ruler over the kings of the earth. To Him who continually loves us and has absolved us of our sins in His own blood, ⁶and has made us a kingdom, priests to His God and Father. To Him belongs glory and complete authority into the ages of the ages. Amen. ⁷Look! He is coming with the clouds, and every eye will see and comprehend, even those who pierced Him. And all the tribes of the earth will wail in despair over Him. This will happen! Amen. ⁸"I Am the Alpha and the Omega," says the Lord God, "who is and who was and who is coming, the All Powerful One."
⁹This is John, your brother and partner in suffering, as well as in the kingdom and patience in Jesus. I found myself on the island called Patmos because of the Word of God and giving testimony about Jesus. ¹⁰I found myself in the Spirit on the Lord's Day, and I heard behind me an overpowering voice, like a war trumpet, ¹¹saying, "record promptly in a book whatever you see, and send it to the seven churches: Ephesus, Smyrna, Pergamos, Thyatira, Sardis, Philadelphia, and Laodicia." ¹²Then I turned to see what sort of voice had spoken with me, and having turned I saw seven golden lampstands. ¹³Among these lampstands was someone who looked like the Son of Man. He was dressed in a full-length garment secured at the chest with a golden wrap. ¹⁴His head and hair were like snow-white wool, and His eyes looked like blazing fire. ¹⁵His feet had the appearance of fine brass glowing in a burning furnace. His voice sounded like rushing waters. ¹⁶There were seven stars in His right hand, a sharp two-edged sword came out of His mouth, and His face shone like the brilliance of the direct sun. ¹⁷When I saw Him, I collapsed at His feet as if dead. But then He put His hand on me and told me, "Do not be afraid; I am the first and the last ¹⁸and the living One who became dead, yet look! I am alive into the ages of the ages, and I have complete authority over death and Hades. ¹⁹This being the case, write down the things you have just seen, the things that are presently taking place, and the things that will soon take place after these things; ²⁰"This is the meaning of the seven stars you saw in My right hand, as well as the seven lampstands: The seven stars are messengers of the seven churches, and the seven lampstands you saw are the seven churches."

**2** ¹"Write this to the messenger of the church in Ephesus: 'The One who is holding the seven stars in His hand and is walking among the seven golden lampstands has a message for you. ²I am aware of your works, your exhausting labor, your patient endurance and your intolerance of those who are evil. You have tested those who claim to be apostles and found them to be liars; ³you have diligently continued on with patience and have worked hard for the sake of My name without quitting in weariness. ⁴In spite of this, I hold against you that you have abandoned your original love. ⁵Think about where you were before you fell; return and do what you were doing then before I come and remove your lampstand from its place, unless you return. ⁶This is in your favor, that you hate the actions of the Nicolaitans as much as I do.' ⁷Anybody with ears – listen carefully to what the Spirit is saying to the churches! 'I will give the overcomers the privilege of eating from the tree of life in God's paradise.'"

⁸"Write this to the messenger of the church in Smyrna: 'The One who is first and last, who became dead and then was restored to life has a message for you. ⁹I am aware of the tremendous pressure you face; living in poverty though you are actually rich; ridiculed by those falsely claiming to be Jews, but in reality are Satan's gathering place. ¹⁰Do not fear anything you will suffer. Listen and be assured! The devil is about to put you to the test by throwing you into prison, and this heavy pressure will last for ten days. Become strong in faithfulness, even to the point of death, and I will give you the crown of life.' ¹¹Anybody with ears – listen carefully to what the Spirit is saying to the churches! 'The overcomers will not be hurt by the second death.'"

¹²"Write this to the messenger of the church in Pergamos: 'The One who has the sharp two-edged sword has a message for you: ¹³I am aware of your hard work, and where you live – the place of Satan's rule – and that you hold firmly to My name, not rejecting faith in Me even in the days when Antipas, My faithful witness, who was put to death among you – where Satan lives. ¹⁴In spite of this, I have a few things against you, since you have among you those who hold to the teachings of Balaam, who taught Balak to put an enticement to sin in front of the children of Israel; to eat food sacrificed to idols and to commit sexual immorality. ¹⁵You also have those who adhere to the teaching of the Nicolaitans. ¹⁶Turn back from this or I will come to you rapidly and make war against them with the sword of My mouth.' ¹⁷Anybody with ears – listen carefully to what the Spirit is saying to the churches! 'I will give the overcomer some manna, and I will give him a white stone on which a new name is written which only the recipient knows.'"

¹⁸"Write this to the messenger of the church in Thyatira: 'The Son of God, who has eyes like blazing fire and feet like fine brass glowing in a furnace has a message for you: ¹⁹I am aware of your works, unconditional love, faith, ministry, and your patient endurance; that your recent works are grater than before. ²⁰In spite of this, I have this against you, since you permit that woman Jezebel who says she is a prophetess, to teach and deceive My servants so they commit sexual immorality and eat idol sacrifices; ²¹and I have given her time to repent, and she desires not to turn from her sexual immorality. ²²Watch! I am throwing her and those who share her adulteries with her into a bed of intense suffering unless they turn from what she is doing. ²³I will also strike her children dead, and all the churches will know that I am He who carefully examines the thoughts and motives and will give to each of you according to your works. ²⁴But, this is what I say to those of you in Thyatira, who do not follow this teaching or know "the deep things of Satan," as they say; I will place no other burden on you.

[25] Just hold fast to what you have until I come. [26] I will give authority over the nations to the overcomer and the one who keeps My works to the end. [27] –"He will shepherd them with an iron rod; as the potter's vessels are broken –"as I have received from My Father. [28] I will also give him the morning star.' [29] Anybody with ears – listen carefully to what the Spirit is saying to the churches!"

3 "Write this to the messenger of the church in Sardis: 'The One who has the sevenfold Spirit and the seven stars has a message for you: I am aware of your works, that you have a reputation of being alive – but you are dead. [2] Stand guard! Strengthen what you have left before it dies – because I have not found your works perfect before my God. [3] Because of this you must remember how you received and heard; hang on and repent, because if you do not stay on guard I will come as a thief, and there is no way you can know what hour I will come upon you. [4] But, you have a few names in Sardis who have not soiled their garments, and they will walk with me in white garments, because they deserve it. [5] The overcomer will have white garments placed upon him, and I will certainly never blot his name out of the Book of Life, but I will openly confess his name before My Father and His angels.'
[6] "Anybody with ears – listen carefully to what the Spirit is saying to the churches!"
[7] "Write this to the messenger of the church in Philadelphia: 'The One who is set apart from evil and is the ultimate truth; having the key of David who opens and no one shuts, who shuts and no man opens, has a message for you: [8] I am aware of your works. Look! I have given you an opened door and no one can close it, because you maintain a small amount of power, have kept My Word and not denied My name. [9] Look! I will give out of the synagogue of Satan who claim they are Jews they are not, but are lying. Watch! I will cause them to come and worship before your feet, and they will know that I loved you. [10] Because you have kept the word of My patience, I will also keep you out of the hour of that trial that is about to befall the inhabitants of the whole world, to put the ones living there to the test. [11] I am coming quickly! Hold on to what you have, not letting someone deprive you of the crown destined for you. [12] I will make the overcomer a pillar in the temple of My God, and he will not ever go out of it any more. And I will write on him the name of My God as well as the name of the city of My God – the New Jerusalem descending out of Heaven from My God – and my new name.'
[13] Anybody with ears – listen carefully to what the Spirit is saying to the churches!"
[14] "Write this to the messenger of the church in Laodicea: 'The Amen, the Witness, the Faithful and True, the Beginning of the creation of God has a message for you: [15] I am aware of your works, that you are neither cold or hot. I wish you were cold or hot, [16] so, because you are lukewarm, and not hot or cold, I am about to vomit you out of My mouth – [17] because you are saying: "I am rich, I have become wealthy and have no needs." You do not understand that you are wretched ones; pathetic, poor, blind and naked. [18] I counsel you to buy from Me gold that has been refined in the fire so that you may be rich; white garments, so that you might put on some clothes, so your nakedness will not be seen; and eye ointment so you can see. [19] All those I love I correct and discipline, so get some enthusiasm and change your ways! [20] Listen! I stand at the door and knock. If anyone listens to My voice and opens the door, I will come in to him and we will eat and be together. [21] I will give to overcomers, to sit with Me on My throne, just as My Father gave Me, as I overcame, to sit with Him on His

throne.' ²²Anybody with ears – listen carefully to what the Spirit is saying to the churches!"

4 After these things I saw an open door in Heaven. The first voice I heard like a trumpet was saying to me, "Come up here and I will show you what must happen after these things." ²I immediately found myself in the Spirit, and saw a throne set in Heaven and Someone on the throne. ³The One seated there appeared like jasper and sardis stones, and there was an emerald rainbow encircling the throne. ⁴I saw twenty-four thrones encircling this throne, and upon these thrones twenty-four elders were sitting, having been clothed in white robes and with gold crowns upon their heads. ⁵Out of the throne continually came lightnings, voices and thunders; and seven lamps of fire continually burning before the throne these are the seven Spirits of God, ⁶before the throne a sea of glass like crystal; and in the center of all and around the throne four living beings, filled with eyes in front and back. ⁷The first living being was like a lion; and the second living being like a young calf, and the third living being having a face like a man, and the fourth living being like an eagle in flight.
⁸Each of the living beings had six wings, around and within full of eyes, and they continue day and night without ever stopping to say: "Holy, Holy, Holy, Lord God Almighty, the One who was, and is and is coming." ⁹The living beings continually give glory and honor and thanksgiving to the One sitting on the throne, the One living into the ages of the ages.
¹⁰The twenty-four elders continually prostrate themselves before the One sitting on the throne, the One living into the ages of the ages, continually throwing their crowns before the throne saying: ¹¹"Worthy are You, our Lord and God, to receive the glory and the honor and the power, because You have created all things, and because of Your desire they were created and stand created."

5 Then I saw on the right hand of the One sitting upon the throne a completed scroll with writing both inside and outside, having been sealed with seven seals. ²I saw a powerful angel proclaiming in a loud voice, "Who is worthy to open the scroll and to remove its seals?" ³There was no one in Heaven, nor upon the earth nor under the earth who had the power to open the scroll or look at it. ⁴Then I wept loudly, because no one worthy was found to open the scroll or look at it ⁵Then out of the elders one spoke to me: "Stop weeping! Look! One has become victorious; the Lion of the tribe of Judah, the Root of David; to unroll the scroll and its seven seals."
⁶I saw in the center near the throne and in the middle of the four living beings and the elders a Lamb standing as having been made a perpetual sacrifice, having seven horns and seven eyes, which are the seven Spirits of God having been sent out into all of the earth. ⁷He had come forward and had taken out of the right hand of the One sitting on the throne. ⁸When He took the scroll, the four living beings and the twenty-four elders fell before the Lamb, each one having a harp and golden bowls full of incense, which are the prayers of the saints. ⁹They continually sing a new song, saying, "You are worthy to receive the scroll and remove its seals, because You were sacrificed and have purchased to God by Your blood out of every tribe and language and people and nation, ¹⁰and have made them a kingdom and priests unto out God, and they will reign over the earth. ¹¹Then I saw and heard the sound of many angels around the throne and the living beings and the elders, and the number of them was

numberless numbers and thousands upon thousands, ¹²saying with a loud voice, "Worthy is the Lamb who was sacrificed to receive the power and the riches and the wisdom and strength and honor and glory and blessing." ¹³I heard every created thing which is in Heaven and on the earth and under the earth and on the sea and all that is in them saying: "To the One sitting on the throne and to the Lamb: the blessing and the honor and the glory and the might into the ages of the ages." ¹⁴And the four living beings said, "Amen," and the elders fell and worshiped.

**6** I watched when the Lamb broke open one of the seven seals; and I heard one of the four living beings speak with a voice like thunder, "Proceed!" ²Then I observed, and look! A white horse! And the one sitting on it had a bow, and a crown had been given to him. And he went out as a conqueror intending to conquer.
³After He had broken open the second seal, I heard the second living being saying, "Proceed!" ⁴Then another horse, fiery red, went out! And the one sitting on it was granted authority to take peace out of the earth in order that they will kill one another. He was also given a great sword. ⁵After He had broken open the third seal, I heard the third living being saying, "Proceed!" Then I observed, and look! A black horse! The one sitting on it had a balance in his hand. ⁶I heard a sound like a voice in the midst of the living beings saying, "A day's supply of wheat for a day's wages, and just a little more low quality barley for a day's wages, but do not harm the oil and the wine." ⁷After He had broken open the fourth seal, I heard the voice of the fourth living being saying, "Proceed!" ⁸I observed, and look! A pale green horse! The name of the one sitting upon it was Death, and the place of the dead followed with him. Authority was given to them over one fourth of the earth, to kill with the sword, with famine and by the wild animals of one fourth of the earth, to kill with the sword, with famine and by the wild animals of the earth.
⁹After He had broken open the fifth seal, I saw underneath the altar the souls of those who had been slaughtered on account of the Word of God and on account of the witness they maintained. ¹⁰And they cried out with a loud voice, saying, "When, holy and true Supreme Master, will you judge and execute vengeance for our blood on those who dwell on the earth?" ¹¹A white stately robe was given to each one of them and they received instruction, in order that they might rest a little longer, until the proper number of their fellow servants and brothers be killed just as they were. ¹²I saw, after He had broken open the sixth seal, and look! A great earthquake occurred, and the sun became black a rough sackcloth made of hair, and the whole moon became as blood. ¹³The stars of heaven fell into the earth, like unripe figs from a fig tree shaken by a mighty wind. ¹⁴The sky was split open, like a scroll when torn and curled up, and every mountain and island was moved out of where it had been. ¹⁵Then the kings of the earth, the authorities, the military leaders, the wealthy, the strong, all slaves and free men went into the dens and rocks of the mountains to hide themselves. ¹⁶They say to the mountains and rocks, "Fall on us and hide us from the face of the One sitting upon the throne and the deep anger of the Lamb! ¹⁷"For that day, that great day of their wrath has come, and who has the power to stand?"

**7** ¹After this I saw four angels standing upon the four corners of the earth, firmly holding the four winds of the earth, in order that the wind should not blow upon the earth, nor upon the sea, nor upon any tree. ²Then I saw another angel coming up from the east, having a seal of the living God. Then he cried in a loud voice to the four angels to whom it was given to harm the earth and the sea, ³saying, "Do not harm the earth, nor the sea, nor the trees until we have sealed the servants of our God upon their foreheads." ⁴I heard the number of those who had been sealed. One hundred forty-four thousand of all the tribes of the sons of Israel had been sealed. ⁵Out of the tribe of Judah twelve thousand had been sealed; out of the tribe of Reuben twelve thousand had been sealed; out of the tribe of Gad twelve thousand had been sealed; ⁶out of the tribe of Asher twelve thousand had been sealed; out of the tribe of Naphtali twelve thousand had been sealed; out of the tribe of Manasseh twelve thousand had been sealed; ⁷out of the tribe of Simeon twelve thousand had been sealed; out of the tribe of Levi twelve thousand had been sealed; out of the tribe of Issachar twelve thousand had been sealed; ⁸out of the tribe of Zebulun twelve thousand had been sealed; out of the tribe of Joseph twelve thousand had been sealed; out of the tribe of Benjamin twelve thousand had been sealed. ⁹After these things I observed, and look! A great crowd which no one could number out of all nations, tribes, peoples and languages; standing before the throne and before the Lamb, having been clothed with white stately robes and palm branches in their hands, ¹⁰crying out with a loud voice, saying, "Salvation to our God sitting on the throne and to the Lamb!" ¹¹All the angels were standing around the throne, and the elders and the four living beings, and fell before the throne upon their faces and worshiped God, ¹²saying: "Amen! The blessing and the glory and the wisdom and the thanks and the honor and the power and the strength to our God into the ages of the ages. Amen."

¹³Then one answered out of the elders, saying to me, "These which are arrayed in the white robes, who are they and from where have they come?" ¹⁴I said to him, "My lord, you know." Then he told me, "These are the ones coming out of the great tribulation, and have washed their robes and made them white in the blood of the Lamb. ¹⁵Therefore they are before the throne of God, and serve Him day and night in His temple, and the One sitting upon the throne will spread His tabernacle over them. ¹⁶They will no longer hunger or thirst, nor will the sun strike them or any other heat. ¹⁷This is because the Lamb who is in the center by the throne will shepherd them and lead them on to fountains of waters of life, and God will wipe away every tear from their eyes."

**8** ¹When He broke open the seventh seal there was silence in Heaven for about half an hour. ²I saw the seven angels who stood before the throne of God, and there was given to them seven trumpets. ³Another angel with a golden censer took his place over the altar, and he was given much incense, in order that he should add it to the prayers of all the saints upon the golden altar before the throne. ⁴The smoke of the incense ascended before God with the prayers of the saints out of the angel's hand. ⁵The angel, having taken the censer and filled it out of the fire upon the altar, cast it into the earth. There occurred thunders and sounds and lightnings and an earthquake. ⁶Then the seven angels who had the seven trumpets prepared themselves in order that they might trumpet.

⁷The first trumpeted, and there came hail and fire having been mixed in blood, and it

was cast into the earth; then the third part of the trees were burned up, and all the green grass was burned up. ⁸The second angel trumpeted, and the likeness of a great mountain burning with fire was cast into the sea, and the third part of the sea became blood. ⁹A third of the living creatures in the sea died. A third of the ships were destroyed. ¹⁰Then the third angel trumpeted, and a great star like a lamp fell out of heaven. It fell on the third part of the rivers and unto the springs of the waters. ¹¹The name of the star is called Wormwood. A third of the waters became wormwood; and many of the men died from the waters, because they were made bitter. ¹²The fourth angel trumpeted, and a third part of the sun, a third of the moon, and a third of the day would not appear, and the night likewise. ¹³I saw and heard an eagle flying in mid-heaven and saying with a loud voice, "Woe! Woe! Woe to the ones dwelling upon the earth out of the remaining voices of the trumpets of the three angels who are prepared to trumpet!"

9 The fifth angel trumpeted, and I saw a star which had fallen out of heaven into the earth. The key to the shaft of the abyss was given to it. ²He opened the shaft of the abyss, and smoke went up out of the shaft as smoke from a great furnace. The sun and the air became darkened because of the smoke of the shaft. ³Out of the smoke came locusts into the earth, and they were given authority as the scorpions of the earth have authority. ⁴They were instructed so that they would not harm the grass of the earth or anything green or any tree, but only such men as have not the seal of God upon their foreheads. ⁵It was given to them that they should not kill them, but instead that they should be tormented five months, and the torment as a scorpion whenever it stings a man. ⁶In those days the men will seek death, and by no means will they find it, and they will long to die, but death will flee from them. ⁷The appearance of the locusts was like horses which had been prepared to enter battle, and on their heads were crowns of something like gold, and their faces like faces of men. ⁸They had hair like women's hair, and teeth as a lion's. ⁹They had breastplates as breastplates of iron, and the sound of their wings as many multi-horse chariots running into war. ¹⁰They also have tails and stingers like scorpions, and in their tails is their power to injure men five months. ¹¹They have over them a king, the angel of the abyss, whose Hebrew name is Abaddon, and in Greek has the name Apollyon. ¹²One woe has gone forth. Look! Two more woes are coming after these things!

¹³Then the sixth angel trumpeted: and I heard one voice out of the four horns of the golden altar before God ¹⁴saying to the sixth angel who had the trumpet, "Turn loose the four angels who have been bound over the great river Euphrates." ¹⁵The four angels were set loose, who had been prepared for this hour and day and month and year in order that they should kill a third of men. ¹⁶The number of the soldiers of this cavalry: two hundred million. I heard the number of them. ¹⁷After this manner I saw the horses in the vision and the ones sitting upon them: they have fiery red, dusky blue and sulfur yellow breastplates, and the heads of the horses like lions, and out of their mouths went fire, smoke and sulfur. ¹⁸A third of men were killed by these three plagues, out of the fire and the smoke and the sulfur going out of their mouths. ¹⁹For the power of the horses is in their mouths and in their tails, for their tails are like serpents, having heads, and in them they do harm. ²⁰But the men who remained, who were not killed in these plagues, did not repent out of the works of their hands, that they should not worship demons and gold, silver, brass, stone and wood idols, which cannot see or hear or

walk about. ²¹They did not repent out of their murders or their mystical sometimes drug induced arts or their sexual immorality or their thefts.

**10** Then I saw another strong angel descending out of heaven, having been enveloped by a cloud. There was a rainbow on his head, his face was like the sun and his feet like pillars of fire. ²He had a little opened scroll in his hand. He placed his right foot upon the sea and his left upon the land, ³and cried with a loud voice, as a lion roars. When he cried out, the seven thunders uttered their voices. ⁴When the seven thunders spoke, I was about to write, but I heard a voice out of Heaven saying, "Seal the things spoken by the seven thunders, and do not write them." ⁵Then the angel, whom I saw standing upon the sea and upon the land lifted his right hand into Heaven ⁶and swore by the One living into the ages of the ages, who created the heaven and the things in it, the earth and the things in it, and the sea and the things in it that time no longer shall be. ⁷But, in the days of the voice of the seventh angel, when he is about to trumpet, then the mystery of God was finished as He had proclaimed to His servants the prophets.

⁸The voice which I heard out of Heaven spoke to me again saying, "Go take the opened scroll in the hand of the angel standing upon the sea and upon the land." ⁹I went away toward the angel, telling him to give me the little scroll. He said to me, "Take it and eat it completely, then it will make your stomach bitter, but in your mouth it will be sweet as honey." ¹⁰I took the little scroll out of the hand of the angel and ate it completely, and in my mouth it was sweet as honey, and when I ate it it was made bitter in my stomach. ¹¹Then they said to me, "It is necessary for you to again prophesy before many people, nations, languages and kings."

**11** A reed was given to me like a staff, and one said, "Rise and measure the temple of God and the altar and those worshiping in it. ²But exclude the court outside the temple, and do not measure it, because it has been given to the nations, and they will trample the holy city forty-two months."

³"Then I will commission my two witnesses, and they will prophesy one thousand two hundred and sixty days, clothed in sackcloth. ⁴These are the two olive trees and the two lampstands standing before the Lord of the earth. ⁵If anyone desires to harm them, fire proceeds from their mouths and consumes their enemies. This is how anyone who desires to harm them must be killed. ⁶These have the authority to close heaven, in order that no rain falls in the days of their prophecy; and they have authority over the waters to turn them into blood and to strike the earth with every plague as often as they desire. ⁷When they finish their testimony, the wild beast ascending from the abyss will make war with them and will overcome them and will kill them. ⁸Their fallen corpses will remain upon the open street of the great city which is called spiritually Sodom and Egypt, where even their Lord was crucified. ⁹People out of the peoples, tribes, languages and nations will look at their corpses three and a half days, and will not allow their corpses to be placed in a tomb. ¹⁰Those who dwell upon the earth will rejoice over them, make merry, and send gifts to one another, because these two prophets tormented those who dwell on the earth." ¹¹Now after the three and a half days the breath of life out of God entered them, and they stood upon their feet, and

great fear fell upon those looking at them. [12]They heard a loud voice from out of Heaven saying to them, "Come up here!" Then they ascended into heaven in the cloud, and their enemies saw them. [13]In that hour a great earthquake occurred, and a tenth part of the city fell, and in the earthquake seven thousand of the names of men were killed, and the rest became terrified and gave glory to the God of Heaven.

[14]The second woe has passed away. Look! The third woe is coming quickly! [15]The seventh angel trumpeted: And there were loud voices in Heaven, saying, "The kingdom of this world has become the kingdom of our Lord and of His Christ, and He shall reign into the ages of the ages!" [16]The twenty-four elders who sat before God upon their thrones fell upon their faces and worshiped God, [17]saying: "We thank You, O Lord God Almighty, the One who is and who was, because You have permanently taken Your great power and reigned. [18]The nations were angry, then Your wrath came, and the time of the dead to be judged, and to give the reward to your servants the prophets and to the saints, and to those fearing Your name, to the small and to the great, and to destroy the ones destroying the earth." [19]The temple of God was opened in Heaven, and the ark of His covenant was seen in His temple. Then there were lightnings, voices, thunders, an earthquake, and the great hail.

12 A great sign was seen in heaven: a woman having been clothed with the sun, the moon underneath her feet, and a crown of twelve stars upon her head. [2]Being pregnant, she cries, suffering labor and distressed to give birth. [3]Another sign was seen in heaven: Look! A great, fiery red dragon having seven heads and ten horns, and upon his heads seven crowns. [4]His tail sweeps a third of the stars of heaven and cast them into the earth. Then the dragon stood before the woman who was ready to give birth, in order that when she delivered he might devour her child. [5]She gave birth to a male child who is about to shepherd the nations with a staff of iron. Then her child was caught up to God and His throne. [6]The woman fled into the desert where she has a place prepared by God, in order that they might nourish her there one thousand two hundred and sixty days. [7]Then war began in heaven: Michael and his angels made war with the dragon, and the dragon made war along with his angels, [8]but they were not strong enough, and there was no longer any place found for them in Heaven. [9]Then the great dragon, the old serpent, called the devil and Satan, the one deceiving the whole inhabited world, was cast into the earth, and his angels were cast with him. [10]I heard a great voice in Heaven saying, "Now salvation, and strength, and the kingdom of our God, and the authority of His Christ have come, for the accuser of our brethren, who accused them before our God day and night, has been cast down. [11]They overcame him because of the blood of the Lamb and because of the word of their testimony, and they did not love their lives to the death."

[12]"Rejoice because of this, O heavens, and the ones who dwell in them! Woe for the earth and for the sea, because the devil has come down to you, having great anger, knowing that he has a short time." [13]When the dragon saw that he was thrown to the earth, he hunted the woman who bore the male. [14]The woman was given two wings of the great eagle, in order that she might fly into the desert, into her place, where she is nourished for a time and times and half a time, away from the face of the serpent. [15]The serpent expelled water out of his mouth after the woman. It was like a river in order that he might carry her away by the flood.

¹⁶The earth helped the woman. The earth opened its mouth and swallowed up the river which the dragon had expelled from its mouth. ¹⁷The dragon was enraged over the woman, and went away to make war with the rest of her offspring, the ones keeping the commandments of God and have the witness of Jesus.

**13** Then I stood upon the sand of the sea, and I saw a beast ascending out of the sea, having ten horns and seven heads, and upon its horns ten crowns, and upon its heads names of blasphemy. ²The beast which I saw was like a leopard, and its feet as a bear, and the mouth of it as the mouth of a lion. The dragon gave its power to it, its throne and great authority. ³One of its heads appeared as mortally wounded, but its deadly wound was healed, and all the world wondered at and followed after the beast. ⁴They worshiped the dragon because he gave the authority to the beast; and they worshiped the beast, saying, "Who is like the beast? Who is able to make war with it?" ⁵It was given a mouth speaking great things and blasphemies, and it was given authority to work for forty-two months. ⁶It opened its mouth in blasphemy toward God to blaspheme His name, His tabernacle and those who dwell in Heaven. ⁷It was given to it to make war with the saints and to overcome them, and authority was given to it over every tribe, people, language and nation. ⁸All those dwelling upon the earth will worship him, whose names have not been written in the Book of Life of the Lamb having been slain from the laying down of the foundation of the world. ⁹If anyone has an ear, let him hear. ¹⁰If any man leads into captivity, into captivity he goes. If anyone kills by the sword, it is necessary that he be killed by a sword. Here is the endurance and faith of the saints.
¹¹Then I saw another beast ascending out of the earth, and it had two horns like a lamb but spoke like a dragon. ¹²It exercises all the authority of the first beast before it, and makes the earth and those dwelling in it worship the first beast, whose stroke of death was healed. ¹³It does great signs, so that it even makes fire come down out of Heaven into the earth before men. ¹⁴It deceives the ones dwelling upon the earth because of the signs which were given to it to do before the beast, telling those dwelling upon the earth to make an image to the beast who has the deadly stroke of the sword yet lived again. ¹⁵Permission was given to it to give breath to the image of the beast, in order that the image of the beast might speak so that those who do not worship the image of the beast be killed. ¹⁶It makes all men, both small and great, both rich and poor, both free and slave to receive a mark upon their right hand or upon their foreheads, ¹⁷so that no one can buy or sell except one having the mark or the name of the beast or the number of its name. ¹⁸Here is wisdom. Let the one having reason calculate the number of the beast, for it is the number of a man: the number of it is 666.

**14** Then I watched, and look! The Lamb standing upon Mount Zion, and with Him one hundred forty-four thousand, having His name and the name of His Father written upon their foreheads. ²I heard a voice out of Heaven, like the sound of many waters and like the sound of great thunder, and the voice which I heard was as harpers playing their harps. ³They sang a new song before the throne and before the four living beings and the elders; and no one could learn that song except the hundred and forty-four thousand who had been purchased from the earth. ⁴These are the ones who did not defile themselves with women, for they are celibate. These are the ones following the Lamb wherever He might go. These were purchased from mankind as firstfruits to God and to the Lamb. ⁵There was no lie found in their mouths – they are unblemished.

⁶I saw another angel flying in mid-heaven, having eternal good news to proclaim to those sitting upon the earth – to every nation, tribe, language and people; ⁷saying in a loud voice, "Fear God and give Him glory, because the hour of His judgment has arrived. Worship the One who has made the heaven and the earth and sea and springs of water." ⁸Another angel, a second, followed saying, "Fallen, fallen is Babylon the great, which has caused all the nations to drink out of the wine of the anger of her fornication." ⁹Another angel, a third, followed them, saying in a loud voice, "If anyone worships the beast and its image, and receives a mark upon his forehead or upon his hand, ¹⁰he himself shall also drink out of the wine of God's anger having been mixed undiluted in the cup of His anger, and will be tormented in fire and sulfur before holy angels and before the Lamb. ¹¹The smoke of their suffering goes up into the ages of ages, and they have no rest day or night, the ones worshiping the beast and his image, and if anyone receives the mark of his name." ¹²Here is the patience of the saints; those keeping the commandments of God and the faith of Jesus.

¹³I heard a voice out of Heaven saying, "Write: 'Blessed are the dead, the ones dying in the Lord from now on.'" "Yes," says the Spirit, "in order that they may rest out of their labors, for their works follow with them." ¹⁴Then I saw, and look! A white cloud, and One sitting upon the cloud like the Son of Man, having upon His head a golden crown and a sharp sickle in His hand. ¹⁵Another angel then came out of the temple, crying out with a loud voice to the one sitting upon the cloud, "Thrust in Your sickle and begin to reap at once, because the harvest of the earth is overripe and dry." ¹⁶So the One sitting upon the cloud thrust His sickle upon the earth, and the earth was harvested. ¹⁷Another angel went out of the temple in Heaven. He also had a sharp sickle. ¹⁸Another angel came out from the altar. He had power over the fire, and he spoke in a loud voice to the One with the sharp sickle. He said, "Thrust in Your sharp sickle and gather the clusters of the vine of the earth, because her grapes are in their prime." ¹⁹So the angel thrust his sickle into the earth, and gathered the vine of the earth and cast it into the winepress of the great anger of God. ²⁰The winepress was then trampled outside the city, and blood came out of the winepress up to the bridles of the horses for about 200 miles.

## 15

I saw another great and wonderful sign in Heaven: seven angels having the last seven plagues, for in them the anger of God is concluded. ²I saw what looked like a sea of glass mixed with fire, and those coming out with triumph over the beast, out of his image, out of his mark and out of the number of his name. They were standing upon the glassy sea with harps of God. ³They are singing the song of Moses, the servant of God, and the song of the Lamb, saying: "Great and marvelous are Your works, Lord God Almighty! Righteous and true are Your ways, King of the ages! ⁴Who will not reverence and give glory to Your name, for You alone are holy? Because all the nations will come and will worship before You, because Your righteous acts of judgment have been revealed."

⁵After these things I saw that the temple of the tabernacle of the testimony in Heaven was opened. ⁶Seven angels came out of the temple, having been clothed in shining

linen with golden sashes wrapped around their chests. They brought out the seven plagues from the temple. ⁷Then one out of the four living beings gave to the seven angels seven golden bowls filled with the wrath of God who is living into the ages of the ages. ⁸The temple was filled with smoke out of the glory of God and out of His power, and no one could enter into the temple until the completion of the seven plagues of the seven angels.

**16** I heard a loud voice out of the temple saying to the seven angels, "Go and pour out the seven bowls of the wrath of God into the earth." ²The first proceeded and poured out his bowl into the earth, and a bad, malicious sore came upon the men having the mark of the beast and worshiping his image. ³The second poured out his bowl into the sea, and became as the blood of a dead person, and every living creature in the sea died. ⁴The third poured out his bowl into the rivers and springs of the waters, and they became blood. ⁵I heard the angel of the waters saying: "Righteous are You, the One who is and who was, the Holy One, because of these things You have judged. ⁶Because the blood of the saints and the prophets they have shed, and blood You have given them to drink. They are worthy of this!" ⁷I heard the altar say: "Yes, Lord God Almighty, Your judgments are true and righteous."
⁸The fourth poured out his bowl over the sun, and it was granted to him to scorch men in fire. ⁹Men were scorched in the great heat, and they blasphemed the name of God who had power over these plagues; and they did not repent to give Him the glory. ¹⁰The fifth poured out his bowl over the throne of the beast, and its kingdom was darkened, and men chewed their tongues because of the pain. ¹¹They blasphemed the God of Heaven because of their pains and sores, but they did not repent of their works.
¹²The sixth poured out his bowl over the great river Euphrates, so its water was dried up for the purpose of making the way ready for the kings of the east. ¹³I saw three unclean spirits like frogs out of the mouth of the dragon, out of the mouth of the beast, and out of the mouth of the false prophet. ¹⁴They are the spirits of demons, for the purpose of performing signs, going out upon the kings of the whole inhabited world – to gather them into the war of the great day of the Almighty God! ¹⁵"Listen! I am coming as a thief. Blessed is the one who watches and keeps his garments, so that he does not walk naked and they see his shame." ¹⁶They lead them together into the place called in Hebrew, "the mountain of Megiddo."
¹⁷The seventh poured out his bowl over the air, and a great voice came out of the temple, from the throne, saying, "It is completed!" ¹⁸There were lightnings and voices and thunders. A great earthquake then came, an earthquake such as had not happened since man was upon the earth. ¹⁹The great city was then divided into three sections, and the cities of the nations fell. Then Babylon the great was remembered before God, to give her the cup of the wine of the anger of His wrath. ²⁰Every island fled, and the mountains were not found. ²¹Great hail about the size of a talent fell upon men out of Heaven; and men blasphemed God out of the plague of the hail, because the plague is exceedingly great.

**17** One of the seven angels who had the seven bowls came and talked with me, saying, "Come here! I will show you the judgment of the great prostitute sitting upon many waters, ²with whom the kings of the earth practiced immoral acts, and those dwelling on the earth became drunk with the wine of her immorality." ³He carried me away in the spirit into a wilderness. I saw a woman sitting upon a scarlet beast. It was filled with blasphemous names, having seven heads and ten horns. ⁴The woman was clothed in purple and scarlet, gilded with gold, precious stones and pearls, having in her hand a golden cup full of abominations and the filthiness of her fornication. ⁵A name had been written on her forehead: Mystery, Babylon the Great, the Mother of Harlots and of the Abominations of the Earth. ⁶I saw the woman, drunk with the blood of the saints and with the blood of the witnesses of Jesus. When I saw her, I wondered with great wonderment.

⁷The angel said to me, "Why do you wonder? I will tell you the mystery of the woman and of the seven-headed, ten-horned beast which carries her. ⁸The beast that you saw was, and is not, and is about to come up out of the abyss and go into destruction. Those living on the earth whose names are not written in the Book of Life from the foundation of the world will wonder when they see the beast that was, and is not, and yet is. ⁹Here is the mind with wisdom: the seven heads are seven mountains on which the woman sits. There are also seven kings. ¹⁰Five fell, one is, and the other has not yet come. When he comes, he will remain for a little while. ¹¹And the beast that was, and is not, is himself also the eighth, and is out of the seven, and is going to destruction. ¹²The ten horns which you saw are ten kings who have not received a kingdom as yet, but they receive authority as kings with the beast for one hour. ¹³These have one purpose, and they will give their power and authority to the beast."

¹⁴"These will make war with the Lamb, but the Lamb will overcome them, for He is Lord of lords and King of kings; and those with Him are called, elect, and faithful." ¹⁵Then he said to me, "The waters which you saw, where the harlot sits, are peoples, crowds, nations, and tongues. ¹⁶And the ten horns which you saw, and the beast, these will hate the prostitute, make her desolated and naked, then eat her flesh and burn her in fire. ¹⁷For God has put into their hearts to fulfill His desire, to be of one mind, and to give their kingdoms to the beast, until the words of God are accomplished. ¹⁸And the woman whom you saw is the great city having a kingdom over the kings of the earth."

18 After these things I saw another angel descending out of Heaven, having great authority, and the earth was illuminated by his glory. ²He cried out in a strong voice, saying, "Fallen, fallen is Babylon the great, and has become a dwelling place of demons, a place of banishment for every unclean spirit and unclean and hated bird! ³For all the nations have drunk of the wine of the wrath of her immorality, the kings of the earth have committed immorality with her, and the merchants of the earth have become wealthy through the power of her arrogant luxury." ⁴I heard another voice out of Heaven saying, "Come out, my people, out of her, so that you do not become a partner in her sins, and out of her so you do not receive her plagues. ⁵For her sins have joined to one another until they have reached to Heaven, and God has remembered her unrighteous acts. ⁶Pay back to her as she has paid back to you, double it according to her works; in the cup which she has mixed, mix double for her. ⁷By the things she glorified herself and lived in arrogant luxury, give her as much torment and sorrow; because she says in her heart, 'I sit a queen and not a widow, and will never see sorrow.' ⁸Because of this her plagues will come in one day – death, sorrow and hunger, and she will be consumed in the fire, because the Lord God who judges her is strong."

[9]"The kings of the earth who practiced immorality and lived in arrogant luxury with her will weep and wail over her whenever they see the smoke of her burning. [10]Standing far off because of the fear of her torment, they say, 'Woe! Woe! That great city Babylon, that strong city! Because in one hour your judgment has come.' [11]The merchants of the earth mourn and sorrow over her, because no one buys their products any longer: [12]products of gold, silver, precious stones, pearls, fine linen and purple, silk and scarlet, every kind of citrus wood, every kind of vessel of ivory and precious wood, bronze, iron and marble; [13]cinnamon, incense, fragrant oil, frankincense, wine and oil, fine flour and wheat, cattle and sheep, horses and chariots, and bodies and souls of men. [14]The fruit your soul has desired has gone from you, and all the things which are sumptuous and shining have gone from you, and you will never find them again. [15]The merchants of these things, who became rich by her stand far away because of the fear of her torment, weeping and wailing, [16]saying, 'Woe! Woe! The great city that was clothed in fine linen and purple, gilded in gold, precious stones and pearls! [17]Because in one hour such great wealth was made desolate.' Every pilot, every traveler, every sailor and as many as work on the sea stood at a distance [18]and cried out seeing the smoke of her burning, saying, 'What can compare to this great city?'" [19]They threw dust on their heads and cried out, weeping and mourning, saying, "Woe! Woe! The great city, in which all who had ships on the sea were made rich by her wealth! Because in one hour she was made desolate. [20]Rejoice over her, O Heaven, saints, apostles and prophets, because God avenged on her what she has judged concerning you." [21]One strong angel lifted a stone as great as a millstone and threw it into the sea, saying, "With this kind of violent rush the great city Babylon will be thrown down, never to be found again. [22]The sound of harpists, musicians, flutists and trumpeters will not be heard in you again. No workman of any trade will be found in you again. The sound of a millstone will never be heard in you again. [23]The light of a lamp will never shine in you again. The voice of bridegroom and bride will never be heard in you again – because your merchants were the great men of the earth; because in your mystical sometimes drug-induced arts all nations were deceived. [24]In her was found the blood of prophets, saints, and all who were slain on the earth."

**19** After these things I heard a loud voice like a great multitude in Heaven, saying, "Alleluia! The salvation and the glory and the power belongs to the Lord our God! [2]Because His judgments are true and righteous, for He has judged the great prostitute who defiled the earth with her immorality; and He has exacted vengeance for the blood of His servants shed by her hand." [3]A second time they said, "Alleluia! Her smoke ascends into the ages of the ages!" [4]The twenty-four elders and the four living beings fell down and worshiped God who is sitting on the throne, saying, "Amen, Alleluia!"

[6]I heard a sound like a great crowd, like the sound of many waters and like strong thunderings, saying, "Alleluia, because the all powerful God reigns! [7]Let us rejoice with enthusiastic gladness and give Him the glory, because the marriage of the Lamb has arrived, and His wife has prepared herself." [8]It was granted to her to be clothed in fine linen, pure and bright. This is because this linen is the righteous acts of the saints. [9]Then he spoke to me, "Write: 'Blessed are those who have been called into the marriage supper of the Lamb!'" He also said to me, "These are the true words of God." [10]I fell before his feet to worship him, but

he said to me, "See that you do not do that! I am a fellow servant with you and your brothers who have the witness of Jesus. You worship God! For the witness of Jesus is the spirit of prophecy." [11]I then saw that Heaven had been opened, and look! A white horse! The One sitting on it was called Faithful and True, and in righteousness He judges and makes war. [12]His eyes were like a flame of fire. There were many crowns upon His head, and He had a name written that no one but Him knew. [13]He had been clothed in a blood-dipped robe, and He had been named The Word of God. [14]The armies in Heaven, having been clothed in white, clean, fine linen, followed after Him on white horses. [15]A sharp sword proceeds out of His mouth, in order that He may strike the nations He will shepherd them with a staff of iron. He treads the winepress of the wine of the burning anger of the wrath of the all-powerful God. [16]He has upon His garment and His thigh a name written: King of Kings and Lord of Lords. [17]Then I saw an angel standing in the sun. He cried out in a loud voice, saying to all the birds flying in mid-heaven, "Come, be gathered together into the great supper of God, [18]so that you may eat pieces of flesh of kings, commanders, mighty men, horses and those who sit on them, and the flesh of all; both free and slave, small and great." [19]I saw the beast, the kings of the earth and their armies, standing assembled to make war with the One sitting on the horse and His army. [20]The beast was taken into custody, and with it the false prophet who performed signs before it, in which he deceived those having received the mark of the beast, and those worshiping its image. These two were thrown alive into the lake of fire burning with sulfur. [21]The rest were killed with the sword which proceeded from the mouth of the One sitting on the horse. And all the birds were filled with the pieces of their flesh,

**20** Then I saw an angel coming down out of Heaven, having the key of the abyss and a great chain upon his hand. [2]He took the dragon into custody, who is the ancient serpent, Devil and Satan, and bound him for a thousand years. [3]He threw him into the abyss, then shut and sealed it over him so that he would not deceive the nations any more until the thousand years are completed. After these things he must be set loose for a little while. [4]I saw thrones and those seated upon them. Judgment was committed to them, I saw the souls of those beheaded because of the witness of Jesus and because of the Word of God, who did not worship the beast or its image, who did not receive its mark upon their foreheads or upon their hands. They lived and reigned with Christ for a thousand years. [5]The rest of the dead did not live until the thousand years were completed. This is the first resurrection. [6]The one who has a part in the first resurrection is richly blessed and holy. The second death has no authority over such individuals. Instead, they will be priests of God and Christ, and will reign with Him for the thousand years. [7]When the thousand years are completed Satan will be released out of his prison. [8]He will go out into the four corners of the earth to deceive the nations Gog and Magog: the number of them is like the sand of the sea, to bring them into the war. [9]They spread out over the land and surrounded the camp of the saints and the beloved city. Then fire came down out of Heaven and completely consumed them. [10]The Devil, who deceived them, was thrown into the lake of fire and sulfur to join the beast and false prophet. They will be tormented day and night into the ages of the ages.

[11]I saw a great white throne and the One sitting upon it. Heaven and earth bolted

from His presence, but there was not found a place for them. [12]I saw the dead, great and small, standing before the throne. Books were opened, and another was opened, the Book of Life. The dead were judged according to their works by means of the things written in the books. [13]The sea gave up its dead, and Death and Hades gave up the dead in them. Then each one was judged, according to their works. [14]Then Death and Hades were thrown into the lake of fire. This is the second death, the lake of fire. [15]If anyone is not found written in the Book of Life, he was thrown into the lake of fire.

**21** Then I saw a new heaven and earth, for the first heaven and earth passed away – the sea is no more. [2]I saw New Jerusalem, the holy city, coming down out of Heaven from God, having been prepared as a bride beautifully adorned for her husband. [3]I heard a loud voice out of the throne saying, "Look! The tabernacle of God with men! He will live with them and they will be His people. God Himself will be with them. [4]"God will wipe every single tear out of their eyes. Death will no longer exist, no sorrow, no anguish cry: pain will no longer exist, because the first things have passed away." [5]The one seated upon the throne then said, "Look! I make all things new!" Then He said, "Write, because these words are faithful and true." [6]Then He said to me, "It has come to completion! I am the Alpha and the Omega, the Beginning and the End. I will freely give water out of the fountain of life to the thirsty one. [7]"The overcomer will inherit these things. I will be God to him, and he will be son to Me. [8]But to those fearful, unbelieving, saturated with evil vices, murderers, sexually immoral, practitioners of mystical sometimes drug induced arts, worshipers of something other than God, and all liars have their part in the lake burning with fire and sulfur, which is the second death."

[9]Then one of the seven angels who had the seven bowls, having been filled with the seven last plagues came out and talked with me. He said, "Come, I will show you the bride, the wife of the Lamb." [10]He carried me away in Spirit onto a huge, high mountain, and he showed me the holy city Jerusalem, coming down out of Heaven from God, [11]having the glory of God (the light of it as a precious stone like jasper, clear as crystal). [12]It had a great, high wall with twelve gates and twelve angels upon the gates. Names were inscribed on the gates, which are the twelve tribes of the children of Israel [13]from the east, three gates; from the north, three gates; from the south, three gates; and from the west, three gates. [14]The wall of the city had twelve foundations, and upon them twelve names of the twelve apostles of the Lamb. [15]The one speaking with me had a golden reed in order to measure the city, its gates, and its wall. [16]The city forms a square. Its length is as great as its width. He measured the city with the reed: twelve thousand furlongs its length, width and height are equal. [17]He measured the wall, which was one hundred forty-four cubits, a measure of a man, which is of an angel. [18]The wall was made of jasper, and the city was pure gold, like clear glass. [19]The foundations of the city's wall were adorned with every precious stone. The first foundation was jasper, the second sapphire, the third chalcedony, the fourth emerald, [20]the fifth sardonyx, the sixth sardius, the seventh chrysolite, the eighth beryl, the ninth topaz, the tenth chrysoprase, the eleventh jacinth, and the twelfth amethyst. [21]The twelve gates were twelve pearls. Each individual gate was of one individual pearl. And the broad street of the city was pure gold, like transparent glass. [22]I did not see a temple in it, for the Lord God Almighty and the Lamb are

its temple. ²³The city did not need illumination from the sun or moon, because the glory of God was its light, and the Lamb its lamp. ²⁴The nations shall walk around in its light, and the kings of the earth continually bring their glory into it. ²⁵The gates will never be closed during the day there will never be night there. ²⁶They will bring the glory and honor of the nations into it. ²⁷Nothing profane will ever enter in, or anyone who makes an abomination and a lie. The only ones are those having been written in the Lamb's Book of Life.

**22** He showed me a river of water of life, brilliant as crystal, going out of the throne of God and of the Lamb, ²which flowed in the middle of the city's wide street. The tree of life was on both sides of the river. Twelve fruits were produced each month, with each tree bearing its fruit. The leaves of the tree are for the healing of the nations. ³There shall never again be any curse. The throne of God and of the Lamb will be in it, and His willing servants will render Him service. ⁴His servants will see His face, and His name will be on their foreheads. ⁵Night will no longer exist there. They will not need the light of a lamp or the light of the sun, because the Lord God will shed light upon them. They will reign into the ages of the ages.

⁶He said to me, "These are faithful and true words. The Lord, the God of the spirits of the prophets, sent His angel to show His servants the events which will quickly take place. ⁷Listen! I am coming quickly! Rich blessedness belongs to the one keeping the Words of this prophecy of this Book." ⁸I, John, am the one seeing and hearing these things. When I heard and saw I fell to worship before the feet of the angel showing these things to me. ⁹He told me, "Don't do that! I am your fellow servant, and of your brothers the prophets and of the ones keeping the Words of this Book. You worship God!"¹⁰He told me, "Do not seal the Words of this Book's prophecy, for the time is near. ¹¹Let the unjust one continue to act unjustly, and the filthy one continue being filthy. Let the righteous one continue to be righteous, and the holy one continue in holiness. ¹²Look! I am coming quickly, and My reward is with Me, to reward each man according to his work. ¹³I Am the Alpha and the Omega, the First and the Last, the Beginning and the End." ¹⁴Blessed are those who are washing their stately robes, so that they will have a right to the Tree of Life and enter into the city through the gates. ¹⁵Outside are the dogs, those practicing mystical sometimes drug induced arts, the immoral, the murderers, the idolaters and everyone loving and making a lie. ¹⁶"I, Jesus, sent my angel to testify these things to you in the churches. I am the Root and the Offspring of David, the Bright Morning Star." ¹⁷The Spirit and the bride say "Come!" Let the one hearing say "Come!" Let the thirsty one come, and drink freely as he wishes. ¹⁸I testify to everyone hearing the Words of the prophecy of this Book. If anyone makes an addition to these things, God will add, upon him, the plagues which have been written in this Book. ¹⁹If anyone takes away from the Words of the Book of this prophecy, God will take away his part from the Tree of Life, out of the holy city and of the things written in this Book.

²⁰The One testifying to these things says, "Yes, I am coming quickly." Amen! Come, Lord Jesus! ²¹The grace of the Lord Jesus be with all!

Printed in the United States
17666LVS00002B/82-303